France, 1715–1804: Power and the People

Gwynne Lewis

PEARSON

Longman

Harlow, England • London • New York • Boston • San Francisco • Toronto • Sydney • Tokyo • Singapore
Hong Kong • Seoul • Taipei • New Delhi • Cape Town • Madrid • Mexico City • Amsterdam • Munich • Paris • Milan

Pearson Education Limited

Edinburgh Gate
Harlow CM20 2JE
United Kingdom
Tel: +44 (0)1279 623623
Fax: +44 (0)1279 431059
Website: www.pearsoned.co.uk

First edition published in Great Britain in 2005

© Pearson Education Limited 2004

The right of Gwynne Lewis to be identified as author
of this work has been asserted by him in accordance
with the Copyright, Designs and Patents Act 1988.

ISBN 0 582 23925 7

British Library Cataloguing in Publication Data
A CIP catalogue record for this book can be obtained from the British Library

Library of Congress Cataloging-in-Publication Data
Lewis, Gwynne.
   France, 1715–1804 : power and the people / Gwynne Lewis.
      p. cm. — (A social history of Europe)
   Includes bibliographical references and index.
   ISBN 0–582–23925–7 (pbk.)
      1. France—History—18th century.   2. France—Social conditions—18th century.   3.
   France—Economic conditions—18th century.   4. France—Social life and customs—18th
   century.   5. France—Intellectual life—18th century.   6. Social classes—France—18th century.
   I. Title. II. Series.
   DC131.L49 2004
   944'.034—dc22
                                                                                                2004044194

10 9 8 7 6 5 4 3 2
08 07 06 05 04

Set by 35 in 9.5/12.5pt Stone Serif
Printed and bound in Malaysia,VVP

The Publisher's policy is to use paper manufactured from sustainable forests.

For Dewi and May Lewis and Glyn and Muriel Rosser.

Contents

General editor's preface

For far too long 'social history' was regularly, even routinely, defined dismissively and negatively along the lines of 'history with the high politics, economics and diplomacy left out'. Over the latter decades of the twentieth century, however, a virtual revolution in the sub-discipline of 'social history' gathered momentum, fuelled not only by historians but also by specialists from such established academic disciplines as anthropology, economics, politics and especially sociology, and enriched by contributors from burgeoning cultural, demographic, media and women's studies. At the cusp of the twenty-first century, the prime rationale of the recently launched 'Social History of Europe' series is to reflect the cumulative achievement and reinforce the ripening respectability of what may be positively yet succinctly defined as nothing less than the 'history of society'.

Initiated by the late Professor Harry Hearder of the University of Wales, the 'Social History of Europe' series is conceived as an ambitious and open-ended collection of wide-ranging general surveys charting the history of the peoples of the major European nations, states and regions through key phases in their societal development from the late Middle Ages to the present. The series is not designed to become necessarily either chronologically or geographically all-embracing, although certain pre-eminent areas and periods will demand a systematic sequence of coverage. Typically, a volume covers a period of about one century, but longer (and occasionally shorter) time-spans are proving appropriate. A degree of modest chronological overlap between volumes covering a particular nation, state or region is acceptable where justified by the historical experience.

Each volume in the series is written by a commissioned European or American expert and, while synthesizing the latest scholarship in the field, is invigorated by the findings and preoccupations of the author's original research. As works of authority and originality, all contributory volumes are of genuine interest and value to the individual author's academic peers.

Even so, the contributory volumes are not intended to be scholarly monographs addressed to the committed social historian but broader synoptic overviews which serve a non-specialist general readership. All the volumes are therefore intended to take the 'textbook dimension' with due seriousness, with authors recognizing that the long-term success of the series will depend on its usefulness to, and popularity with, an international undergraduate and postgraduate student readership. In the interests of accessibility, the provision of notes and references to accompany the text is suitably restrained and all volumes contain a select bibliography, a chronology of principal events, a glossary of foreign and technical terms and a comprehensive index.

Inspired by the millennial watershed but building upon the phenomenal specialist progress recorded over the last quarter-century, the eventually multi-volume 'Social History of Europe' is dedicated to the advancement of an intellectually authoritative and academically cosmopolitan perspective on the multi-faceted historical development of the European continent.

Raymond Pearson
Professor of Modern European History
University of Ulster

Acknowledgements

I am indebted to Colin Jones for reading the entire manuscript of this book. His encouragement, advice and criticism have truly been invaluable. I also owe Roger Magraw an inestimable debt of gratitude for the many amicable discussions and debates on French history that we have enjoyed over several decades. Both Colin and Roger are still teaching at Warwick University, where I learned so much from colleagues and students and spent some of the happier days of my teaching life. My happiest, non-teaching days have been spent living in Paris and New Milton where this book was researched and written.

I must also record my gratitude to the Leverhulme Foundation for awarding me a research grant that facilitated my work in France.

Gwynne Lewis
2004

The publishers are grateful to the following for permission to reproduce copyright material:

Pearson Education for Map 1: Administrative and fiscal divisions of France under the ancien regime, reprinted from *The Longman companion to the French Revolution* by Colin Jones © Pearson Education, 1990.

A. Poitrineau, *Revue d'histoire moderne et contemporaine*, 1962, ix. Reproduced by permission of the *Revue d'Histoire Moderne et Contemporaine*.

In some instances we have been unable to trace the owners of copyright material, and we would appreciate any information that would enable us to do so.

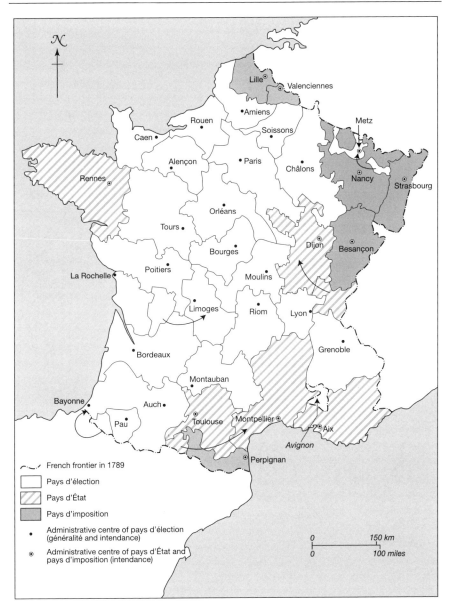

Map 1   Administrative and fiscal divisions of France under the ancien regime.
© Pearson Education 1990. Reprinted from *The Longman companion to the French Revolution* by Colin Jones (1990), by permission of Pearson Education.

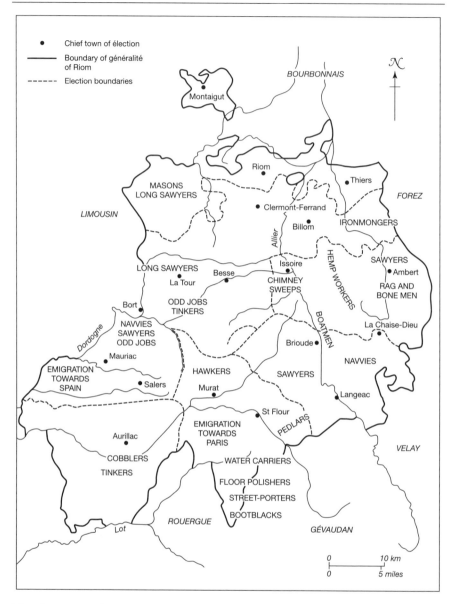

Map 2   Regional trade specialisation of temporary emigrants from the Auvergne in the eighteenth century. (After A. Poitrineau, in *Revue d'histoire moderne et contemporaine*, 1962, ix.)

Map 3   The 83 Departments of France, 1790 (excluding Corsica). The Revolution created an administrative structure which has lasted to the present day. Paris became the Department of the Seine; Rhone-et-Loire was divided into Rhone and Loire. As a result of the first annexations, Mont-Blanc – i.e. Savoie and Haute-Savoie, came from Savoy; Alpes-Maritimes from Nice and Monaco; Mont-Terrible – i.e. Territory-de-Belfort – from the district of Porentruy; and Vaucluse from Avignon and the Comtat-Venaissin. By 1799 there were 90 Departments in all.

Introduction

The intention of this work is not to provide a general history of eighteenth-century France. Its main focus is the relationship between the decline of an aristocratic and ecclesiastic state, the rise of the bourgeoisie and the reaction of *le peuple* to both of these historical evolutions. We will argue that it was the complex, often violent, deconstruction of this relationship that played a crucial role in the fall of the Bourbon monarchy, the course of the Revolution of 1789 and the shaping of the modern French state. *'Le peuple'* is one of those capacious, umbrella terms that altered its meaning as the century elapsed and political and socio-economic relationships altered, which is why we chose to delay a detailed analysis of its social composition and political significance until chapter five.

When assessing the political significance of, and the threat from, *le peuple*, we were mindful of James McMillan's salutary warning that 'Traditional historians have rightly been sceptical of a kind of social history that dwells on the lives of the obscure and the powerless but has nothing to say about those in positions of authority, and this trivialises the key historical issue of power.'[1] We agree, in general, with this comment, although we will challenge the idea that poor people were necessarily 'powerless'. Indeed, we will argue that the actions of the poor and the disenfranchised made a greater impact upon the course of French history, both during the ancien regime and the Revolution, than many historians have suggested.

In order to explain the threat *le peuple* posed for both aristocratic and bourgeois elites, we set the problem within the context of the socio-economic, cultural and political changes that shaped the eighteenth century. To achieve this, we charted the expansion of commercial capitalism and rejected the hypothesis that *'the* Enlightenment' was a unitary and linear movement. We also focused upon the political and religious power structures that ultimately wove the patterns of ordinary people's daily material and spiritual lives. By tackling these different themes, the reader may think that we exchanged analytical depth for methodological breadth, and we would plead guilty to this charge. In the fairly recent past, however, social history has been forced out of the methodological and ideological ghetto that too rigid and structuralist a reading of Marxism had placed it, prompting two leading French historians to write that 'Only the innocent are surprised by the existence of

1

links between the economic, the social, the political'.[2] Following their lead, we have not provided separate chapters on social 'classes', convinced that the richness, as well as the dynamic, of eighteenth-century French history emerges from the *interaction* of political, social, economic and intellectual events and movements rather than from the conflict of nineteenth-century 'class struggles' as defined by Karl Marx.

Thus, the structure and foci of this work, its tripartite division and its separation into nine chapters are founded upon the following premises. First, that it is more illuminating to analyse eighteenth-century France as a society of 'orders', 'estates' and 'corporations' rather than one of 'classes' in the Marxist sense (i.e. related to changing modes of production). Second, that the imposition of any rigid division between the period before the 1750s and that between the 1750s and 1789 is fundamentally misleading. Third, that '1789' represents a political and administrative, *as well as* a social, revolution. Consequently, part one of this study deals with long-term structures of French society and economy – *la France profonde*. Part two examines the movements and ideas that challenged fundamental ancien regime assumptions, beliefs and power structures. Part three examines the consequences of what we could describe – somewhat grandiloquently – as a 'clash of civilisations'.

The chapters in part one focus upon the fundamental political and administrative institutions, cultural attitudes and socio-economic structures of French politics and society, some of which would survive, with important modifications, into the twentieth century. The understanding of French history that we have acquired through teaching and researching modern French history for some thirty years confirms the validity of epistemologies, whether Burkeian, Braudelian or Marxist, that prioritise the *longue durée* approach. Peter Campbell has argued that the court politics of the 1780s were not fundamentally different from those of the late seventeenth century, and this contentious conclusion reminds one that social history is the history 'des lenteurs de l'histoire'.[3] Hence, chapter one of this book provides a general introduction to '*La France profonde*' – its geography, its political, financial, socio-economic and cultural institutions and values. Thereafter, the accent is placed on the *interdependence*, rather than the class specificity, of elites and masses: 'aristocratic archbishops and plebeian *curés*' in chapter two; 'rural seigneurs and small-owning and land-less peasants' in chapter three; and 'bourgeois masters and working men and women' in chapter four. Chapter five is entirely devoted to *le peuple*. Its aim is to provide discernible features for this amorphous social group – representing, we should remind ourselves, the majority of the population – as well as to emphasise its increasing importance in the political sphere.

Part two, consisting of chapters six and seven, switches the focus to address the 'winds of change' that were driven, primarily, by the forces of world capitalism and consumerism and the ideas of what is often misleadingly described as '*the* Enlightenment'. How did French society and the state endeavour to harness these winds of change? The spur to action was unquestionably France's defeat at the hands of the British during the Seven Years War (1756–63). Royal ministers and their critics all agreed that fundamental changes had now to be made, but just how much liberal capitalism and democracy could the Bourbon absolutist system take? A string of reforming ministers, from the duc de Choiseul in the 1760s to Charles-Alexandre Calonne in the late 1780s, would attempt to marry liberal capitalist values to absolute monarchy, only to find that they were strange bedfellows. Behind the scenes, the rise of the modern, bureaucratic French state mirrored the rise of the bourgeoisie. For many liberal and conservative observers in France today, the power of the ancien regime and Revolutionary state is still all too evident. Guy Sorman, in his recent, tongue-just-in-cheek account of France at the end of the 1990s, cites the example of government tax inspectors, those 'servants of the French State, following rites that baffle me . . . The inspectors are clearly discernible in our old history books that sing the praises of our great public servants who allegedly "made France".' Revealingly, Sorman adds that 'In these history books, the people are absent or only appear as abstract figures.'[4] The gap between the governed and the governors is an historical constant. It became of increasing concern to ministers of both Louis XV and Louis XVI.

Part three is composed of chapters seven, eight and nine. They focus upon the failure of the Bourbon monarchy to adapt itself to the new political, economic and social realities of the late eighteenth century, as well as the Revolution's failure to create stable and durable political structures to accommodate the epochal changes that were introduced between 1789 and 1795. For *le peuple*, these years represent a period of exaggerated hopes leading to an almost inevitable sense of disillusionment and despair. From 1795 to the creation of the Napoleonic Empire in 1804, the expansion of the militarised, bureaucratic state drained the strength of popular resistance – from the revolutionary left and the counter-revolutionary right – thus securing the rather fragile and partial 'triumph of the bourgeoisie'. Constant war, civil and foreign, accounted for the lives of hundreds of thousands of poor 'citizens'. Modern social revolutions, especially the French, the Russian and the Chinese, all unleashed demands for greater political participation and the relief of poverty, all eventually flattering only to deceive. The poor were left to pick up the cheque, paid in their own blood. In France after 1795, having helped the bourgeoisie to secure victory in their historical struggle against the aristocracy, ordinary people were punished for their audacious, Revolutionary assumption that they were now bona fide members of the (political) nation. In fact, they would have to wait for another 100 years – 150 in the case of women – before their hopes were fully realised. The chapters in part three are more narrative in style than others, because, as Peter McPhee has explained, there were 'times when huge numbers of people were directly involved in and affected by political processes, when social and political history become inseparable and need to be fused into a "social history of politics"'.[5]

In general, we have placed women under the umbrella of *le peuple* rather than winnowing them out to be discussed as a separate historical species. However, there were issues, within individual chapters, when a sharper focus on gender roles was required; for example, their treatment by the Catholic Church and by the medical profession, or their political exclusion after 1795. We have argued throughout that if the poor suffered most under the ancien regime, poor women took the brunt of that suffering. Both ancien regime and Revolutionary administrations failed to solve the fundamental 'social question' of the eighteenth century, the problem of mass poverty. On the eve of the Revolution, that perceptive diarist of French politics and society, Arthur Young, recorded a meeting with the comte de la Bourdonnaye. Young remarked that, from his observations of Brittany at least, France 'seemed to have nothing in it but privilege and poverty'. La Bourdonnaye simply smiled, prompting Young to write that 'no nobleman can ever probe this evil as it ought to be done, resulting as it does from the privileges going to themselves, and the poverty to the people'.[6] It is true that Brittany was a province that contained extremes of noble wealth and peasant poverty, but the evil of mass poverty, in our estimation, lies at the heart of the political dilemma confronting all modern political systems that claim to have the interests of the majority of their populations at heart – from the eighteenth century to the present.

Our emphasis on the poor throughout this work is not predicated upon a belief in the supposed religious or moral virtues of poverty, nor in the alleged progressive potential of 'the dictatorship of the proletariat'. We pose far more basic questions – why were the poor denied a legitimate voice, at national level, in deciding the shape of their own lives, and what were the consequences of this denial? These questions were not first placed on the political agenda of governments in the eighteenth century. One hundred years before the publication of the *Encyclopédie*, the Dutch philosopher Baruch de Spinoza was pouring scorn on the belief that the 'common people' were too 'irrational' to merit any real stake in political affairs, arguing instead that 'all men have one and the same nature: it is power and culture which misleads us'.[7]

PART ONE

La France Profonde

Chapter 1

Louis XIV and the Regent: war and peace

During the personal reign of Louis XIV (1661–1715), popular participation in affairs of Church and state was primarily a matter of participating in Sunday mass and paying taxes. The 'Sun King', for the vast majority of the French people, was a remote and semi-divine figure; the court at Versailles, 'a reflection of the cosmos'. At least, this was the image that the 'spin doctors' of the day – priests, poets and painters – had fabricated. This picture of the most powerful monarch in Europe was enlarged by identification with classical gods. To celebrate France's victories over the Dutch in the 1670s the court painter Lebrun had painted nine scenes for the *grande galerie* in Versailles, including one with Louis sitting in a chariot holding a thunderbolt, accompanied across the Rhine by Minerva, Hercules and personifications of Glory and Victory. As for ordinary mortals, 'Confronted with a king who was God's lieutenant on earth, sacred and enlightened by divine grace, his subjects had only duties, the first of which was that of obedience'.[1] Louis's successors would find it increasingly difficult to defend a 'divinity' that was losing its mystery, confronted by the rise of a more literate and secularised society, the first of the profound contradictions that would characterise the politics of the eighteenth century.

The 1680s had witnessed the meridian of the Sun King. The following decades were to be characterised by military defeat and religious intolerance, the latter encouraged by his last wife, madame de Maintenon, formerly the governess of his illegitimate children. The Revocation of the Edict of Nantes (1685), which led to the persecution and expulsion of hundreds of thousands of his Calvinist subjects, the disastrous wars of the League of Augsburg (1689–97) and the Spanish Succession (1701–14) profoundly, and adversely, affected popular, and elite, perceptions of Louis XIV. The vast majority of his subjects feted rather than mourned his death in 1715. Nonetheless, despite his fall from grace, his policies reshaped the nature of Bourbon absolutism and altered the geographic contours of modern France. Pierre Pluchon has argued that by 1700 France was not only the most powerful country in Europe, it was also a leading world power. As early as 1666 François Charpentier, a member of the *Académie française*, had suggested that 'The French nation cannot be contained within Europe. It must reach out to the far corners of the world. Barbarians must experience in the future its beneficial domination and be refined in the process.'[2] France's oft-quoted *mission civilisatrice* was taking shape, and it was this dual objective – the pursuit of both continental and colonial supremacy – that would weigh most heavily upon the French in modern times, and never more obviously than in the eighteenth century. Torn between fighting in Europe on the one hand and in the Channel, West Indies, lower Canada and the Indian Ocean on the other, French strategy was repeatedly in danger of falling between two stools.[3] This was the second, increasingly precarious position that the Bourbon monarchy was forced to adopt. We will argue that the failure to resolve the conflicts inherent in the two major issues of the eighteenth century – absolute or constitutional monarchy, and continental or colonial supremacy – would precipitate the collapse of the ancien regime in 1789. English financial and political elites, confronted with similar choices in the seventeenth century, had traded divine right absolutism for commerce and colonies.

The chances of retaining an absolutist system of government, as well as a leading place in world affairs, still appeared to be favourable at the beginning of the century, however, despite the many military reversals. France, with over twenty-two million inhabitants, was, by far, the most populous country in western Europe, around three times the numerical size of England or Spain. Most people – as in most ancien regime states – lived and worked in, or depended upon, the countryside. Ancien regime France was synonymous with agrarian France: the Church and the nobility, as well as a high percentage of the bourgeoisie, lived off the peasantry and the land. The farm, not the factory, would remain the basic unit of eighteenth-century French economic life until well into the nineteenth century; indeed, the reality and myth of rural culture would continue to influence its socio-economic and socio-cultural institutions well into the twentieth century. As Fernand Braudel explained: 'At ground level, the settlement patterns of villages and bourgs formed the living base on which everything else would depend. These aggregates were reproduced indefinitely, on a model that did not radically vary from one end of the country to the other.'[4] The basic units of ancien regime France were her 36,000 communes. Around 1700, 70 per cent of the population lived in communities of fewer than 300 households. The majority of these communes depended upon neighbouring small towns (*bourgs*), which, in turn, were linked to regional urban centres. In 1700, France possessed only 59 cities or large towns of 10,000 or more inhabitants. If we exclude Paris, this would represent less than 7 per cent of the total French population (fixing the benchmark for a town at 2,000 inhabitants, as some historians do, would, of course, increase the urban percentage). By the 1780s, there would be 88 large towns which, given the overall increase in population, means that the percentage figure for the urban population remained in single figures. England's urban population had reached 10 per cent by the 1670s, and would rise to 25 per cent by 1800. Paris, with a population of

510,000 in 1700, was five times as big as France's second city, Lyon; but, whereas over 10 per cent of the total population of England lived in London, less than 3 per cent of the French people lived in Paris.[5] The monarchy had moved to nearby Versailles after its completion in the 1680s following the mid-century Parisian rebellions (Frondes). Versailles would be shaped into an architectural icon of monarchical power. Paris, which would reclaim the monarchy during the Revolution of 1789, would continue to represent the threat of popular power.

In political terms, France had taken a very different road from that followed by England after the mid-seventeenth century European crises. In England, the Glorious Revolution of the 1680s had confirmed the transition from an absolute to a constitutional monarchy, a transition that had begun in earnest with the Civil War of the 1640s. In France, this process would be reversed: royal power would triumph over parliamentary power, an historical fact of profound significance. Although the roots of French absolutism may be traced back at least to the reign of Francis I (1515–47), they penetrated more deeply between the 1620s and the 1660s as a result of war and the centralising policies of the two cardinals, Richelieu and Mazarin. The rebellion of the Parisian Fronde in August 1648 had provoked a reaction that strengthened, rather than weakened, the Bourbon monarchy; it had also increased the historic fear of popular power, especially when it was associated with noble, political ambitions. It would be the alliance of a liberal noble and bourgeois elite with the popular classes (*le peuple*) that would finally undermine the Bourbon edifice in 1789. The long reign of Louis XIV, however, saw the suppression, not the destruction, of princely, parliamentary and popular power as, initially, success on the battlefields of Europe and the wider world propelled France to unprecedented heights of glory. Mankind had only experienced four great ages, according to Voltaire, those of the Greeks, the Romans, the Italian Renaissance and the French under Louis XIV – and the greatest of these, for Voltaire at least, was 'the age of Louis XIV'.[6]

Bourbon absolutism

In order to comprehend fully the complicated, and rather antiquated, machinery of French government and administration, the absolutist system of Louis XIV should never be confused with despotism, or even with a rigidly centralised political system. The great authority on these matters, Michel Antoine, pours polite scorn on those who support, uncritically, the thesis of Alexandre de Tocqueville – that centralisation and state bureaucracy destroyed French liberties, leading to the fall of the Bourbons and the rise of Napoleonic dictatorship.[7] A number of anti-Marxist, 'revisionist' historians have recently provided variations on Antoine's theme, arguing that the foundations of modern democracy are to be found in the ancien regime. The French Revolution, especially the Jacobin Terror of 1793–4, would, allegedly, lay the foundations of modern dictatorships, not democracy.[8] The French state would certainly become more efficient and bureaucratised over the eighteenth century, but, as late as the eve of the Revolution, some ministers were pushing ahead with the creation, or rehabilitation, of some of the provincial estates that had been abolished by Louis XIV!

France was a country in which the challenge of 'modernity' constantly collided with the claims of the past. French absolutism was the product of historic collisions and compromises, of military conquests, dynastic marriages, religious warfare and political and social conflict. Negotiation and compromise, the search for consensus, was always the vital prerequisite for survival. If Louis XIV was more 'absolutist' than his predecessors, or, indeed, his successors, it was primarily because the princely and popular Frondes of the mid-seventeenth century – which had threatened the very existence of the monarchy – was a very recent and painful memory. Just a few miles across the channel in England a king had actually been executed and a republic proclaimed in the 1640s. Both Louis XIV and Louis XV believed that only the personal authority of the monarch, representing the body politic of France, could provide the necessary linkage between the multiple historic, disparate institutions, corporations (*corps*) and cultures that constituted the kingdom. Historic disunity legitimised the centralising absolutism of the monarchy. However, both Louis XIV and Louis XV also realised that centralising policies, if pushed too fast and too hard, could provoke potentially explosive reactions. As Pierre Goubert explains: 'Government institutions . . . reflected above all a type of society, that of an [aristocratic] government, structured around the king and a few ministers, to achieve the material and moral conquest of a country. In plain language, a conquest of other social groups, with other institutions, other customs, another esprit – let's use the word, other "civilisations". . . . For these groups, every agent of the state represented a stranger, an intruder.'[9]

The king stood at the apex of the pyramid of 'government' (and this modern expression began to be employed more widely after the 1720s) – the head of the executive, the legislature and the judiciary; he was God's lieutenant on earth, the embodiment of 'national' unity. Most political theorists, however, from Jean Bodin (1529–1596) to Jacques-Bénigne Bossuet (1627–1704), agreed that, although the king held absolute and, especially for Bossuet, divine authority, he had duties as well as rights. There were the 'fundamental laws' of the kingdom that all monarchs had to obey. For example, the Salic Law. The French crown was not, strictly speaking, hereditary, since, when a king died, his successor was chosen 'in accordance with the fundamental law of the kingdom', and that law stipulated that the French Crown was a male preserve. It was also 'fundamental' that, although the king's word was to be regarded as final, it should not be uttered until other voices had been heard. The most insistent voice was the voice of God. Bourbon kings were consecrated in Reims cathedral where they were christened with holy oil, alleged to have been delivered by a dove when the king of the Franks, Clovis, had been baptised in 496. God's blessing conferred the gift of healing scrofula upon kings, and, in a royal lifetime, he might 'heal' thousands of his subjects. There was, then, a divinity that shaped the ends of even the most absolute of Bourbon kings. Royal justice should be dispensed in the name of God. In periods of political or economic crisis, there was also the voice of the nation's elite, channelled, theoretically, through an Estates General of the realm, divided into the first order, representing the clergy, the second, the nobility, and the third, the bourgeoisie. The mass of the ordinary people (*le peuple*) had no official voice; they were lumped together in a 'Fourth Estate' of relative poverty. It was significant, however, that the Estates General had not in fact been convoked since 1614. During the long reign of Louis XIV, Bourbon absolutism would be rewired to receive only voices coming 'from above', not 'from below'. However, even Louis XIV's sleep had been disturbed during his last years by the occasional rumour that influential, aristocratic voices were suggesting that the Estates should be recalled.

Every Bourbon king governed through royal councils. For most of the eighteenth century, they would be five in number – the king's council (*conseil d'en haut*), the council of despatches (*conseil des dépêches*), the council of conscience (*conseil de conscience*), the finance council (*conseil royal des finances*) and the commercial council (*conseil royal du commerce*). Of these, the king's council was the most influential since it had originally dealt with both the external and internal affairs of state. It met, like all royal councils, in the king's private apartments and was composed of an intimate and influential group of advisers who alone were entitled to call themselves 'ministers of state' (*ministres d'états*). Under Louis XV, the council of despatches would vie in importance with the king's council, the former covering the internal affairs of the kingdom, the latter, foreign affairs. The council of conscience was created during the Regency of the duc d'Orléans (1715–23) and dealt, in the main, with religious issues concerning Protestant and Jansenist 'heretics'. The other two councils formed part of the extensive financial empire carved out by one of the most powerful ministers of the crown, the controller general (*contrôleur général*), although meetings became less frequent as he and the king increasingly resorted to private meetings. In addition to the controller general, the once all-powerful figure of the chancellor would regain under Louis XV some of the authority he had lost under the Sun King. There were usually four secretaries of state (*secrétaires d'état*), responsible for the royal household, the navy, war and foreign affairs. These were prestigious positions, and incumbents almost always ended up in the king's council as ministers of state.

Apart from the royal councils and the key offices of state, two centralising institutions stood clearly above and apart from the rest by the 1700s: the sovereign courts, and the provincial Intendants. They both received their orders directly from Versailles. The sovereign courts included the thirteen Parisian and provincial 'parlements' of the realm, the nine *chambre des comptes*, the four *cours des aides* and the two *cours des monnaies*. The *chambres des comptes* – one in Paris and eight in the provinces – were responsible, primarily, for the supervision of the financial affairs of the country and of the royal domain. The *cours des aides*, situated in Paris, Clermont-Ferrand, Montauban and Bordeaux, dealt with matters relating to taxation and customs duties. The *cours des monnaies,* one in Paris, the other in Lyon, were responsible for matters pertaining to currency and counterfeiting. Positions in the parlements and the sovereign courts were highly prized since they often conferred noble status on successful applicants. Magistrates and officials in these institutions represented the top echelon of the judiciary and the administration – the robe nobility (*noblesse de robe*), a term used to distinguish them from the traditional sword nobility (*noblesse de l'épée*).

The thirty or so Intendants linked the machinery of the central government to the provinces. They have frequently been compared with the Napoleonic Prefects, although the size of their jurisdictions (entire provinces rather than departments) makes such comparisons dubious. Originating with the masters of requests (*maîtres des requêtes*) of the mid-seventeenth century, they were based, geographically, upon the old financial jurisdictions, the généralités. Trained as jurists, and experienced in the workings of the royal bureaucracy, the Intendant was responsible for the maintenance of public order, matters of taxation and justice and a host of other duties, including the promotion of trade and industry. Beneath each Intendant there were several sub-delegates (*sous-délégués*), invariably chosen, unlike their superiors, from the local legal elite. There has been a tendency in recent years to question the extent of the Intendants' authority, but there can be no doubting their crucial importance in ensuring the efficient administration of the state from the 1650s to the Revolution. Michel Antoine describes them as 'the coping stone of monarchical authority in the provinces'. He also points to one of the most remarkable features of Bourbon administration – the heavy load of responsibility carried by just a handful of officials, often not more than ten in each Intendancy.[10]

If the Intendants were by far the most powerful representatives of the monarchy in the provinces, the officials (*élus*) who staffed financial districts (*élections*) also carried considerable authority. They were responsible for the collection of government taxes in the historic central regions of France, the *pays d'élection*. The structure of the financial system was incredibly complicated, since the crown had mortgaged much of its authority over the centuries in return for money to finance its foreign and domestic policies, especially its wars. Government taxes were collected in a variety of ways, and by a variety of government and private agencies and individuals. Rich bankers and financiers, like the Protestant banker, Samuel Bernard, and the Crozat brothers, bailed the monarchy out in times of crisis. The more systematic collection of direct taxes (the *taille*, a land tax, being the most important) was different in the regions directly administered by the crown (*pays d'élection*) from the practice in the provincial estates (*pays d'état*). In the former, taxation was under the control of the Intendants; in the latter, it was in the hands of the officials of the provincial estates.

Indirect taxes had long been 'farmed-out', first to rich individuals, then to a financial syndicate, or 'Tax Farm' (*ferme générale*). This rather shady institution made huge profits, first by charging interest on the money they advanced to the Crown, and then by 'creative accounting' on the taxes they were then allowed to collect from taxpayers. It is not surprising, then, that tax-farmers (*fermiers généraux*), as well as their agents and enforcers, were deeply unpopular. By the end of the ancien regime, the Tax Farm had become 'a state within a state', with 58 offices in Paris employing 685 people and 228 provincial offices with 28,762 employees. It had won the right to collect the lucrative salt tax (*gabelle*) and taxes on wines, soap and oil (the *aides*) in 12 provinces of the centre and west, as well as duties on goods entering their customs zone. At times, half of the money going into the royal coffers came from tax farmers. Anomalies abounded. In the *pays de grande gabelle*, like the Paris Basin, the compulsory salt tax was generally high; in the *pays de petite gabelle*, like Provence and Languedoc, it varied; in Brittany, Artois, Flanders and many other regions, it was low or non-existent.[11] As a result, smuggling from high to low tax regions, along the border between Normandy and Brittany, for example, became 'a cottage industry'. The financial and fiscal systems of ancien regime France were inefficient, inimical to the growth of trade, anomalous and inequitable.

Finally, the royal system of justice exhibited most, if not all, of the confusions and complexities associated with this theoretically centralised and absolutist form of government. Apart from the 13 parlements that acted as appeal courts, there were around 400 provincial courts known, after the judicial areas they covered, as *bailliage* courts in much of the north and east, but as *sénéchaussée* courts in the west and south. Above these courts – though often staffed with the same judges – was the local appeal court, the *présidial*. Not too confusing perhaps, but add to this the municipal and consular courts in the towns, the thousands of seigneurial courts of justice in the countryside and, then, the ecclesiastical courts dotted throughout the country, and we can begin, at least, to appreciate the scale of the problem. Michel Antoine suggests that, since most of the magistrates who provided the personnel for these courts of justice had bought their posts and were thus 'independent' of government, we might find here the origins of the salutary modern practice

13

of separating the executive from the judiciary.[12] The argument has merit, but we need to remember that the king remained the head of the judiciary. Only the king could issue the arbitrary *lettres de cachet*, enabling ill-disciplined sons and enemies of the state to be locked away without trial. Around 2,500 victims of these royal warrants were imprisoned in the Bastille during the reign of Louis XIV; others might languish for years in provincial prisons.

Checks and balances

Many forces militated against the effective operation of Bourbon central-isation, the most obvious being historical geography. The king's writ ran throughout France, but the further it travelled from Versailles, the less authoritative it became. The extensive province of Brittany had been acquired in 1491, but it continued to exhibit strong manifestations of independence until the Revolution of 1789, and beyond. The province of Lorraine was only added to France, officially, in the eighteenth century. From an administrat-ive and fiscal standpoint, there were, in fact, two Frances: the France of the *pays d'élection*, composed of the old Capetian lands at the centre of the kingdom and governed directly from Versailles, and the France of the *pays d'état*, the peripheral provinces that had been acquired through marriage or conquest. Several of the latter, including Guyenne, Normandy, Quercy and Rouergue, had lost their political independence in the seventeenth century, leaving Burgundy, Dauphiné, Brittany and Languedoc – representing around a quarter of French territory – to carry on the fight against state centralisa-tion. Of these four, however, only Brittany and Languedoc wielded real political clout. France was a centralised monarchy in theory, but 'corporatist' in practice, with power being diffused through a bewildering variety of independent and semi-independent bodies representing provincial estates, duchies, bishoprics, ports and cities. In addition, there were the many cor-porations and guilds that represented barristers and doctors, as well as trade and craft organisations.

The second major constraint on absolutism was institutional, represented by the thirteen parlements of the realm, the Paris parlement being by far the most influential since its jurisdiction covered almost half of the country; the other twelve parlements were situated in the peripheral *pays d'état*. The func-tions of these medieval institutions were primarily judicial: they were the highest appeal courts in the land. It was their political power, however, that provoked conflict with the monarchy. The Paris parlement had the right to register royal edicts and, in some cases, including those relating to taxation and religion, the right to refuse to register edicts considered to be inconsist-ent with the 'traditional liberties of the kingdom' (the right of *remonstrance*). It is true that the king could appear before the parlement in person and, in a display of his regal power, force it to act (a *lit de justice*), and, if further resistance was forthcoming, even exile its officials to some boring retreat in the country. However, this procedure was always fraught with danger and employed only when all else had failed. One can detect historic parallels here with the struggle between the English monarchy and Parliament, and, by the mid-eighteenth century, some political theorists were beginning to think in these terms, but the analogy should never be pushed too far. For one thing, there were the twelve, provincial parlements that did not always agree with the Paris parlement, or, indeed, with each other, especially when 'national' rights conflicted with provincial rights. More importantly, the peculiar evolution of the French parlements had drained them of much of their early authority. Louis XIV had severely curtailed their political powers in 1673. The full restoration of their authority after his death would mark a significant turning point in the constitutional history France. The repeated conflicts between the monarchy and the parlements during the eighteenth century would reveal an everwidening gap between the defenders of Bourbon absolutism and those who supported constitutional change, albeit along aristocratic lines.

The independent note struck by the parlements may be explained, in part, by the fact that many of their members had bought their offices, not just for themselves, but for their descendants. French governments had been selling state offices since the fourteenth century. In 1604, these venal offices were made hereditary on the annual payment of one-sixtieth of their purchase price, a practice that became known as *la paulette* after the founder of this lucrative fiddle. During the latter part of Louis XIV's reign the sale of state offices reached unprecedented heights. From the top positions in the sovereign courts to judicial and mayoral posts in small provincial towns, down to the menial offices of bailiffs and town criers, the state had mortgaged much of its authority over its financial, administrative and judicial personnel in return for hard cash. In theory, the state could have regained the right to sack incompetent officials by offering to repay the original cost of purchasing the office, but it rarely had the money to do so. By the end of the seventeenth century, the state had just 300 non-venal officials compared with the 45,000 offices it had sold to the highest bidder. Ancien regime governments had 'farmed-out' control of their administrative, financial and judicial personnel to finance their wars. Louis XIV's gross exploitation of the system – abolishing an office only to 'reinvent' it for more cash, or selling the same office to three purchasers – helps to explain growing hostility towards it. Nonetheless, offices continued to be sold by the government until 1789. David Parker argues that venality had its advantages, including a degree of independence from the state. He concludes, however, that 'It was precisely the widespread unreliability, dishonesty, and unproductive rivalry of the office-holders that explain the enormous array of responsibilities bestowed on the . . . Intendants.' It seems that 'independence' was bought at a very heavy price.[13]

Finally, in terms of 'checks and balances', there were the acute problems associated with the dissemination of government information. When assessing the real nature of Bourbon centralisation, we must begin by rejecting facile comparisons with twentieth-century states, whose agents exploit the advantages of an electronic age. Today, instructions and information can reach the furthest outposts of any state, or indeed any foreign country, within seconds; in 1700, it could take several days for government officials in Rennes or Marseilles to receive orders from Versailles. Administrative time in the eighteenth century travelled as fast as horses' hooves and poor roads permitted, favouring the time-honoured technique, adopted by many a local official, of *immobilisme*, or 'forgetting' to reply to government communiqués! Widespread illiteracy and linguistic diversity aggravated inadequate means of communication. As late as 1789, over one-third of the French population could neither read nor write, although rates of literacy obviously varied according to class, gender, geographic location and cultural milieu. More surprisingly, perhaps, around two-thirds of the French population did not use French (the official language since 1539) in daily conversation; indeed, for the mass of the poor, it was a foreign tongue. Even by the end of the century, the millions who lived in the north, parts of the west and the centre, preferred to speak in their local Picard or Burgundian dialect. In the *langue d'oc* regions of the south, those speaking Provençal would have experienced great difficulty in communicating with their Limousin or Auvergnat compatriots. Add to all this a few million Flemish, Breton, German, Basque and Catalan-speaking inhabitants and we realise that eighteenth-century French men and women spoke with many tongues.[14] Revolutionary governments in the 1790s would begin to impose more linguistic conformity: speaking Breton, for example, would constitute a 'counter-revolutionary' act. This was serious state 'centralisation'!

Louis XIV – 'absolutism reinterpreted'

If, on his death-bed, Louis XIV actually did say, 'L'état, c'est moi', then he died in ignorance. It is more probable, however, that he died saying, 'I shall pass away, but the state will continue,' since his most lasting achievement was to complete the task started by Richelieu and Mazarin of ending the nobility's pretension that, because it was coeval, it was also coequal with the monarchy. Louis XIV and his chief ministers, Colbert and Louvois, scotched the threat of aristocratic rebellion, not least by placing overall control of the armed forces in the hands of military intendants (*intendants de l'armée*); henceforward, the escutcheoned aristocracy would be given room and board in the draughty garrets of Versailles. During the 1690s, the feudal duty of the king's vassals to supply him with troops (*ban et arrière-ban*) was finally consigned to the historical dustbin. By this time, Louis had gathered around him at Versailles the top 300 or so aristocrats, including princes and peers of the realm, to indulge themselves in a fantasy world of plays, balls, fêtes and fireworks – all the 'folies de grandeur'. The French aristocracy would be given a cultural facelift; they would be 'born again' by studying the neoclassical texts of Racine and Corneille. They would not exactly 'turn their swords into ploughshares', but they would henceforth only use them on foreign rather than on domestic soil, an historic reorientation of power. The monarchy, of course, would have to pay a price for this surrender, but that price would be paid, in the main, by the peasantry in the form of seigneurial dues. There was also the lavish distribution amongst his favourites of gifts, pensions and lucrative positions in the Army. Louis XIV regarded himself primarily as the head of a military state. Of the 318 medals struck during his reign to honour his achievements, 218 portrayed him as Mars, the God of War, and only 17 as Apollo, the Sun God. Averaged out over the entire reign, war expenditure under Louis XIV consumed half of all government revenues. Versailles may have been the hub of the civil administration of France, but it was also 'a whole society in miniature', the abode of 1,000 or so nobles and 4,000 servants – including the 300 top aristocrats whose cultural formation, and professional expectation, would remain that of a pre-capitalist, warrior caste.[15]

Peter Campbell is one of those historians who question the Tocquevillian thesis concerning the centralisation of France under the Bourbons. Extending the thesis of Susan Kettering, he argues that, up to the Revolution of 1789, ancien regime governments would operate through aristocratic clans and cabals at court and networks of clientage and patronage in the provinces.[16] Privilege and patronage had been, and would continue to be, the name of the ancien regime political power game. The top echelon of the aristocracy, *les Grands,* were given not only prestigious positions, such as provincial military governors, thus enabling them to develop new networks of clientage and patronage, but also plum posts in the army and navy. From the reign of Louis XIV to that of Louis XVI it would be more difficult for a non-noble, or even a minor noble, to become a marshal or an admiral than for the proverbial camel to pass through the eye of a needle. As was the case with the sale of administrative and judicial offices to the robe nobility, the monarchy was bribing the sword nobility in return for its assistance in running the state. There was also an additional, and more valuable, reward for both sections of the nobility. In return for their support, the monarchy would sustain, with increasing difficulty, a decaying, pre-capitalist, landed system. The problem of the relationship between the state and the nobility was similar in Eastern Europe, though the solutions here were different.[17]

In addition to his support for feudal aristocracy, Louis XIV also strengthened the authority of the Bourbon state by nominating leading aristocrats – the Rohans, the Fitzjames, the Noailles – to the top ecclesiastical offices of the Church, thus weakening its political independence and reliance upon

Rome. Louis realised that bishops and priests were far more important in shaping the daily lives of the masses than any provincial Intendant or *élu*. As John McManners explains: 'The theoretically absolute monarchy of France, though becoming more responsive to public opinion throughout the eighteenth century, was primarily looking for approval to the aristocracy: Versailles, where the nobles glittered around the king in self-interested subordination, was the heart and symbol of the monarchy's power. Over-simplifying, it can be said that the nobles had yielded up their anarchical local domination in return for bribes offered by the Crown, and the source for the bribes was the wealth and splendour of the Gallican Church.'[18] The Concordat of Bologna with the Papacy in 1516 had given the French State the right to nominate to all bishoprics in the country. Under Louis XIV, nominations went to the aristocracy. Although he curtailed the practice of allowing aristocrats to keep their posts in the family, aristocratic control of archbishoprics and wealthy religious houses would continue right up to the Revolution. Of the 1,416 nominations to sees from 1516 to 1789, 1,227 were nobles and 62 were commoners (the status of the remaining nominees is unknown). Half of these commoners were nominated between 1560 and 1588 when the power of the crown was weak. The most sought-after (financially rewarding) sees went to the 300 members of *les Grands*, although the percentage fell from 25 per cent or more under Louis XIV to 18 per cent after 1726. It was the aristocracy that cemented the union between throne and altar.

But it was the attack on 'heresy', almost medieval in conception and intensity, which, apart from the identification of the regime with war, gave the reign of Louis XIV its unique character, and which bequeathed the most burdensome legacy to its successors. Richard Bonney has recently focused our attention on what he terms 'confessional absolutism'. He explains that the origins of Louis XIV's Revocation of the Edict of Nantes in 1685 can be traced back to the 'confessional absolutist' beliefs of Cardinal Richelieu half a century earlier. Like Elizabeth I of England, Richelieu had equated heresy with rebellion against the state. It was the salvation of the state, not the individual soul, which was at stake.[19] Although it is now widely accepted that the Revocation represents the greatest mistake committed by Louis XIV, it is worth noting that it elicited favourable comment in the media of the day: 'confessional absolutism' unquestionably had its supporters, from archbishops to farm-labourers.[20] The implementation of the Revocation undoubtedly strengthened the historic bond between the Catholic Church and the Bourbon State. Calvinist temples were destroyed, their congregations obliged to choose between resistance, conversion or exile; children of Calvinist marriages had to be raised as Catholics. Over 200,000 Calvinists emigrated, their financial and manufacturing skills welcomed in Prussia, England, Holland and Switzerland.

There is no need to dwell on the acute suffering of those who chose to stay in France and resist: McManners has provided a grim, national portrait of the brutality of the royal troops, the rapes, the torture, the hangings.[21] The relevant issue here is the legacy of hatred and religious division that would poison French society for a century or more. Its most immediate and violent consequence was the guerrilla war, known as the *Guerre des Camisards*, that erupted in the Calvinist stronghold of the Cévennes mountains in the southeast from 1702 to 1704. Terrible atrocities were committed by the Camisards (the word derives from the local word for the shirts – *chemises* – worn by the guerillas) as well as by the royal troops sent to crush them. And the fact that this rebellion broke out at a time when Louis was engaged in a major European war meant that Calvinists now had the words 'traitors' and 'republicans', as well as 'heretics', stamped on their brows. Their treachery convinced many sceptics that the Crown had been right all along – heresy would destroy the state.

The Jansenist controversy was to be less brutal, far less bloody, but, from a political and constitutional perspective, far more important in challenging the fundamental aims of Bourbon absolutism, since Jansenists claimed, unlike Calvinists, to be part of the Catholic family. For Louis XIV, however, Jansenism was the bastard offspring of Calvinism. The term 'Jansenism' is derived from the writings of Cornelius Jansen, bishop of Ypres. In his work on Saint Augustine, *l'Augustinus*, which had appeared in 1640, Cornelius had stressed the importance of going back to the true Augustinian faith, with its emphasis upon predestination, the austere moral life and personal salvation only through grace. Jansenists believed unreservedly in original sin and, more disturbingly for the official French Church, questioned the final authority of the pope and his appointed bishops in matters of faith and doctrine. Although they refused to leave the Catholic Church, regarding themselves as the true, primitive Catholics, their opponents in Rome and Versailles detected a poisonous, democratic odour of the 'priesthood of all believers' in their theology, a dangerous concept with worrying political and constitutional spin-offs, as Elizabeth I of England had found. Versailles was also none too keen on all this talk about sexual depravity and the need for a moral, austere lifestyle!

There were, in fact, several 'Jansenisms', one variant for the upper clergy, one for the magistrates of the parlements, another variant for the lower clergy and the laity.[22] In very general terms, however, Jansenism drew most of its strength from its compatibility with two profoundly French, 'nationalist', religious movements, Gallicanism and Richerism. The history of the former goes back at least to Francis I's Concordat of Bologna with the papacy in 1516 which gave the state the power to nominate candidates for bishoprics, leaving the papacy to grant them his spiritual authority. In 1682, Louis himself pressed the pope to accept the four 'Gallican Articles' that would govern the relationship between France and the papacy until 1789. It was agreed, after years of discussion, that (a) the pope should have no authority over the temporal affairs of France; (b) that the authority of the General Assembly of the French clergy was superior to that of Rome; (c) that Gallican liberties were unassailable; and, crucially, (d) that on matters of faith, papal pronouncements had to receive the assent of the French Church. The 'Four Articles' represented a major assertion of the independence of the French Church.[23]

If Gallicanism was a doctrine that appealed to all levels of the clergy, Richerism – based upon the ideas of the early seventeenth-century cleric, Edmond Richer – drew its main support from the lower clergy. It was a radical, democratic doctrine that advocated the full participation of *curés* in the governance of the French Church; it also preached in favour of clerical marriage and the state nationalisation of Church property! The supporters of Richerism – and they were numerous amongst the lower clergy – would have to wait for the French Revolution before these ideas were translated into practice. And this is interesting, for if we dispense with the religious terminology and contemporary theological disputes in which Gallicanism and Richerism were wrapped, we find that the first was essentially a 'nationalist' and the second a 'democratic' movement. What we are dealing with here, in effect, is the birthpangs of a nation, a nation that the Revolution of 1789 would deliver.

Having forced the papacy to toe the French line over the Four Articles in 1693, it seems perverse, at first glance, that Louis XIV should have begged Pope Clement XI for his assistance in crushing the revival of Jansenism twenty years later. Louis was, of course, getting old by this time, his thoughts, influenced by his pietistic wife, madame de Maintenon, and his Jesuit confessor, Le Tellier, were turning increasingly towards the afterlife. There was, however, no major contradiction, as Louis XIV saw it, between his own salvation and that of his country. Both Louis and the traditional French Catholic Church were keen to defend their 'national' rights and liberties against Rome. But they were both just as keen, as was the papacy, to defend the French Catholic state against 'heresy', and this included 'heretics' at home and abroad. Abroad, England, having already executed one Catholic king, Charles I in 1649, had exiled another, James II, in 1688, replacing him with France's enemy, William of Orange. Louis XIV thus had to face Protestant rebellions at home and Protestant enemies abroad.

Jeremy Black thinks that: 'Louis established himself as the enemy of Britain . . . more by his real and apparent backing for the [Catholic] Stuarts and their British supporters than by his activities on the continent'.[24] Both Louis XIV and Louis XV would shelter Stuart pretenders to the English throne. If this were not enough to explain Louis's crusading zeal during the last decades of his reign, there was the 'second wave' of Jansenism. Pasquier Quesnel, a Jansenist priest, had published his *Nouveau Testament en français* in 1692. It was a book that combined Jansenist, Gallican and Richerist themes in one explosive combination. A few miles south of Versailles the ideas of Quesnel began to attract hundreds of sympathisers to the convent of Port-Royal. By 1711, Louis XIV had not only closed down Port-Royal, but demolished the actual buildings. Two years later, hoping to finish with the Jansenist devil and all his works, Louis XIV pressed Pope Clement XI to issue the bull *Unigenitus*, a full-frontal attack upon Quesnel's *Nouveau Testament*. It turned out to be the last, but certainly not the least, of the poisoned chalices the Sun King would hand on to his successor.

The Regency: a failed revolution?

The last decade of Louis XIV's reign had been one of the most miserable in French history, the result of seemingly endless warfare and atrocious weather. It had also been the most miserable period in the life of the Sun King. His son and presumed successor had died of smallpox on 14 April 1711. Less than a year later, the grim reaper called in two grandsons, the duc de Bourgogne, who died of scarlet fever, and the duc de Berry, the victim of a riding accident. This left two great-grandsons as heirs to the throne, the duc de Bretagne, aged four, and the duc d'Anjou (1710–1774), who was two years younger. On 8 March 1712, the much-feared smallpox had carried off the young duc de Bretagne, proving that the only effective instrument of social equality in eighteenth-century France was death. All of these royal victims had been treated in accordance with current medical practice: they were bled and purged by a cabal of doctors. The life of the little duc d'Anjou – the future Louis XV – had only been saved by the courageous action of the ladies of the Court who refused to allow a doctor anywhere near him! Although it was thought that he was too sickly to reach adulthood, he would, in fact, reign for over half a century. As for his great-grandfather, in poor health, the days of war, wine and mistresses long gone, he slowly sank into the redemptive arms of his last wife, madame de Maintenon, not for sexual pleasure, but for protection and religious solace.[25]

Louis XIV had chosen his nephew to act as Regent until the young Louis XV came of age. In common with most of his contemporaries Louis XIV thought that the Regent, Philip, duc d'Orléans, was a disaster, too fond of wine, women and orgies and therefore – minus the orgies – too much like Louis XIV had been in his salad days. The Orléans family was a cadet branch of the House of Bourbon, and if the young Louis XV did succumb to the many killer diseases of the time, Philip was next in line to the throne. He was as rich as Croesus and owned the duchies of Orléans, Valois and Chartres, as well as one of the most visited tourist spots in Paris today, the Palais-Royal. Despite his uncle's contempt and the widespread, but erroneous, popular belief that he had poisoned the King's offspring to get closer to the throne, there was more to the Regent than Louis XIV, or the scurrilous lampoons of the day, imagined. His capacity for a tight working day was as large as his appetite for loose women. He was also, according to his close friend, the duc de Saint-Simon, intelligent, eloquent and perceptive.[26]

Given the misery of the mass of the French people, allied to the fact that the government was virtually bankrupt, a programme of peace and reconstruction was a necessity, not an option. Furthermore, the Regent was determined to keep his own chance of becoming king on the front burner, and therefore had no interest in undermining the political system he had inherited in trust for the young king. Overall, government policy would continue to be influenced by traditional, hierarchical and privileged power structures; by the extensive influence of the Church; by the political and institutional resistance of parlements and provincial estates; as well as by the dead weight of rural France, *la France profonde*. But, as Colin Jones has observed, previous Bourbon rulers had always given absolutism 'an individual twist'[27], and the Regent proved to be no exception to the Bourbon rule. A few historians have suggested in recent years that some of the new initiatives taken during the Regency bordered on the revolutionary. They point out that in Europe and the wider world economic, cultural and diplomatic forces were combining to create a new, more secular and capitalist society, and that the duc d'Orléans, an intelligent and adventurous soul, was anxious to participate in this brave new world. After all, not every piece of the ancien regime jigsaw could be put back in its customary place. There was change, hope and a desire for more freedom in the air; a spirit of opposition to absolutist policies had taken hold, even at court.

Emmanuel Le Roy Ladurie is one of those historians who have recently provided us with a radical new interpretation of the Regency period. He divides it into two distinct halves: the 'Liberal Regency' from 1715 to mid-1718, and the 'Authoritarian Regency' from 1718 to the Regent's death in 1723.[28] Does this division simply reflect the fact that the Regent was obliged to be 'liberal' during his early years, given his relatively weak position, and 'authoritarian' once his rule was firmly established? Does he really merit Ladurie's praise as a liberal forerunner of Europe's 'Enlightened Despots'? Ladurie's critics have argued, for example, that the Regent encouraged the brief return of the aristocracy in 1715, as well as the political pretensions of the aristocratic Paris parlement, not just to bolster his shaky personal position, but to further the dynastic interests of his branch of the Bourbon family. It is also possible that the collapse of the liberal phase of the Regency in 1718 was not unconnected with his personal drive for power. A colourful and contentious personality, the duc d'Orléans has provided much grist for the historical mill!

The liberal phase, 1715–18

There is convincing evidence that the early political decisions taken by the Regent were prompted by weakness rather than principle. In the first place, control of government was handed over to the 'reactionary' princes and peers of the realm, *les Grands*. Excluded, in the main, from political power under Louis XIV, the court aristocracy was very necessary now, particularly if the Regent was thinking – as he undoubtedly was – of becoming king on the probable death of the sickly Louis XV. In place of the old departments and secretaries of state, the new system – described as the *Polysynodie* by the duc de Saint-Simon – was composed of seven, separate councils, each headed by an aristocrat or prince of the blood. These councils reported to the Regency Council, whose president was, of course, the duc d'Orléans. It was not exactly what the aristocratic, liberal cabals, led by influential figures such as Fénelon, archbishop of Cambrai, and the duc de Saint-Simon, had been dreaming of for a decade or so, but it was, for them, a move in the right direction. In his classic study, *Robe and Sword: The Regrouping of the French Aristocracy after Louis XV*, Franklin Ford is extremely dismissive of the contribution of the *Polysynodie*. He argues that nothing much could be expected from 'a group of barely literate soldiers and pompous courtiers, who devoted more attention to whether or not a subordinate official might be seated while reporting to a council than they did to the substance of his report'.[29]

The judgement is too harsh. One of the 'barely literate soldiers' was Louis XIV's illegitimate son, the comte de Toulouse, and one of the 'pompous courtiers' was the duc de Noailles, both intelligent and capable men. They were products of that uneven, cultural transformation of the aristocracy that had occurred in many parts of Europe during the seventeenth century. This is of crucial importance in understanding the evolution of the Bourbon regime during the following century. As David Parker explains: 'Fashioning a renewed sense of hierarchy, order and self-discipline out of the disarray into which they [the aristocracy] had fallen, they reshaped their own aristocratic identity. In the process they also gave shape to the absolutist regime.'[30] On political and social levels, it is not so much the 'rise of the bourgeoisie' that characterises our period as the refusal of the aristocracy to fall, a key to unlocking the mystery of the outbreak of the Revolution of 1789.

Ford was right to argue, however, that since Louis XIV had excluded, in large measure, *les Grands* from the domestic administration of the country, many were found wanting when the moment came for them to seize power in 1715. But it could also be argued that it was the operation of the new system itself, rather than the personal inexperience of the aristocracy that led to failure. The infighting and bureaucratic confusion that occurred, aggravated by the secret, personal policies pursued by the Regent, certainly did not help. The reality was that, over previous centuries, a proto-modern, bureaucratic, ministerial system of government had gradually taken shape, and no 'post-feudal' collection of privileged, aristocratic councils could easily replace it.

Then there was the restoration of the political power of the parlements. We have seen that Louis had emasculated the power of the Paris parlement, particularly its right to criticise royal policies, the right of *remonstrance*. However, the parlement had never lost hope of regaining its former glory; it had only agreed to register the papal, anti-Jansenist bull, *Unigenitus*, under duress. The fundamental issue here was not religious, but constitutional, a case of 'who ruled in Versailles'? Was it a 'despotic' monarch, careless of the fundamental laws of the kingdom? Was it a 'foreign' pope, constantly seeking to impose his will over the French people through religious orders like the Jesuits? The parlement insisted that it had evolved in parallel with the monarchy and that, therefore, the two institutions were interdependent. There should be a contract between the king and the people, with the parlements, Parisian and provincial, acting as 'guardians of the people's liberties'. In terms of democratic credibility, the manifesto of these aristocratic bodies of rich magistrates was distinctly suspect; in terms of the evolution of the constitutional history of eighteenth-century France, it was to prove revolutionary. Julian Swann has argued that it would be 'a dangerous combination of princes, parlements, and people that would prove Louis XVI's undoing'.[31]

Louis XIV's death provided the Paris parlement with the moment for which it had long been waiting. The Regent needed the parlement to annul key articles in Louis XIV's will, particularly the recognition of Louis's illegitimate sons, the duc du Maine and the comte de Toulouse, as next in line to the throne. In a fateful move (that would be repeated in 1774 when Louis XVI came to the throne after the powers of the parlements had once again been curtailed), the Regent decided to restore to the Paris parlement the right of *remonstrance*. He also released many Jansenist 'heretics' from prison as well as appointing the cardinal de Noailles, the Gallican-Jansenist archbishop of Paris, as president of the council of conscience. When, in April 1716, an ageing and inflexible pope stated that he would not confirm the appointment of pro-Jansenist candidates for bishoprics, the Regent, an agnostic at best, revealed his liberal sympathies – or his weakness – and refused his support. Unfortunately, both sides in this historic contest, the pro-papal *constitutionnaires*, who wanted to make *Unigenitus* a fundamental law of the kingdom, and the pro-Jansenist – or Gallican – *appelants*, who wanted a general council of the clergy to reject what they interpreted as an attack on Gallican liberties, refused to follow the Regent's moderate line. The intransigence of the papacy did not help matters. The war of words, and pamphlets, became increasingly bitter. On 7 October 1717, the Regent tried to impose a vow of silence on both camps, but in vain. An historic, religious conflict, involving profound constitutional issues, threatened to undermine the regime.

If the renewed authority of the Paris parlement dismayed the old, aristocratic guard, the diplomatic revolution that occurred between 1715 and 1718 incensed them. The rumoured alliance with England, they argued, was not just a case of surrendering to a bunch of arrogant magistrates, it was a betrayal of national interest. For most of Louis XIV's reign, the majority of the French people (excluding the Protestants) had regarded England and Holland as the sworn enemies of France, responsible for much of the misery inflicted on the country. By the Treaty of Utrecht (1713), Louis XIV had been forced to accept that his grandson, who had acceded to the Spanish throne as Philip V in 1700, should renounce his claim to the French throne. However, Philip V had refused to accept the provisions of the Treaty of Utrecht, which meant that the Regent's own claim to the French throne was threatened. The Regent's natural ally in this case, given its determination to avoid the unification of the Spanish and the French thrones at all costs, was England, particularly since England had royal pretenders of its own to worry about. In 1714, the Elector of Hanover had ascended the English throne as George I. If the Regent would now reverse Louis XIV's support for the Stuart pretenders, the English could sleep safely in their beds. An Anglo-French alliance was, therefore, a way of propping up two new, and somewhat shaky, regimes.

All this smacks of personal, dynastic ambition taking precedence over national interest, and Pierre Pluchon is convinced that this was indeed the case. He argues that, led astray by his wily but corrupt former tutor and personal envoy to England, the abbé Dubois, the Regent threw away 'any pretence of a national policy in favour of the interests of the House of Orléans', an interpretation that has attracted considerable support.[32] Guy Chaussinand-Nogaret, however, has recently attributed more selfless motives to the Regent and Dubois. He claims that they sought to replace the era of Louis XIV's catastrophic wars with one of peace and commercial development. The old aristocracy would now have to change their swords into ploughshares (or fishing-nets!) as Dubois and the Regent worked to create 'a little Europe of the north-west [England, Holland and France], linking France to the great maritime powers, symbols of modernity'.[33]

This was a revolutionary project indeed, and one that was in harmony with the spirit of the age. In 1712, the abbé de Saint-Pierre had published his *Mémoire pour rendre la paix perpétuelle en Europe,* a blueprint for future projects of European union. Saint-Pierre, who came to regard Louis XIV as little better than Attila the Hun, had been a member of the liberal, pacifist circle, led by the duc de Bourgogne and archbishop Fénelon, towards the end of Louis XIV's reign. There were other arguments for a major shift in diplomatic alignments. France's old allies Sweden and Turkey were declining powers confronted, respectively, by Russian expansion in the Baltic and by Russian and Austrian expansion in the decaying Ottoman Empire. In addition, Charles VI of Austria, France's traditional enemy, had not been pleased with the Treaty of Utrecht and had designs on territories in Italy, as indeed did Philip V of Spain. The overall situation in Europe was fluid and potentially explosive.

It was in this context that one of the great diplomatic shifts in French history was to occur. In November 1716, Dubois and the English foreign minister, Stanhope, signed a treaty promising French support for the Hanoverian succession in England and English support for the Regent should Philip V of Spain seek to reactivate his rights to the French throne. On 4 January 1717, Holland was brought on board transforming the Anglo-French agreement into a Triple Alliance that would keep the peace, more or less, in Europe until 1731. The 'little Europe' of the maritime powers had been created and the ghost of Louis XIV laid to rest, almost.

If Dubois and the Regent are regarded by many historians as unscrupulous adventurers, they appear to have been models of integrity compared with John Law, the man who was to turn the French economic and fiscal system inside out. According to Antoine Murphy, '1720 would become a year that would be etched on the eighteenth-century calendar in the same way as 1929 would become a financial reference date in the twentieth century. It would be the year of a new European phenomenon, namely stock-market booms and crashes, most notable in France, a French Revolution *avant le nom* and without the Terror.'[34] To pay for Louis XIV's wars, the Treasury had been forced to rely on a number of costly expedients – alienation of the royal domain, a massive increase in the sale of government offices, loans from financiers and the wealthy nobility. More regular sources of income came from the issue of government annuities and, in 1695, a new poll tax (the *capitation*). However, lacking sound actuarial advice, the annuities proved costly to finance, whilst the returns from the *capitation* also failed to reach expectations since the nobility, the clergy and many bourgeois again off-loaded their responsibility onto the peasantry. In any case, new direct or indirect taxes did little to stimulate an ailing economy.

Louis XIV's controller general, Desmarets, had resorted to currency devaluation to clear up the financial and economic mess, but deflationary policies only aggravated the situation. Hard currency, which was losing its value, became harder to find as individuals hid their coins under the bed in the hope of a future revaluation. To resolve this liquidity crisis the Treasury had resorted to the issue of paper money, the so-called *billets de confiance* – in which the public had little or no confidence. They were originally intended to act as government certificates, valid as cash, issued in place of gold and silver coins; but, as with most experiments in paper money, the government could not resist the temptation of printing too much of it (several million *livres'* worth in fact) to pay off its creditors. By 1706, the face value of the *billets* had been halved. The public's distrust of paper money did not begin with John Law.[35]

The financial situation, then, was critical when the Regent came to power. Revenues were only 69 million *livres* to cover government expenditure of around 146 million. Servicing the debt was now costing 165 million *livres* a year. The pattern of ancien regime budgets that would endure, with notable exceptions, throughout the eighteenth century was now being set, and nothing short of a revolution in fiscal policy – which ultimately entailed an attack on privilege, in other words, a social 'revolution' – could alter it. Initial attempts to deal with the crisis did not augur well for the future. Desmarets, a nephew of Colbert, was sacked; a Chamber of Justice was set up to enquire into alleged 'irregularities'; a few financiers were imprisoned and fined. One of the latter, Antoine Crozat, was instructed to return six million *livres* to the treasury, a fine that created a hole in his pocket, but by no means emptied it.

But all this was par for the course at the beginning of a new reign. The revolutionary move was the Regent's decision to turn to a Scottish Protestant adventurer who was wanted for murder (he had killed a man in a duel) in England, and who had gambled his way around Europe to the gates of the Palais Royal. Fortunately, John Law was also a highly intelligent man, well versed in the economic debates of the day. Despite his gambling, drinking and womanising (character traits that probably endeared him to the Regent!), he had found time to write 'a majestic work towering over the contemporary writings of the early eighteenth century', *Money and Trade Considered* (1705). This was early macro-economic theory. It made the revolutionary association not just between money and price levels, but between money and a nation's overall trade. It also sought to show how increases in the supply of money could stimulate employment. Antoine Murphy regards Law as an early precursor of John Maynard Keynes.[36] This was the man that the Regent now unleashed upon a pre-capitalist, *rentier*, Catholic society.

Law began by establishing his own bank, which first opened its doors in the rue Sainte-Avoie in June 1716. It prospered, due to good management, issuing 100 million *livres'* worth of paper money, convertible into silver and gold, in two years. The following year, Law set up his Mississippi Company out of the royal concession that Antoine Crozat had neglected in the territory then known as Louisiana (in honour of Louis XIV). Today, this concession encompasses the American states of Louisiana, Mississippi, Iowa, Arkansas, Missouri, Wisconsin and Minnesota, a huge area, but populated at the beginning of the eighteenth century only by several Indian tribes and a few hundred French colonists and soldiers. The potential of this vast colony fuelled rumours of a new Eldorado, only comparable to that discovered by the Spanish and Portuguese conquistadors, and, within a couple of years, his company was making paupers rich. This success encouraged the Regent to support Law's extraordinary, long-term plan to wipe out all the debts of the state by replacing hard currency with paper money. But why should French investors exchange their gold and silver coins for Law's paper money, having just had burned their fingers with Desmarets's *billets de confiance,* as well as by other government promissory notes? The short answer is human greed, allied to the fact that Law's bank was backed by an alluring Mississippi dream, not an empty Treasury. In England, at precisely the same time, those who were eager to make a 'quick sovereign' (including Law himself!) were investing in what became known as 'the South Sea Bubble'. If Law could work miracles for his own bank, might he not do the same for a state bank? England had created one in 1694.

The authoritarian phase, 1718–23

By the summer of 1718, Dubois and Law, increasingly anxious about resistance from court aristocrats, the Paris parlement, and financiers like the Crozat and the Pâris brothers, decided to convince a rather sceptical Regent that liberal policies were no longer appropriate. The 'old guard' would have to be sacrificed on the altar of 'modernisation'. Dubois, who regarded himself as the reincarnation of Richelieu, was desperate to don a cardinal's hat, and thus had little time for the pro-Jansenist antics of the parlements. Like his role model, he was more than prepared to sup with Protestant devils abroad in order to make France safe for Catholic absolutism at home. His friend Law was also facing increased hostility over his moves to further depreciate the value of gold and silver coins in favour of his paper money.

The Regent, however, conscious of how many political cards were being stacked against him, took some convincing; but his eventual conversion to the authoritarian cause was facilitated by the conspiracies of the duchesse du Maine and the Breton nobility. It is easy, with the benefit of hindsight, to dismiss these events as 'comic-opera', but it would be wrong to underestimate contemporary fears of noble resistance, foreign interference and popular rebellion, in other words, a reversion to the days of the mid-seventeenth century Frondes. A feisty granddaughter of one of the grandest of *les Grands,* the prince de Condé, the good duchesse had been incensed by the Regent's move to 'rebastardise' her husband, the illegitimate son of Louis XIV and the latter's choice as guardian of the young Louis XV. Living in her turreted fantasy land, she succeeded – to most people's astonishment – in getting the Spanish foreign minister, Alberoni, and the Spanish ambassador to France, Cellamare, to join her in a plot to secure both the return of the Stuart pretender to London and the replacement of the Regent in Paris by Philip V of Spain; in other words, to destroy the Treaty of Utrecht.[37]

The duchesse du Maine also became embroiled in a less hair-brained revolt by the Breton parlement – the most independent and aristocratic in the country – over the government's attempt to force new taxes on the province in the spring of 1718. By September, several of the members of the parlement had been arrested or exiled for opposing 'these assaults on the rights and privileges of our estates'. This firm action failed to break the resistance of over 500 Breton nobles, however, some of whom would organise armed resistance, stiffened by vague promises of Spanish assistance, over the following year. Eventually, in November 1719, the leader of the revolt, the marquis de Pontcallec, and three of his co-conspirators were arrested and tried, and finally executed on 26 March 1720. Pontcallec's revolt is a reminder that, although the Bourbon state was gradually imposing its authority on the country, the liaison of the aristocracy with the parlements and the provincial estates could still pose a significant threat to its survival, particularly if there was a danger that *le peuple* might become involved.[38]

It is hardly surprising, therefore, that Dubois should have exploited these acts of rebellion, indeed of treason, to convince the Regent that 'the velvet glove' should now be replaced by 'the iron fist'. In foreign affairs, Dubois managed to convince Austria and Savoy, worried about the expansion of the Spanish fleet and the probability of attacks on Sardinia and Sicily, that they should join France and England in a Quadruple Alliance. It was signed on 2 August 1718. In January of the following year, exasperated by the refusal of Spain to toe the diplomatic line, England and France declared war. Within a year, Spain had been humiliated by the victorious actions of the British fleet in the Mediterranean and the French army in northern Spain. On 17 February 1720, she was forced to join the Quadruple Alliance. Spain's only choice in future, given the increasing vulnerability of her overseas empire, would be to play the junior partner either to France or to England. Meanwhile, Dubois and his English paymaster, Stanhope, had protected the peace in Europe for another decade.

On the domestic front, the triumvirate of Dubois, Law and the Regent had matched their success in foreign policy by establishing their authority over their 'liberal' enemies. As early as January 1718, the duc de Noailles, a key figure in the Treasury, had been forced from office. Marc-René Voyer d'Argenson, one of Louis XIV's pro-Jesuit hard men, determined to clip the wings of the Paris parlement, was brought in as keeper of the seals. On 26 August, the political power of the Paris parlement was once again nullified by the removal of its right of *remonstrance* during a famous *lit de justice*. The duc de Saint-Simon, the ultimate aristocratic snob and hammer of the 'bourgeois superbes' – an ironic term he used for the robe nobility sitting in the parlement – was beside himself with joy. He records in his memoirs: 'It was at this point that I began to savour, with unspeakable delight, the spectacle of these proud legislators, who had dared to refuse us their support, go down on their knees and offer, at out feet, homage to the throne'.[39] It had, indeed, been an historic moment. On 25 September, the discredited *Polysynodie* met for the last time, to be replaced by the ministerial system, run by several of Saint-Simon's 'bourgeois superbes'! Bourbon absolutism, as redefined by the Regent, was back. Now it could be employed to unravel the financial mess bequeathed by Louis XIV, the key to the success or failure of the 'Regency revolution'.

One of the reasons for de Noailles's departure had been his opposition to Law's schemes to transform his bank into a state bank and to replace hard currency with bank notes. Law argued that these moves would restore confidence in the state, lubricate internal and external trade and secure a surplus for the Treasury that could be used to buy back venal offices (offices of state sold as 'personal property' to individuals). Despite considerable and prolonged resistance, even from ministers like d'Argenson, Law won the argument and his bank was elevated to the status of 'Royal Bank' on 4 December 1718. Provincial branches were opened in commercial and manufacturing centres such as Amiens, La Rochelle and Lyon. The Paris parlement refused to register the necessary legislation, but was simply ignored.

The foundation for the confidence now exhibited by a growing band of investors and state creditors was the alleged vast wealth to be tapped in the French colonies, what Jean-Christian Petitfils refers to as 'the second horse pulling Law's triumphal chariot', the first being control of state finances.[40] At the end of 1718, Law purchased the shares of the Senegal Company for 1,600,000 *livres*, and, during the following year, acquired the African and East Indies Companies. He now had a near monopoly of all French overseas trade. In August 1719, he succeeded in convincing the Regent that his renamed Mississippi Company, the 'Company of the Indies' should take control of the national debt (the South Sea Company in Britain would follow suit). Law also seized control of the farming of indirect taxes from the Pâris brothers. Having 'converted' to catholicism, John Law, the former Protestant Scotsman, was made controller general of France on 5 January 1720. In addition to his colonial portfolio, he had now gained control of the state bank, the printing and issuing of paper money, the national debt and most of the nation's taxes. Gold and silver coins continued to be reduced in value, pressurising investors and savers to exchange them for his banknotes. By an astonishing act of reverse medieval alchemy, it seemed that Law was changing gold into paper! Industry began to flourish in the towns; farmers began to pay off their debts in depreciated currency in the countryside. Best of all for the many Saint-Simons of the period, the parlements could only wriggle helplessly, having been bound hand and foot by the Regent. There were even plans to undermine the power of the parlements permanently by buying back the offices their members had purchased. It all seemed too good to be true – and it was!

Law's 'system' had fuelled an unsustainable boom. Fortunes were being made overnight as princes and paupers rushed to Law's offices in the rue Quincampoix to exchange their gold and silver for shares in his Company of the Indies. Paris had seen nothing like it. Shares were being traded in the street; foreigners began to invest in France's 'gilt-edged' securities; stinking basement apartments around Law's offices were rented out for ridiculous sums. Troops had to be rushed in on occasions to prevent bloodshed as people fought over their share of what was rapidly becoming a national lottery. However, in many well-informed circles, confidence in Law's schemes had been evaporating since the beginning of 1720. Rumours were circulating, based upon the reports of travellers, that the Mississippi region was full of 'savages' and mosquitoes, but empty of precious metals. Canny investors, who had amassed sheaves of paper money, began to hedge their bets by rushing to change them back into gold and silver, thus undermining the entire basis of Law's 'system'. Law was going too far too fast, forcing him to introduce legislation that sought to outlaw hard currency as a means of exchange, and, even worse for the *rentier* magistrates of the parlements, placing a cap on interest rates. The collapse of the South Sea Bubble in England during the late summer of 1720 did not help. In May 1720, the share value of Law's Indies Company was 6,138 million *livres*. By July, it had fallen to 1,974 million *livres*, and, by the end of the year, to just 411 million. The game was up; the bubble had burst. Law was eventually forced to flee to Brussels in the company of the duc de Bourbon's mistress, madame de Prie. He died in Venice in 1729.

John Law was the prophet of a modern capitalist system, with its stocks and shares, its booms and bust. However, he was not only well ahead of his time, but seriously out of place in a society that put such a premium on traditional social values, blessed by a Church that still preached the message that borrowing at interest was immoral. His enemies, linked to traditional financial networks and systems, ensured that, as a result of the ruin brought to hundreds of thousands of individuals rich and poor, paper money, state banks and shares in far-distant lands would remain things accursed until well into the nineteenth century. But to understand fully the historic significance of the Law experiment, we must set events within the wider struggle for power between England and France.

Pierre Pluchon, in his provocative study of French colonisation, argues that English perfidy, the greed and treachery of some French government ministers, the parlements and financial cabals, led by the corrupt trio of Dubois, the Regent and Law, set France off on the wrong historic foot at the beginning of the eighteenth century. By failing to effect a permanent rapprochement with Austria and Spain, he argues, the Regent, aided and abetted by his 'creature', Dubois, reduced France to the status of an English satellite. In contrast the English, led by 'the capitalist Whigs', were pursuing a 'truly global' policy. As for Law and his 'Mississippi system', it was all a 'gigantic fraud', a conclusion shared by the lawyer Barbier, chronicler of the Parisian bourgeoisie, who described the experience (he had lost a small fortune!) as 'a frightening massacre'.[41]

31

Not all historians, especially those who seek to rescue French history from the enfeebled hands of Marxist interpretations of history, sympathise with Pluchon's assessment. Apart from Antoine Murphy's lionisation of Law, Le Roy Ladurie is unequivocal in his belief that the Regency marks the beginning of a great economic expansion, and that Law was only pursuing, on a grander scale, policies introduced by his predecessor, Nicolas Desmarets. There is, indeed, more to Law than the proposition that he was simply an intelligent and gifted gambler. His theories did not rest simply on the vain prospect that the French colonies were paved with gold. He realised the importance of paper currency as a means of promoting the growth of trade and commerce; he also knew that work and the expansion of the economy, not dreams of Eldorado, were the basis of a healthy economy. It was during the Regency that the French people, as opposed to government ministers and the 'chattering classes', began to realise how fast the world was changing. Unfortunately, however, it would take another generation, and defeat in the Seven Years War (1756–63), before government and the chattering classes seriously began to explain to the French people how they sought to adapt to this changing world. The Regent and Law had rocked traditional, aristocratic France, defended by the Pâris brothers and the parlements. For them, a pre-capitalist fiscal and landed system based upon the forced expropriation of the country's wealth, was preferable to risky overseas ventures run by fly-by-night financiers like Law.

Law's departure left the abbé Dubois in effective control of power. He had been the Regent's tutor under Louis XIV and the master–pupil relationship remained in place. Dubois's tireless pursuit of a cardinal's hat – which he obtained in the summer of 1721 only after the death of one of his many enemies, Pope Clément XI – has enabled his detractors to dismiss him as an unprincipled roué consumed with personal ambition. But, as with the career of the Regent, it is often difficult to distinguish personal projects from principled policies. For example, English ministers had worked hard to get Dubois his cardinal's hat because of his importance to the Anglo-French alliance. There can be no doubt that the alliance with England was Dubois's greatest single achievement; it would be maintained by his successor, cardinal Fleury. Dubois also kept the Jansenists and their friends in the Paris parlement under control as well as presiding over, and encouraging, the economic recovery that was not unrelated to Law's policies. He died on 10 August 1723, as devoted a servant to Bourbon absolutism as his role model, Richelieu. The duc d'Orléans followed him to the grave four months later.

The triumvirate of Dubois, Law and the Regent had mounted a remarkable and courageous campaign to rescue France from the disastrous state in which Louis XIV had left it. Their policies, however, had done little or nothing to challenge the privileges of the aristocracy, the wealth and power of the Church or the unjust seigneurial system that propped up the entire edifice. This does not mean – as we shall see in part three of this work – that the Revolution of 1789 was 'inevitable'. It does mean, however, that France would be brought closer to the precipice if its rulers refused 'to think the unthinkable' and undertake any meaningful fiscal and social reform, and this would entail alleviating the mass misery experienced by millions of the king's subjects. In most accounts of the ancien regime, *le peuple* appear too often as 'bit players' or as a noisy chorus to this main historical drama. In any major political crisis, however, from the mid-seventeenth century Frondes to the French Revolution of 1789, 'common people' often helped to determine the fate of a nation.

Suggested reading

Blanning, T. *The Culture of Power and the Power of Culture* (Oxford, 2002), pp. 29–52.

Bonney, R. 'Absolutism: What's in a Name', *French History*, Vol I 1987, pp. 93–117.

Braudel, F. *The Identity of France*, 2 vols, translated by Sian Reynolds (New York, 1988, 1990), Vol I, *History and Environment*.

Burke, P. *The Fabrication of Louis XIV* (London, 1992).

Collins, J.B. *The State in Early Modern France* (Cambridge, 1995), chapters three and four.

Doyle, W. *Jansenism* (London, 2000).

Doyle, W. 'Politics: Louis XIV', in W. Doyle (ed.) *Old Regime France* (Oxford, 2001), pp. 169–94.

Jones, C. *The Great Nation: France from Louis XV to Napoleon* (New York, 2002), pp. 1–81.

Murphy, A. *John Law: Economic Theorist and Policy-maker* (Oxford, 1997).

Parker, D. *Class and State in Ancien Régime France: The Road to Modernity?* (London, 1996), chapter six.

Chapter 2

The Catholic Church and French society

Tourists driving through the more rural regions of France today frequently pass through villages, often hanging on hillsides, dominated by the turrets and towers of the castle and the church, enduring symbols of the once mighty power of the seigneur and the priest. For Pierre Goubert, the ancien regime rested upon 'the seigneurie and the tithe (*dîme*)'.[1] The domination of the nobility and the clergy was indeed uncontested at the beginning of the eighteenth century, but it was the clergy who formed the first order of the realm.

This was an accurate representation of social reality since it was the Catholic faith that made the most indelible mark upon the population of ancien regime France: Protestants and Jews were not, legally, members of the state. From the cradle to the grave, in castles and cottages, in schools and hospitals, Catholicism permeated every aspect of daily life. Church bells recorded the passing hours of the day; the Gregorian calendar, the weeks and months of the year. For every victory or royal birth, there was a public, Catholic ceremony (*Te Deum*); for every holiday – 'holy day' – there was a saint. The Church bestowed the sacred attributes of kingship upon the Bourbons during their coronation in Reims. A trio of cardinals, Dubois, Fleury and Loménie de Brienne, would become 'first ministers' during the eighteenth century: Fleury unofficially; de Brienne on the very eve of the Revolution. The payroll at Versailles included no fewer than 200 clerics responsible for the daily rituals that circumscribed the life of a king and his court – formal prayers before getting out of bed, informal prayers after breakfast, mass at noon, prayers before going to bed. Louis XV had to be reminded, repeatedly, of God's sadness over his multiple sexual adventures; his mistresses were often denied the solace of the confessional. Louis XV's wife, the Polish princess Marie Lecsynska, a profoundly religious woman, often meditated in front of a skull, prompting a few ladies of the court to imitate their royal mistress by placing illuminated death's-heads on their dressing-tables. Surrounded by skeletons and other *memento mori*, it is little wonder that Louis XV was obsessed with the fear of death![2]

Catholicism also shaped the features of Bourbon France in the wider world. Louis XIV and his successor supported the many abortive schemes of the Catholic Stuarts to regain the English throne; they also pressed for an alliance with Austria, 'the only means of securing a lasting peace and maintaining the Catholic religion'.[3] In 1756, their wish would be granted, and, in 1770, Louis XVI would cement the relationship by marrying a 15-year-old Austrian princess, Marie Antoinette. Neither the alliance nor the marriage would prosper, possibly suggesting that a new, more secular age was dawning. This was hardly apparent at court, however: the last of the Bourbon absolute monarchs, Louis XVI, would be executed as a Catholic prince in 1793. Overseas, the culture and character of the French colonial empire would be largely determined by the advancing tide of the Counter-Reformation. When Samuel Champlain landed in Canada in 1615 missionaries had accompanied him, and, as Governor in 1633, he had welcomed the Jesuits. On the other side of the world, in China, 60 Jesuit priests, aided and abetted by Franciscans and Dominicans, struggled heroically to forge a 'Confucian–Catholic' culture. According to a recent estimate, the Jesuits may have converted half a million Chinese to Christianity by the beginning of the eighteenth century.[4]

One of the most striking features of the French Church was its vast wealth. It comes as no surprise that the Church was a substantial property-owner, but we must add to its property portfolio its income from one of the heaviest taxes to be levied under the ancien regime, the tithe. The combined revenues from property and the tithe brought in twice the amount raised by the heaviest government tax, the *taille*. As landlords, the Church owned between 6 and 10 per cent of the cultivable land of France. In many regions, its wealth was urban rather than rural: it owned one-third of all property in Rennes, for example, but just 3.4 per cent in 130 parishes surrounding the city – an extreme example, perhaps, but a reminder of its imposing urban presence.[5] The most visible signs of its wealth were to be found in the magnificent churches and abbeys in the north of the country. It owned 30–40 per cent of the property in and around Laon and Cambrai as opposed to 10 per cent in the Touraine region of the centre and just 3 per cent in poor Limoges further to the south. Even in the south, however, important towns like Toulouse and Nîmes contained several churches and monastic houses within, and outside, their walls. Many rich abbeys, such as the abbey of Saint-Denis in Paris, had extensive seigneurial rights, receiving rents and feudal dues, as well as the tithe, from several parishes in the neighbourhood. The abbey of Saint-Vincent in Le Mans exercised seigneurial rights over 55 farms. Some abbeys and monasteries received income from investment in industry, like the Benedictine monastery in the Hainault that had bought shares in a smelting furnace. Studies of the great abbeys of Angers and Rennes have revealed that income from their estates rose slowly up to the 1760s, followed by a very significant increase during the reign of Louis XVI. Does this help to explain the increasing trend of anti-clericalism in France after mid-century?

The second major source of income was the tithe, worth, according to some estimates, around 120–130 million *livres* a year, which means that it provided a higher return for the Church than its property holdings. In theory, it was supposed to cover the salaries of the clergy and provide support for the poor. In fact, only one-third of the *curés* received their meagre salaries – the *portion congrue*, worth a few hundred *livres* at the beginning of the century – from owners of the tithe, whilst support for the poor would dwindle to a level that bordered on the scandalous by 1789. The most dangerous, and expanding, fault-line running through the Church, a line that created fissures in almost every strata of French society, was the gap between the wealth of the aristocratic bishops at the top and the relative poverty of most *curés* at the bottom.

The tithe (*dîme*) was a tax on the produce of the land, divided between *les grosses dîmes*, levied mainly on cereals, and *les menus dîmes*, levied mainly on fruit, vegetables and, as its market importance developed, wine. It was the first tax to be collected, and estimates were based upon the gross value of the harvest. It was levied by a wide variety of individuals – village *curés*, urban bourgeois who had paid churches and monasteries for the franchise to levy the tithe, well-to-do farmers (*fermiers*) who collected it on behalf of seigneurs and agents of lay owners of tithe rights (*les dîmes inféodées*). Like all ancien regime taxes, the incidence of the tithe varied from province to province, often from parish to parish. It could rise as high as one-seventh of the value of the harvest in parts of Lorraine, or one-eighth in Gascony, but fall to an average of one-thirteenth in the provinces of Maine, Berry and Champagne. A percentage as low as one-thirtieth has been discovered in Orléans. In Brittany, the tithe could carry off a tenth of the harvest in one region, but one-thirty-sixth in another. In many parishes, the proceeds from a single tithe collection could be divided between several tithe-owners, often on an annual basis.

Litigation over the tithe became increasingly common over the century, especially when peasants saw wagonloads of their grain being carted off to enrich the abbots and priors of rich monastic houses. One village of 240 inhabitants in the mid-eighteenth century recorded a gross annual income of 11,000 *livres*. Of this sum, the tithe took 2,400 *livres*, seigneurial dues 1,900 and direct taxes 1,975 *livres*, so that well over half of the total income of the village went to the clergy, the seigneur and the government.[6] René Baehrel's study of lower Provence furnished similar examples, but he advised caution when presenting particular cases, given the multiple variations in tithe contracts. Caution must also be exercised when dealing with the profits to be made from the tithe. Baehrel quotes the case of the abbey of Saint-Victor whose gross profits for 1730 were reduced by 40 per cent to cover the costs of levying the tax and contributions towards church repairs and the salary of the local clergy. By no means every tithe-owner reneged on his or her duties to support the Church. The abbey of Lessay in Normandy paid 6,000–7,000 *livres* a year to meet its obligations. The abbey de Saint-Victor's net profit from the tithe represented only 12 per cent of the total income it derived as seigneur of the 22 priories it controlled. Furthermore, Baehrel establishes that, although landowners benefited over the century from the rise in rents, many tithe-owners 'became neither wealthier nor poorer', given the impact of inflation and the fact that the amount levied, when paid in cash, remained fixed.[7] Most tithe payments, however, were made in kind, and their value rose substantially as prices rose over the century.

Profits for the tithe-owner, then, can sometimes be exaggerated; but this does not affect the initial heavy burden laid on the tithe-payer in most cases. The latter, of course, could volunteer to reclaim scrub or marshland, which, after a government initiative of 1761, was declared exempt from the tithe for fifteen years, or change to growing crops that did not carry the penalty of the tithe. If this was not feasible, peasant communities – most peasants acted through their *communauté* – could join the growing band of critics attacking the general principle of paying any kind of tithe. Voltaire, an occasional ally, posed the rhetorical question: 'Did God come down to earth to award a quarter of my income to the . . . abbot of Saint-Denis?' This, of course, was before he became the tithe-owning seigneur of his Ferney estate on the Swiss border! As anticlericalism became endemic, and attacks on the Church increased, so many of the faithful, in town and country, would ask that the tithe be given to local communities to fund schools, hospitals and the relief of poverty, rather than to rich aristocratic abbots and archbishops. This was a very significant, and frequently overlooked, shift from a conception of the state that rested upon privilege, and distinct corporations like the Church, to one that encompassed 'the community', foundation stones of the emerging nation.

The example of the community of Le Coudray-Macouard, which I discovered whilst on a working holiday in the Saumurois, provides a microhistory that illustrates the complexity of Church–community relations. The right to levy half of the tithe belonging to the priory in the village had been bought by a monk, Dom Welch, the other half by the village *curé*. Around 1750, the priory belonged to the abbey of Saint Aubin in Angers, which, in turn, had been a dependency of an English Benedictine house. Dom Welch, however, lived in Paris and, it seems, had never visited the quite beautiful village of Le Coudray-Macouard. In 1765, a legal battle began between the tithe-owners and the village community to determine who should pay the costs of repairing the dilapidated village church. It took eleven years to settle the case! Dom Welch agreed to pay one half of the repair costs, the village community the other half. The *curé* of Coudray-Macouard, also a tithe-owner, refused to pay anything, arguing that his predecessor should have paid it before leaving the previous year.[8]

Church and state: 'the jealous sisters'

If there was one thing above all else that defined the ancien regime in France it was the union of 'throne and altar'. Until the introduction of the Civil

Constitution of the Clergy in 1790, Church and state continued to be 'joined at the hip', indissolubly linked in places, but also, in many respects, retaining separate identities. This is why it would be an exaggeration to think in terms of a theocracy, since ultimate power lay with the Crown: medieval jousts between emperors and popes had clarified this point, more or less. Nonetheless, the Church remained 'the eldest daughter of the Roman Church' and the twin sister of the monarchy. It performed a crucial administrative function through the agency of its clergy; it provided the Crown with financial assistance; and, most important of all, it spearheaded the assault on 'heretics', many of whom carried the dreaded virus of republicanism, especially since the Reformation, thus threatening both Church and state. As Pierre Goubert concludes: 'The Church's presence was almost universal; its collaboration with the civil power was constant and multiform.'[9]

At the highest administrative level, abbés tutored kings. From 1715 to 1743, cardinals Dubois and Fleury became the two most important political figures in France. Another cardinal, Louis Antoine de Noailles, controlled state finances during the early years of the Regency. Archbishops and bishops held powerful positions at court; they also presided over some provincial estates, particularly the Estates of Languedoc. Their influence with ministers on the one hand, and with the public on the other, was extensive. At the lowest level, *curés* were responsible for one of the most important administrative tasks in any state – keeping the registers of births, deaths and marriages. They had done so, with varying degrees of competence, since the sixteenth century. And this was, arguably, the least important of the duties and responsibilities laid upon the backs of the village *curés*. In terms of their relationship between 'power and the people' they were the most important figures in ancien regime France, which is why we will be returning to them later in this chapter.

The financial relationship between Church and state was fraught with difficulties, the latter, more often than not, coveting the wealth of its rich sister, particularly in times of war and recession. Unfortunately for the Church, from the sixteenth century to the early eighteenth century, wars and recessions had occurred with indecent regularity. The Estates General of the realm had toyed, seriously, with the idea of taking control of the Church's property as early as 1560. After all, Henry VIII of England had done pretty well out of his dissolution of the monasteries! In France, however, the second half of the sixteenth century had been plagued with religious warfare, and the Catholics had won. If Henry IV of France, raised a Protestant, had not reached the opportunist conclusion in 1594 that 'Paris is worth a mass', the history of France might have been different. But he did, which does not mean that Henry IV, like all his successors, stopped coveting the Church's wealth. The compromise, officially recognised in 1670, was the *Don gratuit*, a free gift to be paid by the Church to the state every five years, the exact amount to be determined by the Assembly of Clergy. It was a compromise that reflected how much the monarchy depended upon the Church, but its consequences were to be extremely serious. In the first place, the tax privileges of the Church – which did not pay the *taille*, and which paid just eight million *livres* in 1711 to secure its exemption from the extraordinary tax, the *dixième* – attracted increasing resentment and criticism as the weight of government taxes and feudal dues increased over the century. Secondly, it has been estimated that the total value of the *Don gratuit* between 1715 and 1788 was only 268 million *livres*, or just about four million *livres* a year. This was less than the Estates of Provence – which also enjoyed considerable tax privileges – paid in state taxes on the eve of the Revolution.[10]

Why was the monarchy so generous? Basically, because it felt that this was the price worth paying for the Church's invaluable assistance in dealing with 'heresy', or, in layman's language, opposition to the principles of Louis XIV's concept of absolute monarchy. Louis XVI, as late as 1775, insisted on retaining the traditional oath during his own coronation that emphasised the crown's obligation 'to exterminate, in all lands subject to my rule, the heretics declared to be so by the Church'. We have already noted that Louis XIV's 'confessional absolutism' had evolved within the context of the Church's post-Tridentine (after the Council of Trent, 1545–63) onslaught against the Reformation. Gabriel Audisio suggests an even longer historical perspective: 'The return of heretics to the Church was the main objective of the seventeenth century. The spirit of Catholicism continued to be profoundly influenced by the myth of the Crusades.' It is important to note, however, that, although the Assembly of the Clergy had accepted the decrees of the Council of Trent, they were never enshrined in state law. Gallicanism, that ecclesiastical manifestation of early nationalist sentiment, had always made it difficult for the two 'jealous sisters' to walk to church in step. Audisio suggests that the refusal of the state to recognise, officially, the work of the Council of Trent marks the first, hesitant step of its march in the opposite direction: 'the secularisation of politics'.[11]

On the other hand, the Catholic Church and the Bourbon monarchy shared the belief that heresy was a cancer that threatened them both. The *dévot* party at court, counselled by the Jesuits, fought hard to continue the repressive religious policies of Louis XIV. In their eyes, Protestantism remained the most malignant form of cancer to affect the body politic, even though, officially, it had ceased to exist since the Revocation of the Edict of Nantes. Jansenism was also thought to possess the Augustinian theological gene of predestination that also made it susceptible to the disease. Protestantism would continue to require invasive surgery; Jansenism, only regular purgatives. The work of the Counter-Reformation was not over.

For the better part of the eighteenth century, French Protestants had no legal civic existence. They were ineligible for public office; they were denied burial in parish cemeteries, although sympathetic *curés* would often record their births, marriages and deaths under the rubric 'nouveaux convertis', even when, as often happened, their conversion to Catholicism was a fiction. We discovered another 'micro-history' to illustrate this point in a brief entry in the parish registers of the village of Vergèze, situated in the Cévennes region of the south-east. On 23 September 1727, the *curé* wrote: 'It has been brought to my attention that Marguerite Fontayne Gaufrès, nouvelle convertie, aged fifty-six, has died without the *curé* being asked to attend.'! This was undoubtedly Marguerite Gaufrès's final insult to the village priest as she passed into her unknown.[12] In most Protestant regions, in Paris, around Bordeaux, in certain Normandy villages, but mainly in the Cévennes – that south-eastern bastion of *'résistance'* – pastors risked execution or a living death in the galleys to baptise, marry and bury the faithful. Nonetheless, a small group continued to perform these duties, and to preach in remote valleys, hillsides or private homes. From the 1680s to the 1750s, thousands of Calvinists were thrown into prison or sent to the galleys accused of illegally practising their faith or attempting to emigrate. Their ministers suffered most. Pastor Dortial was hung in Nîmes in 1742; ten years later, pastor Jean Rocque suffered the same fate in the same place. This long period of exclusion and persecution would be commemorated in the Protestant collective memory as 'the sojourn in the desert'.

Commemoration of the persecuted past became one of the characteristics of French Protestantism. The collective memory of martyrdom from 1685 to the 1750s would create a unique Calvinist culture, complete with its 'cult of the martyrs'. One of my most memorable research visits was to the Tour de Constance in Aigues-Mortes where a female prisoner, Marie Durand, who had been imprisoned for decades, had scratched on the wall *'Résister'*, a short word that enshrines a long history of human courage.[13] In spite of the horrors of persecution, however, the early decades of the eighteenth century marked the emergence of a new Church. Under the inspired leadership of pastors like Antoine Court and Paul Rabaut, Calvinism, now accounting for less than 5 per cent of the total French population, would be reorganised, complete with its local consistories and national synods (the first was held at Monobled in 1715). On a broader front, the rise of religious toleration after 1750 would provide the prospect of reintegration within the modern nation that was gradually being formed, although it was only during the Revolution that this fond hope would be transformed into reality.

The small Jewish community in France – some 40,000–50,000 strong – was regarded as a separate historic, ethnic and cultural species. They did not have to obey the law of 17 May 1724 compelling subjects of the king to baptise their children within twenty-four hours; they were prevented from entering public office, and were not allowed to own land. The result was that, in the main, French Jews were involved in the commercial and financial sectors of the economy. However, united by their religious and cultural heritage, they were profoundly divided by wealth and geography. Many of the 4,000 or so Sephardim Jews of Bordeaux and Bayonne, whose forefathers had fled persecution in Spain and Portugal in the fifteenth century, were rich, educated and influential. They spoke French and Spanish, rather than Yiddish; several were extremely wealthy bankers, ship-owners and wine exporters. One Joseph Pereyre, became a baron and owner of a seigneury despite the legislation against Jews owning land; another became a physician to Louis XV. Their money did not buy just influence but acceptance, at least by equally wealthy and educated Catholics.

At the other end of the spectrum, we find the Ashkenazim Jews of Alsace, whose roots were in Eastern Europe. They were the most numerous (*c.*30,000), and, by far, the poorest of all French Jews. The uglier manifestations of anti-Semitism could all be found among the poorer sections of the Alsatian peasantry, dependent upon Jewish moneylenders and itinerant traders. Similar examples of prejudice and 'ghettoisation' (ghettos were easier to tax!) could be found in the papal enclaves of Avignon and Carpentras. However, whatever the degree of racial and religious prejudice they faced, not all Jews wished to sell their cultural birthright for assimilation into the wider community. Many preferred to live by their own laws and customs, interpreted by their own elders, dreaming that, one day, they would return to their own 'Holy Land'.[14]

No Jansenist bishop or *curé* was hung in the eighteenth century, but many adherents of this 'methodism of the Catholic Church' were imprisoned during the periodic waves of repression that occurred during the Regency and the reign of Louis XV. The advent of the duc d'Orléans as Regent in 1715 had seemed to herald a period of religious peace and reconciliation. The 'authoritarian' period of the Regency in 1718, however, had marked the beginning of a less tolerant approach. In 1720, the Regent had decreed that all sides in the debate should observe a vow of silence, a temporary solution to a serial problem that had, by this time, united Jansenists and Gallicans, as well as an influential minority of members of the Paris parlement. The first major crisis in the relationship between the parlement and the Crown occurred from 1727 to 1732. Peter Campbell suggests that it was during these years that Jansenism developed a coherent agenda and strategy for action, one that would be employed to greater effect in the second important crisis of the early 1750s. If Campbell is right to argue that the prime concern of the Jansenists during the first period was 'doctrinal . . . not political', then the more politicised nature of the conflict in the 1750s, especially the more prominent role played by the parlements and the public, again suggests that the transition from a religious to a secular political culture was gaining momentum.[15]

The crisis of 1727 was precipitated by an obscure, 79-year-old, Jansenist bishop in an obscure Jansenist diocese. Bishop Soanen was one of those rare ecclesiastical birds – a commoner in an age of aristocratic bishops. He had long been a thorn in the side of the government, refusing any compromise with the supporters of the 1713 papal bull, *Unigenitus*. In September 1727, a provincial Church council in Embrun demoted Soanen to the ranks of a layman and exiled him to the abbey of Chaise-Dieu. It proved to be a major tactical error. In the eyes of many people, not all of them Jansenists, a saintly old 'bishop of the people' had been 'persecuted' by a council full of Jesuits and aristocratic toadies of Fleury. Clerics and lawyers now began scouring the archives for medieval examples of papal theocratic attacks on the authority of French kings, thus feeding popular resentment against Rome and its militant outriders, the Jesuits.

It was in crises such as these that André Hercule de Fleury, effectively first minister from 1726 to his death in 1743, revealed the iron, anti-Jansenist fist in the velvet politique glove. He worked tirelessly, and cunningly, to undermine Jansenism 'from below', by rooting out pro-Jansenist sympathisers in parishes, colleges and convents, while using his wide powers of preferment to appoint, 'from above', anti-Jansenist bishops and archbishops to vacant posts. By December 1729, he had effectively taken over control of the Sorbonne, forcing its learned doctors to declare the validity of *Unigenitus*. The unkindest cut of all for the Jansenists came on 24 March 1730 – Fleury's announcement that the papal bull would become a law of the French state. McManners suggests that Fleury's arbitrary employment of *lettres de cachet* to imprison Jansenist sympathisers represents 'a towering example of the misuse of political power in the service of religious intolerance'.[16]

By the spring of 1730, the crisis appeared to be over. In fact, the most worrying phase for the government was just beginning. If troublesome priests had been brought to heel, members of the Paris parlement and their public cheerleaders, *le peuple*, had not. Fifty barristers attached to the parlement had put their names to a pamphlet in October 1727 denouncing the treatment that had been meted out to bishop Soanen. The parlement itself refused to register the decree making *Unigenitus* a law of state when it was published in March 1730, declaring that such a move raised the historic question of the relationship between the papacy and the French Crown. Instead, it raised the fundamental and explosive issue of who ruled in Versailles, the pope or Louis XV? Did not the parlement have the right to defend the 'fundamental laws of the kingdom' which, in this case, included the four Gallican articles signed by Louis XIV himself in 1682? Fleury, through a *lit de justice* on 3 April 1730, made it clear that he did not think they did. The stakes were raised even higher in October with the appearance of a pamphlet published by Parisian barristers which stated that the parlements were 'the Nation's Senate'. This was revolutionary talk, hardly calculated to cool tempers. In March 1731, Fleury resorted to the tried and tested expedient of imposing an 'oath of silence' on all parties. Some things were better left unsaid, a sure sign of a changing religious culture.

If the parlement could be silenced, however, *le peuple* could not. The most significant aspect of the crisis of 1727–32 was the further development of Jansenism as a 'popular movement', facilitated by the expansion of the press. The Richerist element in Jansenist doctrine, such as the greater involvement of priests and the laity in the governance of the Church, had already laid down the foundations of a more democratic movement. The appearance in 1728 of one of the earliest and most influential newspapers of the eighteenth century, the *Nouvelles ecclésiastiques,* provided the means of disseminating the faith (and anti-Jesuit propaganda) to thousands of readers in Paris and parts of the provinces. In 1731, mass hysteria broke out in Paris as a result of rumours that miraculous cures had taken place in the cemetery of Saint-Médard over the grave of a young Jansenist deacon named François de Pâris. Pâris had apparently died of exhaustion as a result of his work on behalf of the poor in the *faubourg* Saint-Marceau. The curious who came to visit the cemetery were to witness quite extraordinary scenes as worshippers went into convulsions, stabbing themselves to imitate the suffering of the saints and prophesying the downfall of Jesuit 'anti-Christs'. The response of the government was to brick up the walls of the cemetery of Saint-Médard in January 1732. Despite this firm action, Parisian barristers and magistrates, exploiting the popular wave of Jansenism, continued to challenge the government from inside the walls of the parlement. They even sought to bring the administration of justice to a standstill during the summer by going on strike. Fleury responded by trying to curtail, *à la Louis quartorze*, their right of remonstrance. Thus, the now ritualised eighteenth-century ballet-à-deux between the Crown and the Paris parlement was played out until a truce was called at the end of 1732.[17]

Another *pas de deux* between the crown and the parlement would be staged in the early 1750s, on this occasion over the attempt by the Jesuit archbishop of Paris, Cristophe de Beaumont, to deny holy sacraments to dying Jansenists. This 'billets de confession' crisis revealed the increasing strength of Jansenism in the corridors of the parlement, although, as Julian Swann points out, the parlement was essentially a law court staffed by around 130 magistrats of whom only 15 to 20 may confidently be described as Jansenists. Following the line taken by William Doyle and John Rogister, Swann warns us that it would be wrong to see the parlement as essentially 'anti-monarchist', dedicated to the task of providing a 'parliamentary' constitutional alternative to the Crown. Traditional political rhetoric, rivalries and objectives continued to characterise the struggle. The warning is salutary. Nonetheless, Swann himself concludes that by the 1750s Jansenist magistrates, through their prolonged opposition to the papal bull, *Unigenitus*, as well as their fierce

43

opposition to archbishop Beaumont's policy over the denial of sacraments to suspected Jansenists, had become the 'dominant' faction within the parlement of Paris. He also states that certain Jansenist magistrates 'played a crucial role in integrating the constitutional theories of lawyers such as Le Paige and La Monnoye into the daily vocabulary of the Parlement and, consciously or not, sapped the intellectual foundations of the monarchy'.[18]

In his erudite, event-driven study, Rogister denies that 'public opinion' played any significant role in these periodic crises. This denial is too strong. One of the main strengths of the Jansenist-dominated parlement in Paris was popular support, especially in certain parishes such as those of Saint-Médard and Saint-Nicolas-des-Champs. William Ward actually suggests that there was a link between popular responses to the religious and constitutional crises of the 1730s and 1750s and the ideology of the sansculottes during the Revolution of 1789.[19] Such linkages are obviously open to criticism, but there can be little doubt that the above crises did revolve around matters of great religious, constitutional and *democratic* significance. They involved rising nationalist sentiments and the demarcation of power between Church and state. Perhaps there should be a written contract between the monarchy and the people, with the parlements acting as its interpreters and guardians? Should France, as a young lawyer named Voltaire was suggesting, borrow some of the better constitutional practices of the English? Should the Church be disestablished? As grave matters of state, foreign wars, economic modernisation, fiscal crises and cultural change began to overwhelm the crown, bitter quarrels between the 'two jealous sisters', Church and state, were undoubtedly weakening both of them.

The organisation of the Catholic Church

By 1789, 170,000 clerics, secular and regular (members of religious houses and monastic orders), would be employed by the Catholic Church. They would include some 26,000 monks and friars, 56,000 nuns, 60,000 *curés* and curates (*vicaires*), 15,000 canons and 13,000 other clerics with no permanent office or regular pastoral duties. Eighteen ecclesiastical provinces, encompassing 136 dioceses or bishoprics, would form the administrative armature of the Church. A metropolitan bishop, or archbishop, ran the province; a suffragan bishop was in charge of each diocese. As was the case with almost every other ancien regime administrative body, there was no comparability between dioceses, especially in size and influence. The diocese of Rouen covered 1,388 parishes; that of Grasse, just 23. Immediately below archbishops and bishops we find the vicar generals (*grands vicaires*), numbering almost a thousand. The General Assembly of the Clergy that met in Paris once in every five years ran the national affairs of the Church. These assemblies, divided into two orders, bishops and lower ranks, dealt with major religious and financial affairs, from ways of dealing with the periodic crises over *Unigenitus*, to determining the exact amount of the *Don gratuit* to be paid to the Crown.

The regular clergy were distinguished from their secular counterparts by their membership of religious orders and by taking vows of poverty, chastity and obedience. Their numbers included twice as many females as males. The Commission on the Regular Orders, set up in July 1766, estimated that there were 26,674 monks and 8,000 lay brothers in France. Monasteries and abbeys were concentrated more in the north-east, from Flanders to Lorraine, and the south, across lower Languedoc and lower Provence, than in the centre. Over half of the total number of regular clergy were friars belonging to the mendicant orders. The Franciscans were 8,780 strong and were divided into five groups, the Cordeliers, the Capuchins and the Récollets being the most important. There were 1,492 Dominican friars – or Jacobins as they were known in France, 1,194 Carmelites and 884 Augustinians. There were also several offshoots from the main monastic branches, like the fifteenth-century Minims and the Trappists. Benedictine monks represented around one-sixth of the regular clergy (if one includes their Cistercian and Cluniac offshoots), with around 660 religious houses and 6,000 monks, followed by the Carthusians with 1,004.

The religious orders had been created at different times in response to different challenges. The contemplative Benedictines had been around since the sixth century; friars like the Franciscans and Dominicans had been created by the religious culture of the thirteenth century. The Jesuits and the majority of the female orders were products of the Counter-Reformation. Time had conferred a certain laxity on the Benedictine Order, and many of their members lived in considerable luxury. Wealthy nobles and bourgeois would use abbeys and monasteries for travel breaks and longer, spiritual retreats. The wines and gastronomic fare at the Cistercian abbey of Saint-Sulpice at Bugey elicited universal praise from weary travellers. Many monks were renowned agriculturalists and winegrowers. Dom Leronge had made a name for himself by publishing the *Principes du cultivateur*, whilst a certain Dom Pérignon, bursar of the abbey of Saint-Pierre d'Hautvilliers, helped to give champagne its sparkle. Particular vocations or skills were associated in the public mind with particular orders. Capuchin monks ran the fire services in many towns. Capuchins, Lazarists and Jesuits served as chaplains on ships-of-the-line or on convict galleys. Some Cordeliers were practised at running prisons, although not all of them attracted the notoriety of Saint-Pierre de Canon in Provence where the gatekeeper 'was a drunkard, the bursar could not read, and the chaplain had affairs with peasant women'.[20]

In terms of promoting the Roman Catholic religious culture of the Counter-Reformation and performing the more mundane Christian tasks of caring for the poor and the sick, however, it was the Jesuits and the many seventeenth-century female religious orders that left the boldest imprint on French culture and society. The Jesuit Order, created by Ignatius Loyola and set up in Paris in 1534, were the assault troops of the reformed papacy, devoted to the extinction of heresy. Of the 25,000 Jesuit priests scattered throughout the world, 3,300 had been sent to the five French Jesuit 'provinces' and 1,000 of these to Paris. Jesuit missionaries were also dispatched to Canada and China. They were confessors to kings and tutors to generations of secondary schoolchildren. The papacy often thought that they were getting too big for their robes! Unlike their Jansenist adversaries, who leaned towards Calvin's theory of predestination, the Jesuits preferred the ideas of Luis Molina (1536–1600). Molinists believed that God had dispensed just about enough free will to enable His children to choose between good and evil, provided, of course, that they practised good works and followed the teaching of the Catholic Church. Devoted supporters of the union of throne and altar, the Jesuits were to be deserted by both kings and popes when the waves of nationalism began to sweep over the Bourbon decks after the 1750s.

The secular clergy, the archbishops, bishops, vicar-generals, canons, *curés* and curates, were responsible for the daily administration of the Gallican Church. Required to be celibate and obedient to kings and popes – but not necessarily in that order – they were divided between an episcopate that was aristocratic, almost to a man, and a lower clergy that was commoner, almost to a man. Although clearly senior in terms of administrative authority and influence, an archbishop was regarded by the more radical bishops as being little more than a *primus inter pares*. The effective administrative head of the Church in France was the General Assembly of the Clergy.

Archbishops and bishops represented the strongest link in the chain that bound the Church to the state, a link that was forged in the aristocratic crucible of Versailles. Bishops, with very few exceptions, were chosen from the ranks of the nobility until the Revolution of 1789; a fifth of the richest sees were reserved for the sons of the court aristocracy, some 300 families. Apart from the obvious exception of Paris, worth around 300,000 *livres* in annual income, the most sought-after archbishoprics and bishoprics were to be found in the north of the country. Arras and Verdun brought in around 80,000 *livres* a year, whilst the diocese of Marseille could only manage 50,000, and Vence just 12,000. But this was only the 'basic salary'. Court favourites were also showered with abbeys and priories. The Regent's favourite, Dubois, was rewarded with a cardinal's hat and seven abbeys (Cardinal Richelieu had done much better – 20 abbeys!). Cardinal Dominique de la Rochefoucauld doubled his income of 172,000 *livres* as archbishop of Rouen by pocketing roughly the same amount from his position as abbot of the great abbey of Cluny. And the old sword nobility, like the Rohans and the Castellanes, managed to keep these marks of royal esteem in the family, passing down the mitre with the money, from uncle to nephew.[21]

Chosen by the Crown, but confirmed in office by the papacy, the Council of Trent had required the episcopate to be 'the pivot of the policy of Reform in the diocese', and the majority of post-Tridentine bishops did their best to oblige. The aristocratic leadership of the Church guaranteed the state that 'heretics' and 'republicans' would not triumph in France as they had elsewhere in Europe, a 'mutual security pact' that lies at the heart of ancien regime politics. If many bishops never bothered to tour their diocese, preferring the luxuries of Parisian life to the privations of tramping the mountains of Haute Provence, most appear to have taken their duties as the king's messengers quite seriously. The eighteenth century was a good time for pastoral visitations, if only because things were better organised through the adoption of standard procedures, with vicar-generals deputising for busy bishops. And many archbishops and bishops were men of integrity, carrying out the decisions of the Assembly of Clergy, supervising the ecclesiastical affairs of the diocese and, in some instances, presiding over meetings of provincial estates. There were, of course, some exceptions to this episcopal rule. The bishop of Lodève was accused of not believing in God and of living openly with women, but 'all this was forgiven him for his name was Phélypeaux' (one of the great robe families at court). A minority of bishops even began to reveal disturbingly enlightened views on religious toleration as the century progressed. In general, however, the episcopate faithfully fulfilled its part of the bargain as an administrative arm of the Catholic and aristocratic ancien regime state. Government policy would be relayed, through the Assembly of Clergy, to the episcopate, and through the latter, the crown could control both the regular and the secular clergy. An aristocratic episcopate buttressed an aristocratic Bourbon state for most of the eighteenth century, until, in 1789, the weight of privilege proved too heavy for the nation to bear.

Waiting in the wings to share the wealth, power and historic burden of struggling against the tide of secularisation were the vicar-generals, first lieutenants of the bishop. Their numbers would rise to around 1,000 by 1789, reflecting the increased administrative load placed on every diocese. A sizeable minority were nephews of the bishop they served and, therefore, of noble lineage. Although the sons of the oldest aristocratic families might be allowed to short-circuit the system and leap straight into a bishop's chair, less favoured nobles would have to serve their apprenticeship, either as canons or vicar-generals, sometimes as both. The vicar-general of Pontoise only became the bishop of Avranches in 1774 after fourteen years in the lower ecclesiastical ranks. Their professional formation improved over the century in line with the increased administrative burdens placed upon them. They did not usually receive a salary, but those who were obliged to stoop this low to make noble ends meet were usually given the income from one or more cathedral chapters or abbeys.

Finally, at the lowest level of the higher clergy, we find the 15,000 or so canons attached to the 136 cathedral chapters and over 500 collegial churches, or private chapels and foundations. Job descriptions varied. Some worked as administrative assistants to the bishop; some were in charge of the liturgy; others specialised in theology, music or teaching. Their famed independence of mind arose, in part, from the many different ways they were appointed – by the king, cathedral chapters, seigneurs or lay individuals. Their impact on urban life was visible and significant, especially in cathedral towns like Chartres where they numbered almost a hundred. Not only did they supervise the daily rituals and festivals of religious life, they also served as local magistrates, judges or schoolmasters. Many cathedral chapters were infected by the customary vices of ancien regime society. There was, for example, the pervasive odour of privilege. A few chapters – in Besançon, Lyon and Strasbourg, for example – were reserved for noble candidates; the cathedral chapter in Chartres would become a noble club after 1777. Then there were the usual complaints about non-residence and sexual licence. There can be no doubt, however, that canons – with colourful and dishonourable exceptions – fulfilled key roles in the urban life of eighteenth-century France.

For every canon there were 50 *curés* in France. In town and country, daily life was lived on the level of the parish, and the linchpin of parish life was *le bon curé*. Pierre Goubert has reminded us that most of the communes in France today can be traced back to the old parish: 'the old Christian geography remains very much a reality'.[22] Unlike today, however, the *curé* not only provided for the spiritual needs of his parishioners, he was their most important cultural and political broker with the outside world.

To qualify as a priest, one had to pass, theoretically, through seven stages, from the symbolic cutting of hair (*la tonsure*) to the final nomination to a living. This journey might begin at seven and end at twenty-five. The social composition of the priesthood obviously reflected the regional variations of French society. Overall, less than 1 per cent of priests hailed from noble backgrounds by the eighteenth century, but, as one might expect, certain Breton towns like Tréquier (18 per cent) and Vannes (6–12 per cent) bucked the national trend. Of the 326 priests who ministered in Boulogne over the century, 157 were the sons of well-off farmers (*laboureurs*), and 52 the sons of merchants. In the diocese of Lisieux on the other hand, 54 per cent of priests came from merchant backgrounds, 20 per cent from the legal and professional class, and 21 per cent were farmer's sons. Some parts of Normandy specialised in producing *curés*, particularly for Paris: in Coutances, 75 per cent of serving priests came from farming backgrounds. In general, then, *curés* were recruited from across the social spectrum, but the majority were the sons of reasonably well-off farmers, artisans and merchants. *Curés* and curates were also better trained as the century progressed, the result of a marked improvement in the seminary education they received. Finally, *curés* tended to stay within their own locality. Again we find obvious exceptions to the rule: whereas two-thirds of Parisian *curés* would be 'foreigners' by the end of the century, in Reims, in 1774, 88.8 per cent were local.

There were, of course, many kinds of livings apart from being responsible for a parish. Priests were needed in religious houses, private foundations, schools and colleges. Many of these posts were filled by abbés, men who had joined the priesthood, or who had left a religious order, but did not want, or could not find, permanent posts. There were many rich, noble abbés at court; many poor ones were floating around the country. Attired in their little white collars, short coats and wigs, they were frequently seen as parasites, operating on the shadier side of the ecclesiastical road. Many lived off private incomes, or worked as tutors or Grub Street journalists. A few, like the novelist Prévost, made notable contributions to the literary and intellectual achievements of the age.

Parish *curés* fell into two main categories – the *curés décimateurs*, who owned the right to levy the tithe personally, and those who were appointed by tithe-owning seigneurs, abbots or laymen. The latter received a salary, or *portion congrue*, hence the term, *curés congruistes*. The following list, for 1760, illustrates some of the variations which existed throughout the country:

Diocese	*curés décimateurs*	*curés congruistes*
Bordeaux	74%	26%
Clermont Ferrand	49%	51%
Limoges	76%	24%
Paris	71%	29%
Rodez	37%	63%[23]

Salaries for *curés* reveal similar variations. The average salary fell between 500 and 1,500 *livres* a year, with curates being paid far less than this. *Curés congruistes* appear to have been paid something like 300 *livres* in 1686, rising to 700 by the Revolution. This was a very low salary by any standard, not much above that of a farm labourer in some instances. One could add to these sums the fees most *curés* charged for officiating at funerals and weddings – much resented by parishioners by the way – but this would still leave the majority on the bottom rungs of the income ladder. Many *curés décimateurs* did better. A study of 50 *curés* working in the region of Saumur at the end of the ancien regime found that 32 had incomes lower than 2,000 *livres* a year, 11 received between 2,000 and 3,000 *livres*, and 15 had over 3,000 *livres*. There are also examples of *curés* (possibly noble by birth) in Tréguier earning between 2,400 and 4,000 *livres* annually, which would certainly have allowed them to live in some comfort.[24]

It is clear, then, that not all *curés* were poor. It is equally clear that almost all curates were poor, at least in terms of remuneration. The curate of Le Coudray-Macouard received a salary comparable to that of an agricultural labourer, around 300 *livres* a year. However, social status is not to be measured in money alone, particularly in the highly status-conscious society of ancien regime France. The clerical life was, after all, a vocation, and a priest in a cassock was far more highly regarded than a grain merchant who earned five times his salary. Parishioners undoubtedly supplemented meagre clerical salaries with gifts of food, wine and the occasional chicken. There was also the fact that the clerical order was the only one of the three orders of society that allowed, theoretically at least, a rapid climb up the social ladder. Nonetheless, the low material returns experienced by parish priests assume greater significance when we examine their contribution to the state. Not only were their pulpits the medium for government news and propaganda, their churches, after Sunday mass, the sites for the exercise of local government, but village *curés* often tended the sick, buried the dead, taught children the catechism and instructed parents in the mysteries of having sex without enjoying it! Although some tithe-owning priests were hated for exploiting the meagre resources of the village, and some men hated the Church for challenging their right to knock six village bells out of their wives, most *curés* it seems were loved, or at least respected, as family friends and protectors. In times of famine and sickness, the *curé* was also an important cog in the machinery of the Catholic Church's ersatz 'welfare state'.

It is almost impossible to provide a comparable account of the contribution made by pastors to the lives of the 700,000 or so Protestants in France, if only because the Protestant Church did not exist, legally, until the Revolution. The main concern for pastors, at least until mid-century, was not 'pay and conditions' but avoiding prison, the galleys or, *in extremis*, the gallows. Local accounts of their heroic struggle to keep the Protestant Church alive refer constantly to experiences that can only be compared with those of Jesuit priests risking death to defend their faith during the reign of Elizabeth I of England. There is a Protestant *Muséum du désert*, situated near the village of Mialet in the Cévennes hills. According to its founders, it serves as a memorial to 'the obscure host of unknown martyrs who, for a century, from the Revocation of the Edict of Nantes to the Edict of Toleration in 1787, died in order to preserve and perpetuate the Reformation in France'.[25] The words 'perpetuate the Reformation in France' are highly significant, emphasising as they do the reality of the politico-religious conflict that always lay just beneath the surface of ancien regime life.

We do know that there were perhaps fewer than 800 pastors for around 900,000 Protestants on the eve of the Revocation of the Edict of Nantes in 1685, and that the number of pastors was decimated during the religious wars and persecution of the early decades of the eighteenth century. There is evidence to show, however, that post-Revocation pastors benefited from a good education and training in Swiss Protestant seminaries, and that the basic institutions of the Church were rebuilt from the 1710s to the 1740s. One social fact is also relevant here: both Catholic and Protestant *curés* and pastors moved closer to their parishioners during the eighteenth century, and the gap between the higher and lower levels of their respective hierarchies widened as the century progressed. This was to be of crucial significance when hard political, and religious, choices had to be made in 1789.[26]

The Catholic Church: 'in sickness and in health'

By the beginning of the eighteenth century, the process of centralising and institutionalising medieval charitable organisations was well advanced, especially in towns and certain dioceses. The upheavals of war and economic decline, as well as religious and cultural change, had undermined medieval hospitals and, more visibly, the nursing systems that ran them. Audisio refers to a 'double evolution' that began in the late fifteenth century: in the first place, a challenge to the influence of the Church on the part of local, lay authorities; in the second, the increasing intervention of the state.[27]

An early example of lay power may be seen in the case of the hôtel-Dieu in Paris. Founded in the seventh century, the control of the cathedral chapter of Notre-Dame was replaced in 1505 with an eight-man board of governors. However, the Counter-Reformation, and the related 'confessional absolut-ism' of Richelieu and Louis XIV, placed certain checks on this process of secularisation. For example, the creation of scores of religious orders during the sixteenth and seventeenth centuries, many of them female, launched a second wave of hospitalisation which was to peak in the eighteenth century. Kathryn Norberg found that in Grenoble at the end of the seventeenth century, 'one looks in vain in the Hospital records for even the slightest trace of the parish clergy. Then, in 1700, the *curés* of Saint Laurent, Saint Hugues, and Saint Louis parishes begin to appear consistently . . .' The 1680s to the 1730s, then, represent an important period of structural change in the hospital and charitable sectors. By 1789, France would be endowed with over 2,000 town and country hospitals (*hôtels-Dieu*), as well as almost 200 poor houses (*hôpitaux généraux*). Changing attitudes in the provision of poor relief was an inevitable corollary of this institutional 'revolution'. Norberg has described how the elite of Grenoble 'abandoned the punitive stance of their predecessors' between the 1680s and the 1730s, leading to a greater involvement in social policy by a widening spectrum of society. She provides a salutary reminder, however, that this period was also one of considerable economic recession and social misery. In other words, it might have been the consequences of war and famine, as much as Christian zeal, that was afflicting the conscience of the Grenoblois elite.[28]

51

In many other provincial cities, bureaucratic and efficient organisations like the *bureaux de charité* and the *Miséricordes* were working to channel individual acts of charity into more community-based schemes, particularly hospitals and poorhouses. In some instances, they chalked up a significant degree of success: about two-thirds of the income of the *Miséricorde* in Montpellier in the 1740s came from private charity – donations, benefactions and legacies.[29] And the Church continued to play a major role in all these changes, with a minority of bishops providing an example, not only in terms of leadership, but also Christian charity. In 1744, for example, the archbishop of Bourges left nearly 300,000 *livres* to repair buildings and support local seminaries and hospitals. By 1700, most of the larger provincial towns had an *hôtel-Dieu* and an *hôpital général* within their walls. We must beware, however, of simplistic analogies with present-day hospitals. The *hôpital général* bore a closer resemblance to a poorhouse, frequently doubling up as a prison for vagabonds and prostitutes, than to our concept of a hospital, whilst most *hôtels-Dieu* provided medical care for the poor.

Most *hôtels-Dieu* attracted a clientele with well-defined characteristics. In Lyon, patients were drawn from the ranks of domestic servants, the textile industry and semi-skilled artisans. In Blois, they fell into three main categories: artisans, country-dwellers and soldiers; female patients came, in the main, from farms, domestic service and semi-skilled trades. Diet was simple, mostly bread, soup and vegetables, though, at Chartres, fish and butter made the occasional appearance. It seems that it was the food, rather than the medical treatment they received – 'bleeding and purging' in the main – that cured the majority of patients. However, not all eighteenth-century hospitals were death traps. Although rates were high in the over-crowded *hôtel-Dieu* in Paris, where one in four left in a shroud, deathrates in the provinces were between 10 and 20 per cent, varying according to location.[30]

Patrick Thinard's study of the *hôtel-Dieu* in Roanne, near Lyon, will provide us with a fairly typical provincial example. The original building had been built in the fourteenth century for a Capuchin convent, and it was not until 14 June 1638 that the archbishop of Lyon agreed to its use as an *hôtel-Dieu*. On 28 November 1724, it had just 20 beds for 30 patients of both sexes. This low figure is not unusual: a quarter of the 2,189 hospitals officially registered by 1789 had fewer than 10 beds. Anyone with the money, particularly in the countryside, to make alternative arrangements for medical care was treated either in a private foundation or at home. 'Care in the community' is not a modern concept. The total annual expenditure in 1724 for Roanne's *hôtel-Dieu* was 614 *livres*, and meeting even this modest financial commitment was only possible with the help of the town council.

Notwithstanding, a new extension (which is still in existence today) was built between 1744 and 1747 at a cost of 524 *livres*, and the hospital's archives reveal continuing financial support from the town council, supplemented by donations from the clergy and the aristocracy. The new extension had only been built after prompting from the *curé* of the church of Saint-Etienne; whilst, in 1765, the wife of the seigneur de Chantois contributed 3,000 *livres* to extend the men's dormitory of the hospital. Here we have a revealing example of the local operation of the Church and state alliance. A *maison de charité* had been opened for children of the poor who could not gain access to the hospital three years earlier. By the 1780s, however, the Roanne hospital had fallen on bad times, in common with many other comparable institutions. In 1782, there was 'pas un sous en caisse', and, in August 1785, it was recorded that distributions of bread to the poor – another common charitable practice – would have to end. The following month, the nuns left the *maison de charité*.[31]

A similar emphasis on the centrality of religion in people's daily lives characterises the work of the Church in the field of education. Religion, during the ancien regime, played a vital role in the expansion of education and the rise of literacy, both of which contributed to the rise of a national consciousness. In the 'land of my own fathers', Wales, the translation of the bible into Welsh, and the ability of ordinary people to read the scriptures in homes and Sunday Schools, proved to be some of the fissiparous rocks upon which Welsh nationalism was constructed. The crucial role played by the French Catholic Church in the expansion of education helped to secure the birth of a nation and, paradoxically (at least for the more pious village *curé*), the advance of a more secular and scientific culture. If 'Luther made necessary what Gutenberg made possible', then the Catholic Church also made necessary what Gutenberg and the Reformation had made possible – the expansion of 'the Word' to ordinary people through the publication and circulation of words. Protestantism had led the way, whilst Jansenism not only facilitated 'the progress of the human spirit' through its long-running periodical, the *Nouvelles ecclésiastiques*, and its translations of the scriptures, it also made a signal contribution to the advance of education by publishing works such as the *Grammaire générale* and *Logique*.[32]

The history of eighteenth-century education is punctuated with contradictions and paradoxes as Church, state and local communities struggled to keep – in some cases, find – their feet in the face of the advancing tide of literacy, scientific knowledge and the demands of an expanding capitalist economy. David Bell has suggested that Jansenism, with its emphasis on a mysterious and invisible God, was not totally incompatible with the 'new science' of the Enlightenment, the science that produced a Newtonian 'watchmaker God'.[33] However, despite the fears of many priests – and some *philosophes* – who thought education was too good for the masses, it was the official Catholic Church which 'developed nothing short of an ideology of the school in the course of the seventeenth and eighteenth centuries'. In 1680, the bishop of Angers enjoined priests to consider the Church itself 'as

a school, in which Jesus Christ is the schoolmaster'.[34] Government legislation in 1695 and 1724 reveals the emergence of a joint Church–state alliance
on education.

Two points emerge clearly from a reading of this legislation. Firstly, that
a Christian education was regarded as vital in the fight against ignorance
and 'heresy' (the period between these two decrees marks the peak of the
struggle against Calvinism and Jansenism); secondly, that the *curé* should
be in charge of appointing schoolmasters. In the region of the Var between
1660 and 1750, 40 per cent of teachers appointed were clerics. In many cases,
it was the local seigneur and the *curé* who decided things. Ninety inhabitants
of the parish of Saint Léger de Montbrun, gathered outside the church
after mass on 26 May 1764, were told by the local seigneur, Charles Brinault
de Rigny, that he had hired a curate as the village schoolmaster. He added,
however, that it would be the job of the village *curé* to decide which children
should be allowed to attend. The control of the Church was less obvious
in the capital and large provincial towns. Of 103 schoolmasters appointed
in the archdiocese of Paris across the eighteenth century, 54 were laymen,
40 were curates and 9 *curés*. The Church educated rich and poor alike in
Paris with 166 fee-paying schools, for boys and girls, and 80 free schools
(most of them founded in the eighteenth century), 24 of them for girls,
as well as schools attached to convents, private religious and lay foundations.[35] In the countryside, the Church's control of education was even
tighter.

It was in the primary sector that Church influence was most evident. Diocesan instructions make it abundantly clear that the goals of an elementary
education were, first and foremost, the formation of a Christian, followed by
the ability to read, write and count, all this crowned with moral improvement. The diocesan synod of Boulogne in 1744 decreed that the catechism
should be 'the first reading book for children who have learned the alphabet',
and that schoolmasters should lead the children in prayers morning and
afternoon. The acknowledged experts in the indoctrination of generations
of French schoolchildren were the Brothers of the Christian Life (*Frères
des écoles chrétiennes*), founded by Jean-Baptiste de La Salle in Reims in
1679. The Brothers, like the Jesuits, 'were to be uncompromisingly orthodox, giving total obedience to the pope, and set in flint-like opposition to
Jansenism'. Their *petites écoles* expanded rapidly in the first half of the
eighteenth century: by 1747, they had trained 800 teachers and opened 80
schools. Thirty years later, the Brothers would be teaching 30,000 pupils in
over 100 schools. This was to be the high water mark of La Salle's 'Counter-
Enlightenment'. On the eve of the Revolution, the Catholic Church would
be responsible for nearly 500 elementary schools in Paris, most of them free.
As the century progressed, French, or occasionally the local patois, would
replace Latin as the language of instruction.[36] The mental world of the

eighteenth-century child was constructed out of the vocabulary of Catholic priests, monks or nuns.

The contradictions inherent in the struggle to root out heresy by inculcating the values of the Catholic faith, whilst simultaneously confronting the demands of an embryonic capitalist and bureaucratic state, were hardly detectable in the elementary field. They would become increasingly manifest, however, in the secondary and tertiary sectors of education. We shall examine universities in a later chapter, if only because, during the eighteenth century, the *collèges* (the French equivalent of British grammar schools) in the secondary sector became the principal arena for the battle between religious and secular education. Around 48,000 students would be attending *collèges* by 1789, which means that one in fifty boys, aged from eight to eighteen, succeeded in gaining admission. An increasing number of these boys came from noble or wealthy bourgeois backgrounds, a few from the ranks of rich artisans and peasants; the majority, however, were sons of merchants and professional bourgeois. The most prestigious *collèges* – the Oratorian establishment at Juilly, Louis-le Grand in Paris – were also the most aristocratic in composition. Sons of the lower orders tended to enter late and leave early, a practice common to many fee-paying educational systems.

Until the Revocation of the Edict of Nantes in 1685, control of education in the *collèges* had been contested between Protestants and Catholics. After 1685, the field was cleared for the main Catholic teaching orders, primarily the Jesuits, the Oratorians and the Doctrinaires. Pursuing their individual strategies, this holy trinity of religious orders would compete with parlements and other provincial bodies to endow their towns with a *collège*, some of them directly linked to local universities. They never succeeded in imposing complete control of education since many *collèges* had been endowed by lay bodies and retained their secular characteristics: 10 of the *collèges* in Paris remained in lay hands, whilst Bordeaux and Reims housed both Jesuit and secular *collèges*. The battle between secular and religious values, fought in many different arenas, was a distinctive feature of ancien regime politics and society. The heyday of the Jesuits had been reached at the beginning of the seventeenth century when they had taught around 40,000 students; by the mid-eighteenth century they ran 151 *collèges* compared with the 72 that were in the hands of the Oratorians and the 60 belonging to the Doctrinaires. Most of them were to be found in the larger towns (over 10,000 inhabitants). Their domination was challenged in the west and the north by the Oratorians, and in the south by the Doctrinaires. Although the Jesuit establishments laid greater emphasis on the link between religion and education, every *collège*, to a greater or lesser degree, operated within the constraints of a Catholic culture.[37]

If one wanted the best for one's children, and one had the money to achieve this, education could be a very expensive item indeed. Madame Delehants, a financier's wife, estimated that it cost 10,000 *livres* to cover the living costs and fees of the two sons she sent to the *collège* des Grassins in Paris between 1725 and 1730. Families of the nobility of the sword sent their sons, at eight to ten years old, to the even more expensive colleges of Juilly and Louis-le-Grand. For the old nobility, an expensive education was increasingly perceived as a way of protecting one's top spot in society. The cost of sending the eight-year-old son of the d'Ourvilles from Valognes to the Louis-le-Grand *collège* in 1755 was 2,500 *livres* a year. To meet 'the challenge of the new', most *collèges* had to respond by increasing the amount of teaching they did in French, by providing more classes on history and geography (Jesuits were well-versed in these disciplines) and by altering the balance between medieval and modern science. Science classes were still infrequent but – another sign of the changing times – they do appear to have increased in number as the century progressed. Roger Chartier and Dominique Julia state that, comparing the eighteenth and sixteenth centuries 'the progress of scientific teaching in *collèges* during the final years was remarkable'.[38] All this would contribute to the scientific and secular character of the mid-century French Enlightenment.

From this perspective, the final expulsion of the Jesuits in 1764 would mark a very important watershed in the history of French education and culture. The Jesuits had often led the way in introducing science, geography and modern languages into their curricula, but always with a religious emphasis. Their approach had exercised a powerful influence over the minds and opinions of adolescents over two centuries. Their defeat would encourage those – not all of them to be found amongst the *philosophes* – who had always believed that educational establishments should not act, essentially, as transmission belts for religious beliefs and values. The Oratorians and the Doctrinaires, who now became the dominant, 'modernising' forces in secondary and higher education, differed from their Jesuit counterparts in that they did not all see their careers lying solely in the priesthood. For every one Oratorian who entered the priesthood by 1789, six became teachers. They were, therefore, more responsive to the pressures coming from families paying high fees for an education that, they hoped, would train their offspring for the modern world, not the world to come – a very important existentialist shift in attitudes.

Oratorians and Doctrinaires had been teaching some French from the 1700s; almost all their teaching would be in French by the 1780s. Even the diehard anti-Jansenist Brothers of the Christian Life felt that they had to move with the commercial times, adapting their curricula to suit the career prospects of their students. Hydrography would be taught in Vannes and Nantes by the second half of the century; commercial courses would be on offer in Boulogne; horticulture, surveying and accounting could be taken in Reims and Montpellier. The Brothers of Saint Jerome would try to resolve the contradiction between traditional religion and the demands of a commercial society by explaining to their students that numbers had mystical powers, and that the parable of the unjust steward and the talents demonstrated 'the importance of learning to add up bills and calculate interest'! The principal of the Lille *collège* would order his management committee in 1772 to change the syllabus, explaining that history, not the classics, was the key to understanding change in society. He still insisted that one should study sacred history first, but the very idea of studying 'social change' sent shivers down the spines of more traditional and orthodox priests.[39]

Religion, women and 'the public sphere'

It was the Catholic Church, rather than capitalism or Rousseau, which laid the foundations for the subordination of women to men. The Judeo-Christian tradition had consistently downgraded the importance of women in public life, and, although Protestantism and Jansenism had accorded women a more positive role, 'Adam' always remained superior to 'Eve'. Bonnie Anderson and Judith Zinsser write that, 'when it came to assumptions about women's functions and role and to descriptions of her nature and her body, no new assumptions were formulated'.[40] The dalliance in the Garden of Eden provided biblical justification for regarding women as potentially more lustful and, hence, more sinful than men. Rousseau, accompanied by several other Enlightenment writers, would secularise this religious discourse by insisting on women's peculiar ability, and duty, to raise children for the new civic Garden of Eden. The heartfelt cry of Euripides' anti-heroine, Medea, remained relevant: 'I was born unfortunate, and a woman.'

Rousseau's patronising comment on women, 'It is fortunate when your chaste power exercised solely in conjugal union, makes itself felt only for the glory of the State and public happiness' was loaded with the ideology of the Counter-Reformation, despite the fact that he was a Protestant. Ordinary women could best realise their potential as wives, primarily in the bedroom, the nursery and the kitchen. This focus on the reproductive and maternal aspect of women's biology and psychology explains, in great measure, the dominant role they played in the 'caring professions'. In the early 1630s, women who entered religious orders, primarily to serve the poor and the sick, would finally be released from their medieval cloisters and relocated in the hospital ward and the schoolroom, though not in the wider public sphere. In the hospital, nurses would be subordinate to the doctor; in the schoolroom, to the local bishop or *curé*. In return for this relative freedom, the Counter-Reformation episcopacy would ensure that the extraordinary contribution of female religious orders to the cultural and psychological formation of generations of young women would be directed, essentially, towards the production of 'Christian wives and mothers'.

The Brothers of Saint-Jean-de-Dieu ran the best hospitals in France, employing some of the best surgeons. At their central hospital in Paris,

60 Brothers, 8 doctors and surgeons and 24 lay servants cared for just 200 patients, a remarkable doctor–patient ratio. The Brothers also ran the vast naval hospital at Brest, as well as four military hospitals in San Domingo. But these hospitals were exceptions, the product of a well-endowed religious order enjoying considerable royal patronage. Women, dedicated to caring for the poor and the sick, ran the great majority of hospitals. The image of the nun as a cloistered 'bride of Christ' changed when, in 1633, Vincent de Paul and Louise Marillac created one of the most influential of all the female religious orders of the period, the Daughters of Charity (*Filles de la Charité*).[41] By the early eighteenth century, they were providing nursing care in 200 localities; by 1789, they would be running 426 hospitals in France, as well as many in Poland and Austria. Their recruitment was predominantly lower middle class.

The *Filles* who ran the hospital at Roanne near Lyon in the mid-eighteenth century trained auxiliary staff (*servantes*) for six months before deciding whether or not they were capable of taking on qualified nursing care. Working under a hospital board that included a bishop and a local priest, they assumed responsibility for nursing care, administration of drugs, admission registers and day-to-day financing of their institution. Their pharmacy – an innovation by the Daughters of Charity – included an allegedly therapeutic cocktail of pills, powders, syrups, herb teas and flower petals. Holistic medicine *avant la lettre*! Whatever they dispensed to patients, the *Filles* in Roanne were never allowed to forget that they were nuns before they were nurses. Saving souls was, for most of them, the primary goal. The daily routine for the children in the orphanage attached to their hospital was to rise at 5.00 a.m., make their beds and then walk silently to the assembly room for prayers. This was followed by work and, at 7.30 a.m., mass. At 8.00 a.m., back to work. The teaching of the catechism and lessons on reading and writing preceded lunch, at 10.15 a.m. From midday to 4.00 p.m., the children were sent back to work, after which they read the New Testament – in French. Supper was at 6.15 p.m., followed, at long last, by an hour's play. Everyone had to be tucked up in bed by 8.30 p.m. – after prayers![42]

Jones and Brockliss conclude that the Daughters of Charity 'exemplified an important strand of post-Tridentine piety: a pragmatic commitment to charitable activity in the world and the inculcation of godliness into those adjudged most in need of it, namely the poor'.[43] However, the Daughters of Charity were only the biggest and best of the female religious orders caring for the sick and the poor, often with no fees attached. The *Soeurs de l'Annonciation*, the *Soeurs grises du Tiers Ordre de Saint-François* and urban foundations such as the *Soeurs de Saint-Charles de Nancy* were just a few of the many orders who formed part of the nursing profession under the ancien regime.

Female religious orders also left their indelible imprint upon education for women in the seventeenth and eighteenth centuries, and it comes as no surprise that one of their champions was an archbishop. François de Salagnac de Lamothe Fénelon (1651–1715), archbishop of Cambrai, was one of the most advanced thinkers of his time; his writings form an intellectual bridge between the 'confessional absolutism' of Bossuet and the 'secular republicanism' of Rousseau. His Homeric fable, *Télémaque* (1699), proved to be one of the most influential books of the century, and we shall return to it. In 1687, he had dared, as an archbishop, to declare that women were, potentially, as important in the construction of human knowledge and experience as men, and the way for women to realise their potential was to obtain an education, one that went beyond embroidery and learning to dance. He opens his *De l'éducation des filles* with these words, 'Nothing is more neglected than the education of girls.' This was both a statement of fact and a call for radical change, but, again, within the parameters of the Christian faith.

One year before the appearance of Fénelon's educational tract, Louis XIV's morganatic wife had founded *la communauté de Saint-Louis* at Saint Cyr for 250 daughters of the nobility of the sword. The girls entered between the ages of seven and twelve and could remain until they were twenty. It proved to be a model – albeit of the highest class – for many schools attended by young ladies. The curriculum was radical enough, with history and languages being taught along with embroidery and dancing. The ultimate aim, however, was the transformation of the immature girl into the mature wife and mother, or, as Fénelon would have preferred, the future, educated, wife who would have 'a house to run, a husband to keep happy, and children to bring up'.[44]

The religious orders of the Ursulines and the Visitandines were to the schoolroom what the Daughters of Charity were to the hospital. The Ursulines, founded in Italy in 1535, had opened 300 religious houses in France by 1670 and were to become the leading force of their day in female education. The Visitandines, founded in 1610 at Annecy by Jeanne de Chantal and François de Sales, developed as one of the many hybrid female orders in France. They catered for those who wished to remain within the cloister as well as for those who, taking temporary vows, wished to work in the world. They had opened 87 schools for girls by 1641. Unlike the Daughters of Charity, however, both the Ursulines and the Visitandines taught, and were recruited from, the nobility and the wealthier bourgeoisie. A study of 198 Ursuline nuns in Rouen between 1619 and 1787 reveals that 42.9 per cent were daughters of either the sword or the robe nobility, whilst 29.3 per cent came from families attached to the world of trade and commerce. The Visitandines acquired an even more aristocratic veneer, and were particularly successful in reproducing themselves: of 403 Visitandine nuns who died between 1667 and 1767, one in two had been educated 'in-house'. It is all too easy to forget the courage of girls from wealthy homes, often dumped by their parents in religious houses as family marriage fodder, who struggled to give social, and existential, meaning to their lives, either as nuns, teachers or nurses.

Fees for places in the thousands of female schools available by the eighteenth century ranged from the exorbitant to the nominal. At the primary level, of course, girls from poor families would often receive a free education. It has been estimated that, in Paris by 1789, there would be 'nearly five hundred establishments of elementary education which depended on the Church and which were available more or less free to children from modest homes'.[45] The *Congrégation des Soeurs de Saint-Charles* in Lorraine, responsible for 45 religious houses by 1789, was just one of the many provincial and local bodies providing a range of social services – clothes for the poor, soup for the hungry, medicines for the sick and elementary education for the illiterate. In Paris, the Daughters of Saint-Geneviève taught, nursed the sick and organised workshops for girls seeking employment. Originally, the Ursuline order had dedicated itself to the instruction of the poor, but, as education became a more marketable commodity, money began to talk louder. Aristocratic girls, accompanied by their servants, who were sent to school in the Abbaye-aux-Bois in Paris could set their parents back by 30,000 *livres* a year! However, this was quite exceptional: the less well-heeled ladies who attended the school run by the Ladies of the Panthémont in the rue de Grenelle paid only 800 *livres* a year.[46]

As for the curriculum, it obviously varied, often according to class and market price. No central direction was imposed on the hundreds of Ursuline schools. In general, however, eighteenth-century education for women remained fixed within the Fénelonian pious context of the 'good wife and mother'. Sophie, the mother of Rousseau's *Emile*, was the literary child of Fénelon. For the good archbishop, as for Luther before him, 'Women must be taught because they are teachers', teachers of their children and, on the wider front, of the manners and morality of a Christian civilised culture. Needlework was thought to be a particularly Christian pursuit and was taught almost everywhere, as, indeed, was 'household economy', but, in the better schools, there were lessons in history and modern languages. Methods of teaching in the best fee-paying schools were often based on the Jesuit model, with groups of 10 or 12; in the larger, poorer establishment, large classes were certainly not uncommon, with the best pupils often teaching the worst. It was not so much the curriculum as the convent-based setting that the *philosophes* would attack.

This is hardly surprising since the exclusivist and frequently intolerant religious ideology of the post-Tridentine Catholic Church provided the text for teaching in the vast majority of schools, from those run by parish priests to the aristocratic houses run by nuns. The Ursuline order had played a significant role in the conversion of Protestant girls after the Revocation of the Edict of Nantes. The Visitandines were equally devoted to the task of promoting the Catholic religion inside, and outside, the classroom. Another famous, and successful, female teaching organisation, the Congregation of the Ladies of Saint-Maur, founded in 1621 and linked to the Benedictine Order, had expanded their influence in the Midi following invitations from Catholic local authorities to convert the daughters of Protestant families. Until the Revolution, attendance at mass and daily prayers remained a common practice in schools run by female religious orders, which is one of the reasons why Merry Wiesner is convinced that, in many ways, 'European religion had been feminized during the seventeenth and eighteenth centuries.'[47]

However, by 1789, the culture of the post-Tridentine world was to be irrevocably changed by the culture of what is usually described as 'the Enlightenment', and schools and hospitals could not remain unaffected. For example, if most girls' schools for the wealthy would continue to train young women for marriage, the institution of marriage itself would change. What is really surprising when researching religious orders in late eighteenth-century France is the multi-faceted nature of their activities. In addition to religious, medical and educational work, they occasionally acted as unofficial 'marriage bureaux', hotels for paying guests and retirement homes, as well as soup kitchens and 'people's dispensaries'. And, unlike present-day welfare states, the selfless devotion of hundreds of thousands of monks, nuns, priests and lay volunteers meant that they were remarkably 'cost-efficient'. This would only become apparent during the Revolution when the entire religious and charitable edifice collapsed and, with it, a world the Catholic Church had lost.

Suggested reading

Aston, N. 'The Golden Autumn of Gallicanism? Religious History and its Place in Current Writing on Eighteenth-Century France', *French History*, Vol 13 (1999), pp. 187–222.

Bell, D. 'Culture and Religion', in W. Doyle (ed.) *Old Regime France* (Oxford, 2001), pp. 79–104.

Campbell, P. *Power and Politics in Old Regime France, 1720–1745* (London, 1996), pp. 193–318.

Hudson, D. 'The Regent, Fleury, Jansenism and the Sorbonne', *French History*, Vol 8 (1994), pp. 135–48.

Jones, C. *Charity and Bienfaisance: The Treatment of the Poor in the Montpellier Region, 1740–1815* (Cambridge, 1982).

McManners, J. *Church and Society in Eighteenth-Century France* 2 vols (Oxford, 1999).

Norberg, K. *Rich and Poor in Grenoble, 1600–1814* (Berkeley, 1985).

Rogister, J. *Louis XV and the Parlement of Paris, 1737–55* (Cambridge, 1995).

Swann, J. 'Parlement, Politics and the *Parti Janséniste*: The *Grand Conseil* Affair', *French History*, Vol 4 (1992), pp. 435–61.

Swann, J. 'Politics: Louis XV', in W. Doyle (ed.) *Old Regime France* (Oxford, 2001), pp. 195–222.

Wiesner, M. *Women and Gender in Early Modern Europe* (Cambridge, 1993).

Chapter 3

The nobility and the seigneurial system

The nobility, of sword and robe, was the dominant political and social group in ancien regime France. It monopolised the top posts in the government, the Church, the armed forces, the parlements and the royal administration. Not all seigneurs were of noble birth, and it was both old and new nobility that dominated life in the countryside, for if the parish shaped the religious experience of the mass of the French rural population, the seigneury shaped its political, social and economic life. Gail Bossenga puts it succinctly: 'The seigneurial system was intimately bound up with the ideal of living nobly: it was designed to let seigneurs consume what peasants produced.'[1] Seigneurial authority did exist in towns, and seigneurial dues were levied on urban properties just as they were on rural farms, although, to a very considerable extent, towns had emancipated themselves from seigneurial control during the Middle Ages. During the course of the eighteenth century, however, those associated with the military life and 'living nobly' would increasingly be influenced by the rise of capitalism and consumerism. The sword nobility would be called upon to fight on two fronts: against the encroachment of the new robe nobility, with its modernised vision of a strong administrative state, as well as against the related 'rise of the bourgeoisie', with its vision of a more commercialised market economy.

French agriculture: custom and modernisation

For the influential, mid-century school of French economic theorists, the physiocrats, an agrarian society was composed of three 'classes': the land-owning class, the productive class and the unproductive class (*la classe stérile*). The land-owning class included the tens of thousands of seigneurs, from the king at the top of the pyramid to the smallest fief holder at the bottom, who were the recipients not only of landed rents, but also of the feudal dues and tithes attached to a fief. Land, for the physiocrats, was the true and original source of a country's wealth, not commerce or industry. This is hardly surprising since, in 1735, France had roughly 20 million country-dwellers and under 4 million town-dwellers. France was an agrarian country; her economy was dominated by the agricultural sector. For the sword and robe nobility, as well as for the wealthier sections of the bourgeoisie, rents remained the key to a stable and prosperous life. However, the physiocrats had been convinced that a more modern type of capitalist contractual property rights should replace the existing archaic and complex type of feudal property rights. This part of their programme, first formulated in the 1750s, would only be fully implemented after 1789.[2]

The debate over the performance of agriculture during the ancien regime has been fierce and prolonged. It is generally agreed that there was some improvement as more land came under cultivation, population increased and regional and international markets expanded; less agreement, perhaps, that it was the dominant seigneurial system that militated against long-term revolutionary, managerial or technological change. Ernest Labrousse's detailed statistical analyses, conducted in the 1930s and 1940s, argued that agriculture, not commerce or industry, provided the motor for general economic growth, with a sustained rise in the production of basic agricultural commodities of around 60 per cent between 1726–41 and 1771–89. Jean-Claude Toutain estimated that national agricultural production rose by around 60 per cent over the entire century. Most economic historians now prefer the more modest conclusion of Joseph Goy and Emmanuel Le Roy Ladurie, a net rise of between 25 and 40 per cent. There was, then, no agricultural 'revolution' in ancien regime France.[3]

Agriculture at the beginning of the eighteenth century was far more vulnerable to cycles of 'boom and bust', the consequence of primitive farming methods and a dependence upon a narrow range of crops, mainly wheat, rye and oats in most areas, maize, chestnuts and olives in parts of the south. Owing to a shortage of fertiliser, too much land was left fallow. Crops were only planted every other year in good farming land in the north, once in every three years in the south. Minor roads were extremely poor; river and canal communication networks were burdened with an infinite number of tolls and seigneurial dues, all of which inhibited the development of regional and national markets. In the absence of alternative sources of food and a sophisticated market system, the vast majority of farmers, large and small, were peculiarly susceptible to poor weather conditions.

In recent years, the science of climatology has advanced hypotheses to explain why there was no significant and sustained improvement in agricultural productivity until the early nineteenth century. Empirical, statistical evidence of the links between the climate, harvests and epidemics was lacking until the Royal Society of Medicine, encouraged by a leading doctor, Vicq d'Azyr, and a clergyman, Father Cotte, launched a scientific enquiry in the 1770s. However, researches by glaciologists, archaeologists and geologists have suggested that Europe may have experienced 'a little ice age' between the late sixteenth century and the mid-nineteenth century, with colder winters and warmer summers. A few historians have even speculated that, within this 'little ice age', there were shorter spells of a half a century or so when temperatures dropped to new lows, thus helping to explain the miserable decades from the 1680s to the 1710s.[4] The evidence appears to be thin, but should not be rejected out of hand.

Whatever the link between long-term 'ice ages' and short-term cycles of good and bad weather, there can be no doubt that climatic conditions exercised a powerful influence on farming methods, as well as on the many regional variations that characterised French agriculture. Jean-Marc Moriceau has stressed the impact of the dire weather conditions of the late seventeenth century upon the rich farmers of the Île-de-France, who were forced to introduce widespread marling (the mixing of clay and lime with the soil) to improve fields sodden with continual rain. According to Peter Jones: 'Climate left a deeper imprint [than transport problems] . . . for no other country of Europe experienced the range of weather patterns to which France was susceptible.' Regions in the north, west and south-west were affected by moist and temperate Atlantic airstreams, while the south and the south-east experienced the more favourable Mediterranean climate. It was, primarily, the climate that dictated why the best wheat was grown in the north and the east; why pastoral farming, along with the cultivation of rye, was widespread in the west and the western parts of the central highlands; and why vines, olives and chestnuts competed with arable farming in the south-east. Given the constraints of the climate, and the post-feudal system of land exploitation, experimental change could easily spell starvation rather than profit.[5]

This is not to say that, within the above constraints, many peasants did not try to improve their lot. Exceptions to the rule that farming was 'backward' or 'stagnant' did exist, and were significant. Over half a century ago, Jean Meuvret challenged the notion that traditional commercial farming was incompatible with emerging forms of capitalist development by concentrating his research upon the importance of concrete and identifiable aspects of market organisation. For Meuvret, food crises during Louis XIV's reign were, primarily, a problem of social and economic organisation, not peasant resistance to change. He argued, firstly, that the demand for increased grain production from Paris was undermining traditional village autarkies; secondly, that the key factors in reducing bottlenecks in grain supplies were improvements in transport and better market relationships between town and country. Finally, he concluded that the 1720s and 1730s marked a significant turning point in the history of these problems, 'a time when different strands of institutional and economic change began to weave themselves into a fundamentally new and more open kind of economic organisation'.[6]

The more recent, equally exhaustive research of Jean-Marc Moriceau provides support for Meuvret's arguments, particularly with reference to the importance of market organisation and market demand. Moriceau analyses the impact of rising Parisian demand upon the wealthier farmers of the Île-de-France, demand that encouraged the concentration of farms, as well as diversified and more productive methods of farming and cattle husbandry. This 'processus de modernisation' begins, for Moriceau, in the mid-seventeenth century and accelerates during the first decades of the following century. After 1720, farm prices, particularly of grain, start to rise appreciably and the region enters 'une conjoncture de prosperité'. Although some of this improvement is explicable in terms of a recovery from the dismal performance of farming during the seventeenth century, Moriceau argues that what we are witnessing in the Île-de-France between 1670 and 1730 are 'capitalist transformations in the scope and orientation of large-scale farming'.[7] The main conclusion to be drawn from the work of both Meuvret and Moriceau is that modernisation of ancien regime agriculture was possible given an appropriate combination of good farming land, market demand, adequate transport facilities, the existence of a reasonably wealthy and enterprising community of farmers and, of course, good weather conditions. But the Île-de-France, with its massive Parisian market at the centre, was not typical of France; and even Moriceau suggests that the long-term capitalisation of agricultural production in his advanced region was restricted by the ambitions of many wealthy merchant-farmers to became noble seigneurs and fief-holders.

Patrick O'Brien's work, focusing upon contrasts in labour productivity, provides illuminating comparisons with the evolution of British agriculture. Adopting the long-term approach, O'Brien suggests that between 1520 and 1910, labour productivity probably multiplied twice as fast in Britain than in France. There were, of course, many reasons for this contrast, including, *inter alia*, the geography of the two countries, their different climates and their political, economic and fiscal systems. But O'Brien also focuses upon the key issue of contrasting attitudes to land ownership. As opposed to what happened in France, the exodus of farmers from the countryside in Britain, from the sixteenth to the eighteenth centuries, pushed urban wage rates down, leading to the increased profits and higher capital formation necessary for the development of an urban, industrialised economy.[8] Similar movements were taking place in France, but not on the scale witnessed across the Channel. France, for example, did not experience enclosure movements comparable to those that transformed the nature of British farming. In contrast to what occurred in England, the French state, after the 1660s, often defended communal lands, as well as the open-field system of agriculture. The policy of the government, influenced by the lay and ecclesiastical owners of vast seigneuries, was to encourage the survival of communal pasture and peasant livestock, thus cushioning millions of peasants – who supplied the ruling elite with seigneurial dues – from the economic recessions that led to the massive expropriation that occurred in England.

The link between the seigneurie and the exploitation of the peasantry is reinforced by Hilton Root's study of the Burgundian peasantry. Root stresses

65

that there was 'no community-wide consensus in favour of abolishing the right of free pasture rights [*vaine pâture*] or the three-field rotation system . . . because most members of the community identified their interests with the preservation of the open fields. It was the demands of the seigneury, not the open-field system, that peasants, rich and poor alike, saw as obstructing their economic goals'.[9] In other words, it was the feudal economic exploitation of the peasantry by seigneurs, the majority of whom were noble, that acted as a brake on agricultural reform. The physiocrats realised this and campaigned for the abolition of what remained of an anachronistic feudal land system. Another important, and often ignored, explanation for the separate development of the French economy is to be found in the prolonged dependence on protoindustrialised forms of production. The dispersion of textile and other forms of domestic manufacturing into the countryside and small towns was certainly a feature of the British 'transition to capitalism' during the early modern period. In France, however, the phenomenon of peasants, trapped within the seigneurial system, forced to obtain a supplementary wage from industry in order to pay the dues necessary for the retention of their small plots, persisted for far longer than in England, and affected many more communities.

A 'feudal' or a 'seigneurial' ruling class?

In England, 'the commercial nature of agriculture meant that [landed] . . . investments continued to work in a capitalist way'; in France, the official realisation that greater prosperity in the agricultural sector was desirable was 'in practice subordinated to the short-term interests of a ruling class which was very far from capitalist'. Joel Félix reminds us that around a third of all land, and a far higher proportion of good farming land, was owned by the nobility and the clergy.[10] Was this ruling class 'feudal' or 'seigneurial'? The question has provoked bitter, often barren, debate over many years. The answer depends, to a large degree, upon the period one is discussing. The ruling class that indulged in medieval jousting in the Italian Wars during the reign of Francis I was not the same ruling class that was domesticated and then 'reinvented' by Richelieu and Louis XIV a century later; neither was it the more commercially minded nobility that collapsed with Louis XVI in 1789. One could define medieval feudalism as a set of juridical, social, economic and military relationships that linked the king to his lords, and those lords to their vassals and serfs. However, to define eighteenth-century society in this way would produce a caricature out of a simplification. For Sharon Kettering, medieval feudalism was being transformed as early as the fifteenth century into 'clientelism', a more political system of reciprocal relationships between 'patrons' and 'clients', pursued by Cardinal Richelieu and other ministers in the seventeenth century to tie provincial power brokers to central government. Whether we are dealing with 'feudalism', 'bastard feudalism', 'clientelism' or 'kinship', the possession and exploitation of land was always of crucial importance.[11]

Much of the confusion surrounding the terms 'feudalism' and 'seigneuralism' is based upon the confusion that existed between feudal and bourgeois concepts of property ownership. Again, the physiocrats recognised the problem and frequently denounced 'the tyranny of feudal law', thus paving the way for a more modern concept of property rights. Thomas Kaiser argues that, by the eighteenth century, French property law was indeed moving towards a modern, 'bourgeois' definition of private property rights. However, these rights were still 'conditioned by local customary right, seigneurial law and sovereign power'.[12] In some regions, even the power of the sovereign did not go uncontested. Lawyers attached to the Estates of Languedoc argued that, since the legal system of much of southern France was based on Roman Law (which favoured a modern interpretation of private property), land not attached to a seigneury should be subjected neither to the authority of the seigneur nor to the Crown. Such arguments moved the Estates of Languedoc a few steps nearer the belief in 'absolute, inviolable property rights' as expressed in the Declaration of Rights of 1789. Given the confusion that reigned before the Revolution, one can now see why Revolutionary jurists would insist upon the inclusion of those twin, explosive adjectives, 'absolute' and 'inviolable', in their definition of property rights. The clarification was of historic importance: it created a clear demarcation line between the legal fog of the 'feudal' past and the relative legal clarity of the 'bourgeois' present. However, let us note that it took four years (1789–93), a European war and several major peasant uprisings for jurists to reach this historic judgement!

Should we, then, dispense with the term 'feudalism' altogether? To do so would neither be justified in terms of ancien regime property law, nor in terms of social reality. Pierre Goubert, an acknowledged expert, concluded that there has been too much hair-splitting over the meaning of feudalism: 'it is clear that the members of the Constituent Assembly (in 1790) had no problem with using the term, that they were perfectly aware of its significance . . . demonstrating that the so-called feudal regime constituted one of the foundations of the Ancien Régime'.[13] For the peasantry, the ancien regime was associated with the nobility and feudalism, and the institution through which this historic, unholy alliance had been forged was the seigneury. In purist terms, the ownership of a seigneury entailed the simultaneous possession of a fief, courts of justice and a landed estate. The fief represented the legal and judicial rights transferred by a lord to his vassal on the purchase of a seigneury. The courts of justice gave the new owner the power to implement those rights.

The land attached to the fief was divided into two parts, the *réserve seigneuriale* and the *directe seigneuriale*. The former was that part of the estate owned and farmed either by the seigneur himself using hired labour or, in the cases of large noble estates, through a steward or manager. The latter described the land which was leased out to farmers and sharecroppers, in return for a truly bewildering variety of feudal and seigneurial dues, as well as obligations to work on the seigneur's estate and use his mills, ovens, and winepresses.[14] As one might expect, confusion reigned in some regions over the distinction – or lack of one – between a fief and a seigneurie. In Brittany, the *directe seigneuriale* was frequently referred to as 'a fief', and the seigneur could lease out parcels of land to anyone, noble or peasant, creating new 'mini-fiefs'. The barony of Chateaubriand near Combourg was comprised of 224 'fiefs'! In Burgundy, too, we often find that the terms 'fief' and 'seigneurie' were synonymous, although more often than not the former referred to the seigneur's own lands (the *réserve*).

The eighteenth-century noble

It is almost as difficult to provide a precise definition of an ancien regime noble as it is to describe a seigneury. What real unity could have existed between a millionaire, aristocratic courtier at Versailles and an impoverished noble scraping a living by his wits in a one-roomed apartment in Bordeaux; or between a very rich Parisian receiver-general of taxes and a poor provincial noble ploughing his few hectares of land in Brittany? It is true that they were all (if they had the necessary genealogical proof!) bound together by being members of the second estate of the realm. They had the legal right to carry a sword and to have a reserved pew in their local church, and most nobles escaped government taxes, the salt tax and excise duties. These, and similar, privileges certainly marked them out from the common herd, but it is equally clear that what divided them was infinitely greater than that which united them. If this is true, what meaningful categorisation can we employ to clarify what eighteenth-century society perceived a noble to be?

The nobility represented only a small fraction of the total population, around 1.5 per cent. The exact percentage is hard to establish with any degree of exactitude since contemporary estimates varied between a low of 100,000 to a high of 400,000 individuals. If the government had not weeded out thousands of 'false nobles' from time to time, the latter figure might have been fairly accurate.[15] Based upon a careful assessment of the available statistics, Franklin Ford suggested that, in 1715, there were probably around 190,000 nobles in France, while Guy Chaussinand-Nogaret went even lower, arguing that we should 'settle for 110 or 120,000, or about 25,000 noble families', by 1789.[16] Whichever figure we accept, can we place these individuals into meaningful categories?

Historians who place considerable emphasis on culture as opposed to class, and upon the reality of legally recognised estates, guilds and corporations as opposed to class differences related to new methods of production and wealth creation, suggest that a system of traditional, and widely accepted, values defined the nobility – honour, rank, privilege. Gail Bossenga concludes that 'orders and corporate groups may best be considered status groups, where status is defined as ranked positions in society based upon shared perceptions of social honour'. Status certainly 'co-opted wealth' as Bossenga suggests, but it is very difficult to accept her argument that 'from the old regime to the early nineteenth century, the class structure of France underwent little change: it remained a country of wealthy landlords; small impoverished peasant proprietors; and dispersed protoindustrial activity'.[17] As we shall see below, a significant minority of peasants were neither 'small' nor 'impoverished', and, on more general grounds, capitalism exerted a powerful, and disruptive, influence on peasants, bourgeois and, indeed, the nobility as the century progressed. France in 1789 was certainly not the France of Louis XIV.

Guy Chaussinand-Nogaret divides the nobility into five groups based on wealth rather than social background or profession, arguing that, in an increasingly commercialised and consumerist society, cash was beginning to talk louder than caste. At the very top we find 'the plutocratic kernel', those in receipt of an annual income of 50,000–200,000 *livres*, occasionally far more; perhaps 200 families, 'who effortlessly dominated the whole nobility of the kingdom by their luxury and standard of living'. In the lowest category, with incomes of less than 1,000 *livres* a year, we discover nobles who were 'indistinguishable from peasants; some were even worse off and lived a wretched life of dependence on alms'.[18] Franklin Ford, using the tax brackets for the 1695 poll tax (*capitation*) returns, agrees that different income levels undoubtedly help us to separate the 'plutocratic' goats from the pauperised sheep. Both historians also agree that there was a 'fusion' of the two principal categories of nobility – the 'old' sword nobility and the 'new' robe nobility – as the century progressed. However, for Chaussinand-Nogaret, this fusion led to the virtual extinction – or radical transformation at least – of the 'feudal' sword nobility, while Ford lays far greater emphasis on the ways in which the robe nobility evolved as parliamentary and legal defenders of the privileges of both sections of the nobility. The latter interpretation is more plausible.

In stark contrast to the 'fusion' hypotheses advanced by several historians, however, Richard Andrews insists that the robe nobility in the parlements and the sovereign courts believed that they were a distinct group, partly because the old sword nobility rejected them as members of their exclusive club. 'In the collective vision of the military-seigneurial aristocracy', he writes, 'the *robin* remained essentially bourgeois.' More importantly, from the standpoint of the evolution of French society and government, Andrews argues that his influential judicial officers (or 'themistocrats' as he calls them) formed an important bridge between the third and the second estates. They evolved

69

over the seventeenth and eighteenth centuries into a distinct judicial category, their noble status remaining 'marginal to the abiding professional identity, recruitment and existence of all but a few high-ranking themistocrats'.[19] This radical interpretation has merit. Fifty years ago, Albert Soboul singled out 'the great families of the magistrates of the parlements whose intention it was to control the royal government and take part in the administration of the state'.[20] There is also David Bell's study of Parisian barristers, which also reveals 'the long process by which magistrates became the nucleus of a new nobility'. Of particular interest, given our emphasis on the importance of Louis XIV's 'confessional absolutism', is Bell's argument concerning the king's 'final, convulsive attempts to rid his kingdom of the Jansenist "heresy"'. It was during this momentous struggle that the Parisian barristers transformed themselves into a combative organ of public opinion in order to shore up the resistance of the Paris parlement.[21] The role of lawyers and magistrates in defining the character and discourse of ancien regime politics should not be underestimated.

The various categorisations chosen by the historians discussed above are based, in large measure, upon conflicting ideological interpretations of the ancien regime and the Revolution. Chaussinand-Nogaret seeks to undermine any Marxist-inspired thesis relating to the inevitability of class conflict between distinct bourgeois and aristocratic groups, insisting that the supposed unity of the nobility was simply a post-1789 creation, inspired by the real political conflict between 'revolutionary' bourgeois and 'counter-revolutionary' nobles. He argues that, during the first half of the eighteenth century, the nobility of the sword had finally ditched its attachment to notions of 'honour' and military prowess in favour of the bourgeois values of personal merit and involvement in the new capitalist world. From the 1760s on, 'there was no longer any significant difference between nobility and middle classes'.[22] This stretches credulity a little too far.

Ford's thesis was more sophisticated. The robe nobility, with its recent bourgeois economic and cultural values, he suggested, did make some impact upon the traditional value systems of the nobility of the sword. However, in the very process of undermining these values, the robe nobility itself became infected with old 'feudal' values, such as 'landed prestige, military connections, [and] pride in family'. Ford, then, concludes that there was a 'fusion' between robe and sword nobles, but that certain 'class distinctions' (relating to socio-cultural rather than socio-economic values) remained.[23] If one seeks to resolve the conflict between the hypotheses of Ford and Chaussinand-Nogaret, one could begin by noting that the former is dealing, primarily, with the first half of the eighteenth century, while the latter is chiefly concerned with the period after 1750. Finally, Richard Andrews adopts an approach that recalls the influence of Michel Antoine and his insistence upon the pre-eminence of politics and the rise of the modern administrative state. Both are convinced that education, professionalism and high moral purpose are the hallmarks of robe magistrates: class interests are subsumed in the process of creating a modern judiciary for a modern state.

Below, we examine in more detail four categories of nobles and the relationship of these groups, constituting the ruling elite, to the 'feudal' or 'seigneurial' system of landownership.

Categories of nobles

The sword nobility (*noblesse de l'épée*)

It is probable that of our total of under 200,000 noble individuals, only one-third could trace their family origins back to pre-1600, and only a relatively small fraction of this number could find ancestors of pre-1400 vintage. In theory, a noble had to possess a pedigree dating back to the medieval period before he could be presented to Louis XIV at Versailles; in practice, as the Grim Reaper took his toll of the medieval noble families, only diehard traditionalists continued to defend the purist line. This does not mean that, under Louis XIV, the old distinctions between 'sword' and 'robe' became obsolete, far from it.

In terms of wealth, the princely sword nobility could be found in the first of the 22 tax brackets – covering those who paid over 2,000 *livres* – used for the *capitation* of 1695. However, the sword nobility, counts, viscounts and barons, was also present in class seven alongside magistrates of the sovereign courts, paying 250 *livres*. In class fifteen, relatively poor fief-holding provincial nobles, paying only 40 *livres*, found themselves in the same category as municipal officials. Finally, we find petty nobles, owning neither fief nor castle, in class nineteen, paying just over six *livres* in taxes, the same sum as master artisans![24] Diehard sword nobles, like the duc de Saint Simon, were being 'fused' by the fiscal state with the robe nobility and, even, the bourgeoisie, the ultimate fall from aristocratic grace! Modernisation of the state was slowly dissolving the boundaries between the peerage, the nobility and the rest of society.

This threat to the old nobility gave birth to a political and philosophical reaction, spearheaded by aristocrats such as archbishop Fénelon (1651–1715) and comte Henri de Boulainvilliers (1659–1722), whose significance in the long struggle against the Catholic absolutist state has too often been ignored. We paid tribute to Fénelon's pioneering work on behalf of women's education in the previous chapter. Le Roy Ladurie describes Fénelon as a man 'of very high intelligence, a precursor of pacifism, of modern education theory, even of socialism'.[25] Praise indeed, and probably somewhat exaggerated. In more measured terms, Roger Mettam believes that the Fénelonian reformers 'made an intelligent assessment of the difficulties besetting France before offering detailed methods of avoiding them in future'. These methods included the possible convocation of the Estates General and a government run by an aristocracy of merit. They also included 'councils' that would be real units of power in which the aristocracy would learn, or relearn, the arts of governing, obviously prototypes for the *Polysynodie* that operated during the early years of the Regency. Finally, there would be stronger links between provincial institutions, culminating in a 'hierarchy of consultative bodies with the Estates General at the apex and new provincial estates and local assemblies beneath'.[26] This programme of reform contains striking similarities with those introduced, or advocated, on the eve of the Revolution of 1789. The more liberal and intellectual wing of the aristocracy was present at the birth of 'modern France'.

For Jonathan Israel, the writings of Boulainvilliers formed part, not of any intellectual 'feudal reaction', but of the 'early Radical Enlightenment'. For too long, critics of Boulainvilliers have concentrated on the anti-democratic and racialist themes in his writings. His *Essai sur la noblesse française* was, indeed, 'racist' in that it traced a (mythical) racial line of descent from the German Franks, who had conquered the Gallo-Roman population of early France, to the ancien regime aristocracy. By the second half of the century, the *Essai* could be found on the bookshelves of every self-respecting – or self-deluding – sword noble; it became an icon of sword identity, a tenet of traditional noble faith. Boulainvilliers's dismissal of the 'common people' is, again, a feature of his political theory; he was no democrat, as Israel points out, but a supporter of a 'quasi-republic of the nobility', a stout defender of the seigneurial system, courts of justice included. However, Montesquieu, one of the founding fathers of the 'High Enlightenment', shared much of contemporary racist opinion, while anti-democratic sentiment is common amongst 'radical and revolutionary' thinkers such as Voltaire.

The relevant point to grasp about Boulainvilliers, living, it should be remembered, under the autocratic rule of Louis XIV, is that his concept of a reformed, desacralised monarchy, advised by the sword nobility, was the very opposite of the Sun King's 'confessional absolutism'. His *Essai de métaphysique*, written in the late 1700s, was a revolutionary attack on traditional Catholic theology, an attempt to interpret the meaning of the Bible through the use of reason. There is validity in Chaussinand-Nogaret's assertion that Boulainvilliers 'was the primitive painter who . . . sketched in bold colours, though with a rather heavy hand, the political thought of the Enlightenment'.[27] We should not automatically lump all sword nobles with the 'reactionary past' and robe nobles, like Montesquieu, with the 'enlightened future'.

The provincial nobility
The provincial sword nobility was divided by geography as well as by history and 'race'. Breton nobles, for example, retained a powerful sense of their

historic identity. This was true of most of the provinces that had been integrated into the French kingdom in relatively recent times; they had brought their privileges, including their privileged aristocratic estates, with them. The Intendant of Languedoc, Bâville, writing at the beginning of the century, explained that the long history of religious warfare in his region had produced a unique noble identity. In the first place, the 4,486 'familles de gentilshommes' he mentions were not distinguished by their wealth: excluding a handful of court aristocrats, only 15 possessed an annual income of over 20,000 *livres*. Secondly, the continual, and bloody, wars of religion appear to have dulled their appetite for fighting: 'They are not even attracted to the military vocation,' Bâville concluded, sadly. But other regions also exhibited distinctive characteristics. In the Touraine, 65 per cent of the old nobles studied by Luc Boisnard could trace their roots back at least to the sixteenth century.[28]

As the century progressed, the provincial sword nobility could frequently be found amongst the poorest as well as the richest sections of the noble estate, a fact that further widened the gap between the provincial and the court aristocracy. In Brittany, Jean Meyer discovered that half of the nobility lived in straightened circumstances, and that 38 per cent of these existed on the poverty line. They belonged to the 'noblesses populaires' who had gradually become accustomed 'to a peasant existence not unlike that of their non-noble neighbours'.[29] One Breton noble, Collas de la Baronnais, was left with just 2,000 *livres* a year to bring up 20 children during the 1760s and 1770s. Emile Léonard, the eminent Protestant historian, revealed that one of his distant, noble relatives, Jean Mabelly, had been raised to the officer class in March 1707, after 20 years' service. In 1714 he was sent into retirement with a miserable pension of just 200 *livres*.[30] The resentment of disgruntled army officers would prove to be one of the most persistent sources of discontent within the ranks of the provincial nobility. Legislation was passed between 1718 and 1727 to reserve officer posts in the army for 'la vraie noblesse', but without real success. As late as 1781, the Ségur Ordinance would be introduced to restrict officer positions in the army to persons possessing four degrees of nobility. William Doyle suggests that bourgeois opinion was 'shocked' at this reactionary piece of legislation, proof of the degree to which bourgeois money had already undermined the exclusivity of sword noble influence.[31]

The robe nobility

The robe nobility carried none of the medieval, military, frondeur baggage of the sword nobility. It was primarily a 'service nobility', looking more to the future than the past, a future that was inextricably linked to the expansion, not the contraction, of central government. By 1778, over 50,000 government offices would be up for sale; in 1515, the figure had been around

5,000. According to Richard Andrews, the real nobility of the robe – those holding hereditary, ennobling titles – only existed for 146 years, from 1644 to 1790, since, prior to 1644, no magisterial office in any of the sovereign courts had conferred nobility on its members. Certainly, as we have seen, many of the top positions in government, the armed forces and the Church were still earmarked for the old nobility of the sword. However, we must make a distinction between these appointed secretaries of state, archbishops, admirals and generals, recruited almost exclusively from the sword nobility, and the increasingly powerful and wealthy administrative robe families like the Ormessons or the Phélypeaux, who ran the show behind the aristocratic scenes. By 1789, the robe nobility, whose influence would now extend from the corridors of power at Versailles to the courtrooms of provincial towns, had considerably weakened the old sword nobility by becoming the power behind the emerging modern fiscal state. Robe nobles also figured prominently in the parlements, the main source of opposition to the Bourbon monarchy by 1789.

Two main avenues led to the privileged position of robe nobility: the first, and most common, was the purchase of an office that carried with it the coveted prize of life, or hereditary, nobility; the second was through direct ennoblement by the king. During the eighteenth century, over 5,000 families would eventually be lifted into the second estate by the purchase of ennobling offices, around 1,000 by the personal gift of the king. Around two-thirds of all nobles by the end of the eighteenth century would belong to the *noblesse de robe*. All of the top offices in the sovereign courts and the parlements, as well as many in provincial fiscal, judicial and administrative offices, now conferred noble status on the purchaser. One could also buy into the nobility by purchasing, at considerable cost, the honorific title of *secrétaire du roi*. By the mid-eighteenth century, Louis XV's 'virtual reality' court was blessed with hundreds of them! Some important offices and titles conferred full, transmissible noble status upon the purchaser after 20 years, or after death in office – magistrates in the parlements of Paris, Besançon and Grenoble, for example. Most, however, entailed a lengthy stay (in some cases four generations) in social purgatory before a family could enter the pearly gates of the nobility – offices in the Parisian *cour des aides* and *cour des comptes* as well as in many of the provincial parlements and *bureaux des finances*.

However, robe nobility became an increasingly expensive way of climbing to the top of the ancien regime pole. The sinecure of a secretaryship in the Grand Chancellory cost around 70,000 *livres* in 1700, but 120,000 by 1780. Many provincial offices, particularly those of mayor, cost one-fifth or even one-tenth of this sum. This meant that applicants for the top ennobling offices of state tended to be drawn, in the main, from the higher echelons of society, indeed, in some cases, from those who had already acquired noble status. The parlement of Rennes was the most aristocratic of all the provincial parlements. Of its 216 magistrates in 1670, 136 could trace their noble ancestry back to the Middle Ages. Richard Andrew's exhaustive research into the magistrates of the Parisian sovereign courts and parlement confirms the general impression that recruitment was drawn mainly from the ranks of existing nobles. Of the 288 magistrates in the parlement of Paris in 1715, just over 80 per cent were noble, and, as was the case with the parlement of Rennes, these percentages did not change significantly during the course of the eighteenth century. As one would expect, the lower grades of the administration and the judiciary produced fewer noble candidates: only 37 per cent of the 130 judges in the Châtelet between 1735 and 1789 were of noble rank on assuming office. However, for Andrews, what distinguishes the members of both the Paris parlement and the Châtelet is not their noble blood, but the self-preservation of a nearly autonomous professional group. In other words, the judicial ranks of the robe nobility formed a 'caste', not a 'class', a professional identity that increasingly marked them out from the old sword nobility, and, increasingly, from the feudal component of the monarchy itself.[32]

The noblesse de cloche

Those ennobled by their service as municipal officials, whether as mayors or town councillors, were snobbishly dismissed by most sword (and some established robe nobles!) as 'nobles of the town hall bell'. However, if we start with the fifteenth century, it is likely that more families were ennobled through the purchase of municipal office during the ancien regime than by any other procedure. By the eighteenth century, this pool of 'town-hall nobles' was shrinking in size. The route to the lowest rank of noble status was now only available in a few towns such as Poitiers, Angoulême, Lyon, Toulouse and Nantes. In Toulouse, councillors (*capitouls*) were kept firmly in their non-noble place by the parlement of Languedoc. Few established nobles sought these municipal posts. Most recruits came from the legal, administrative and mercantile bourgeoisie.[33]

In addition to those who were elevated to the robe nobility by purchasing offices in the eighteenth century, approximately 1,000 individuals were ennobled by *lettres royales de noblesse*. This practice of rewarding servants of the crown was not new: Francis I had ennobled 183 candidates in 32 years during the first half of the sixteenth century. Once again, however, it was Louis XIV, anxious to finance his costly wars and associate persons of wealth and influence with the Crown, who brought the system into disrepute by increasing substantially the number of offices available for sale. Many members of the old nobility thought this scandalous; they argued that the sale of public offices was responsible for undermining 'honour, valour and pedigree as the foundations of true nobility'.[34] The flood abated somewhat in the eighteenth century when the privilege was increasingly reserved for officers in the armed forces and legal administrators, as well as for a growing number of merchants and industrialists.

Landownership: 'This bizarre system'

David Parker has argued that during the eighteenth century a ruling elite, composed of sword and robe nobles, the upper clergy and the urban bourgeoisie, 'derived its wealth from a capacity to appropriate through a combination of rents, feudal perquisites and fiscal devices, the "surplus" wealth generated by the peasantry'.[35] Over 250 years earlier, the marquis d'Argenson had launched a withering attack upon what he described as 'this bizarre system', by which 'the greatest authority over the nation was in the hands of certain principal usurpers who had beneath them other subordinate usurpers'.[36] Who were these 'principal' and 'subordinate' usurpers, and how much authority, in terms of seigneurial power, did they exercise over the rest of the nation?

On the eve of the Revolution, the clergy probably owned less than 10 per cent of the cultivable land of France, the nobility 20–25 per cent, the bourgeoisie around 30 per cent and the peasantry 35 per cent or more, the remainder being common land. Unsurprisingly, extreme diversity between, and within, regions was the rule: 'In some places, wealthy nobles might own practically everything; a few kilometres away, almost nothing. In the north, the Church held up to a quarter of the land, and sometimes more, but in the Midi, less than a twentieth. Around the towns, the peasantry owned almost nothing; in the centre of the Auvergne, they sometimes owned everything.'[37] Can we add some precision to mitigate the offence of using these broad generalisations?

Let us begin with the nobility, since the great majority of seigneurs on the eve of the Revolution were still noble, although bourgeois wealth was challenging its domination. For this ruling elite, fiefs and seigneuries, with their rents, feudal dues and courts of justice, formed the basis of their wealth and power. The nobility owned 23 per cent of the land in 215 parishes in Savoy in 1700, and a similar percentage in 37 parishes around Beauvais. On the eve of the Revolution, the nobility would still own as much as 68 per cent of the land in the future department of the Seine-et-Oise, 60 per cent in the Angevin region of the Mauges and 40 per cent in the Brie near Paris. In contrast, it controlled only 22 per cent of the land in the future department of the Nord, 15 per cent in the Quercy and the diocese of Montpellier and just 11 per cent in the Haute-Auvergne.

The greatest beneficiaries of this seigneurial system of land ownership, were Chaussinand-Nogaret's 'plutocrats', the court and Parisian aristocracy. In 1700, the Condé family enjoyed a vast, landed fortune worth around twenty million *livres*, providing an annual income of 700,000 *livres*. In Brittany, the duc de Rohan's fief was composed of no fewer than 257 noble seigneuries. The maréchal de Castries, a favourite of Marie Antoinette, owned a huge estate at Gaujac in the Corbières. In March 1777, Castries purchased the premier fief in Languedoc, the county of Alais, for 770,000 *livres*.[38] The Choiseul family would remain one of the richest landowners in the future departments of the Sarthe and the Seine-et-Marne, despite its losses during the Revolution. Natalie Coquery's detailed research into the Parisian aristocracy reveals that the top 60 aristocrats in the kingdom, the majority living in Paris or Versailles, amassed huge fortunes from their landed incomes: the duc de Mortemart, for example, around 500,000 *livres*, the duc de Chevreuse, 400,000.[39]

As we have seen, the court aristocracy also monopolised the top posts in the Church. Abbeys, priories and convents owned fiefs and seigneuries in every corner of France. The Order of Malta, which owned no fewer than 650 estates in France, even owned 17 hectares of land at the beginning of the eighteenth century in the small village of Coudray-Macouard.[40] All the land owned by the Church was divided between a small number of very big estates, exploited by aristocratic bishoprics and great abbeys, and a large number of medium and very small fiefs and seigneuries, owned by priories, even by humble *curés*. Overall, its land holdings were more widespread in the north and east of the country than in the south and west. By 1789, the Church would own 20 per cent of the land in the north, 14 per cent around Paris, 11 per cent in Burgundy and 15 per cent in Berry, but only 5 per cent in the province of Anjou and 2 per cent in Brittany. To the north, around Laon and Cambrai, for example, Church property accounted for some 30 to 40 per cent of the land. In the upper regions of the Anjou, in contrast, only 14 out of 142 parishes reveal any indication of clerical ownership; while in Brittany, the Church owned just over 300 out of a total of 3,905 seigneuries. In the Béarn, clerical share of land fell to a low of 0.003 per cent.[41]

Most of the 'fiefs' owned by the robe nobility were different in kind from those in the hands of the old sword nobility, often little more, in fact, than accretions of small, non-noble farms bought over several centuries. However, the monarchy and the sword nobility had long been aware of the threat that bourgeois money posed to noble status. As early as 1579, the Edict of Blois had decreed that the purchase of a seigneury would no longer automatically confer nobility on the purchaser. Non-noble purchasers of seigneuries would be obliged to make a payment to the Crown, the *franc-fief*, to underline the fact that the land had fallen into the grubby hands of the bourgeoisie. But, after a generation or two, payment of the *franc-fief* might lapse and a bourgeois landowner might be translated into a 'noble' seigneur. Time gilded the escutcheons of many a parvenu noble! In addition, the purchase of the more prestigious venal offices, like *secrétaires du roi*, exempted

77

robe nobles from paying the *taille* and most feudal dues. Robe nobles were also spared the indignity, suffered by roturier (non-noble) purchasers of noble land, of paying the *franc-fief* to the Crown. Finally, some aspiring nobles bought 'virtual fiefs' (*fiefs en l'air*), purchases that brought no land with them, but which did provide the opportunity of levying feudal dues, thus improving their suspect social position in the noble hierarchy.[42]

We have seen that Richard Andrews seeks to exonerate one group of robe nobles, the Parisian magisterial nobility, from alleged contamination by the feudal system: 'Their familialism was not feudal . . . Their ultimate subservience was to law and vocation, not to kings.'[43] In general, this may well have been true. However, this did not prevent the wealthiest of them from investing heavily in noble real estate. Andrews' 'themistocrats' owned about a third of all the non-royal and non-ecclesiastical estates in the immediate vicinity of the capital in the eighteenth century. Thomas Maussion, a magistrate in the Châtelet, bought no fewer than seven estates, three of them substantial, whilst Jean Thévinin acquired a marquisate, a barony and eight other seigneuries, mostly in Burgundy. This is not to dismiss out of hand Andrews' contention that his 'themistocrats' were 'anti-capitalist'; that the main economic dynamic of their investments 'was conversion of money into fixed capital/land and office not of capital into money: the polar opposite of a capitalist economy'. Top judicial and administrative officials, in Paris and the provinces, shared the widely held view that money invested in land and office offered greater security than shares invested in mines or factories or overseas trade, particularly after the Law crash of the 1720s. The purchase of public offices was undoubtedly a diversion on the road to modern capitalism.

Outside the charmed circle of the high magistrature, many of those who had acquired noble status by purchasing venal offices were committed to make profits within feudal economic and legal structures. The Castaniers were extremely wealthy textile magnates whose business activities were centred in and around Carcassonne in Languedoc. In 1720, they bought into the nobility by purchasing the office of *secrétaire du roi*. They went on to invest the profits from their business activities in the purchase of noble estates and titles. When Guillaume IV of the Castanier dynasty died in 1725, he owned 23 seigneuries and 45 large properties worth, perhaps, 20 million *livres*. Guillaume V married the daughter of the president of the Paris parlement. On his death in 1765, the family fortune, which was 'essentially proprietorial and seigneurial', went to Catherine Poulpry, who eventually became a lady-in-waiting to Marie-Antoinette's sister-in-law. She helped to finance her lavish Parisian lifestyle from the 8,000 *livres* a year in rent and produce that she exacted from the hundred or so families in the village of Pomas, supplemented by the 2,113 *livres* collected in seigneurial dues.[44] Thus, as was the case in other textile-producing regions, merchants and manufacturers translated themselves into nobles by purchasing noble seigneuries and/or offices. Whether they lost any sleep over the issue or not, their lifestyles were enhanced, in large measure, by 'this bizarre system' of feudal land ownership.

Finally, the urban bourgeoisie. The erosion of noble and ecclesiastical landed wealth at the hands of the bourgeoisie represents one of the major structural transformations of French society during the early modern period, and, as one would expect, bourgeois control spread outwards from urban centres. Around Meudon, today a suburb of Paris, 'perhaps a fifth of the land was already in bourgeois hands by the early sixteenth century'.[45] Jean-Marc Moriceau's work traces the rise of wealthy merchant and farming families in the Île de France back to the decline of the old nobility following the Hundred Years War, gaining momentum during the period from the fifteenth to the seventeenth century.[46] Roger Dugrand's research in the 1960s revealed how the many bourgeois in towns like Marseilles, Nîmes and Montpellier had invested in rural property, rather than in trade or industry, for centuries, a further example of ancien regime, 'anti-(industrial) capitalism'.[47] The north-western region of the Corbières had long been a happy hunting-ground for wealthy merchants seeking seigneuries. One son of a wealthy textile merchant, Joseph d'Airolles, turned his back on the family firm and transformed himself into a landed nobleman. In 1769, he bought the seigneuries of Leuc and Cavanac for the considerable price of 68,400 and 150,000 *livres* respectively; the latter included 221 hectares of land.[48]

This is not to say that enterprising nobles – and they did exist – did not challenge the increasing threat from the bourgeoisie by competing in the land market.

The exploitation of a seigneury

The seigneury impacted upon the lives of almost everyone in the countryside and 'more often than not they encountered it first in the guise of surplus extraction'.[49] Pierre Goubert refers to the extraordinary diversity of ancien regime contracts concluded between seigneurs and the peasantry, contracts that were complex enough, he writes, 'to stupefy us'.[50] Peasant dues might be fixed or variable; they might be paid in cash or in kind, or both. Contracts could last for a few years, frequently for nine, but they could also cover periods of 27, 54 or even 99 years. In the west, contracts remained markedly feudal in content and language. With the possible exception of 'a partridge in a pear tree', every kind of payment of fowl, fish or vegetable, every conceivable device for squeezing physical labour out of the peasantry, every demeaning act of *hommage* to a lord, can be found in one or other of the thousands of ancien regime charters. What follows is, of necessity, a simplified and abbreviated analysis of this 'stupefying' system of economic, judicial and political exploitation.

We first need to distinguish between 'feudal', or 'seigneurial', dues, and those that were, in effect, landed rents. No easy task! During the early years of the Revolution, the dismantling of the seigneurial regime would require 'the combined energy of three legislatures and the promulgation of well over a hundred decrees'.[51] We can simplify our task, however, by learning from their exhausting experience. The lawyers who sat deconstructing the 'feudal complex' on the Feudal Committee of 1790 were pretty clear on one or two key issues. The ecclesiastical tithe (*dîme*) should be abolished outright in view of the Church's association with the feudal past and its economic exploitation of the peasantry. They also had few doubts about condemning serfdom (*mainmorte*), the most obvious, and degrading, link with the feudal past. Perhaps a million peasants, many of them on Church lands in Franche-Comté and the Nivernais, could be described as serfs, and variations on this feudal survival could also be found in Champagne and in Brittany (*quevaises*). Among other feudal obligations that were abolished, without indemnity, were the *franc-fief*, the due paid to the government by non-nobles when purchasing noble land; the *cens*, usually a small cash payment made in recognition of a seigneur's authority over his tenants (*censives*); seigneurial *corvées*, the restriction on personal freedom involved in forcing peasants to work, periodically, on the seigneur's estate; and the *banalités*, the right to force peasants to have their bread baked in the seigneur's mill and their wine to be pressed in the seigneur's winepress. Finally, *la chasse*, the seigneur's widely hated and often exclusive right to hunt on peasant land, was also, theoretically, consigned to the dustbin of history.

When it came to annual dues like the *champart* (referred to as the *tasque* in many parts of the south) and occasional dues on the sale and purchase of land like the *lods et ventes*, the jurists of the early 1790s had to pause for breath. It was true that, in many instances, it was almost impossible to separate what was 'feudal' in these dues from what were 'landed rents', particularly given the feudal terminology employed in many old charters. But how could these onerous dues be abolished when they furnished seigneurs (who were only too ready by 1789 to see them described as 'landed rents'!) with a sizeable part of their income? Such dues were heaviest in many parts of the south-west, in the provinces of Poitou and Quercy, as well as in the Massif Central. In provinces where the seigneurial burden was relatively light – in parts of Brittany and Provence, for example, as well as in Artois in the north – the Church tithe was liable to be heavy. The *champart* was a heavy due, usually paid in kind and based on the size of the harvest. The proportion levied varied from a third to a twentieth according to the region: in most cases, it was around one-twelfth of the harvest. Collected immediately after the tithe, it was often the heaviest burden imposed upon the peasant. *Lods et ventes*, payable whenever a non-noble vassal of a seigneur bought or sold land, most commonly represented one-fifth or one-sixth of the purchase or sale price, although it could drop to as low as one-twelfth in certain regions. For those seigneurs owning considerable tracts and types of property, the *lods et ventes* could prove very remunerative indeed.[52]

For the peasantry, the burden of feudal and seigneurial dues could, in extreme cases, be crippling, especially when one adds the obligation of paying the Church tithe and the government *taille*. Liana Vardi, in her study of the Cambrésis in the north, found that in the mid-eighteenth century a rural textile worker, earning around 100 *florins* a year, would contribute 15 *florins* to local and state taxes, 10 to the Church, and 2 in seigneurial dues. Peter Jones cites a comment made in 1780 by the Provincial Assembly of Upper Guyenne: 'land subject to the right of champart is condemned to barrenness'. Out of a dozen sheaves of corn, 'the seigneur takes three, the tithe owner one, while [government] taxes absorb two more'. Peter McPhee estimates that in the mid- to late-eighteenth century, the community of 100 or so families in the village of Pomas in the Corbières paid 20 per cent of their produce to the Church and the seigneur, and perhaps 15 per cent to the state.[53] But the last two cases refer to the south-west where dues tended to be particularly burdensome; in the south-east and the east, dues were generally much lower.

The above résumé of the weight of feudal or seigneurial dues applies, in the main, to the middling and poorer peasantry. It has to be remembered that the top rank of the peasantry was rich, or, at least, comfortably off, and we shall discuss the historic significance of this privileged minority below. By the same token, we should not lump all seigneurs together as wealthy exploiters of the peasantry. Hundreds of provincial seigneurs were as poor as church mice, and, even for the court aristocracy, feudal dues might only represent a relatively small percentage of their total landed income. In 1746, the duc de Bourbon-Penthièvre obtained around a quarter of his income from what we may describe as feudal sources, but only 10 per cent of this amount came from his landed domain. Most of his wealth was derived from royal gifts and pensions, together with his exorbitant salary as an Admiral of France. Further information relating to the proportion of feudal dues in the overall income of seigneurs – 30 per cent for some seigneurs in the Haute Auvergne, but only 17,950 *livres* out of a gross income of 247,795 *livres* for the comte de Choiseul-Gouffier – only serve to illustrate the striking contrasts between regions and indeed, between one seigneurie and another.[54]

The key issue here concerns the secular transformation from a 'feudal', archaic and anarchic system of land ownership to that founded upon the advent of a more monetarised, commercial market economy. This profoundly important process of change had made very little impact upon the more remote regions of the west, the centre and the south-west, but was well advanced in many parts of Burgundy, the Île-de-France, upper Normandy and the wine-producing Bordelais. Moriceau's research into the rents and dues paid by farmers in the Île-de-France suggests that feudal dues were rapidly being replaced by rents during the eighteenth century. He estimates that only 10 to 15 per cent of his wealthy farmers were still paying the *champart*. The steward of one of the marquis de Castries's estates in the southeast, making his annual return at the end of the century, recorded that only 4,210 *livres* had been received in feudal dues, but 17,108 *livres* from renting out farms. In many regions of the south, there was a perceptible, if uneven, move towards renting out farms for cash, replacing sharecroppers with farmers who rented properties for specific periods of time. Finally, a study of several Savoyard seigneurs reveals that only one-third of their income came from cash rents in 1730, a proportion that had risen to 58 per cent by the 1780s. Change was obviously taking place, but, like most things under the ancien regime, it was uneven, piecemeal and messy.[55]

The coercive power of the seigneury

If the fate of the ancien regime system of land ownership had depended upon the economic importance of feudal dues alone, it would have collapsed long before 1789. It was the willingness of the monarchy to maintain decaying, aristocratic structures of political power – lay and ecclesiastical – at Versailles, and the continued existence of the judicial and political powers attached to thousands of seigneuries throughout the country, that extended its life. Although, over the centuries, the Crown had largely emasculated the military and political power of the nobility, it continued to defend its social and economic power through seigneurial courts of justice and seigneurial agents.

No fief worthy of the name was complete without its court of justice. However, just as there were many different kinds of fiefs, so there were corresponding variations in the judicial powers attached to these courts. They were divided into three main types – courts of high justice (*haute justice*), middle justice (*moyenne justice*) and low justice (*basse justice*). The first was authorised to judge most crimes committed within the jurisdiction of the seigneurie (even murder in the first instance); to seize the possessions of persons condemned to death; and to rule on disputes relating to the payment, or non-payment, of seigneurial dues. *Seigneurs hautes justiciers*, as they were called, had gallows erected on their property as potent, if macabre, symbols of their judicial power. Courts of middle justice dealt with less important cases and could exact fines of up to three or four *livres*. They could also deal with certain civil cases and settle property disputes. Courts of low justice dealt with minor cases and could only exact fines of under three *livres*. Like the higher and middling courts, however, their main function was to settle matters pertaining to the levying of dues and the resolution of property disputes. If litigants were dissatisfied with the justice meted out by any of these seigneurial courts, they could appeal to the royal courts of justice at the *bailliage* level.

Let us look at two examples of seigneurial judicial power, one general, the other particular. In 1711, Brittany, over-endowed with seigneuries from the vast to the miniscule, possessed no fewer than 282 ecclesiastic and 3,518 lay seigneuries endowed with courts of justice, an average of two for each parish. 1,500 of these seigneuries had courts of high justice, an exceptional figure.[56] In the poorer central parts of France, where rich seigneurs were thin on the ground, one would have had to walk many kilometres to find any seigneurial court of justice. At Pontivy in Brittany, the principal seat of the duchy belonging to the plutocratic Rohan family, the duc's high courts of justice often met three times a week, although, in other parts of the province, low courts of justice might only meet three times in a year.[57]

Our particular example concerns the town of Alès, several hundred kilometres to the south-east in lower Languedoc. What happened here enables us to illustrate, in all its feudal, Byzantine splendour, the relationship between the seigneurial and the royal systems of justice at the beginning of the eighteenth century. Alès was blessed with a seigneurial court of appeal (*cour d'appeaux*) that tried cases from all the lower seigneurial courts within the county, as well as from the barony of Alès, a jurisdiction covering some 60 parishes. In theory, if a litigant did not receive justice from the lower seigneurial court belonging to the baron d'Alès, he or she could appeal to the higher court run by the comte d'Alès. If satisfaction was not forthcoming here, the case could be moved to the appeals court in Alès. Failure at this stage meant switching the case – at considerable cost of course – to the royal *présidial* court in Nîmes. Nor was this the end of the judicial line. If the litigant had not yet exhausted his financial reserves, or his patience, it was possible for the case to be heard by the parlement of Languedoc, and, *in extremis*, by the Royal Council in Versailles! Given the tangled web of noble and royal interests involved in all this, one may be forgiven for wondering if serious reform of the ancien regime was ever possible – if, that is, it had to be undertaken by nobles and kings.

The economic, administrative and judicial business of the seigneurie was conducted by a small army of officials, providing employment for tens of thousands of individuals. In Brittany, the biggest seigneuries included judges, councillors, tax officials, tax collectors, notaries, stewards, bailiffs, gaolers, archivists and, occasionally, apothecaries and doctors. The prince de Guémené boasted a feudal entourage that included 88 'gentilshommes et gens de notre conseil'.[58] Even seigneurs exercising only rights of low justice employed a judge, a clerk of the court, a court sergeant and a jailer. The essential administrative trinity was the magistrate (*sénéchal*), the financial expert (*procureur fiscal*) and the clerk of the court (*greffier*). In Artois, the most important seigneurial official was the *bailli* or lieutenant. Many seigneurial offices had been bought, and were treated, like venal state offices, as family property. At the higher level, seigneurial officials were recruited from the ranks of local, often semi-trained lawyers; lower down, the positions of constable or jailer could be filled by landless peasants.

Seigneurial officials acted, alongside the *curé*, as intermediaries with the outside world, acting not only on behalf of the seigneury, but the wider community. They were very important people, exercising considerable political power within the parish – or parishes – that constituted a seigneury, on behalf of their influential noble masters. Seigneurs often determined, and controlled, village representatives on municipal councils, or the choice of village teacher. Challenging a seigneurial official might lead to the loss of one's lease, given that it was the seigneur who ultimately decided the fate of his tenants, unless, of course, with the backing of the village assembly, one had the courage to fight the case in the royal courts. In many regions, peasant communities increasingly discovered the courage to do just this, with important consequences for the political education of the peasantry and the fate of what remained of a feudal system of land ownership. Hilton Root advances the intriguing and convincing thesis that, in their struggle to question the validity not just of individual feudal dues but the entire land-owning system upon which the collection of such dues rested, peasant communities in Burgundy were assisted by representatives of the state. By the 1760s, with the feudal land system itself increasingly on trial, 'Royal administrators encouraged communities to question their obligations to their feudal lords'.[59] It was an issue of money and power: the peasantry simply could not continue paying higher taxes to the Church, the king and the seigneur. In the historic struggle between the development of a costly modern administrative state system and an exploitative hierarchical aristocratic system, there could be only one winner, as the Revolution of 1789 would demonstrate.

'Apprentice seigneurs': *fermiers* and *laboureurs*

In his prophetic diatribe against the feudal land system, the marquis d'Argenson referred not only to the noble and ecclesiastical 'usurpers' of the land, but to the 'subordinate usurpers' who were the apprentices of 'la classe dominante'. Prominent among these 'apprentice seigneurs' were the wealthiest members of the agricultural community, the *fermiers* and the *laboureurs*. During the ancien regime, social groups were never immobilised within their 'class' or 'estate': fluidity across 'peasant', 'bourgeois' and 'noble' categories was the norm, particularly as old certainties began to collapse under the impact of capitalist and consumerist values.

Defining a *fermier* or a *laboureur* is notoriously difficult. The former could be a substantial farmer and merchant collecting seigneurial dues and rents for an aristocrat or an abbot. The wealthiest of them in the Île-de-France were placed at the summit of the rural social hierarchy, well advanced on the road that led to the purchase of a seigneury and, possibly, the purchase of a noble office. On the other hand, in the poorer parts of the country, a *fermier* could be living and working on his farm, running another farm for a rent paid in cash, and reasonably well-off, but not wealthy enough to invest in the purchase of a seigneury or an ennobling office. A *laboureur* (referred to as a *ménager* or *cultivateur* in parts of the south) was usually a well-to-do farmer, particularly if he worked in Picardy or on the great cereal plains around the capital. He could, on the other hand, be independent, but farming just a few hectares with the assistance of a few oxen. Belonging to what was widely regarded as the upper echelons of peasant society did not guarantee success: personal failings, combined with limited natural resources and climatic disasters, led thousands of erstwhile wealthy peasants down the road to insolvency rather than up the road to nobility.

Let us begin with *laboureurs*, the less influential of the two groups at the summit of the peasant hierarchy. For Jean Bart, the well-to-do *laboureur* should be defined 'by his income if not by his lifestyle, which was way above that of the ordinary peasant'. He suggests that if the *fermier* who collected dues for the seigneur was 'an entrepreneur of the fief', then we should think of the *laboureur* as 'a bourgeois peasant', someone who worked the land, usually with a paid workforce, and produced for the local or regional market. Georges Lefebvre described the laboureur as a 'coq du village'.[60]

The Andrieu brothers, farming in the Beauvaisis region in the 1690s, provide a typical example of successful *laboureurs*. François worked 32 hectares of arable land, 2.5 hectares of woodland and scrub and 3 hectares of grazing land and apple orchards. He kept four horses, one chicken, three cows, two heifers, two calves and seven pigs. He paid the relatively high sum of 106 *livres* a year in government taxes. He was obliged to borrow money from time to time, but easily managed to pay the annual interest. His brother, Charles, helped on the farm, as well as owning 11 hectares of land set aside for grain. Although he reserved one-third of his grain harvest for seed, delivered one-eighth of the harvest to the church tithe-collector and a similar amount to settle seigneurial dues and the salt tax (*gabelle*), Charles could still afford to live comfortably enough. This was the life of independent *laboureurs*, comfortable farmers who did not, like the *fermiers*, derive a significant part of their income from the collection of seigneurial or ecclesiastical dues.[61] Many of Jean-Marc Moriceau's *laboureurs* in the Île-de-France had reached this level of comfortable living by the sixteenth or seventeenth centuries. A good minority, assisted by the development of a thriving market economy around Paris, exploited their profits and contacts at the beginning of the eighteenth century to become *laboureurs-marchands*, often farming 50 to 100 hectares and making considerable profits from the sale of grain and other farming produce. The Petit family rose from the status of comfortable *laboureurs* to become typical Schumpeterian agricultural capitalists in a couple of generations.[62]

Beneath the dynamic *laboureurs-marchands* of Moriceau's Île-de-France, we find various gradations of wealth and influence. In Artois, *laboureurs* made up 15 per cent of the working farming community, and a quarter of those who owned their own farms. Some of them farmed more than 30 hectares; the majority between 5 and 30 hectares. At the opposite end of the country, in Provence, *laboureurs* often worked between 10 and 20 hectares, the wealthiest of them possessing teams of horses or oxen, and at least 10 cows and 50 sheep. In the Haute-Marne, the top 5 per cent of farmers also worked between 10 and 20 hectares; hardly anyone farmed more than 50 hectares. In the region of the Vivarais in lower Languedoc, we find a counterpart to Moriceau's *laboureurs*, in terms of social ascension if not of wealth. The Pastré family had also expanded their horizons in the parish of Saint Germain between the late seventeenth and the mid-eighteenth century. Antoine Pastré had purchased land cheaply during the crisis years of the 1700s, exchanging fields with his neighbours to rationalise his estate. Part of his land was on the domain of one of the most powerful seigneurs in the south-east, the comte de Vogué, to whom the family paid seigneurial dues like the *cens*. In 1729, Antoine married his eldest daughter to Guillaume Gascon, one of the biggest landowners in the village of Saint Germain. Both Antoine and his son died within days of each other in 1751, leaving his daughter-in-law, Madeleine Villedieu, in possession of his large farmhouse and one of the biggest farms in the region. This case provides a salutary reminder that *laboureurs* and *fermiers* could be either male or female.[63]

We have included *laboureurs* in this chapter not because, like most *fermiers*, they were directly involved in managing the finances of a seigneurie, but because their influence in village social and political life often weighed as heavily as that of their *fermier* neighbours. Seigneurial power was weak or non-existent in many regions of France. In the village of La Nouvelle (Normandy), 15 *laboureurs*, representing just 5 per cent of the total population 'controlled the village's principal resources in much the same way that merchants dominated the resources of the nearby town of Pont-St.-Pierre'.[64] Similar examples could be found in Artois, the Île-de-France and Burgundy. However, if the *laboureur* often carried considerable social and political clout, the *fermier*, particularly if involved in the 'farming' of seigneurial dues (the *fermier receveur-seigneurial*), usually wielded more. This was due, in no small measure, to his or – far less frequently – her position as a collector of dues for some lay or ecclesiastic seigneur. *Fermiers* were the social hinges between the rural bourgeoisie and the nobility, not fully integrated into the seigneurial dominant class, but usually very ambitious to join. They created the essential conduits through which the hard-earned profits of the peasantry were transferred to the ruling class.

Jean-Marc Moriceau suggests that the most successful of his *fermiers* in the Île-de-France represented a new social group in the French countryside, a 'rural gentry' no less: 'Towards the end of Louis XIV's reign, these notables became more numerous and more ambitious. If the majority of *fermiers* benefited from the strong economic growth of the period, for the most powerful of them, it opened up unprecedented social horizons. In the course of the first half of the eighteenth century, they gave birth to an aristocracy that would look in future towards the town as much as the country-side ... We are talking here of *gentilshommes-fermiers* rather than *fermiers-gentilshommes*.'[65] One or two *fermiers* bought offices in the king's household which brought with them immediate noble status for the family; a few were rich enough to buy the costly, honorific office of *secrétaire du roi*, which, after 1727, conferred transmissible noble title upon the recipient after just 20 years in office. Others, less wealthy, perhaps more provincial in outlook, were satisfied with the purchase of judicial or financial offices in their locality which only conferred noble status after four generations. The purchase of these minor provincial offices seems to have increased during the last 30 years of the ancien regime.

Nor was the Île-de-France the only nursery for the birth of this new social group: Jessene confirms the socio-economic and political pre-eminence of the *fermiers* in the province of Artois. Although the majority could not compete with the wealthiest of Moriceau's 'rural gentry', in some regions they owned two-thirds of the cultivable land. Their economic power ensured that they played a disproportionately important political role in the village. Although they only represented 5 per cent of the population in the villages studied by Jessene, they dominated the top positions of lieutenant and *bailli*, key positions for the transmission of seigneurial power: 113 of the 119 holders of both these offices were 'fermiers de principal seigneur'. The discovery of the *fermier* as a new 'social type' is not, in fact, as new as it would appear. Pierre de Saint Jacob, in his influential work, *Les Paysans de la Bourgogne du Nord*, published in 1960, wrote that in Burgundy, 'the installa-tion of the *fermier* at the heart of the fief was one of the great events of agrarian and social history of the century'. The *fermier* is central to Régine Robin's description of the ancien régime socio-economic system as 'trans-itional', a hybrid of feudalism and capitalism. For Robin, the *fermier* is also 'the farmer who had full barns, who speculated on the high price of grain and who controlled the parish through the debts he was owed'. Hilton Root agrees: the *fermier* had the capital reserves to dislocate the old market pattern: 'The peasants resented the penetration of urban financial interests into the countryside and held the seigneur responsible for introducing those interests in the person of the *fermier*.'[66]

Although there was a degree of 'fusion' between the robe and sword nobility during the eighteenth century, the latter retained their social supremacy.

The rise of the robe nobility reflected the development of the modern administrative state. The sword nobility may have retained their leading place in society in terms of honour, rank and status, but these values associated with a society of estates and orders would be increasingly undermined by values related to an emerging capitalist society. The state was also becoming more powerful, increasing its judicial and fiscal power, and protecting many village communities against rapacious seigneurs. So far as the countryside is concerned, what is most striking is the emergence of those 'entrepreneurs of the fief', the *fermiers*. They were the importers of rural commercial capitalism, adapting the seigneury to the requirements of a market economy whilst continuing to act as 'rent collectors' for noble landlords. In the next chapter we shall examine, *inter alia*, the impact of the urban bourgeoisie upon the countryside.

Suggested reading

Andrews, R. *Law, Magistracy, and Crime in Old Regime Paris, 1735–1789* Vol I: *The System of Criminal Justice* (Cambridge, 1994) pp. 103–278.

Bossenga, G. 'Society', in W. Doyle (ed.) *Old Regime France* (Oxford, 2001), pp. 42–77.

Braudel, F. *The Identity of France* Vol II, *People and Production* (London, 1990), pp. 227–410.

Chaussinand-Nogaret, G. *The French Nobility in the Eighteenth Century: From Feudalism to Enlightenment* (Cambridge, 1985).

Cobban, A. *The Social Interpretation of the French Revolution* (Cambridge, 1964), pp. xiii–xiix, chapters four and five.

Dewald, J. *Pont-St.-Pierre, 1398–1789: Lordship, Community, and Capitalism in Early Modern France* (Berkeley, 1987).

Félix, J. 'The Economy', in W. Doyle (ed.) *Old Regime France* (Oxford, 2001), pp. 7–41.

Ford, F. *Robe and Sword: The Regrouping of the French Aristocracy after Louis XIV* (New York, 1965).

Parker, D. *Class and State in Ancien Régime France: The Road to Modernity?* (London, 1996), chapters four and five.

Root, H. *Peasants and King in Burgundy: Agrarian Foundations of French Absolutism* (Berkeley, 1987).

Chapter 4

The ancien regime bourgeoisie

The word 'bourgeois' is charged with explosive, ideological significance. Any reference to 'the bourgeois Revolution of 1789' is calculated to raise the blood pressure of historians who have never paid intellectual homage to Karl Marx. They insist that the concept of a 'revolutionary bourgeoisie' is an ideological invention, devoid of all social reality, especially when applied to the period before 1789.[1] Their preferred option is 'the ancien regime bourgeoisie'. A 'revolutionary bourgeoisie' conjures up images of factory owners, industrialists, bankers and entrepreneurs, the harbingers of a modern capitalist bourgeoisie; in other words, a nineteenth-century socio-economic class. An 'ancien regime bourgeoisie' suggests an amalgam of diverse, 'bourgeois' groups – landowners, lawyers, *rentiers*, doctors, merchants and master craftsmen, the heirs of a medieval social and economic system. The term also focuses attention on the continued 'professionalisation' of bourgeois corporations and guilds, a process that channelled public authority and power further away from women towards men. This chapter will trace the 'rise of the bourgeoisie', beginning with a résumé of the significant economic changes that promoted the gradual shift from a predominantly rural and seigneurial socio-economic system to the more urban, commercial and consumerist society of the later eighteenth century.

Confusion often reigns when historians attempt to define the bourgeoisie. Elinor Barber, in a study published half a century ago, thought that a diagram might clear some of the confusion. On the right-hand side of the page we find 'the Professions', composed of intellectuals, lawyers, doctors, the lower clergy, law clerks and 'assistants'; on the left, we have financiers and wholesale merchants and bankers (*négociants*), industrialists and merchant-manufacturers, retail merchants and shopkeepers.[2] The glaring omission here is the absence of the *rentier* and the landed bourgeoisie, reminding us of the misleading assumption that the bourgeoisie should be identified exclusively with urban society. Albert Soboul, more fully apprised of the rural and seigneurial nature of eighteenth-century France, proposed a much broader definition: 'an inactive (i.e. parasitic) class of *rentiers* living on the interest from invested capital or on income from real estate . . . "the liberal professions", lawyers, doctors, intellectuals; the group of artisans and shopkeepers, the lower or middling bourgeoisie . . . the great, upper-middle class of the world of business . . . the merchant wing of the bourgeoisie'.[3]

Given the wide range of occupations and professions that historians of all ideological persuasions have employed, one is tempted to reject any attempt to categorise the bourgeoisie and shut down one's word processors in despair! Guy Chaussinand-Nogaret moved in that direction, convinced that 'nothing specific identifies the bourgeoisie: they certainly did not constitute a "class" – this amorphous mass with no centre of gravity'.[4] He preferred the concept of an 'elite', composed of bourgeois and nobles. David Garrioch opens his study of the Parisian bourgeoisie with this uncompromising statement: 'There was no Parisian bourgeoisie in the eighteenth century. There were merchants and lawyers, teachers, manufacturers, *rentiers*, bourgeois de Paris. But they did not form a united or a city-wide class ... The political and social institutions of the city served to fragment rather than to unite the middle classes'.[5] Garrioch emphasises the importance of metropolitan and national political and social power structures, and bourgeois control of these structures was certainly weak before the historic assault upon the structures of ancien regime aristocratic and seigneurial power in 1789.

In contrast, Christine Adams has suggested that it is possible to discover positive evidence of the existence of a bourgeois class before 1789 if one looks in the right places. For Adams, 'the quintessential bourgeoisie – as illustrated by Balzac, Zola, and Flaubert – lay in the provinces'. Cohesive and established social 'classes' are certainly more difficult to identify in a capital of over half a million people, a good percentage of them being transient, than in small provincial towns.[6] Documentary evidence for the existence of a provincial bourgeoisie is certainly not lacking. In 1768, an anonymous manuscript, written in Montpellier, identified them with *'l'homme des loix*, that is, the magistrate who is not a noble, barristers, doctors, solicitors, notaries, financiers, merchants, and those who derive their income from no particular profession'.[7] This fits rather neatly into the etymological definition of a bourgeois: someone who was a well-established property-owner in a town or *bourg*, enjoying certain political, social and fiscal privileges, such as voting rights for the municipality and exemption from the *taille* and military service. This is a far cry from the Marxist stereotype of a person involved in modern business and industrial practices, prepared to reinvest capital in plant and machinery; an exploiter of the urban working-class rather than the peasantry. It is possible to discover such types in eighteenth-century France, but they were few and far between. Modern mining methods and factory production were still in their infancy.

One fairly obvious, but crucial, point needs to be raised concerning class definition. When one is dealing with a country that was experiencing rapid change as a consequence of the expansion of world trade, as well as the consequences of an intellectual revolution, we need to be as precise as possible over 'time zones'. The definition, and self-consciousness, of a 'bourgeois' living around 1770 was appreciably different from that of his counterpart in

1700. We have, therefore, chosen the term 'ancien regime bourgeoisie' primarily because the 'revolutionary bourgeoisie', as a composite historical phenomenon, whether defined in political or socio-economic terms, is difficult to discover before 1789. Thereafter, and particularly during the 1790s, it is certainly permissible to refer to 'the revolutionary bourgeoisie'.

'The rise of the bourgeoisie'

Whatever disagreements may exist over the concept of a cohesive, class-specific eighteenth-century bourgeoisie, there is little doubt that the number of people who belonged neither to the traditional nobility nor to the *classes populaires* increased significantly as the century advanced. William Doyle tells us that 'the dominant classes' numbered about two and three-quarter million, 'and all of them, except a few hundred thousand nobles and clerics, were members of the middle class – the bourgeoisie'. He goes on to suggest that there may have been 'three times as many bourgeois in the 1780s as there had been at the beginning of the century'.[8] The 'rise of the bourgeoisie', then, appears to be a statistical fact, even if sociological definitions tend to be rather vague.

We also know, albeit in approximate terms, that the population of Europe increased from 75 million in 1650 to 123 million by 1800, and that France's population rose from 21.5 million in 1700 to 28.5 million by 1789. This was not a very different rate of growth from that recorded in England – approximately 7 million in the 1700s to 10 million a century later, although, significantly, France, unlike her neighbour across the Channel, failed to sustain this rate of growth after the 1760s. However, if we turn to the urban sector, and decide that a town in an age of increasing industrialisation should have a population of over 10,000 inhabitants (as opposed to the 2,000 inhabitants of the ancien regime small town, or *bourg*), then the comparison with England reveals a very different scenario. Although the number of French towns of this size increased from 60 in 1700 to 93 by the 1800s, giving us an urban population of around 12 per cent, the urban population of England had reached almost 25 per cent of her total population by 1800. French and English pathways to a modern capitalist society, as defined by rapid urban population growth and industrialisation, were moving further apart, and would only really begin to converge again after the Second World War. More people would live in the countryside than in towns in France until the 1930s.[9]

The definition of a town cannot, of course, be determined by population size alone. As Bernard Lepetit explains, 'in one case the urban label might be applied to any community which was walled and enjoyed privileges; in another, the title of town might be reserved for agglomerations of over 2,000 inhabitants'.[10] In Brittany, 42 towns were defined not by the size of their populations but by their right to send deputies to the Provincial Estates. In the south, the *bourg* was a small town, often with fewer than 2,000 inhabitants, 'where festivities and solemn processions took place. It reigned over a rural district which needed its services – but which also provided its sustenance, for the *bourg* itself could not otherwise have existed.'[11]

A brief examination of the demography of those regions and towns that prospered, as well as those that stagnated, during the course of the century will throw some light on the distinctive evolution of the French economy. In the first place, it is not surprising to find several commercial and manufacturing centres expanding. The Normandy woollen town of Rouen, for example, increased its population from 64,000 at the beginning of the century to 75,000 by the 1780s. Lille, the commercial and textile capital of the north, rose from 55,000 to 69,000 over the same period; Amiens in Picardy, also an important centre for the production of woollen goods, increased its 1700 population of 30,000 by 50 per cent. Pride of place in the demographic league, however, went to France's 'second capital', the historic and beautiful city of Lyon. An important administrative, financial and judicial town, the real jewel in its crown was its international trade in luxury silk products. Between the 1700s and the 1780s, its population would rise from 97,000 to 152,000. In the second place, the Atlantic ports obviously benefited from the expansion of world trade. Bordeaux recorded one of the highest growth rates, from 50,000 in 1700 to 83,000 on the eve of the Revolution; Nantes increased the number of its inhabitants from 42,000 to 57,000 over the same period. In contrast, the great port of Marseille, with a population of 75,000 in 1700, only managed an increase of 10,000 between 1700 and the 1780s, a slow rate of growth reflecting the shift of world trading routes from the Mediterranean to the Atlantic.

Many well-established inland towns, like Tours and Orléans, also stagnated, or experienced slow rates of growth: the population of the former actually declined, from 30,000 in 1700 to 23,000 by the 1780s, whilst that of Grenoble, capital of the Dauphiné, only managed a rise of 5,000, admittedly from the low base of 20,000. A few administrative and commercial centres did reasonably well. Nancy, in the recently annexed province of Lorraine, experienced one of the highest rates of growth, from 15,000 to 35,000; Toulouse, rose from 38,000 to 54,000. The old administrative town of Montpellier, also in the Midi, fared less well with a rise of just 6,000 from a population of 25,000 at the beginning of the century. In contrast, the rise in population of the capital of Franche-Comté, Besançon, from 17,000 to 25,000, mirrored pretty accurately the demographic and economic success of a region that was well situated on the trade routes to Germany and Switzerland. Almost directly across France to the west, however, the fall of Rennes from eleventh place to sixteenth in the table of towns with populations of over 10,000 inhabitants, reflects the decline of certain sectors of the Breton economy.

Demographic change in Paris provides a striking and instructive contrast with that of London. With a population of 510,000 in 1700, rising to 576,000 by 1759, and 604,000 by 1780, Paris was one of the largest cities in Europe. However, even though France boasted a total population three times that of England, London was a bigger city than Paris by the 1730s. For all her historic grandeur and architectural beauty, eighteenth-century Paris never assumed the dominant position enjoyed by London. The main problem with the French capital, for Fernand Braudel, was not the size of its population, but the fact that, lacking a direct outlet to the sea like London, it 'was not dynamic enough to animate the French economy. In France, the role of economic stimulus was divided among several towns, whereas in England there was little challenge to London, and in the Low Countries little challenge to Amsterdam.'[12]

Nonetheless, the early decades of Louis XV's reign witnessed not only the highest demographic growth recorded during the eighteenth century, with urban populations rising faster than those in the towns, but also a major recovery in the economy. Le Roy Ladurie believes that, from an economic standpoint, 'the reign of Louis XV was one of the most brilliant in our entire history'.[13] This is an exaggerated conclusion: 'revival' might be a more appropriate term for what happened from the 1710s to the 1750s than 'take-off', if only because growth occurred within the prevailing structures of a traditional socio-economic system. There was little significant *technological* change, as François Crouzet pointed out 50 years ago; and, despite the dramatic increase in trade with the colonial sector, accompanied by less impressive growth with the rest of Europe, the agricultural sector continued to dominate the entire economy. In the manufacturing sector, the massive expansion of domestic protoindustrial textile production, not that of heavy industry – coal, iron and steel – continued to form the basis of economic growth.

Statistics relating to national and regional economic growth tend to vary disconcertingly. Markovitch, representing the 'optimist' school, produced the rather high figure of 1.9 per cent for France's annual industrial output 1700–80, leading him to conclude that France, not England, was the leading global industrial power, at least until the 1760s. Forty years ago, Jean-Claude Toutain argued that agricultural production might have increased by some 60 per cent during the same period. O'Brien and Keydor, focusing attention on the rise in *per capita* incomes rather than upon indices of industrial growth, suggested that economic growth in France was as good, in some instances, better, than in Britain. On the other hand, François Crouzet has concluded that French annual industrial growth was no higher than 1.1 per cent, while Peter Jones has recently supported the compromise that growth in the agricultural sector produced 'a net rise of between 25 and 40 per cent'.[14]

Given the dubious authenticity of precise, eighteenth-century statistics, 'orders of magnitude' prove to be less contentious. On France's external trade, for example, it is widely accepted that, from the 1710s to the 1780s, the value, in *livres*, of all foreign trade quadrupled, trade with Europe trebled, while France's colonial trade increased tenfold. By 1789, French foreign trade was higher in value than that of England, but, whereas the percentage of manufactured goods in the total volume of French exports did not record any significant rise, British exports now consisted mainly of manufactured articles.[15] By the end of the eighteenth century, Protestant Britain was well on her way to becoming an urbanised, industrial society; France, in contrast, was still operating within the constraints of a Catholic, seigneurial society.

Colonial trade represented one of the most dynamic sectors of the entire French economy. In terms of profit, however, it was focused upon the Antilles (the French Caribbean islands), particularly the islands of Saint Domingue, Martinique and Guadeloupe. Trade with this region flourished in proportion to the decline, and, in some cases, fall, of trade with India, Africa and North America. The Antilles was unquestionably the honey pot – perhaps 'sugar pot' would be more appropriate – of France's overseas empire. The value of imports of sugar and indigo from Saint Domingue alone increased seventeen-fold between 1713 and 1756, reflecting the insatiable appetite of Europeans for sugar. In 1700, the English Caribbean islands (principally Barbados and Jamaica) had produced 20,000 tonnes of sugar a year, Brazil around 20,000 and Saint Domingue 10,000. Forty years later, Saint Domingue had overtaken Jamaica as the most productive sugar island in the region, and, down to the Revolution of 1789, her output never fell below 40 per cent of the sugar produced by the English and French Caribbean islands combined. By 1789, English production was 89,000 tonnes, France's 100,000, four-fifths of it being produced by Saint Domingue alone. This dramatic increase was only possible as a result of the slave trade. In 1780, out of a total population of 455,089, Saint Domingue had 27,717 whites and a staggering 427,372 blacks.[16]

Too sharp a focus on the Antilles, however, masks the central feature of French commerce – the European trade. It is all too easy to forget the obvious when criticising French governments for failing to compete with England in the New World: France was a continental country, Britain was not. In 1716, Europe absorbed 91 per cent of all French exports and provided 66 per cent of its imports (valued in *livres*); by 1787, the respective percentages were still high, at 82.8 per cent and 57.5 per cent. The middle decades of the century saw a significant increase in French global trade, significant because it predated the disaster of the Seven Years War (1756–63). Imports rose in value from 112.8 million *livres* over the period 1740 to 1748 to 155.6 million between 1749 and 1755. France did even better in the export field: 92.2 million *livres* between 1740 and 1748, but 257.2 million between 1749 and 1755. Trade with the Antilles continued to rise faster than with any other colonial region, but, by 1789, imports from the Antilles still counted for just one-third of goods imported from European countries, while exports represented just under one-quarter of France's European trade.[17]

The notable expansion of European and overseas trade was reflected in the increasing wealth and power of the great Atlantic ports. Saint Malo (whose 'glory days' had been founded on the profits from Newfoundland cod), the Breton cloth trade, privateering and trade with South America, may have been fading as early as the 1730s, but, in the same period, Bordeaux, strategically situated for the Atlantic trade on the Garonne estuary further south, was being transformed. As early as 1664, the ports of Le Havre and Saint Malo had despatched 97 and 61 fishing boats respectively to the Newfoundland fishing grounds. Between 1715 and 1765, the volume of Bordeaux's trade would increase by 5 per cent annually, falling to around 3 per cent thereafter. Following a visit to the port in 1787, Arthur Young reported: 'Much as I had read and heard of the commerce, wealth, and magnificence of this city, they greatly surpassed my expectations. Paris did not answer at all, for it is not to be compared with London; but we must not name Liverpool in competition with Bordeaux.'[18] In south-eastern France, the port of Marseille was expanding at a rate of 1.5 to 2 per cent a year in good times. This was not as impressive as the growth recorded in Bordeaux, but, as we noted above, global trading routes were changing, away from the Mediterranean towards the Atlantic.

Good news for the inhabitants of the major ports also brought prosperity to towns and villages lying on internal trade routes. The depiction of the French economy as composed of a booming periphery and a stagnant centre requires major revision. It is true, however, that the further one travelled from major commercial and manufacturing centres, the less visible the impact of market capitalism became. Peter Jones tells us that a traveller, 'crossing the waist of France from Bordeaux to Rodez, a small town in the central highlands, at the end of the ancien regime would have found himself moving from a maritime to a mule-pack economy in the space of a few days'.[19] Nonetheless, it was increasing interdependence, not separation that was now shaping the contours of France. France was becoming a mosaic, the fragments bound together 'by constraints, by complementary differences, by the trade and communications that have tirelessly woven links between pays and regions, villages and bourgs, bourgeois towns, provinces and nations'.[20] The town of Montauban, for example, situated almost 200 kilometres to the south-east of Bordeaux, tripled its grain exports through the port to North America during the first half of the eighteenth century. Exports of brandy from Cognac through the Atlantic ports reached their peak *for the century* in 1720. According to one historian, the growth in the production of spirits became 'one of the phenomena of the age'. Finally, trade with the Levant through Marseille revived significantly after the 1700s. James Thompson's work on the cloth industry in Clermont-de-Lodève illustrates how important these international ports were in sustaining the woollen industry which had expanded into most parts of lower Languedoc during the late seventeenth and eighteenth centuries.[21]

If international commerce was one of the principal engines of capitalist growth throughout the eighteenth century, it was the textile industry that dominated the commercial and manufacturing sectors of the economy. As was the case with agriculture, however, expansion occurred primarily within the traditional, protoindustrial mode of production, although there were individual entrepreneurs and industrialists who sought to challenge old methods of production and managerial practices. Technological change and the concentration of industry, often related to the introduction of cotton manufacturing, only really began to make an impact after mid-century. Even then, the weight of government regulation, the prevailing seigneurial system and the reliance on wood and water as sources of power rather than coal and steam meant that France continued to follow a traditional, rather than a modern, path to industrialisation. Her economy would continue to be sustained primarily by agricultural products, by the protoindustrial production of textiles from Picardy, Brittany, Normandy, Languedoc and Provence, as well as by wines and brandies, fine porcelain and glassware, silks and designer dresses from Lyon and the hundreds of 'articles de Paris'.

Protoindustrial forms of production provided the commercial networks that linked a miserable, non-French speaking village, or even hamlet, with urban manufacturing centres that traded in turn with Russia, Spain, Latin America and the Far East. For Franklin Mendels, who fashioned the concept in the 1970s, protoindustrialisation was not the medieval system of rural domestic industry, but 'the production of goods for distant, often international, markets by peasant manufacturers; it grew out of, but was distinct from, traditional cottage industries for local consumption'. Protoindustrial work increasingly provided cash supplements for the poorer sections of rural society. When we think of an eighteenth-century French 'peasant' we should imagine a man or woman who was as familiar with a spinning wheel and a loom as with a scythe and a plough. It was this dual relationship with the land and the loom that brought peasants closer to capitalism, to a cash economy, to commercial, as opposed to heavy industrial, capitalism. As the century progressed, some regions began to concentrate on agriculture, others on domestic manufacturing, 'developing in the process dynamic and symbiotic regional economies, organised and financed from towns, where rurally made protoindustrial goods were finished and sold'.[22]

Research on protoindustrial systems of production has helped to relegate the idea that capitalism was the exclusive concern of the urban bourgeoisie to the historical dustbin. The study of a small village called Montigny, situated in the northern region of the Cambrésis, demonstrates that peasants could also be endowed with entrepreneurial gifts. Villages like Montigny were not isolated rural retreats, but way-stations in a series of exchanges and complex relationships. It is argued that 'Peasant entrepreneurship existed and without it rural industry could not have flourished the way it did ... Montigny's peasants saw further than the farm gates and the village boundaries. Their connections to the world beyond were dynamic, born out of a mixture of necessity and response to opportunity. Given that only a minority could live off the land, the remainder had to search for alternative sources of income'.[23] In other words, necessity became the mother of invention, occasionally in an entrepreneurial and technical sense. And what was true of Montigny was also true of a thousand more villages around Lille in the Nord, Amiens and Beauvais in Picardy, Rouen and Elbeuf in Normandy, Tours in the Touraine, Le Mans and Angers in the Pays de la Loire, Carcassonne and Nîmes in Languedoc, Grenoble in the Dauphiné and, of course, around Lyon and the Lyonnais.

This issue is crucial to our understanding of the ancien regime industrial and manufacturing bourgeoisie, caught up in the complex webs of rural-urban and national-international processes of production and exchange. Yes, there were a few factories and mines employing hundreds, even a few with thousands, of workers by the end of the century, but these would be very much the exception rather than the rule. Yes, the town was essential to the spread of rural industry, crowning the regional edifice of protoindustrialisation. But, as Gay Gullickson warned in her study of a Normandy village, it was the complementarity of urban and rural needs that provides the key to protoindustrialisation. Maxine Berg has long supported this line of argument, explaining that, 'In practice it was and is very difficult to make clear-cut divisions between the traditional and the modern, the tradable and the non-tradable, as there were rarely separate organisational forms, technologies, locations or even firms to be ascribed to either. Eighteenth- and nineteenth-century cotton manufacturers typically combined steam-powered spinning in centralized factories with large-scale employment of domestic hand-loom weavers using traditional techniques.'[24] We are reminded again of Régine Robin's hybrid transitional society which is a more accurate depiction of eighteenth-century France than any simplistic, structuralist account of one based on sharp class divisions related to new forms of capitalist production, or on rigid contrasts between 'town and country'. Modern forms of capitalism *were* developing in eighteenth-century France, but slowly.

For example, there was significant growth in the heavy industrial sector during the second half of the century as new techniques and working practices began to percolate through. Again, confusion over definitions about what exactly is covered by the term 'industry' means that reliable statistics are rare. Nonetheless, it is clear that, if we exclude the craft, protoindustrial production of textiles and household goods and focus upon 'heavy industry', as we define it today, then progress was visible. France would be producing far more cast iron than England by 1789. Coal production would rise to under three-quarter of a million tonnes, although, significantly, this represented only one-tenth of British output. The Anzin coal mines in the north, however, were beginning, at least, to challenge Newcastle's collieries: the former would employ 4,000 workers by 1789. As for 'King Cotton', production increased sharply after the 1740s, eventually reaching the very respectable annual figure of 4 per cent per annum. Rouen, where production of cotton goods tripled between 1730 and 1750, became known as 'the Manchester of France'. Oberkampf's 'factory' at Jouy-en-Rosas, not far from Paris, would be employing over 800 workers by the 1780s. Also, although there were just a few dozen steam engines and a few hundred spinning jennies operating in France by 1789, a few notable technical innovations were recorded. Vaucanson's loom was transforming the production of silk; technical improvements at the Saint-Gobain works in Picardy would enable it to manufacture some of the best sheet glass in Europe. France may have been technically 'retarded' in the production of coal and iron, but, when it came to the production of luxury goods, porcelain, wines and brandies, she was one of the most advanced countries in the world.

Signs of modernity, then, but, James Thompson was not very wide of the mark when he wrote that, 'the impressive French growth in the eighteenth century, if Languedoc's example was representative, which I believe it was, was not part of a modern economic growth, a movement towards industrialization, but a pre-industrial cycle'.[25] Bernard Lepetit, summarising his detailed assessment of urban change, goes much further: 'Manifestly . . . the period 1740 to 1840 marks the end of a traditional phase before the urban question acquired an altogether different dimension under the impact of industrialisation and massive rural outworking.'[26] Certainly, it would be a gross exaggeration to describe France as an eighteenth-century version of contemporary 'third world' societies, although, in terms of mass poverty, there were certain parallels as we shall see in our next chapter. What happened was that economic growth continued to evolve within the structures of a pre-industrial society and economy, one in which agriculture still provided up to three-quarters of the gross national product. The engines of growth were moving up a gear, but the drivers were still aristocratic. What *was* changing, indeed, what *was* 'revolutionary', was the relationship between France and the wider, increasingly capitalist, world.

Typology of the bourgeoisie

Two of the chief warriors of the historical 'Cold War' in the 1960s were Albert Soboul and Alfred Cobban, the former representing the Marxist-Leninist, the latter, the liberal camp. They disagreed profoundly over many fundamental issues of historical interpretation. On one basic issue, however, they were in complete agreement: 'The bourgeoisie was diverse, it did not form a homogenous class.'[27] Very few historians would now challenge this statement. Hetereogeneity, not unity, corporatism, not class, characterised the ancien regime bourgeoisie.

Over a century ago, Albert Babeau defined the traditional 'bourgeois' as a *rentier* living in an impressive town house and/or country mansion. Bourgeois were privileged local worthies, filling positions on town councils, on school or hospital boards. They represented 'a community of bourgeois living like lords (*vivant noblement)'*.[28] The *rentier* formed the backbone of this traditional bourgeoisie, involved in property acquisition, the supervision of family estates; investing in the money market, or providing loans for anyone from a shopkeeper to an impecunious noble. Security, not speculation or risk, was the key to success. Anything to do with government paper money or shares in foreign bonds would be treated with considerable suspicion. John Law was a name with which to frighten children. Above all, *rentiers* were propertyowners. Property was a relatively safe form of investment, and the more property they owned, the safer they felt. Government venal offices represented a form of property, especially since they could be kept within the family, so the more prosperous *rentier* might buy offices that could be passed on to the next generation. *Rentiers* might also purchase seigneuries in the countryside, particularly if they brought with them the promise of noble status.

By the mid-eighteenth century, urban residence was not the essential hallmark of the bourgeoisie; indeed the higher you stood in the social scale the more likely you were to own property in the country, even if you continued to be based in a town. Wills made by the bourgeois inhabitants of the Norman town of Bayeux usually included a reference to stocks of grain, the produce of their country properties that maintained them during the year. Around Angers, 'Almost all the bourgeoisie . . . owned property in the countryside, spent part of the year there, and derived a greater or lesser part of their income from it in cash or kind.' As Claude Nières explains: the urban bourgeoisie 'lived in symbiosis with the surrounding countryside, but they did not identify themselves with it'. The *rentier-propriétaire* represented one arm of the bourgeois domination of the countryside (the other, of course, being the merchant-manufacturer (*marchand-fabricant*). A detailed study of the village of Chaponost, not far from Lyon, reveals that by mid-century half of its territory, representing up to two-thirds of the value of its land, had been bought by the Lyon bourgeoisie. Of the 66 bourgeois whose profession is known, 13 were described as 'bourgeois de Lyon', 19 as members of the professional classes, and 34 as merchants.[29]

Lawyers were by far the most numerous and influential of the liberal and professional classes. Ancien regime France was an extremely litigious society. Its imploding feudal system, operating in parallel with an expanding modern state apparatus, created a plethora of courts associated with the seigneurie, the Church and the state. Apart from the magisterial elite in the parlements and the other *cours supérieurs*, which was, as we have seen, predominantly noble, an army of lawyers, the majority poorly trained, battled with the arcane complexities of feudal, criminal, civil and canon law.

Ancien regime legal nomenclature can be most confusing. David Bell tells us that thousands of men 'held the title of "barrister" (*avocat*), but only a small percentage of them belonged to the Parisian Order of Barristers, whose members had the sole right to practice before the Paris parlement and the other courts of the city'. He places the average Parisian barrister 'squarely in the upper middling ranks of society, better off than artisans and most tradesmen, but far below the glittering heights of the magistrature and high finance'.[30] As was the case with many professions, practising law was frequently a family affair. Two-thirds of Parisian barristers between 1661 and 1715 were sons of barristers or other legal officials. In the provinces, the wealthier and better-educated members of the bourgeoisie, many of whom longed to join the ranks of the nobility, often staffed the *bailliage* courts. Barristers were not all rich, but success brought considerable public esteem. An *avocat au parlement* could wear ermine robes and sit next to the *conseillers au parlement*, and these councillors were next in the legal hierarchy to the presidents and high magistrates of the court.

The great majority of lawyers from the lower ranks of the bourgeoisie had little chance of becoming magistrates or barristers in the parlements; they counted themselves lucky if they obtained a senior position on one of the 400 *bailliage* courts. Their likely fate was to live out their lives as notaries, *procureurs* or clerks to seigneurial courts. They aimed, primarily, at 'notability', hence the keen desire to purchase an office from the Crown, whether in a minor law court or a tax office. A son with a safe ecclesiastical position served a similar purpose.[31] Sébastien Mercier in his popular play, *L'Indigent*, contrasts the 'parfait notaire', endowed with probity and common sense, with the *procureur*, often a more aggressive and dubious character. The function of a French *notaire* was similar to that of an English notary – dealing with minor legal matters, including the drawing up of wills and property conveyance. The *procureur au parlement* in the provinces acted as a prosecuting attorney, and could be a person of some wealth and influence. On the other hand, a *procureur* in a small provincial village might perform some of the functions of an English solicitor, but, to make a reasonable living, he was frequently obliged to become an estate agent or even a moneylender. Most *procureurs* were obliged to purchase their offices from the Crown. They formed a highly visible section of the variegated *gens de la loi*, who Nicole Castan identifies as the dominant force in the administrative and judicial life of small towns and villages in Languedoc.[32] Beneath the notaries and *procureurs*, a motley crew of 'practiciens', whose training and acquaintance with the law was often nominal, plagued the lives of the poorer peasantry.

Lawyers, by virtue of their involvement in the potentially explosive human business of money transfers, property transactions, wills, neighbourhood violence and disputes over seigneurial obligations were possibly the most hated figures in French society. Many village notaries and solicitors supplemented their meagre salaries by moneylending, or by collecting taxes, tithes or feudal dues. Lawyers acting as judges (*baillis*) of seigneurial courts often performed similar functions in royal courts, making it rather difficult for peasant litigants to obtain justice. By the 1780s, there would be no fewer than 52 minor legal officials employed in the seigneurial courts of Joyeuse, les Vans and Saint Ambroix in lower Languedoc. Although the root causes of the bloody confrontations that erupted in these regions during the 1780s and the Revolution were related to the wider issue of commercial and industrial change, the immediate targets of popular hatred were 'those people who devour village communities' – small-town lawyers and moneylenders.[33]

Legal incomes obviously varied according to status and location. A handful of barristers attached to the Parlement of Paris almost managed to reach the dizzy heights of the millionaire magistrate, but what is striking is the great disparity in incomes. Of 50 Parisian barristers plying their trade between 1760 and 1790, the lowest earner received just 3,630 *livres*, while the highest was rewarded with the princely and exceptional sum of 882,500 *livres*. The average, however, was around 50,000 *livres*. But this was Paris, and monetary rewards rose appreciably once you entered the city gates; earnings were far lower in the provinces. It is true that, as early as 1677, the top position in the *bailliage* court of Troyes (*lieutenant-général*) cost 83,000 *livres* to buy, but this was pretty exceptional. Only three of the 84 *procureurs au Parlement de Rennes* in the 1750s earned more than 10,000 *livres*, while 28 received between 5,000 and 10,000 *livres*, and 53 less than 5,000 *livres*.[34] At the bottom end of the legal hierarchy, incomes could be on or below the subsistence line. We are referring here to village solicitors with little legal education, notaries, court clerks and bailiffs. In Bayeux, some *procureurs* only made between 200 and 300 *livres* a year, bailiffs between 50 and 222 *livres*. Clearly, this would have meant living on the bread line, almost literally, since it is generally accepted that an annual income of around 300 *livres* was the minimum necessary to survive during the second half of the eighteenth century.

By the end of the seventeenth century, the medical profession had been in serious danger of losing the confidence of the elite it had mistreated for so long; it had never enjoyed much credibility amongst the masses. Molière had pilloried doctors, while, in 1688, the famous society intellectual, madame de Sévigné, had denounced them for their medieval approach to healing, 'their mania for bleeding and purging'.[35] By 1789, a much healthier mania for science would have gone some way towards repairing the reputation of the profession. Colin Jones records a dramatic increase in the size of the medical household during the reign of Louis XVI, for example.[36]

The medical profession, like its legal counterpart, was corporate in character. In 1700, there were 43 colleges of physicians and 300 corporations of surgeons, together with a similar number for apothecaries. This corporatist structure survived until the Revolution, but significant change would occur during the century, firstly, in the relationship between the medical profession and the state, and, secondly, in the status of surgeons and dentists. In 1743, the surgeons finally emancipated themselves from the medieval guild of surgeon-barbers (*chirurgiens-barbiers*), thus following the lead of the apothecaries, whose break with the spicers (*épiciers*) had been more gradual. By mid-century, encouraged by the intervention of the state, the training of both physicians and surgeons had improved significantly. As early as 1707, the Edict of Marly had rationalised, and 'nationalised', the training and work of the former, while another edict, passed in 1730, dealt with the surgical wing of the profession. Gradually, the aristocratic aloofness of the physician, who seemed to regard touching patients as an act of manual labour, would be challenged by the 'hands-on' procedures of surgeons and dentists. Advances in surgical technique, associated with professional changes within the medical world, would gradually provide 'a favourable context for the emergence of a more systematic understanding of the human body, including the mouth, favouring a new, audacious approach to operations conducted on teeth and the mouth'. Molière would certainly have been amazed, and amused, by the emergence and proliferation of dentists after 1750: 58 had even been accepted – rather than welcomed – into the corporation of surgeons by 1789. The rise of dentistry had begun to put a smile on the public face of France.[37]

Traditionally, doctors vied with lawyers as solid representatives of the bourgeoisie, physicians representing the middle and upper ranks, surgeons the lower. Both law and medicine tended to be family affairs. The restrictive nature of the many medical corporations was designed to perpetuate the rule of the bourgeoisie, entry being restricted 'to the well-heeled and the well-qualified'. In Paris, it cost 7,000 *livres* to become a registered physician, 3,000 in Lyon and Reims. Even in Montpellier – the innovative place to study medicine according to those who taught there – fees were not on the Parisian scale. To secure the social status of surgeons, who were still soaped with the barber's brush in the popular mind, the membership of the Parisian corporation of master surgeons was limited to 235 in 1789, just as it had been in 1715! Despite this move to exclusivity, physicians, with their university training and their working acquaintance with the classics, retained much of their superior social status. Their numbers increased markedly in Paris over the century, many opening practices in the western parts of the capital, such as the *faubourg* Saint-Germain; surgeons tended to live in the centre and east of the city. You would find it difficult to find a top physician in the country-side, whereas trained surgeons (as opposed to untrained 'bone-setters'!) were rather more visible.[38]

In terms of income, physicians attending the royal family or running a fashionable practice in Paris might dare to walk alongside magistrates of the *parlement*. A Doctor Dumoulin purchased the seigneurie of Villejuif and died in 1755 worth 800,000 *livres*. Even the king's dentist, Etienne Bourdet, left 250,000 *livres*. Some Parisian physicians, acting as good bourgeois, invested their profits in the relatively safe *rentes sur l'Hôtel de Ville de Paris*, or in the purchase of venal state offices; others took the more risky option of placing their spare cash in commercial ventures. Although a handful of Parisian surgeons might earn up to 200,000 *livres* a year, two-thirds earned an annual sum that lay on the lower borderline for the Parisian bourgeoisie, around 5000 *livres* a year. Many provincial surgeons did not earn appreciably more than small-town lawyers, that is, an income of 1000 *livres* or less. A great deal depended on the size of one's practice. Doctors depended on fees, and these were obviously easier to obtain in towns than in villages. Jacques Long, a country doctor treated only 25 patients a month in the 1770s. Thomas Hérier, who practised in the small village of Saint-Christophe-de-Chalais, south of Angoulême, appears to have earned less than 300 *livres* as late as the 1780s. Perhaps he was more interested in the flora and fauna of Saint-Cristophe than he was in the flatulence of his patients. By the end of the century, many bourgeois men and women, caught up in the general enthusiasm of the Enlightenment, had begun to fancy themselves as amateur scientists.

Fitting intellectuals into a bourgeois frame is fraught with danger, given that they were well represented among the clergy and the nobility, as well as the third estate. Progressive ideas, relating to the evolution of a more scientific and capitalist world, had never been the preserve of the bourgeoisie. Fénelon, archbishop of Cambrai, had established himself as one of the most influential reformers of the century long before the *philosophes* had made their takeover bid for the intellectual world. The ideas of Newton, Locke and Descartes impacted upon archbishops in their palaces as well as nobles in their castles and, dare we say, intelligent individuals among the *classes populaires*. As Didier Masseau observes, 'Instead of separating the clergy from civil society, we should see that the dividing line between philosophy and anti-philosophy runs through the Church itself as well as through the elites that held the reins of political power.'[39] Eighteenth-century France was a society in intellectual ferment as well as social formation.

One of the most revealing works to appear recently on the relationship between social status and the 'Republic of Letters' is the two-volume *Dictionnaire des journalistes*. It contains the biographies of no fewer than 810 individuals. The social origins of just over one-third of the total number studied are unknown. Of the remainder (64.3 per cent), 78.1 per cent hailed from bourgeois backgrounds, 15.1 per cent had noble parents, while 6.8 per cent came from the *classes populaires*. Of the 713 whose professions are known, 35.8 per cent were writers, 26.7 per cent were public officials, 22.9 per cent professors, 15.2 per cent booksellers and 15 per cent clerics. 14.7 per cent of the sample were teachers, 8.5 per cent barristers, 5.7 per cent doctors, 5.5 per cent *rentiers* and just 1 per cent were artisans.[40] The fact that the *Dictionnaire* covers both the seventeenth and the eighteenth centuries obviously weights the results in favour of ancien regime social structures and ideas, but this is not inappropriate to the purpose of the present chapter.

If we now turn, finally, to the banking, commercial and industrial sectors, we find the financier in pole position. According to Guy Chaussinand-Nogaret, financiers 'were a group who were common in origin, noble by recent eleva-tion, whose wealth was based on the manipulation of public funds and on various banking and commercial operations'. Eager to sustain his general thesis concerning the fusion of bourgeois and nobles, however, he adds that 'They belonged both to the third estate, where some of their families were still stuck, and to the upper nobility with whom they intermarried and shared sinecures and positions of power.'[41] From the reign of Louis XIV to that of Louis XVI, financiers colonised the corridors of power at Versailles as the monarchy sought massive injections of cash to keep the sinking ship of state afloat. Financiers and *traitants* signed 'treaties' with the Crown, promising to advance huge sums of badly needed cash in return for the right to collect, on the Crown's behalf, direct or indirect taxes. One of Louis XV's favourites, madame de Pompadour, who hailed from a family of financiers, opened many a back door at Versailles to prospective tax farmers.

Financiers and tax farmers represented one of the richest and most power-ful sections of the French population. To take a single, but not unrepres-entative example, Samuel Daliès de la Tour (1635–1713) had ascended the first few steps to fame and fortune by working for his father as a government tax collector in Montauban. He subsequently moved to the Dauphiné and, through his position as a receiver-general of taxes – and a confidant of Louis XIV's finance minister, Colbert – became a controller-general of the state tax farm, the *gabelles et greniers à sel de France*. Daliès exploited his wealth and political influence to make several fortunes out of supplying shipping companies operating both to the Americas and to the Levant. His business interests also included the discovery and production of iron ore in the forests of Franche-Comté, Burgundy and Provence. These financial and industrial magnates built, or renovated, many of the great castles around Paris and along the Loire valley, as well as elsewhere in France. They formed the elite of that financial group of intermediaries who controlled the economic com-munication lines between power and the people: the *fermier*, who collected rents and dues for absentee seigneurs; the *receveur des biens du clergé*, who collected tithes for absentee abbots; the customs official, responsible for the collection of local taxes. They were the essential cogs that activated the complicated, and often corrupt, machinery of government at Versailles, machinery geared to ensuring the passage of money from the pockets of the poorest to the coffers of the richest subjects of the king.

Négociants (wholesale dealers and bankers) were involved in national and international dealing, covering everything from guns and grain, the slave trade and textiles, to coal and cognac; given the absence of a national banking system, they also acted as finance and investment specialists for other traders. The elite of this group was to be found in the capital, in seaports and the main commercial cities and towns. François Véron de Forbonnais (an influential critic on capitalism and taxation) was a wealthy *négociant*, the son of a rich textile merchant from Le Mans. He acquired an international status by working for 25 years in France, Spain and Italy for his uncle, a ship-owner in Nantes. In Saint Malo, *négociants* had given birth to financial dynasties, whose economic, political and family interests were closely intertwined. Meslé de Grandclos, another ship-owner, diversified his activities, devoting one-fifth to the slave trade, one-fifth to fishing, another fifth to commerce with the West Indies and the rest to the coastal trade. Ship-owners were also involved in the provisioning of ships they did not own. Grandclos, for example, shared in the provisioning of 36 ships belonging to other *négociants* and *armateurs* between 1757 and 1768.[42] In the Cévennes region of south-eastern France, as in many other regions of the country, *négociants* controlled the economic life of entire valleys, responsible not just for the textile trade but for most of the goods entering or leaving towns and villages. The typical intermediary figure was the *marchand-concessionnaire*, who bought, or exchanged, silk, cloth, leather and chestnuts for raw materials, oil and wine on behalf of the big wholesale trader. Many *négociants* at the centre of this commerce 'were also investment bankers, even moneylenders, in a region where hard currency was rare and the inhabitants in debt. Repayments on loans were often made in kind at prices fixed by the buyer. The price at which goods were bought and sold was always established by rich and powerful *négociants*.'[43]

Merchants and merchant-manufacturers (*marchands-fabricants*) formed the bridges that linked a rapidly expanding world economy to commercial and manufacturing centres throughout France. The import of silks, fabrics, spices and porcelain from the East Indies, and sugar, coffee and spices from the West Indies, changed fashions and tastes in France in much the same way as manufactured goods and fashions from Paris, Lyon, Lille, Rouen and Nîmes added colour and style to the lives of men and women from St. Petersburg to Peru. Some merchant-manufacturers could compete with *négociants* in terms of wealth and social status. The Danse brothers of Beauvais, for example, were wealthy textile merchants, descended from *laboureurs* and *fermiers*, who had assumed international status by the early eighteenth century. They collected raw woollen cloth from the countryside, and had it bleached and finished in the town, before exporting it to European, West Indian and American customers. Gabriel Danse bought the office of *valet de chambre* to the Regent, the duc d'Orléans, in 1717 and thus elevated himself to the ranks of the nobility. One of his nephews would become a hereditary noble by purchasing the influential position of *secrétaire du roi*, for 80,000 *livres*, in 1773. The Danses provide a typical example of social ascension, from commoner status as farmers in the sixteenth century, rising, through trade and industry, to the coveted heights of hereditary nobility by the end of the eighteenth century.[44]

As the century advanced, the increase in wealth of the top 5 per cent of the population provided work for a legion of merchants, artisans and shopkeepers, all devoted to the task of gilding the lives and properties of the rich and the super-rich. If France became famous for the production of luxury goods, it was primarily because her social elite lived in luxury. Merchants who sold pictures, centrepieces of gilded copper and bronze, cut-glass chandeliers, clocks and watches, expensive furniture and furnishings were intermediaries between the customer and the artisans' corporations of goldsmiths, cabinetmakers and joiners, metal-founders and engravers, glaziers and dealers in porcelain and inlaid ware. The merchants and dealers of Paris and the provinces 'had understood the power to expand possessed by trade in the service of a clientele that was itself at the top of the world of wealth and prestige'.[45] Natacha Coquery's inventories of the houses of the Parisian aristocracy reveal how luxury goods and furnishings were being purchased in an increasing frenzy of 'conspicuous consumption'. This development transformed not only the interiors, but also the exteriors of mansions along the western *faubourgs*, 'producing, in consequence, a new organisation and a metamorphosis of urban space'. France entered the consumer society on the backs of the court and the aristocracy.[46]

In small provincial towns, the term *négociants* was often employed to distinguish any kind of wholesaler, large or small, from the retailer. Anduze was a small textile and commercial centre in the Cévenol hills. Its taxation records for 1760 reveal the modest condition of this group. 'Merchants' are divided into three categories. In the first, we find eight *'négociants'* who were, in reality, small wholesale traders in mules, pigs, grain and chestnuts. Their average capital was estimated at just 18,000 *livres*. Small-scale wholesalers and retailers, and sellers of cloth, satins and heavy woollen goods, were included in the second and third categories. The average value in capital of the 14 cloth-merchants in the second category was just 6,000 *livres* a year. Below these came the *facturiers* who were clearly master craftsmen who owned more than one loom. Not one of them, who made fairly miserable annual profits estimated at 100 *livres*, owned more than three looms. This small Protestant town in lower Languedoc had seven notaries, five master-surgeons and two apothecaries who obtained their drugs from the local grocer. The five master-surgeons also made just 100 *livres* a year profit.[47]

At these lower levels of bourgeois society, merchants and artisans were not confined to the towns. Linda Vardi's work on the Cambrésis shows that, through the process of protoindustrial production, many peasants were being transformed into small merchants. She also argues that the more entre-preneurial individuals no longer acted as simple intermediaries, organising the transport of cloth to nearby towns and waiting for wholesale merchants to buy it before returning to pay their weavers, they were laying out capital to purchase the cloth made by their fellow weavers, which they then sold directly to urban brokers. Capitalism was spreading in the countryside entail-ing the usual transformation of social relationships. But, as any student of capitalism knows, periods of boom are inevitably followed by periods of bust, frequently associated with the consequences of war. Jean Pierre Lantier was a village merchant who had benefited from the expansion of the textile industry in Montigny only to see many of his dreams collapse during the Seven Years War. In 1759, he complained that his dealings with unprin-cipled *négociants* in the region had lost him 1,500 *livres*. By 1763, he was bankrupt, owing 9,000 *livres* to various merchants and farmers.[48]

Should we include master artisans in our typology of the bourgeoisie? Edmond Barbier, that intelligent contemporary analyst of the impact of cap-italism upon Parisian society, thought that we should: 'successful artisans and merchants had emancipated themselves from their former states. They no longer belonged to the people.'[49] An artisan, of course, could often be described as a 'shopkeeper', since many had their workshops at the back of their houses, and counters for selling their goods in the front. It is inter-esting that, in eighteenth-century France, 'shops' and 'workshops' should both be referred to as *boutiques*. Master artisans 'owned or leased workshops, sometimes formed partnerships or took on subcontracted work, bought in materials and equipment, employed a certain number of journeymen, sought outlets for the goods they produced and sold them to a great variety of inter-mediaries or final customers'. The fundamental structure of employment was a core of masters with relatively large workshops, usually employing two dozen or more workers but, very occasionally, over 100, and a periphery with a large number of masters employing a handful of workers. In the eight-eenth century, small was still beautiful, but big was becoming more produc-tive. Here again, capitalism was transforming, gradually, the old processes of production, and, consequently, the social relations between 'masters and men'. Artisans now had to be far more flexible and pragmatic in their deal-ings with both workers and customers, obliged to deal with 'a wide variety of possible clients, merchants and outlets'.[50]

In terms of income, Etienne Martin Saint Léon (using government figures for 1707) informs us that earnings varied between twelve *sous* a day for the less prestigious trades – cobblers, masons, seamstresses – but up to 30 *sous* for drapers, locksmiths and goldsmiths. Since a working year often constituted no more than 250 days (it did not include Sundays or fête-days), this suggests a rather low, annual income of 150 to 350 *livres* at the beginning of the century. However, Michael Sonenscher tell us that wages for journeymen in Lyon rose, on average, by around 80 per cent between the late 1720s and the 1780s, and that the income of some master artisan silk workers was 1,800 *livres* in 1744, increasing to 1,944 *livres* by 1786. The problem for journeymen and apprentices, particularly those employed in the larger workshops was the cost of becoming a master, the capital investment required to get started. Entry fees were certainly prohibitive in the more highly regarded trades, unless you had well-to-do parents, which was not unusual. Many of the large-scale hatters in Lyon, for example, were sons of merchants or professional families. The cost of becoming a master draper in Paris was as high as 2,500 *livres*; 1,200 for goldsmiths, 1,000 for furriers, but far less for lowly professions like weavers and seamstresses. But it varied from place to place, and was obviously lower in the smaller towns. In Niort, for example, a master baker's certificate could be obtained for just 150 *livres* at the end of the seventeenth century.[51]

Most skilled urban artisans belonged to trades that were run as corporations, regulated by law and run by committees of elected masters. No fewer than 117 trades, with a total membership of around 35,000 master artisans, were operating in Paris during the 1720s. At their head stood the 'Six Corporations', the powerful organisation that represented all the trades in public ceremonies. It consisted of 190 drapers, 640 grocers, 2,167 mercers (general traders), 47 furriers, 540 hosiers and 500 goldsmiths. The representatives running these six prestigious corporations were usually men of considerable wealth and social standing. Outside this charmed circle, the tailors' corporation was composed of 1,882 masters, the shoemakers 1,820, couturiers 1,700 and wine merchants 1,500. Many of the most successful members of these corporations were very rich men indeed.[52] Artisan corporations in the provinces were more visible in the north and south of the country, particularly in towns with a strong tradition of local government such as Lille in the north and Toulouse in the south. Poitiers' 25 corporations in 1650 had increased to 43 by 1717; those in Tours had risen from 22 in 1479 to 53 by 1776.[53]

'The lawyer, the ironmaster, their wives and children': case studies

Daniel Lamothe (1683?–1763) was 41 years of age, and had been a barrister in the parlement of Bordeaux for 19 years when he married Marie de Sérézac (1699–1773) in 1724. Marie gave birth to ten children, but only five boys, Delphin, Alexis, Jules, Victor and Alexandre, and two girls, Marie and Marianne, survived into adulthood. Three of the sons followed in their father's footsteps and became lawyers; Jules became a priest, Victor, a doctor.

Neither of the two daughters married, 'allowing them to act as surrogate wives to their unmarried brothers (none of the brothers married while their sisters were alive) and to manage the household along with their mother'.[54] Although this marriage pattern of the Lamothes was unusual, it was far from being unique: if a choice, in terms of careers and personal fulfilment, had to be made in the interests of the bourgeois household, the short, self-sacrificing straw almost always went to the women.

Daniel and his sons were proud of their education and professional status, and nothing was more typical of the average, eighteenth-century bourgeoisie than this; after all, doctors, lawyers and theologians were unique in having enjoyed professional status since medieval times. The three sons who became lawyers imitated their father's love of hard work, as well as his scholarly attempts to contribute to the growing corpus of property law. They appropriated Enlightenment notions of utility, public service and charity and applied them in Bordeaux's 'public sphere'. They were members of the *Académie royale des belles-lettres de Bordeaux*. Doctor Victor Lamothe became a consultant on the board of a foundling hospital in the city. His brother, Alexandre, decided to turn his back on the bright lights of Paris – he had toyed with the notion of purchasing the post of a *procureur au Châtelet* for 20,000 *livres* – and return to the bosom of the family in Bordeaux. This was the kind of loyalty to provincial town and region that would lie behind the Federalist revolt against Paris during the Jacobin Terror of 1793.

The financial affairs of the Lamothes reveal the concern for prudence and the acquisition of property, and for public recognition and public office that was typical of so many bourgeois families. The father had purchased no fewer than seven town houses, valued at 74,500 *livres*, by the time of his death. His investments in government bonds added another 15,500 *livres* to the family coffers. The Lamothes also purchased two small country estates, Muscadet and Goulards, for around 28,500 *livres* apiece, both situated in the wine-producing region around Bordeaux. Muscadet, in the Entre-deux-Mers wine-producing district was a noble property, a seigneurie which, although it did not transform the Lamothes into nobles (they presumable paid the *franc-fief* to the Crown as recognition of their non-noble status), nonetheless moved them nearer the borders of the promised land. In 1767, Delphin would render homage to the lord of the region for 'the noble house of Muscadet'; in 1778, he would make an apparently unsuccessful attempt to acquire the precious letters of nobility. Wine was produced on both properties and a few barrels were even exported to Holland. Farming land available for rent on the Lamothe's estates was leased out to sharecroppers, a common practice in the south-west.

The Lamothes appear to have enjoyed success in business and happiness in their personal lives, apart from the loss of three children. Letters between the siblings reveal how much they valued their home and their friends.

Although Paris appears to have briefly exercised its magnetic appeal for Alexandre and Victor, the *grands boulevards* of the capital were ultimately exchanged for the *grandes quais* along the Gironde river. Jules, who had entered the Church, was there to offer first-hand moral advice, advising his brother Victor that when he went to the 'wicked' town of Montpellier to study medicine he should see himself 'as did the Israelites in the land of Babylon'! The Lamothes were a deeply religious family: Voltairian scepticism was tempered by the father's example of obedience to the teachings of the Catholic Church. This did not seem to have involved a life of grim, puritanical behaviour. The entire family appears to have enjoyed the festivities that accompanied the wine harvests on their estates and the parties organised by the Lamothes in their town houses.

The history of the Chaussade family, in contrast to that of Daniel Lamothe, was characterised by huge swings of fortune, underlining the difficulties confronting businessmen and industrialists who chose to operate on the grand scale. Pierre Babaud de la Chaussade, the eventual director of one of the biggest industrial empires in France, was a national, indeed an international rather than a provincial figure. Born in 1706, he would live to see the fall of the Bourbons in 1792. The historical significance of Pierre Chaussade is that he possessed the vision, energy and ambitions of a nineteenth-century entrepreneur, but was forced to live and work within the constraints imposed by an eighteenth-century Catholic seigneurial society. In this light, it is not a contradiction that he began his professional life as a timber merchant and ironmaster, but ended it as a seigneur and a *rentier*. To a greater degree than was the case with Daniel Lamothe, Pierre Chaussade's fate was determined by the economic and political culture of the ancien regime, by the accidents of war and ministerial favour.[55]

The foundation of Chaussade's fortune was the family acquisition of the forge of Guérigny in the 1720s and his marriage, in 1734, to Jacqueline Masson, the 14-year-old daughter of an entrepreneur and businessman who had cultivated links with the immensely wealthy and influential Pâris brothers. By the early 1750s, Chaussade was running an empire, based primarily upon the export of timber and the forging of anchors for the French navy, which was worth hundreds of thousands of *livres*. Guérigny, on the river Nièvre, became the business headquarters of the *Forges Royales*, the nearby town of Cosne, 40 miles north-west of Nevers, the major centre for the production of anchors. Apart from his family inheritance and his marriage to Jacqueline Masson, two main factors explain Pierre Chaussade's success: his courtship and ultimate embrace of the nobility, and his cultivation of Louis XV's ministers, particularly the comte de Maurepas, minister of the navy.

In his introduction to his study of the Chaussades, Paul Bamford argues, with considerable justification, that it was the confusion and contradictions inherent in an over-regulated economy and the repeated failures in foreign policy that made life difficult for manufacturers and industrialists. On the first point, for example, there was the contradiction between the department of the navy's support for direct control of anchor production and the minister's preference for awarding contracts to private concerns. In Chaussade's case, it was the intervention of 'his friend in high places', the minister Maurepas, which secured, in 1736, a 12-year contract for the *Forges Royales*. In the sphere of foreign policy, Bamford argues that diplomacy under Louis XV continued to be associated more with dynastic than state interests, and that the military ethos of the Court meant that the army, not the navy, continued to represent France's 'primary tool of war'. The navy, in fact, was starved of funds for many years. When the Seven Years War broke out in 1756, Chaussade was promised lucrative contracts. This seems to have been a case of 'too little, too late': the disasters that befell the navy during the first two years of the war led to the cancellation of production for the government. In 1760, Chaussade, with his large workforce on the brink of starvation, was describing himself as 'the most unhappy of men'.[56]

Finally, there was the prevailing aristocratic culture that demoted the social position of merchants and manufacturers to the status of second-class citizens. This cultural ethos was not simply a veneer of class snobbery, it exercised a direct influence upon the way that economic power was distributed. In many cases, the social status that accompanied the purchase of a noble office was essential for business success. As Bamford remarks: 'Catholic aristocrats of robe and sword were the real governors of France. Its king was advised, and sometimes led, by members of the first and second estates, who formed a powerful bureaucracy and a highly privileged Catholic aristocracy, the *de facto* fount of law and privilege in the state.' Pierre Chaussade was well aware of this. In 1743 he bought the noble office of *secrétaire du roi au Grand Collège* for the considerable sum of 100,000 *livres*, 'to acquire greater favour and acceptance among aristocratic government officials . . . to improve his bargaining position as a government contractor'. Thirteen years later, Pierre Chaussade's daughter married the Chevalier Marquis de Guiry. The guest list included no fewer than three of the king's ministers of state. Pierre Badaud de la Chaussade, the son of a Protestant family, had become a Catholic and noble ironmaster, *secrétaire du roi au Grand Collège*.

Once endowed with noble status, it was natural to acquire the attitudes and trappings of the noble life. The headquarters of the *Forges Royales*, Guérigny, had originally been purchased as a seigneury, complete with seigneurial courts of justice, and Pierre Chaussade played the part of a seigneur with some enthusiasm. He oversaw the appointment of the *curé* of Guérigny; he even built a church on his estate. Thus, from the very beginning, the history of Chaussade's *Forges Royales* was associated with the seigneurial system. Many historians have stressed the importance of the seigneurial privileges of the nobility in relation to land; few have stressed the point that

111

French absolutism, and the society that had created it, 'was shaped to prioritise noble control of business'. It has to be remembered that nearly all the forges and mills in the Nivernais, as in many other regions, were dependencies of seigneuries.

By the 1780s, Pierre de la Chaussade was exploiting his business experience and acumen in the interests of his family's property portfolio. He sold his *Forges Royales* to the merchant-manufacturers, Sabatier and Desprez for the huge sum of 2.5 million *livres* (though he never received the full payment). He then bought and managed a clutch of seigneuries in the Nivernais, which he had obtained from the prince de Soubise for 330,000 *livres*. His first act after obtaining these properties was to employ feudal lawyers (*feudistes*) to ensure that the maximum income could be derived from feudal and seigneurial dues. This provides an excellent example of Alfred Cobban's interpretation of the 'seigneurial reaction' on the eve of the Revolution – the application of business techniques to the running of an estate. Just before his death in 1792, at the age of 86, Chaussade, one of France's great industrialists, was buying up property in Paris.

In the public world of the bourgeoisie, women became less visible as the eighteenth century advanced; in the domestic sphere, they reigned supreme. A gross generalisation no doubt, but this was certainly the case in the Lamothe household. As we have seen, Daniel Lamothe's wife and daughters devoted their lives to the success and happiness of the father and the brothers. The fact that Marie and Marianne received little formal education, and that they never married, suggests that the Lamothes operated as a bourgeois unit on behalf of the male members of the family. Marriage for the daughters would mean a dowry, more servants, less home comforts for the men. As it was, the women did the knitting and sewing; they washed their brothers' dirty linen – in private – and wrote to comfort them when they were absent. Madame Lamothe, who belonged to the generation that had never been taught to write, left epistolary matters to her daughters. She did insist on knowing something of the family's overall sources of income, however, since this was important in determining what she received as household and personal expenses. She never abused her position, describing herself in a letter to her son Victor on 8 February 1758 as 'Madame l'économe'. The women also made a major contribution to the respectable image that the Lamothes presented to the outside world: they avoided public ballrooms, went regularly to Mass and assisted the Sisters of Charity in the local hospital. We might agree with Merry Wiesner, when she states that the professional bourgeoisie 'regarded wives and daughters who did not engage in productive labor as a requisite of bourgeois status', only if we think that the lifetime's sacrifice and devotion of the Lamothe women was 'unproductive'.[57]

The case of the Lamothes undoubtedly reveals a few 'home truths' of the lives of women in a professional, bourgeois household. The picture is very different, however, when we examine the role of women at the top and bottom strata of bourgeois society. The history of the Chaussade family, for example, reveals something of the importance of women's 'productive' roles at the top level of industry, especially when they were widowed. Pierre Babaud de la Chaussade's brother, Jean Babaud, had married Marie Boesner in 1728. Jean did not enjoy good health and during the final years of his life, Marie appears to have taken an increasingly important role in the business. When her husband died in 1738, Marie continued to trade for a while under the name 'Widow Babaud and Company', but, within a year, she decided to marry one of the partners in the Chaussade-Masson empire, Jacques Masson. This was evidently a marriage of business convenience rather than of love, with Marie doing all she could to protect her own and her daughters' interests. When Jacques Masson died suddenly in 1741, Marie again fought to protect the best interests of her family – she now had two children from each of her marriages – by making an agreement with Pierre Babaud de la Chaussade that he should buy out some of her interests in her husband's company. The eventual settlement formed the basis of Pierre's eventual control of the entire timber and iron empire.

According to her biographer, Marie was highly intelligent and probably played an important role in the many, extraordinarily complicated, business affairs of her two husbands. She was, after all, the daughter of a very rich merchant from Blois. It was the legal system that made it difficult for her, as for many other widows, to play a more active role, forcing her on several occasions to accept the advice of lawyers and advisers. Nonetheless, Marie Boesner maintained, over more than two decades, a very close interest in the financial affairs of the Babauds and the Massons, eventually receiving in the 1750s a final settlement of 105,000 *livres* from Pierre Babaud de la Chaussade for her interests in the forges of Cosne.[58] Marie Boesner's case was by no means unique. A detailed study of *négociants* in Saint Malo during the decades of the 1680s–1720s reveals that women played far more than a peripheral role in the economic success of the Breton port. In the *capitation* rolls for 1701, we find no fewer than 15 women listed as *négociants* out of a total list of 148. Unfortunately for the good business reputation of these women, the biggest bankruptcy in the history of the port during this period concerned one of their number, Françoise Patard, who went bust to the tune of a million *livres* in December 1715.[59]

On the bottom rungs of the bourgeois ladder, the wives and widows of artisans and shopkeepers were often crucial to business success. A few master artisan corporations did allow women to become members – the drapers and innkeepers of Dijon, the drapers and goldsmiths of Caen, for example. A few of the Parisian trades were exclusively female: linen-makers, female hairdressers, seamstresses and midwives all had their guilds and statutes, functioning in much the same way as the male corporations: 'Girls were apprenticed to a mistress just as boys were to a master. They were lodged, fed and instructed in the trade for a fixed period of time, in the case of seamstresses for three years, four years for linen-makers.'[60] Arlette Farge has reminded us that, in Paris, masters' wives performed a wide range of managerial tasks in the workshop. They also exercised their authority over journeymen, servants, apprentices and shop hands.[61] If her husband died, a woman might be allowed by his corporation to continue the business, particularly if she employed journeymen and apprentices to guarantee the quality of the work produced. No doubt 'widow Jacques du Pont, retail draper', whose name appears in the 1760 *vingtième* tax rolls for Anduze is a case in point.[62]

Although women played a far more active role in ancien regime economic and political life than would, at first glance, be apparent, their overall influence in public affairs diminished during the eighteenth century. The law ensured that a woman could not sit on the French throne or the bishop's chair, or the judicial bench. The advance of bourgeois values widened the gap between male public and female private spheres, exiling women from the consulting room and the counting house. In shops and workshops, too, they were usually obliged to exercise their unquestioned influence behind the scenes, in the shadows of the law. The French Revolution would extend the domination of men in public life by denying women the vote.

'The rise of the bourgeoisie' during the eighteenth century was obviously related to the advance of world capitalism during the early modern period. However, the permeability of class barriers in France, as well as the way in which power was distributed through the court, the Church and the professional corporations, masked the gradual formation of a cohesive bourgeois class identity. Christine Adams may well be right to insist that 'the creation of a specific bourgeois mentality – with its emphasis on prudence, virtue, filial restraint, and a healthy sense of public worth – began among the urban professional as early as the mid-eighteenth century'.[63] However, the exchange of this social, economic and cultural capital into effective political power was inhibited under the ancien regime by the control exercised over the nation's affairs by an aristocratic Church and court. As David Garrioch has pointed out, the essence of bourgeois class identity was the association of wealth with [male] political power.[64] It was only with the defeat of aristocratic structures of power and privilege by the combined forces of the bourgeoisie and the popular classes in 1789, and the subsequent bourgeois rejection of 'the Popular Movement' in 1794, that the bourgeoisie would seize control of the nation's affairs. Even then, its victory would not go unchallenged. The Catholic and aristocratic structures of *la France profonde* would not be dismantled overnight.

Suggested reading

Adams, C. *A Taste for Comfort and Status: A Bourgeois Family in Eighteenth-Century France* (Pennsylvania, 2000).

Bamford, P. *Privilege and Profit: A Business Family in Eighteenth-Century France* (Philadelphia, 1988).

Bell, D. *Lawyers and Citizens: The Making of a Political Elite in Old Regime France* (Oxford, 1994).

Crouzet, F. *Britain Ascendant: Comparative Studies in Franco-British Economic History* (Cambridge, 1990).

Cullen, L. *The Brandy Trade under the Ancien Regime: Regional Specialisation in the Charente* (Cambridge, 1998).

Duplessis, R. *Transitions to Capitalism in Early Modern France* (Cambridge, 1997).

Garrioch, D. *The Formation of the Parisian Bourgeoisie, 1690–1830* (London, 1996).

Lepetit, B. *The Pre-Industrial Urban System: France, 1740–1840* (Cambridge, 1994).

Maza, S. 'Luxury, Morality, and Social Change: Why There Was No Middle Class Consciousness in Prerevolutionary France', *Journal of Modern History*, Vol 69 (1997), pp. 199–229.

O'Brien, P. and Keyder, C. *Economic Growth in Britain and France, 1780–1914: Two Paths to the Twentieth Century* (London, 1978).

Thomson, J. *Clermont-de-Lodève, 1663–1789: Fluctuations in the Prosperity of a Languedocian Cloth-Making Town* (Cambridge, 1982).

Vardi, L. *The Land and the Loom: Peasants and Profit in Northern France, 1680–1800* (London, 1993).

Chapter 5

A 'fourth estate' of poverty

Theoretically, the third estate represented the millions of poor subjects in eighteenth-century France. But those who bothered to think about it knew that this was a fiction: historically, the third estate had provided a platform for the demands of the urban bourgeoisie, and, in any case, the Estates General had not met since 1614. Certainly, the more 'respectable', the more skilled you were, the better your chances of being recognised by the law: successful farmers dominated the village assemblies (*communautés des habitants*), master artisans were integrated into the legally recognised guild system. The poorer and less skilled you were, however, the more likely you were to receive the cold embrace of the soup kitchen, the poorhouse or, *in extremis*, the ditch or the gutter.

This failure to respond to the plight of the poor and the dispossessed proved to be the single, most destabilising, socio-political problem confronting the Bourbon monarchy. It was confronted, but not solved, during the Revolution of 1789; indeed, it has never really been solved by modern, 'democratic' regimes, which continue to deny the poorer sections of the community a real voice in economic decision-making processes. Following the shock of popular involvement in the rebellions of the mid-seventeenth century, Church and state worked to shore up the political and socio-economic powers of the monarchy and the aristocracy, assisted by the upper bourgeoisie. Louis XIV had moved the seat of royal power from Paris to Versailles in order to disable the one effective weapon in the armoury of the disenfranchised – the threat of popular violence. The concept of '*le peuple*' was increasingly sanitised to exclude the 'common herd', dismissed in Furetière's Dictionary of 1690 as irrational, cunning and seditious.[1] The division between wealth and power on the one hand, and poverty and relative powerlessness on the other, characteristic of societies ancient and modern, would precipitate the downfall of the Bourbons. However, the poor did fight back. Jonathan Israel has argued that the Enlightenment, particularly in its earlier, radical manifestations during the late seventeenth century, was 'a drama which profoundly involved the common people, even those who were unschooled and illiterate'. The 'common herd' was present at the creation of our modern, democratic world, indeed, it was a major actor, though its presence has too often been dismissed in the text as 'noises off'.[2]

One of the most striking social phenomena of the eighteenth century was the rising tide of poverty. It has been estimated that the constant fear of poverty affected not less than 50–70 per cent of the urban population in times of crisis. In the countryside, 30–50 per cent of the population – a higher figure in periods of famine – have been identified as poor and indigent.[3] There is, of course, a major problem in determining what terms such as 'poverty' and 'pauperisation' actually involved, and how definitions of poverty changed as the eighteenth century progressed. In his erudite endeavour to provide answers, Daniel Roche suggested that, in Paris, 'the world of the workers, the backbone of the lower orders, made up between two-thirds and three-quarters of the population'. He accepts George Rudé's estimate that there would be between 350,000 and 400,000 Parisian workers (over half of the city's population) under Louis XVI, representing 'the ceiling of pauperism; a mass comprising ease and distress in a complex relationship, but always fragile; a self-contained society with as yet no true social zoning even if certain areas, though wide apart, saw concentrations of people on the poverty line'. As for the fundamental change in definitions of poverty, that emerged from the mid-century Enlightenment's new focus on levels of income and comparative needs. This was a time when the keys to the relief of poverty and social exclusion were exchanged, 'passing from churchmen and philosophers to men of power and action'. It was a move that accelerated 'the movement to marginalise the resourceless poor that began at the end of the middle ages and continued with the *renfermement* [incarceration] of the seventeenth century'.[4]

This chapter will endeavour to provide further clarification of the personnel and problems of the 'fourth estate' of poverty. It will introduce us to subsistence farmers, sharecroppers and farm labourers; protoindustrial and industrial workers, journeymen, apprentices, migrant workers and street vendors; domestic servants, beggars, prostitutes and African slaves. The crucial question of changing concepts of poverty raised by Roche – the politicisation of the problem of mass poverty by 'men of power and action' after the 1750s – will be addressed in subsequent chapters. It constitutes a central feature of the changing relationship between 'Power and the People'.

Dependency and poverty in the countryside

Between two and three million families lived on the wrong side of the track that divided the independent farmer (dealt with in chapter three) from the dependent farmer. The latter included 'micro-landowners or the landless, micro-farmers or micro-sharecroppers, owners of a few sheep or cattle rather than large herds; they were workers lacking the necessary tools'.[5] According to Expilly's *Tableau de la population de France* (1780), well over half of the total agricultural workforce did not own enough land to raise, comfortably, a medium-sized family of four or five. Even in good times, they were obliged to supplement their meagre incomes by working for others, either as day labourers, odd-job men or textile workers. If work was not available, then they were forced to join the ragged armies of migrant workers and beggars that disturbed the sleep of property-owners in the countryside.

To give some definition to the featureless mass of 'the peasantry', we shall take, as our starting-point, Pierre Goubert's four-fold typology – the subsistence farmers (*haricotiers*) of the north and parts of the Île-de-France, the share-croppers (*métayers*) of the west and south-west, the peasantry of the Midi and the peasant-artisans of Picardy.

Haricotiers (or *manouvriers* as they were known in many regions of France), were peasants who owned a few hectares of land, basic farming implements and farmyard animals to produce milk, butter and eggs. For this group, the garden was often more important than the house, the latter used primarily as somewhere to eat and sleep. The garden, or allotment, represented the 'private sphere' of the peasant family. This was where the children played; where vegetables and fruit, perhaps even some grain, were grown; where vines might be planted to produce cheap wine, either for private consumption or public sale. In fertile districts, a minority of these small-owning peasants might do more than just survive. Wives and daughters, in addition to running the household, might sell surplus goods, agricultural or manufactured, in the neighbouring town; husbands and sons would strive to make a small profit out of the land, and, perhaps, buy or rent another field or two. These were still families which inhabited the borderlands of dependency, dependent upon 'an urban or rural employer . . . the seigneur, the political elite, the Church, in the person of its tithe collectors and its sermonisers'.[6]

Jean-Jacques Clère's detailed study of the future department of the Haute-Marne, south-east of Paris, reveals structural changes in land ownership and social relationships between rich and poor farmers that were replicated in many small-owning regions. By the 1780s, 2.5 per cent of independent farmers would own more than 20 hectares of land, and 5 per cent over 10 hectares. But 54 per cent of the total farming population owned less than 1 hectare of land, and 18 per cent, mainly agricultural labourers and village artisans, no land at all. Here, as elsewhere in France, the lengthy process of dispossessing the marginal, dependent peasant in favour of the independent farmer was well advanced. There were, however, contrasts as well as similarities between regions. Whereas in the Île-de-France, with its huge Parisian market, concentration of property was producing many large, highly productive farms, the high percentage of ecclesiastic and noble property in the Haute-Marne – one that perpetuated a traditional, seigneurial system of land ownership – worked in favour of many small-owning families. Each region of France had its distinct characteristics, shaped by climate, communication networks and particular geographic and historic processes.[7]

Sharecropping (*métayage*) was a system of subsistence land ownership that flourished in many regions with poor soils and high population density: it was particularly widespread in the west and the south-west. Leases were short – usually from one to nine years – which did not exactly encourage the sharecropper to invest more time and effort in his work than was necessary. Contracts included a bewildering variety of obligations but, in most cases, the landlord leased the land to the sharecropper and took half of the harvest in return. In parts of Brittany, a *métairie* usually referred to a substantial farm, sometimes up to 20 hectares in size, but then the Bretons liked to be different, at least, from 'the French'! In regions like lower Brittany and Poitou, where the bright lights of capitalism had failed to penetrate the feudal gloom, contracts continued to be drawn up in accordance with feudal custom. They included acts of homage and ritual offerings of a chicken or a bunch of grapes, as well as obligations to work in the lord's personal domain. Sharecroppers known as *quévaisiers*, found mainly in the bishoprics of Tréguier as well as around Cornouaille and Saint-Brieuc, were typical survivors from a feudal past. They were peasants who often lived on reclaimed land, one *quévaise* being the term used for the plot of land allocated to one family. *Quévaisiers* were obliged to pay feudal dues on their crops and undertake manual work for their lord, but, on the positive side, they paid neither Church nor state taxes. The system of ownership known as the *domaine congéable*, widespread in certain regions of Brittany, represents another typical compromise between the feudal past and the capitalist present.[8]

Shareholding survived (into the twentieth century in a few regions) because it allowed poor peasants to keep at least one foot on the land. As George Frêche's studies of the Toulousain reveal, however, even this difficult balancing act became more problematic as the practice of leasing land to tenants for cash incomes gradually replaced sharecropping and payments in kind. Where the latter did persist, the landlord's share often rose from a third or a half to two-thirds of the harvest. By the end of the eighteenth century, many sharecroppers would have one foot on the land and the other (if they had not lost it in one of the many accidents that occurred on farms and in workshops) in the local workhouse.[9]

The peasants of the Midi generally fared far better, whether as small farmers or sharecroppers. If the soil was less fertile than in many parts of the centre and north of France, the weather usually provided adequate compensation. The eighteenth century was the time when the south began to market more of its natural treasures – grain, raw and manufactured wool and silk, wines and olives, as well as a wide variety of fruit and flowers. In the Cévenol hills of the south-east, thousands of peasants dug and drained the stony soil to plant precious vines and mulberry trees (whose leaves were used to feed silkworms). The Midi also provided pastures for the millions of sheep and goats that provided wool, meat, milk and hides, and that moved seasonally between the plains and the mountains as they had done for millennia. In terms of local consumption, 'American' maize – promising six times the yield of other grains – supplemented the diet of fruit and vegetables. Then there was the traditional chestnut soup and 'bread' that was prepared for me (as a delicacy!) by a Protestant pastor's housekeeper as late as 1963.

André Chambon's study of the small village of Saint Germain in the Vivarais presents a microcosm of peasant society that is not untypical of many parts of the Midi. The village enjoyed a period of some prosperity from the 1740s to the 1770s, due to the creation of more outlets for manufactured goods and the arrival of more sheep in the village, but also an increase in the production of grapes, maize and beans. Two of the six well-to-do farmers in this village paid over 70 *livres* in government tax; they provided annual employment for a farmhand, a female domestic servant and a shepherd, as well as temporary employment for a dozen or so farm labourers. Ten farmers beneath these (small) '*coqs du village*' paid between 40 and 70 *livres*, and 14 households between 3 and 40 *livres*. Fifteen families, paying under three *livres*, lived on the edge of destitution, as did the village's 15 shepherds, 8 farmhands and 6 female domestic servants.[10]

One of the strategies adopted by subsistence farmers to retain their links with the land was to plant, or lease, vineyards. The love affair between the French and their vines is ancient, but it was in only in the seventeenth and eighteenth centuries that the vineyard really became the patrimony of the poor. In 1725, an official report from the Anjou region stated that 'in the past, only the bourgeois and the rich people owned vineyards. Now almost all the peasants have planted their own.'[11] The planting of vines and mulberry trees ensured the survival of many a community in the south-east. *Vin de table* from the Hérault and the Aude departments became a cheap regional product in the eighteenth century, a national and international phenomenon by the twentieth. In the Corbières region around Carcassonne, land reclaimed by poor peasants was planted with vines despite a government decree of 1731 encouraging the cultivation of grain rather than grapes.[12] The ownership of a vineyard, however small, lifted the subsistence peasant above the common farmer. Tending vines became something of a cult, its mysteries a distinctive aspect of French peasant culture. But a few bunches of grapes did not feed a family: like all subsistence farmers, the small-scale *vigneron* also had to find the time to dig his garden, sow his acre of land and look after his animals.[13]

The career of the *micro-propriétaire*, François Moinet, from the small village of Coudray Macouard in the Val Saumurois illustrates the problem confronting peasants who embraced the vine to escape the constant threat of abject poverty. Moinet was born in 1738. He and his wife, Renée, produced five children. He owned just over half a hectare of land, scattered over several neighbouring villages. Most of this land was made up of small vineyards; the rest consisted of two gardens, a couple of fields and a few fruit trees. The Moinets had one pig, worth just 10 *livres*, and one cow, worth over six times as much. If François Moinet's tiny vineyards and his collection of shovels, scythes and sickles lifted him above the lowly rank of a farm labourer, his family's lifestyle could hardly be described as comfortable. Seigneurial dues, including one-quarter of his grapes, were earmarked for the local priory; he also had to pay the *taille*, the salt-tax and the tithe. Little wonder that his estate when he died at just forty-four, was a miserable 150 *livres*. His wife only survived him by 18 months. She, too, died in her forties. Moinet's grandfather had been an independent farmer. The local custom of dividing land equally between all one's children, as well as the (related) concentration of wealth in the hands of a small village elite, guaranteed that the lives of François and Renée Moinet would be back-breaking and relatively brief.[14]

Protoindustrial 'peasant-artisans', factory workers and miners

The association of peasants with manufacturing is essential to our understanding of French eighteenth-century society, as well as to the more specific nature of work in early factories and mines. The origins and work culture of the majority of factory workers and miners at the beginning of the eighteenth century was rural and peasant, not urban and proletarian: 'Solidarity revolved around the *terroir* and agrarian bonds. While textile production would engender greater individualism and fewer controls, economic necessity and sociability would nevertheless keep such traditional patterns alive.'[15]

The peasant-weavers (*manouvriers-tisserands*) of Picardy were the foot soldiers of rural capitalism, whose lives and work transformed the character of the French countryside from the seventeenth to the nineteenth centuries. In 1707, Vauban, Louis XIV's minister, reckoned that subsistence peasants could only avoid begging and the workhouse if their families joined the swelling ranks of protoindustrial workers. He estimated that to make a daily living, a married subsistence farmer would have to work in the fields for at least 180 days a year, receive a fair wage, produce no more than two offspring and have a wife who earned a supplementary income from textile manufacturing. In fact, as the eighteenth century elapsed, entire families would be recruited into the manufacturing sector. The work tended to be sporadic and seasonal, a pattern that suited the merchant manufacturer trying to adapt his business to erratic cycles of demand. In the winters, looms would be rented from merchants in manufacturing centres. In many regions of Picardy, Normandy, Brittany and Languedoc, control over the lives of marginal peasants was passing out of the hands of the first of those twin agents of capitalism in the countryside, the *fermier*, and into the hands of the second, the merchant manufacturer.

121

The impact of protoindustrial work upon the lives of the 'peasantry' has been grossly underestimated. Hundreds of thousands of individuals, from Picardy in the north to Provence in the south, were recruited into the protoindustrial system. In the Breton district of Fougères alone, 1,200–1,500 'peasants' spun and wove cloth at the beginning of the eighteenth century to make the local *étamines* that were then shipped to several parts of Europe and the Americas. By mid-century, the parishioners of Javené were pressurising the authorities to abolish the tithe levied on linen and flax 'because it represents an essential resource for farmers, occupying their wives and children in spinning through the winter months. The income we get from this pays our rents which have risen sharply recently.' The developing cash economy required cash wages to pay taxes and rents and to buy a few of the new consumer goods on the market. To put enough money in their pockets, families were forced to alternate between agricultural and manufacturing work according to the rhythms of the farming calendar and the swings of the economic cycle.[16] By the end of the century, however, a happy balance between agricultural and manufacturing work would become more difficult to achieve as the demographic boom increased the numbers of marginal and landless peasants. Simultaneously, the massive expansion of national and international trade, the invention of more efficient and affordable looms and the emergence of the protocapitalist international commodity trader combined to provide work for this emerging rural proletariat.

Not that all protoindustrial workers were impoverished. Liana Vardi has complained that 'historians have viewed the eighteenth century as progressively disastrous for the peasantry', adding that this was certainly not the case in her study of Montigny in the Cambrésis. This work does not seek to propagate such myths, arguing that 'the peasantry' is far too capacious an expression to contain any meaningful social reality. We saw in chapter three that a minority of 'peasants', and not just the elite of *fermiers* and *laboureurs*, could make a decent living in the eighteenth century, while any balanced examination of the poorer peasantry reveals destitution was not inevitable. Didier Terrier's research on the same region as that studied by Vardi reveals that weavers of the finer linen products (*mulquiniers* and *liniers*) often attained the same social status and independence as the well-to-do farmer. However, Terrier also concludes that a majority of the peasant-artisans in the region eventually became the victims of the 'lengthy process of dispossession from the land'. What *was* unusual – though not unique – was their heroic and lengthy struggle to avoid proletarianisation, a struggle that continued in many regions into the twentieth century.[17]

At the beginning of the eighteenth century, the divide separating 'protoindustrial' from 'industrial' production was not as pronounced as it is today; indeed, the word 'industry' only began to acquire its modern connotation later in the century. This was a society in which many towns included large gardens and vineyards, while hundreds of thousands of homes in the countryside resounded to the noise of spinning wheels and looms. However, the expansion of rural industry, which received its second wind after the 1762 decree encouraging the growth of manufacturing in the countryside by freeing it of guild control, also provided a boost for heavy industry. The era of cheap, mass merchandise had begun, although this manufacturing, 'consumer revolution' was still based in rural cottages and urban workshops rather than in factories, as we know it today. In their detailed study of the Saint-Gobain glassworks in Picardy – described as a 'precocious model of the pre-Industrial Revolution factory' – Maurice Hamon and Dominique Perrin reject any trite comparison between its workforce and that of a modern factory proletariat. For one thing, the original Saint-Gobain factory had been created by Colbert as early as 1665, when industry was still wearing its somewhat tattered, medieval 'arts and crafts' apparel. The very buildings in which its furnaces burned had been converted from the medieval castle of Coucy! Oberkampf's textile factory at Jouy-en-Rosas, which did depend, in great measure, upon a proletarianised workforce, was a product of the late eighteenth century.[18]

Let us narrow the focus at this stage to examine two examples of early industrial workers, the first employed in the Saint-Gobain glassworks in Picardy, the second in Pierre Tubeuf's coal company based in Alès in lower Languedoc. What were their working conditions? Are we dealing with a proletarianised workforce? How did their wages compare with those of rural farmers and protoindustrial workers?

As late as 1787, Saint-Gobain's workforce of 1,000 in the summer and 1,800–2,000 in the winter was still predominantly seasonal. The increase in winter employment was related to changes in the protoindustrial calendar, with hundreds of semi-skilled and unskilled workers, particularly forest workers, seeking manufacturing employment in the winter months. Similar employment practices characterised Tubeuf's workforce in Alès. He was obliged to pay substantially higher wages in the summer to retain even his skilled workers, some of whom still owned, or rented, small farms or vineyards. Given this 'schizophrenic' attitude towards industrialisation, management had to work hard to create a disciplined workforce. In the 1750s and 1760s, Deslandres, one of Saint-Gobain's most successful managers, introduced severe penalties for absenteeism and new working methods that prioritised effective organisation, discipline and productivity. Tubeuf introduced a more draconian regulatory system in his mines in the 1780s. It decreed that miners should lose a day's pay for turning up late (after 3.45 a.m.!), and exacted a heavy fine of a week's pay for drunkeness. Miners were also expressly forbidden 'to play cards underground, to sleep, smoke tobacco, or defecate'.

Some attempt was made by both companies to improve the working environment, but, in the absence of workers' organisations, conditions were often appalling. None but the very experienced glassworker could stand the heat and fumes of the furnaces at Saint-Gobain, while burning embers and molten glass were responsible for multiple accidents. In Tubeuf's coal mines, pockets of gas were dealt with by a man crawling along the ground with a burning stick, his face masked in a wet cloth, in order to achieve a 'controlled' explosion! Black humour and the existence of a profound religious sensibility combined to describe this worker as 'le Pénitent'. Child labour – 7- to 12-year-olds – was common in both companies. They cleared away the burning ashes from under the furnaces in Saint-Gobain; in Tubeuf's pits, they pulled tubs of coal along crude pathways like donkeys. The few *sous* they pocketed were handed over to put bread on the table or to keep the tithe collector from the door.[19]

It is only possible to provide general indications of wage differentials since variable methods of payment – daily, weekly or monthly, fixed wages or piece rates, payment in cash or in kind – make it extremely difficult to produce reliable figures. We have estimated the average number of working days over the year as 220 for industrial workers, a figure that omits Sundays, feast days and days lost due to illness, and represents a compromise between the estimates made by Vauban in 1707 and government tax officials in 1716.

In general, agricultural wages did not rise significantly from 1700 to 1750; an average of around 10 *sous* a day for farm labourers at the beginning of the century might not be too wide of the mark. A male, protoindustrial textile weaver received anything between 10 and 20 *sous* a day. Weavers in the Cambrésis, for example, were paid only 10 *sous* a day in the 1730s; in the district of Fougères, near Rennes, they were receiving up to 12 *sous*, but female spinners only 4. These were 'starvation wages', supporting the conclusion that the situation of many protoindustrial workers 'was no better off and often worse than that of the peasants'. As for industrial workers, it would be more instructive if we moved forward a little to the post-1750 period, when factories and mines were becoming better organised in terms of wage differentials and shift work. In Alès by the 1780s, coalface workers (*piqueurs*) received 20 to 25 *sous* a day, while those who got the coal out of the mine (*sorteurs*) earned between 10 and 20 *sous*. Foreign miners, usually German and Flemish, often earned twice as much as their French counterparts, reflecting both superior skills and the heavy reliance of French industry upon foreign 'elite' workers. In the Saint-Gobain glassworks, unskilled workers were earning between 10 and 25 *sous* in 1751, semi-skilled furnace workers between 24 and 32 *sous*, but experienced, skilled glassworkers up to 60 *sous* a day. These wages are not significantly different from those paid to skilled and semi-skilled workers at Oberkampf's cotton factory.[20]

In most cases, wages for women were 50 per cent, or more, lower than those paid to men. The onset of industrialisation entailed increasing exploitation, not emancipation, for women and children, representing one of the great scandals of the age. Female spinners in Picardy at the end of the seventeenth century received just 5 *sous* a day, half the male wage. Around Annecy near the Swiss border, average wages for harvest workers between 1707 and 1754 were just 6 *sous* for women, but 11 or 12 for men. In the industrial sector, 33 women at Saint-Gobain in 1751 received a miserable wage of just 6 *sous* a day, with 5 earning 8. At Van Robais's textile factory in Abbeville, women spinners received a pittance of 4 *sous* a day. As protoindustrial and factory work became more common, children were also being transformed from household skivvies into factory drudges. At Saint-Gobain, the majority of 'gamins' aged eight or nine were paid 5 or 6 *sous* a day, but an elite of adolescents, performing semi-skilled tasks in the foundry area, were rewarded with 12 to 16 *sous* a day by the late 1760s. To scrape together a living wage, entire families had to put their shoulders to the wheel, often literally. In 1715, a pork butcher was hired at Saint-Gobain to make soup for families of workers, thus encouraging them to stay on site.[21]

Are we dealing here, then, with a 'proletariat'? The word is anachronistic, certainly when applied to the first two-thirds of the eighteenth century, and suspect whenever it is applied to the rural protoindustrial peasant. Karl Marx would never have employed it, and Michael Mann has explained why: 'Agriculture usually generates its own subculture. Farm labourers rarely conceive of themselves as "proletarians" alongside industrial workers.'[22] *Intra*-class, as opposed to *inter*-class, rivalry is the key to understanding social antagonisms in the eighteenth century. It is valid, however, to describe the dispossessed, increasingly impoverished, marginal peasants who lived in the vicinity of the new factories and mines as an emerging proletariat. As Catharina Lys and Hugo Soly explain, the 'gradual crystallisation of this class of workers, dislodged from the land, deprived of all means of production, totally dependent on wage labour, unprotected, was a new phenomenon in history'.[23]

Did the gradual but perceptive shift towards a more urban and industrialised society transform the role of women in the workplace and the home? Again, not dramatically so far as the majority of women in the countryside were concerned, and probably not for most urban women. Although Gay Gullickson has suggested that protoindustrial work did introduce some improvement in the lives of eighteenth-century women, and Hans Medick has hypothesised that it led to greater social and sexual independence, it seems incontrovertible that the impact of early forms of capitalism did little to transform, in any radical fashion, the sexual division of labour. Tessie Liu and Belina Bozzoli, for example, have argued that the process of proletarianisation followed 'a gendered logic'. Far from methods of production determining gender relations, existing relations within the household often determined the shape that capitalism assumed in its different historical phases: men became the weavers, women the spinners, thus replicating existing gender divisions. In and around the textile town of Cholet in the west, the availabil-ity of women contributed to the expansion of sweated, domestic labour. Certainly the mass involvement of women and children in protoindustrial production, in town and country, proved to be one of the keys to its revolu-tionary expansion in the eighteenth and nineteenth century, thus helping to shape the distinctive features of French capitalism.[24]

Urban workers: journeymen, street vendors and migrants

There were between 30,000 and 40,000 master artisans working in Paris, but as many as two or three times this number of journeymen (*compagnons*). Altogether, there may have been a total of around a quarter of a million journeymen working in Paris and the provinces. Of all the people employed in the eighteenth-century trades who formed a corporate identity, journey-men constituted the largest group.[25] They were skilled workers who had often completed lengthy apprenticeships.

To defend their interests, they had formed illegal secret organisations (*devoirs*), complete with initiation rites and ceremonies, and shrouded in a mystique that originated with the building of Solomon's temple in biblical times. Their true origins lay with medieval artisan corporations and religious confraternities. Journeymen's organisations collected fees to insure their members against unemployment and sickness and to assist families after the death of their members. They were early mutual-aid societies, progenitors of contemporary trade unions. It would be quite erroneous, however, to think of them as workers united against a common capitalist foe. The frequent, often bloody, conflicts between regulated workers, obeying the rules of their order, and unregulated workers were a source of continual concern for local authorities. Nonetheless, if division and diversity were the principal charac-teristics of *compagnonnage,* there is also evidence of an increasing unity, albeit fragile, in the face of the increasing number of capitalist innovations that threatened their jobs and their skills. This may explain why the period between 1750 and 1840 proved to be something of a 'golden age' for *compagnonnage,* the only significant organised form of workers' resistance against employers. As the organisation increased numerically, so it expanded geographically. Whereas *compagnonnage* was identified in about 10 pro-vincial towns, including Lyon, Dijon and Marseille, before 1750, 10 more, including Mâcon, Nîmes and Toulouse joined the list after this date. The *compagnonnage* system was weak in Paris reflecting the antagonistic attitude of local authorities and the police.[26] By 1750, journeymen had perfected their *tour de France*, the practice of travelling from one town to another to find work, gain experience and improve their skills. Some journeymen worked in 20 or 30 towns; others might spend several years in one or two places.

Journeymen were easily recognisable, since apparel oft proclaimed the worker in ancien regime France. A Parisian journeyman baker wore a grey-blue shirt and a white cotton hat, sometimes adorned with a red or white cockade.[27] The majority of journeymen would never make the transition to the coveted position of a master artisan; it was just too expensive, sometimes costing several hundred *livres*. By 1789, a journeyman would have to find 800 *livres* if he wished to become a master mason or carpenter, three times this amount if he had ambitions to be a draper. There was also the preference given to the sons of master artisans, keen on keeping the business within the family. Occupational endogamy was common in most French cities and towns: in Rouen, over 60 per cent of the sons of master tailors married the daughters of master artisans. Successful master artisans considered themselves to be 'bourgeois' even if rich financiers, lawyers and merchants sniffed at the idea. It was the master's wife who usually fought to keep the journeyman outside the bourgeois gate. The account of life in a Parisian printing shop by an apprentice, Nicolas Contat, reveals the tragi-comic antagonisms that developed between masters' wives and the workforce. In this instance, they culminated in the hanging of the mistress's favourite cat, a barbaric act replete with sexual and class symbolism. Contat knew that his master's family was bourgeois: they 'ate different food, kept different hours, and talked a different language. His wife and daughters dallied with worldly abbés. They kept pets. Clearly, the bourgeois belonged to a different subculture – one which meant, above all, that he did not work [manually].'[28]

If it was difficult for a journeyman to become a master, it was almost as difficult for an apprentice to become a journeyman in a recognised and reputable workshop. Although the idea of becoming a skilled artisan appealed to thousands of poor, young boys, many failed to stay the distance. For those who did, apprenticeships might last for two, three or, in the case of the more skilled trades, seven or eight years. Candidates had to be good Catholics, of sound mind and submissive to the authority of the master artisan and his wife. Apprenticeships were 'a process of moral and political socialisation as much as an initiation into the trade'.[29] They also provided a system of cheap labour as many a French 'Oliver Twist' discovered. Apprenticeships were also available to a small number of girls since 'female trades', such as dressmaking, millinery, embroidery and shawl-making, had their own guilds and management. Seamstresses and linen-workers, for example, could qualify as apprentices and journeywomen, apprenticeships for the former lasting for three years, four years for the latter. In this sphere again, however, women's work was never given the same status as that undertaken by men. In the main, *compagnonnage* meant 'companionship' for men.[30]

For those apprentices, journeymen and women who failed to make the grade, there was the far less appealing alternative of the unregulated trades (*métiers libres*). In this world, there would be little to hope for but subsistence

127

wages and a lifetime of hard graft and penury. Every city and town had its unregulated trades, its *quartiers* where the *alloués* (hired workers) created their own work culture. Each town produced a different balance between regulated and unregulated trades, determined by the nature of its craft and manufacturing traditions. In 1755, the town of Chartres had 42 regulated and 17 unregulated trades; in Montargis, on the other hand, there was just 1 of the former and 19 of the latter. In Paris, we find highly skilled tapestry and glassworkers from the prestigious *manufactures royales*, regulated and unregulated artisans, as well as tens of thousands of unskilled labourers and odd-job men crowded into their respective *quartiers*. The last group populated the poorest *faubourgs*, such as Saint-Marcel, oiling the wheels of the 'black economy', hired for the day, or for certain jobs, a feature of modern as well as ancien regime economies.

Michael Sonenscher has argued that if anything typified the urban world of work it was flexibility, if not disorder. In town, as well as in many parts of the countryside, it was a world of short-term arrangements, fleeting opportunities and brief associations. For the poor in particular, it conjured up the 'evanescent environment of the bazaar' rather than that of a well-regulated economic system. The best plan for an aspiring journeyman would be to move to the capital or to a large, provincial city. Rouen provided a model: it had a small 'core' of masters who regularly employed two, three or more journeymen alongside a much larger number who did not provide regular employment. It had a minority of journeymen who stayed with the same master over long periods as well as a majority who did not. Finally, there were journeymen staying in lodging houses who supplied regular masters with up to three-quarters of their workforce, but also the minority who lived with their masters or relatives, or who found their own lodgings. In a rapidly changing, capitalist, international economy, many – not all – manufacturers and master artisans put flexibility and impermanence above the regulated and restrictive control of the guilds, corporations and *compagnonnage*.[31] The links between so-called 'free markets', 'globalisation' and a relatively unprotected, mobile workforce began to be forged in the eighteenth century.

If the workshop served as the main unit of manufacturing, the street was the customary site for trade and commerce. Arlette Farge notes that 'Even work had the street for its witness or companion . . . The shop was linked to the street, the workshop at the back of the house to the courtyard.'[32] For a trading day in the life of the capital, read Sébastien Mercier's *Tableau de Paris*. It begins at dawn with the arrival of thousands of villagers carrying or carting their bread and farm and dairy produce into the city from the villages surrounding the capital. It continues with retailers buying their wares from the central markets, 'stacking them up on carts like pyramids and then transporting everything that there is to eat from one end of the city to the other'. There were itinerant and rowdy street traders, selling everything from coffee in enamel urns to cooked meats, fish, rabbits, brooms, crockery, pots and pans and a hundred other everyday necessities. Then the coalmen, black as soot, often bumping on the stairs into the thousands of water carriers who earned just a few *sous* for transporting water from the Seine to private apartments.[33] Whatever one needed to drink, eat or wear could be found in markets or on streets, with women running most of the trade. Deborah Simonton explains how these women developed their own internal disciplines and customs, like the old clothes and furniture dealers who introduced hierarchical systems and even apprenticeship schemes. Female traders were an essential feature of urban life, acquiring through their work 'a sense of achievement less through the identity of skill and more through establishing women's work in the neighbourhood'.[34]

The eighteenth-century French economy, fuelled by wood and water, was carried on the backs of two- and four-footed animals. Mercier saw men carrying loads that would have killed a horse. The human debris of an economic system that relied so heavily on back-breaking physical labour, the thousands of porters and odd-job men and women, their bodies contoured by the heavy loads they carried, was visible to all. Rétif de la Bretonne was walking along the rue Francs-Bourgeois in the Marais district one evening when he spotted an old man sorting out lettuce leaves from some refuse. He explained that, in his younger days, he had been a journeyman carpenter, but with, the onset of old age, he had been forced to clean out gutters and collect old rags. Now he was collecting leaves to feed the 300 rabbits he had bred: 'it occupies my mind; it keeps me happy and feeds me', the old man explained, adding, existentially, 'I have finally found some happiness. I now feel that life itself is precious.'[35]

Migrants accounted for up to a quarter of the total population of Paris by the late eighteenth century. They often huddled together in large, furnished rooms (*chambrées*). They belonged to Arlette Farge's category of 'excluded' workers, 'odd-job men who cleaned mud off one's clothes, water-carriers and stall-holders, itinerant workers, disappearing from one day to the next, moving from one job to another according to circumstances. They formed a group with very fluid frontiers.'[36] Over the century, hundreds of thousands of immigrants from Picardy, the Auvergne, Limousin and Savoy would flood into the capital. They gravitated towards the same suburbs, *quartiers* and streets, much like present-day immigrants. Certain regions specialised in producing migrants with particular skills: agricultural workers often came from Alsace and Lorraine, carpenters from Normandy, masons from Limousin, chimney sweeps from Savoy, coppersmiths and menders of pots and pans from the Auvergne. According to Mercier, they were 'birds that the cold sends to warmer climes. They flee the snow that covers their mountains for eight months of the year. They return every year, give their wives a baby, then leave them again in the hands of the old and the curés.'[37] Regular migrants, like the Savoyards and the Auvergnats, enjoyed a dual culture, their own and the unique experience of life in the capital or a provincial city. Their determination not to submerge their particular identities with that of the Parisians was a constant affront to the latter and the source of irrational fears and hatreds. The police, when 'rounding up the usual suspects' often jumped on immigrants first.

Savoyards, Auvergnats and Limousins migrated to provincial cities as well as to the capital. In 1700, Bordeaux was a town of some 45,000 inhabitants; 50 years later, its population had increased to 60,000. During the third quarter of the century, population increase was faster in Bordeaux than in Paris or Lyon. The pool of immigration that had been local until 1740 became regional around 1770 and national by 1785. Jean-Pierre Poussou's work on Bordeaux reveals that certain villages specialised in providing migrant workers: five groups of villages in what was to become the department of the Creuse provided virtually all the migrants who went to Bordeaux from the region. Maurice Garden's study of immigration to Lyon, based on the records of those who died in the *hôtel-Dieu* between 1751 and 1789, reveals the human cost of migrant life. A high, annual figure of 950 deaths was recorded for the period 1751–1760, rising to 1,400 deaths for 1781–89. Daniel Roche confirms that many migrants reached the promised land of Paris only to die, since, 'whether in the nets of the police or in hospital beds, Paris took in a population mostly provincial, pauperised and sick'. On the brighter side, 208 Limousins and 154 Auvergnats were married in Lyon between 1782 and 1791. Males made up 87 per cent of the migrants to the city, and half were under thirty years of age.[38] Other migration patterns were more localised and restricted in duration. Families from the Île d'Yeu travelled to the Bas-Poitou region to work in August on the harvests; a couple of months later, over a thousand villagers from the Vendée would move down to the Saintonge. There was 'reverse migration', too, with the poor of the cities moving into the countryside to work in the fields and vineyards, just as Londoners from the East End travelled to Kent to pick hops until fairly recently.[39]

Once again, it is extremely difficult to provide accurate data for wage rates. Sonenscher reports that a Parisian journeymen printer earned 13 *livres* in 1768 for a week's work which would have meant an annual salary of around 680 *livres* had he worked every week, but this would have been very much the exception rather than the rule. Journeymen builders said they could earn around 472 *livres* for a 225-day working year if they worked every available day, which, in most cases, they did not. In Lyon, annual wages for journeymen silkworkers were estimated to be 161 *livres* in 1744, a figure that had risen – rather surprisingly – to 374 *livres* by 1786, but this did not include board and lodgings. In the Caen region, carpenters earned 10 or 11 *sous* a day in the 1720s. How do these figures relate to living costs? At the end of the century, a Parisian journeyman builder said that he spent approximately

30 *sous* a day on food, drink and rent, which did not leave much from his daily wage of 42 *sous*. George Rudé estimated that, at the end of the century, a worker had to earn 435 *livres* a year to maintain a family of four at subsistence level, so, yet again, 'The labor of their wives and sometimes their children was necessary for survival.' As for the unskilled labourer, he probably earned around 30 *sous* a day by the end of the century. Pierre Léon confirms that wages could range from 40 to 70 or 80 *sous* for skilled workers in printed fabrics to 10 *sous* for unskilled workers. A study of 13,760 cloth workers in Sedan in 1774 revealed that 72.2 per cent earned less than 20 *sous* a day, and 38.8 per cent less than 10. The customary price for the daily ration of a four-pound loaf of bread was 9 *sous*, meaning that the lowest paid worker was hardly earning enough to keep himself, or herself, alive.[40]

As for women's wages, Rétif tells us that unskilled women earned around 9 *sous* a day, and that one-third of this went on bread, one-third on rent and the final third on supper in a cheap café (*gargote*). Marie-Erica Benabou estimated that, in Paris towards the end of the century, women's wages ranged from 8 to 20 *sous* a day, and that if a wife got 15 *sous* and her husband, or partner, 20, they could exist, but that was all. One young seamstress earned as little as 7 *sous* a day, but this may have been exclusive of board and lodgings.[41]

Servants, beggars and slaves

By 1789, there were up to two million servants in France, 40,000 of whom worked in the capital.[42] The aristocracy and top-ranking magistrates and financiers were the biggest employers. Peers and princes of the blood might employ up to a hundred servants, though most Parisian nobles seemed satisfied with a dozen or so. The duc de Trémoille instructed his tailor to make uniforms for one Swiss porter, one huntsman, one negro, six household servants, one jockey and one ostler. The prestige that accompanied retinues of servants, however, counted for less as one moved from Versailles to the backwoods of the Cévennes or lower Brittany. Nobles in the parlement town of Toulouse represented just nine per cent of all households in 1700, but they employed half of the town's servants, whereas many fairly wealthy Breton nobles managed to survive with very few servants, especially in poorer regions.[43] If a minority of the upper bourgeoisie succeeded in pushing their complement of servants into double figures, those lower down the pecking order were often satisfied with two or three. In that borderline, bourgeois world of artisans and shopkeepers, one servant was the rule. As for the peasantry, only the wealthier *fermiers* and *laboureurs* employed more than a handful of servants. Only 76 out of 404 households in the Breton town of Plouigneau had more than one servant, and of the 335 households in Guisseny, 272 had no male and 291 no female servants.[44]

The great majority of servants came from peasant and artisan stock. The largest single category of fathers of female servants in Paris, Toulouse and Bordeaux was agricultural labourers. A quarter of male servants in the capital around 1750, however, hailed from the lower middle class, and the sons of impecunious schoolmasters, notaries and 'surgeons' could be found in many towns working as servants. Domestic service became the archetypal female occupation of the ancien regime, primarily because it offered a more enticing future than acting as unpaid skivvies at home, as well as the possibility of saving for a dowry and eventual marriage. Marriage was the ultimate goal, the magic wand that just might transform a domestic slave into a domesticated wife and mother. The options for men were less restricted, a minority would take the occupational route and join an elite of faithful retainers; the majority joined the ranks of unskilled transients who moved from employer to employer, whether as servants or in some ancillary capacity. For Sarah Maza, both male and female servants 'knew or believed that their real future lay beyond the pale of service'. For the young, ignorant and relatively defenceless, violence and sexual abuse was an ever-present threat. In 1752, a maid working in Marseille was accused of stealing six *livres*. She was forced to undress, then beaten until she was unconscious. In Aix-en-Provence domestic servants formed the largest single category of women who became pregnant out of wedlock, while the largest categories of seducers were 'first of all, male servants and second, masters and other men of the upper classes'.[45]

As the plays and songs of the period suggest, servants and apprentices were frequently lumped together as petty crooks, troublemakers and 'foreigners'. Mercier tells us that of a hundred men lounging around the cabarets and street corners of the capital, 40 would be servants and 30 apprentices from the surrounding countryside.[46] Doubtless, many of those who entered service because they could find nothing better to do, or who were dumped on the streets by their employers, merited Mercier's condemnation. However, there were servants who became loyal and indispensable members of a household. McManners asks us to remember the faithful devotion of many housekeepers serving *curés*. There were also valets and *femmes de chambre* who dressed and bathed their masters and mistresses, who chose and purchased their children's clothes. The marquis de Coigny ended a letter to his valet, 'adieu my dear Dangé. Never doubt my affection and most tender friendship.'[47] These types of relationship may well have been the exceptions that proved the rule of far less tender encounters: the relationship between master and servant prioritised dissimulation and hypocrisy. However, during the crisis of the 1790s, many a servant would opt for loyalty to his or her employer rather than to the Revolution. Human beings, even at the most menial level of society, do not all march to the structural sociologist's tune.

For the majority of servants, however, there can be little doubt that domestic service meant a life of unrelenting drudgery, frequently interspersed with serious violence. A contract drawn up in 1695 by a well-to-do farmer in Lyon stipulated that his servant would tend the vines, look after the cattle and undertake a variety of other farming duties, as well as doing 'everything that my wife might require for the house'.[48] In terms of cash rewards, too, domestic servants were amongst the most exploited of all working-class groups, although real wages did rise significantly towards the end of the century. In the 1700s, it was customary for servants to be given food and lodgings and the promise of a dowry, legacy or gift at the end of their contract, which might last several years (*gages à récompense*), a practice that placed domestic service on the borderline of slavery. It was also customary, as in other occupations, to pay male servants twice as much as women. Lackeys in Aix around mid-century were paid 90 *livres* a year, maids between 35 and 50 *livres*; a male cook in one aristocratic household received 120 *livres* a year, female cooks exactly half this sum. Parisian salaries were almost invariably higher than those paid in the provinces. In the 1770s, stable boys could earn anything from 120 to 450 *livres* in the capital, but only 60 or 70 *livres* in Toulouse and Bordeaux. By this time, the servile practice of paying *à récompense* was giving way to more modern methods of payment. This may well help to explain the impressive rise in servants' wages – 40 per cent higher for women in 1771–89 than they had been in 1726–41. Male wages recorded a marginally higher rise.[49]

The increase in, and the more regular payment of, wages help to explain the transformation experienced by domestic servants during the 1770s and 1780s. Sarah Maza concludes that the 'increasing physical and psychological segregation between master and servant within the domestic sphere' was just one expression of 'the pangs of fear and self-consciousness that accompanied the birth of middle-class consciousness in Europe'. Was the bourgeois intellectual, Sébastien Mercier, experiencing these birth-pangs when, on the eve of the Revolution, he criticised the pampered and opulent lives of the rich? Mercier was convinced that with 'so many servants given so many different titles', the rich and famous might reach the erroneous conclusion 'that the rest of the world runs along similar lines'![50]

Domestic service was never far away from the begging bowl. In the 1700s, Vauban had estimated that 10 per cent of the population lived off begging, with another 20 per cent hovering on the brink. From 1724 to 1733, Louis XV's ministers would embark upon the first of two concerted programmes to deal with the social consequences of poverty, an important chapter in the history of what Michel Foucault described as the 'Great Confinement'. An indication of the government's increasing unease over the problems relating to vagrancy and crime had emerged as early as 1662 when it decreed that there should be *hôpitaux généraux* – effectively, poorhouses modelled on the general hospital of Paris founded six years earlier – in every French town. Five years later, Louis XIV had created the post of Lieutenant General of

Police in Paris to deal, *inter alia*, with the city's estimated 40,000 beggars, lackeys, ex-soldiers and thieves. However, the social consequences of wars and famine during the last decades of the Sun King's reign meant that begging increased, with no permanent solution in sight. In 1700, a government edict instructed all able-bodied beggars to return to their places of birth in order to relieve urban centres. Unsurprisingly, the edict proved ineffective, as did the policy of rounding up and transporting beggars to the colonies during the Regency period.

In Paris and provincial cities, particularly in the south where mass migration was a way of life, there was a discernible link between migrant workers and vagrancy. The majority of the 506 vagrants registered in the Montpellier general hospital in December 1694 and 1695 came from Rouergue, Gevaudan and Cantal, the traditional reservoirs of seasonal labour for Languedoc.[51] In 1725, Bayeux, a town of just 7,200 inhabitants would be overwhelmed by the influx of 1,800 beggars, including migrants, the situation being aggravated by the presence of a similar number seeking work and charity in the surrounding countryside. 'Professional beggars' frequently included seasonal workers, travelling booksellers and tinkers, fairground entertainers and fortune-tellers. Research on the 'Great Confinement' of the 1720s and 1730s confirms that the vast majority of 'occasional beggars' came from the ranks of the dispossessed and the disadvantaged. They were marginal or landless peasants, protoindustrial textile workers, unemployed artisans, journeymen and apprentices, small traders and domestic servants. Schwartz's research into those arrested in lower Normandy in the late 1720s reveals that two-thirds to four-fifths were wage-earners. Lis and Soly attribute the massive increase in begging to 'the industrial restructuring of Europe, leading to the proliferation of an agrarian and urban proletariat'.[52]

The majority of those confined in the new poorhouses were elderly men, women and children, who, unlike the able-bodied and unencumbered, could escape the attentions of the rural police (*maréchaussée*). Roche found that the world of begging and vagabondage in Paris was 'essentially a masculine one': over 90 per cent of vagrants arrested by the *maréchaussée* between 1750 and 1789 were men. There were exceptions to this rule, however, dictated by time and place. In the 1720s in lower Normandy, the majority of adults arrested were women. They were domestic servants like the 24-year-old Gabrielle Le Cartel, a farm servant chased out of her village near Bayeux in September 1724 because she was pregnant; or Anne Sortin, who was arrested along with her illegitimate 4-year-old daughter. 'Occasional beggars' were often the victims of family breakdown, young children making up another sizeable complement of those arrested and incarcerated. Many of the women detained in the notorious Salpêtrière hospital and poorhouse in Paris were the children of beggars, vagabonds, prostitutes and criminals.[53]

The most obvious conclusion to be drawn from the first interventionist attempt by the state to repress begging was that it failed. In the first place, because the state, with only some 3,000 police at its disposal, simply did not have the repressive machinery capable of tackling the problem; secondly, because the 150 or so hospitals available could not cope with the numbers of those arrested. On the other hand, many historians argue that this phase of the 'Great Confinement' was a significant turning point in state attitudes towards poverty. Schwartz, for example, suggests that the state had the ability to carry out a programme of unprecedented range and scale, including subsidies to cover hospital costs. Arrested beggars were, of course, forced to work: the hospital in Caen had facilities for spinning, brewing and linen-cloth making, while the Salpêtrière in Paris, 'a carceral universe of women, their children, and their guards', had everything from vegetable gardens to a flour mill and a 'factory'. Michel Foucault's problematic work, *Discipline and Punish: The Birth of the Prison* raises some of these issues, particularly those that relate to state control of hospitals and prisons. Foucault has been accused of many academic crimes, including exaggeration, overdramatisation, lack of archival referencing and ignorance of the contribution of religious charitable institutions. However, some of these criticisms do not engage with Foucault's central concerns, which were to discover the common repressive features of poorhouses, prisons and asylums in the modern era.[54]

The move towards more repressive state measures to deal with vagrancy and crime is clearly relevant to our own discussion of the relationship between state power and the repression of social unrest. We will, therefore, return to it in chapter seven, which examines the second phase of the 'Great Confinement'. The immediate point here is that raised by Sharon Kettering, who concluded that beggars and vagrants lacked the solidarities of family and communal life, as well as those of honour and obedience to the state that characterised more established social groups. Would the poor, this 'large, impoverished underbelly of society composed of 40 to 50 per cent of the population', become even more detached during the eighteenth century under the pressure of consumerist and capitalist change, thus contributing to the destabilisation of the monarchy?[55]

Paris was a favoured haunt for prostitutes as well as beggars in the eighteenth century. There were 20,000 'active' prostitutes working in the capital by 1789, which means that 13 per cent of the 150,000 females aged between 15 and 50 were engaged in the 'sex trade'.[56] Many of these women were migrants from the textile towns of Amiens, Rouen and Beauvais, or from the garrison towns of Verdun and Metz. Roughly half of the 2,069 women arrested in the late 1760s were between 19 and 26 years of age; three-quarters were between 18 and 30; 37 were between 10 and 16. Eighty-seven per cent of these women were single. Of those charged with prostitution and imprisoned in the Saint-Martin gaol for the years 1765, 1766 and 1770 there were 940 textile and clothing workers, 300 laundresses, 272 street traders, 263 domestic servants, 94 non-textile artisans and 39 unspecified day-labourers. We are dealing, therefore, with the youngest, the lowest paid and the most exploited strata of the female working classes. If a laundress or a servant lost her job, working for a pimp, or in a brothel, might be her only means of survival, particularly if she was unmarried and deprived of family or village support networks.

On the lowest rungs of the social ladder, clients could be found on the streets, or in wine shops and cheap inns. There were also the dress shops used as covers for prostitution, like the one on the corner of the rue Saint-Martin and the rue de la Corroierie, patronised by pimps, soldiers and vagrants. The owners of several cheap lodging-houses would rent out rooms to prostitutes: one charged 48 *sous*, and retained half of this sum for himself. Madame Dupont, who rented rooms to her 'girls', was well known to the police, who used 'madames' and pimps as vital sources of information. The links between bars, seedy hotels and the police extend from Mercier to Inspector Maigret, and beyond. On the highest rungs, according to the respectable bourgeois diarist, Barbier, fashionable brothels provided 'fixed menus', and the rich could get girls delivered to their town houses for 24 *livres*, a month's salary for a semi-skilled worker. The appropriately named 'Madame Paris', an ex-prostitute, had a very luxurious house in the *faubourg* Saint-Germain, designed for the rich and famous, in which she instructed a dozen or so young girls in the rudiments of sexual excess. Madame Dhosmont, convent educated and a close confidante of the Lieutenant General de Police, Berryer, ran a top-class, discreet whorehouse near the boulevard Montmartre in the 1750s. Among her clients we find magistrates from the Paris Parlement, a canon from the church of Saint-Genevièvre and one of the great court figures, the duc de Richelieu, a *maréchal de France*. One of Louis XV's mistresses, madame Dubarry, had been working the four-poster beds of the rich and powerful before she was elevated to the royal bed at Versailles. Sex, like death, has ever been the 'Great Leveller'.

If the financial cost could be high for clients, the physical toll on the health of the prostitutes was incalculable. The famous courtesan, Marie-Anne Deschamps, a dancer at the Opéra who counted the duc d'Orléans among those received in her luxurious house near the Palais-Royal, died of veneral disease, aged just thirty-four. As for the 'disorderly phalanx of *filles publiques*' who populated the public thoroughfares, or the 'hideous creatures of the Port-au-Bled, the rue Poirier, and the rue Planche-Mibray', many would have been lucky to reach this relatively young age. What agonies they must have suffered if arrested and forced to undergo the 'mercury treatments' in the Salpêtrière prison can only be imagined.

It may be thought that the tiny number of slaves to be found in France (officially, only 4,000–5,000) merits but a passing reference. They were, however, only a surviving fraction of the African slaves who worked, and died, in the French colonies to enrich French slavers and the court aristo-crats who owned many of the Caribbean coffee and cotton plantations. The majority of African slaves who arrived in France eventually settled in Paris and the principle slaving ports of the western seaboard, Bordeaux, La Rochelle, Lorient, Nantes and le Havre. They had arrived with their white masters who had decided to end their lives in the mother country. Some were given their freedom; others continued to act as servants or mistresses. Many former African slaves, however, could be found working as cooks, wigmakers, carpenters and locksmiths, as well as domestic servants. A few, including small children, were employed by the rich to add a hint of 'colour' and the exotic to their luxurious mansions. As a child, Louis XV had played with an Iroquois Indian boy.[57] A few African women exchanged one form of slavery for another, working to satisfy the jaded sexual appetites of the rich in Mademoiselle Isabeau's 'Bordel des Négresses', rue Montmorency, in Paris.

The emergence of a scarcely veiled, racist ideology seems to have emerged as the economic importance of the colonies developed. Until the decree of October 1716, former slaves living in France were deemed to be free, at least in theory. By the 1760s, however, ministers like Choiseul were complaining about their rising numbers, stressing the fearful consequences of mixed marriages. On 29 August 1769, the colonial administration in Saint Domingue decreed that colonists who wished to take slaves to the mother country would have to pay a deposit of 4,500 *livres*. Nor was racism confined to the aristoc-racy. In 1775, the guild of armsmakers decided that blacks and mulattos should no longer be eligible for membership. It is possible that in France, as in many other European countries, a racially based form of nationalism was evolving as the coloured 'wider world' increasingly made its physical presence felt. A more immediate factor, however, was the immense wealth that was being generated in the colonies, especially Saint Domingue, Guadeloupe and Martinique. Slaves were becoming very expensive commod-ities, rising from 400 to 2,000 *livres* each over the course of the century. By 1789, between one and a half and two million black Africans had been imported to the French Caribbean, a quarter of a million of them deposited on the shores of Saint Domingue. France's economic recovery during the period 1680 to 1720 was rooted in the colonies. The slave population of Saint Domingue rose from 9,000 in 1700 to 24,000 by 1715. French exports to the West Indies and North American colonies would increase eight-fold over the century.[58]

All this wealth came at a cost and, for the most part, it was paid by the ruthless exploitation of black slaves. As the French Chamber of Commerce announced on 30 September 1762: 'The African Trade is important in terms of gold and ivory, but it is infinitely more important from the standpoint of the Black [slave] trade.' Statistics cannot possibly convey the inhumanity and sheer brutality that underpinned the plantation economies of the French colonies, the branding, the savage whippings, the murders, the stench that emanated from the buildings in the ports of Saint Domingue reserved for slavers to deposit the sick and dying Africans who could not be sold in its 'cattle markets'. Some figures, however, do convey something of what can only be described as a holocaust: there was an annual mortality rate of 8 to 11 per cent; 50 per cent of slaves died within eight years of entering the colonies.[59] When, in 1784, a government ordinance forbade the inhuman treatment of slaves, it would clearly be a case of far too little, far too late.

Poverty, the pulpit and popular protest

Under the ancien regime, popular protest was frequently couched in biblical and millenarian language. Evidence that research in this field remains undernourished is to be found in Nigel Aston's critical remark: 'Generally, whether the topic is high politics or the Enlightenment, popular culture or constructions of gender, religion seems of restricted significance, an increasingly ineffective brake on modernity and the emergence of civic society in the course of the century'.[60] We shall argue, in fact, that the bitter and prolonged debate over religious conformity and dissent, a debate in which 'the common people' played a leading role, made a crucial contribution to popular protest during the first half of the eighteenth century. It also marked the beginning of 'a learning curve' that swung in the direction of a more pluralist, democratic society.

Jonathan Israel's encyclopaedic knowledge of the early 'Radical Enlightenment' reveals (a) the centrality of religion to the 'new' post-Cartesian philosophy, (b) the concern of *radical* philosophers for the poor and (c) the importance to these same philosophers of religious toleration and social equality. On the first point, Israel makes it abundantly clear that, from the revolutionary, materialist theories of the Dutch radical philosopher, Baruch Spinosa – 'the supreme philosophical bogeyman of the Early Enlightenment' – in the 1660s to the atheistic propositions of La Mettrie and Diderot a century later, the 'chief targets' were revealed religion and ecclesiastical authority. Secondly, Israel insists that the early, radical Enlightenment was a drama that did involve the common people.[61] Spinosa himself rejected the claim that ordinary, even unlettered people were irrational and superstitious, arguing that 'all men have one and the same nature' and that 'it is power and culture which misleads us', a proposition that is central to our own general thesis. Finally, Israel notes that Spinosa was 'the first major European thinker in modern times to embrace democratic republicanism as the highest and most rational form of political organisation'. Radical philosophers did not embrace toleration as a means to personal spiritual redemption (as was the case with John Locke) but as a weapon to fight for individual liberty, freedom of thought and freedom to publish ideas.[62]

But, how did these radical, even revolutionary ideas impact upon popular protest? In the first place, because radical philosophers, their supporters and their critics targeted the common people. In the Netherlands, where the press was relatively free, native radical philosophers and French exiles spread the revolutionary word. The Dutch radical thinker, Van den Enden, had shocked his contemporaries in the 1660s by proposing that the common people should be educated by using everyday language and uncomplicated terminology. He also realised, long before Michel Foucault, that 'knowledge was power' and that the language of doctors, lawyers and scientists should be demystified so that ordinary people could reach a better understanding of the processes and powers controlling their lives. In France, the baron de Lahontan's widely read account of Indian culture in Canada, the *Nouveaux Voyages* (1705), included a 'rejection of the European social system and a harsh assessment of European religion'.

Lahontan produced one of the first protoypes of Rousseau's 'noble savage'. Five years later, one of Spinosa's critics, François Lamy, decided that it was time to fight the 'new philosophy' on its own terms. His *L'Incrédule amené à la Religion*, published in Paris, was 'noteworthy chiefly for its popular tone, being expressly targeted at servants, shopkeepers and tradesmen with little education'.[63] By the early eighteenth century, diehard traditionalists were lamenting the size of the 'popular' audience for these hitherto cloistered and elitist debates. If there are political and intellectual threads, however frayed, linking the Voltairian, moderate Enlightenment with the ideas of the conservative bourgeoisie of 1789–92, then there are comparable threads linking the radical Enlightenment and Rousseau – directly influenced by Spinoza's ideas – with the Popular Movement of 1792–5.

What fuelled the debate between supporters of Church and state, between moderate, mainstream critics and the radical followers of the 'new philosophy' was the massive repression unleashed by Louis XIV in the 1680s. By this date, radical philosophical and political opinions had broken through the barriers insulating French cultural life from ideas emanating from Protestant lands. Hardly surprising since, as Bossuet and Louis XIV were only too aware, France at the turn of the century still harboured hundreds of thousands of Calvinist and Jansenist 'heretics' who were in constant contact with their exiled compatriots in many European countries, particularly the Netherlands and Switzerland. Calvinist and Jansenist scholars spent their lives deconstructing the Bible to furnish support for their particular theologies, frequently with revolutionary results. For monarchs and the propertied classes, the Bible was proving to be, potentially, as explosive and revolutionary a text as Marx's *Das Kapital* would prove to be in the later nineteenth century.

This is why 'popes and princes' fought so desperately to control the message of the scriptures.

Part of the appeal of Jansenism was its republican and democratic bias, despite the denials of its followers who claimed to be, like their fellow Protestant heretics, just simple Christians. In order to strengthen their appeal, Jansenist leaders had made a point of seeking popular support. Pasquier Quesnel, leader of the second wave of Jansenism during the latter decades of Louis XIV's reign, published commentaries on the New Testament that placed Christ's message in the hands of ordinary people.[64] Following the failure of their famous appeal for a meeting of the General Council of the Church in 1721, Jansenist leaders redoubled their efforts to bypass the Catholic establishment and appeal directly to the people. At the very same time, many Calvinist pastors in the south-east of France were encouraging the more popular evangelical and millenarian expressions of their faith that had been stimulated by the bloody *guerre des Camisards* against Louis XIV in the 1700s. The Protestant elite (worried, from the outset, about popular unrest in any form) would adopt a very different tone towards *le peuple protestant* as its richer and more educated members were gradually admitted, reluctantly, into the Bourbon fold after the 1760s.

Both Calvinists and Jansenists exploited the expanding media of print to reach out to the masses. Pierre Bayle (1646–1706), the son of a French Calvinist pastor who became the exiled 'philosopher of Rotterdam', was one of the most widely read and influential thinkers of the early Enlightenment. His *Dictionary* of 1697 and the 'pamphlet war' over his support for toleration of dissenters, atheists and followers of Spinosa made a huge impact on the reading public. In February 1728, the Jansenists launched one of the most popular and influential journals of the eighteenth century, the *Nouvelles ecclésiastiques*. Its articles on the 'reformed' faith as well as on public affairs attracted an early circulation of around 6,000 subscribers, a figure that has to be multiplied many times when one recalls that one copy of the journal in the hands of a Jansenist priest could reach an audience of scores. Other Calvinist and Jansenist publications, especially on the scriptures and religious controversies, unquestionably widened the circle of literacy among ordinary people, whether they ultimately espoused conservative or radical political options.

What was 'revolutionary' about all this was the number of works that were published in French or, in some cases, in local patois. One-tenth of the propositions contained in Quesnel's writings that attracted the condemnation of the Catholic Church were related explicitly to the right of ordinary Christians to read the Bible in their own language. French translations of the New Testament and the psalms were amongst the best-sellers published by the Jansenist press. Translations of religious works into French also help to explain the relatively high degree of literacy to be found in eighteenth-century Calvinist communities. Take the remarkable example of Anne Marguerite Dunoyer, a 22-year-old Calvinist from Nîmes who was forced to flee to the Netherlands as a result of the Revocation of the Edict of Nantes. In exile, she published her memoirs and, in 1707, the first of the seven volumes of her *Lettres historiques et galantes*. Dunoyer was a pioneering feminist, declaring that 'Notre sexe est capable de tout.' She also published a series of savage attacks against Louis XIV and the court aristocracy for their 'barbarism', for employing the power of the state to unleash 'its butchers' at a time when, she argued, Europe had begun to recognise 'the rights of human beings'.[65]

The dangers of allowing the 'untutored masses' to interpret the scriptures according to the principle of the 'priesthood of all believers' – one of the most revolutionary concepts of the age – seemed to be evident in the contemporary wave of evangelical and eschatological movements that affected both Calvinist and Jansenist communities. The Jansenist *'convulsionnaire'* movement spread in the 1730s and was loosely associated with the earlier 'Figurist' interpretation of the scriptures by Jansenist priests like Jacques-Joseph Duguet (1649–1733). Figurism, 'a creed for a persecuted minority', involved a revolutionary reinterpretation of the scriptures, one that sought to arm the followers of the 'true faith' – Jansenist supporters – against the 'apostates' – the Pope and Louis XIV.[66] 'Convulsionists', as the term suggests, fell victim to contortions and convulsive movements; they spoke in strange tongues, delivered prophecies and declared themselves to be cured of physical and sexual ills. Miraculous cures occurred in graveyards, a favourite spot being the tomb in the cemetery of Saint-Médard of the young Jansenist 'saint', the deacon Pâris who had died in 1727. Pâris's life was still being commemorated in the parish of Saint-Médard in 1749.[67] Similar elastic and exotic performances were taking place among Calvinist communities of the south-east. In the Vaunage region of lower Languedoc, men and women declared themselves to be 'inflated' with the Holy Spirit, appearing to swell in size, hence their popular, pejorative description as *'gonfleurs'*.[68]

During the first half of the eighteenth century, both Jansenism and Calvinism attracted the disenfranchised and the disempowered, especially women, although their appeal, in social terms, was obviously more universal. Without necessarily subscribing to Lucien Goldman's thesis that movements like the *convulsionnaires* and the *gonfleurs* provide evidence of class divisions, it would be dangerous to dismiss their practitioners simply as 'sociopsychological' cases. Rather, we should view their actions as contributions to a complex, profound and widespread manifestation of discontent with the established order. The opinions of the mass of the poor and the illiterate were constantly being filtered through, and sanitised by, bishops and *curés* in churches, and by seigneurs and government officials in village assemblies and seigneurial courts. The ensuing discontent, this feeling of exclusion,

141

was common among women, who were very prominent in Jansenist and Protestant popular movements as prophetesses and miracle-makers. Popular religious movements gave women a voice that was totally denied to them in almost every ecclesiastic, governmental and professional organisation. It is hardly surprising that the conservative Jansenist and Protestant elites frequently denounced the political and religious excesses of their lower class co-religionists, or that Figurism should have appealed to the younger generation of Jansenists.[69]

The problem for *le peuple* during the latter decades of the century, as they were excluded – or excluded themselves – from the bourgeois 'public sphere' and the power of religion to challenge the established political and social order waned, would be to find a new voice, a new vocabulary of protest. Royal administrations, especially after the débâcle of the Seven Years War (1756–63), were not insensitive to the problem. Their failure to create a political consensus to implement radical changes favouring the poor, which several reforming ministers sought to introduce, unquestionably weakened the Bourbon monarchy. '1789' was not inevitable, but deep-seated fears concerning the threat of 'popular anarchy' periodically disturbed the sleep of Bourbon kings and princes. They had played an important part in Louis XIV's decision to move the seat of royal power from Paris to Versailles after the mid-seventeenth-century Frondes. They help to explain why, in a bid to court popularity, the duc d'Orléans had chosen to return to the capital when he became Regent in 1715. It seems that, in moments of crisis, the Regent had cause to regret this decision.

On 17 July 1720, as John Law's financial schemes collapsed and the Regency was shaken to its foundations, a 'mob' marched on the Palais Royal, led by those who had lost their life savings. According to the diarist, Edmond Barbier, the duc d'Orléans's face became 'as white as his cravate'. Everyone around him felt that 'The alliance of the people with the [Paris] parlement was nothing less than the Fronde, with all its bloody and devastating consequences.' The Regent decided to bring detachments of the regular army into the suburbs, and the *Gardes françaises* out onto the streets of the capital. On this occasion, the troops remained loyal to the crown and the crowds were dispersed, but it had been a close call.[70] In 1789, the Bourbon regime would fall after a lengthy spell of resistance from the *parlement* of Paris and the failure of the *Gardes françaises* to support the government.

Suggested reading

Chapman, S. and Chassagne, S. *European Textile Printers in the Eighteenth Century: A Study of Peel and Oberkampf* (London, 1981).

Fairchilds, C. *Domestic Enemies: Servants and their Masters in Old Regime France* (Baltimore, 1984).

Kaplow, J. *The Names of Kings: The Parisian Laboring Poor in the Eighteenth Century* (New York, 1972).

Kriedte, P., Medick, H. and Schlumbohm, J. *Industrialisation Before Industrialisation: Rural Industry in the Genesis of Capitalism* (Cambridge, 1981).

Lewis, G. *The Advent of Modern Capitalism in France, 1770–1840: The Contribution of Pierre-François Tubeuf* (Oxford, 1993).

Mann, M. *The Sources of Social Power* (Cambridge, 1993).

Maza, S. *Servants and Masters in Eighteenth-Century France* (Princeton, 1983).

Roche, D. *The People of Paris: An Essay in Popular Culture in the Eighteenth Century*, translated by Marie Evans (Leamington Spa, 1987).

Schwartz, R. *The Policing of the Poor in Eighteenth-Century France* (London, 1988).

Simonton, D. *A History of European Women's Work, 1700 to the Present* (London, 1998).

Sonenscher, M. *Work and Wages: Natural Law, Politics and the Eighteenth-Century French Trades* (Cambridge, 1989).

Tilly, L. and Scott, J. *Women, Work and Family* (London, 1989).

PART TWO

'Winds of change'

'Today, western civilisation still subscribes to – or rather, some would say, remains imprisoned within – this secular vision, the limitless human drive towards economic growth, scientific innovation and human progress, which the Enlightenment developed'.[1] The reference to being 'imprisoned' within the philosophical and intellectual embrace of the Enlightenment reminds us that, in our post-communist, post-modernist age, criticisms – from an extremely diverse group of scholars – of the universalist values expounded in the pages of the *Encyclopédie* have intensified. Foucault mocked as 'shallow and self-serving all manner of Whig or "progressive" views that purported to show the rise in the West of that humane, emancipatory reason blue-printed in the Enlightenment and constructed by bourgeois liberalism'. In Russia, Alexander Solzenitsyn, reacting against a communist, materialist interpretation of history, was fiercely critical of the 'unending, unlimited progress which has been drummed into our heads by the dreamers of the Enlightenment'. Dorinda Outram, summing-up the feminist case against the majority of the *philosophes*, writes that 'Examination of the debates around gender shows us that the Enlightenment, for all its universalist claims, had much difficulty in finding a place for social groups – not just women, but also lower social classes, and other races.'[2]

Comments in part one of this book will have indicated our general sympathy for some of the viewpoints expressed above. The chapters that compose part two will examine in greater detail the emergence and character of a modern, 'public sphere', inhabited by an increasingly wide circle of rebels and reformers, and the response of enlightened ministers of the Bourbon monarchy to the fundamental issues raised by military defeat, the social consequences of introducing free market economic policies and more outspoken, political criticism. Throughout, emphasis will be placed upon the social and political, rather than the intellectual and philosophical, consequences of this mid-eighteenth century crisis of confidence.

Chapter 6

'Enlightenments' and the people

According to Daniel Roche, the *mentalité* of the French people was transformed by the 'biological push' of the second half of the eighteenth century. From 1700 to 1789, the population of France rose by one-third, from 21.5 million to 28.6 million. But what really mattered to human beings living in 1789, when compared with those who had been alive in 1700, is that life expectancy had increased from 20 to 29.6 years.[3] However, these optimistic, general statistics mask the pessimistic reality of an unequal distribution, between rich and poor, of the social, economic and cultural benefits of *le siècle des Lumières*. Universal principles were applicable to all in theory; in practice, they were mainly confined to elites.

France was by no means the only European power to experience a 'biological push': England's population, for example, would double over the eighteenth century. Nor was the general pattern of demographic growth common to all French regions: Brittany, for example, one of the poorest provinces in the country, produced a very different profile from that recorded in Dauphiné. In the former province, population actually fell by 200,000 between 1690 and 1720 to produce a total of 2,200,000 inhabitants. From 1720 to 1770, a meagre increase of 100,000 was registered, while, during the last thirty years of the century, population actually declined by around 3.5 per cent. In the province of Dauphiné, on the other hand, the population rose from 557,307 in 1698 to 769,962 in 1780 – an increase of 38 per cent – the rate of growth accelerating as the century progressed. Paris, as one might expect, was in a class of its own: 510,000 in 1700, 576,000 in 1750 and 604,000 in 1780, figures that reflect steady, but not really spectacular, growth. The capital experienced the typical ancien regime, demographic pattern of high birth rates, accompanied by even higher death rates. In 1780, for example, 19,617 births were registered as opposed to 21,094 deaths. Very high immigration rates compensated for high death rates, poor immigrants, as ever, paying the highest price for the capital's growth.[4]

Throughout France, one, rather faint, sign of the approach of a modern society was the gradual fall in birth rates that accompanied a more significant fall in death rates. Birth rates averaged around 40 per thousand in the 1740s, rising to over 41 per thousand in the 1750s, but then declining to 37–8 per thousand by the 1780s. Many explanations have been advanced to explain this trend – the declining influence of the Church, the emergence of a more market-orientated and consumerist society, the increasing use of contraceptive techniques in a more literate and individualist culture, more affective love for children. However, the increasing use of contraception, particularly *coitus interruptus*, and the late age of marriages appear to have been the major contributory factors. There is clear evidence of 'family planning' among Parisian families after the mid-seventeenth century. Jacques Dupâquier's research on the town of Meulan, 47 kilometres from the capital, provides further evidence of family control, exercised by about a quarter of the population until the 1750s, then by almost a half by the 1810s. Guy Arbellot's study of five communities in the Haute-Marne reveals that peasant families in this region were also following the trend from the mid-seventeenth century. In the rural, Catholic regions of Brittany and the Vendée, on the other hand, there is little evidence of a decline in family size; probably the consequence of ignorance and poverty, possibly the result of better family policing by local *curés*.[5]

The trend for increasingly late marriages, accompanied by an increase in celibacy, was related, in the main, not just to over-population but to the difficulty of making a living in a traditional, technically backward society. There is also the complex issue of legislation governing property ownership and inheritance. Delayed marriages, particularly for women, explain, in large measure, the demographic pattern of the ancien regime. In 1700, men married, on average, when they were 24 or 25 years of age, women when they were 22. By the late eighteenth century, the average marriage age had risen to 27.5 for men and 24.5 for women. Late marriages and the increasing number of unmarried men and women was obviously related to the problem of acquiring enough money to run a home and enough land to provide a living. Legislation governing inheritance under the ancien regime varied from region to region, but, in practice, leaving everything to the oldest son was the exception rather than the rule, and these exceptions were more common amongst the aristocracy. It is true that, in general, whether we are dealing with regions governed by statutory or customary law, eldest sons tended to be favoured. However, in several regions, provision was usually made for all children, with wives and widows playing a far more important role in maintaining control over their dowries, as well as over the management of legacies, than was previously thought.[6]

The slight fall in birth rates was matched by a decline in death rates, although, in both cases, revolutionary change was delayed until the nineteenth century. Death rates fell from around 40 per thousand in the 1740s to just over 35 per thousand by the late 1780s. An important explanation for this fall was the fact that eighteenth-century France was not visited so frequently by those two outriders of early modern Europe, war and plague.

However, smallpox continued to pockmark the faces of French men and women throughout the country, while typhus and dysentery periodically ravaged the populations of particular regions. Provinces in the west and the south-east suffered more than those in the centre and the north. Anjou, for example, was afflicted with dysentery in 1768, smallpox in 1773–4 and then dysentery again in 1779. And disease was not only becoming more regionalised and more localised, but also more class-specific. It was observed that epidemics of typhus, dysentery and tuberculosis were increasingly hitting the poor, suffering from calorific and vitamin deficiency, rather than the rich.

Again, as one would expect, it was the children of the poor who proved to be the main victims of the Grim Reaper. Although death rates for children aged between one and ten would be reduced by one-third between 1760 and 1790, infant deaths would remain high. In Paris, 25 per cent of all children born in a given year during the first half of the eighteenth century would die before they reached their first birthday. A very general, national estimate for the second half of the century would be that well over 25 per cent of children did not reach adult age, although, once again, there were marked regional and class differences. The figure was as low as 14 per cent for Pont-en-Bessin in Normandy during the 1780s, but 28.5 per cent for many of the poorer, rural areas of Brittany and Anjou. The parish of Sennely-en-Sologne recorded a death rate of 37.4 per cent for the period 1680 to 1779.[7]

One of the most disturbing social consequences of rising levels of poverty was a dramatic increase in the practice of child abandonment. The babies left outside the gates of foundling hospitals and monasteries were predominantly illegitimate, but 40 per cent of those abandoned in Nantes were the offspring of married couples who could not afford to feed and clothe them. Poverty gnawed away at the very fibres of family life. The annual number of admissions to the Paris Foundling Hospital rose from around 2,000 in 1700 to 7,676 in 1772, the majority of these babies dying before they were one year old. Urban foundling hospitals could only deal with the massive problems of feeding infants left in their care by putting them out to wet-nurses, mainly in the countryside, although thousands of individuals, from aristocrats to artisans, made their own arrangements. The majority of infants placed in the care of wet-nurses by hospitals in Rouen and Beauvais died before the age of one. Of the 66,259 infants despatched to wet-nurses in Paris between 1770 and 1776, 21,002 died – 'a disguised form of infanticide' as Madeleine Gutwirth has described this human tragedy. Towards the end of the century, hospital doctors and administrators would introduce better diets and a measure of cleanliness, but, in the words of Jones and Brockliss: 'Over the Enlightenment hospital hovered the spectre of the dead baby.'[8]

149

Love, sex and marriage

So far we have painted a rather dismal picture of eighteenth-century 'progress', that Pied Piper of the Enlightenment. This is because, for the great majority of the population, demographic and economic change was as likely to be accompanied by misery and deprivation as by happiness and fulfilment. On a positive note, many historians have suggested that the advent of a more materialist and individualist age brought a measure of liberation to most people, rich and poor, not least in the sphere of love and sexuality. Beatrice Gottlieb, while stressing the importance of the family when choosing the marriage partners of their offspring, writes: 'There seems to have been a gradual change over the centuries in the direction of more freedom of choice for the couple and hence of a greater acceptance of love as the basis of marriage.'[9] Undoubtedly, the dawning – possibly the return – of a more liberated age of love and sexual freedom explains the repeated attempts by both Church and state to defend the institution of marriage and, in particular, its sacramental nature. In 1730, for example, Louis XV condemned the growing practice of clandestine marriages, explaining that 'we owe it to the sanctity of religion to prevent the abuse of a great sacrament'. Marriage under the ancien regime was the coping stone of the edifice of Catholic Western Christendom. Even today, the Roman Catholic Church remains opposed, in principle, to divorce. However, the married family in mid-eighteenth-century France performed apparently contradictory functions – the crucible in which the new ideas and values of the period were normalised and tested, but also one of the most important of the traditional agents of social control. That social control had been especially effective in the later sixteenth and seventeenth centuries as the post-Tridentine state sought to buttress the authority of the *prêtre* and the *père*: the latter led the bride to the altar, the former sent her away with God's blessing. The law threw its weight behind the sacramental act of marriage. Any young man who tried to force a young women into marriage (and we should note that the age of consent for a man was 30, for the woman 25) could be arrested under legislation passed in 1579 and tried for *rapt de séduction*, a crime that, theoretically, still carried the death penalty.[10]

There are, however, problems associated with the neat scenario of the father commanding the family that, in turn, determined the marriage plans of his children. For one thing, family structures and values differed according to rank and region. The recent work of historical demographers has revealed the inadequacy of our conception of the pre-industrial family as 'a tightly-knit, stable and supportive unit'.[11] The notion that the extended family was the norm in traditional societies and the nuclear family the norm in modern societies no longer commands widespread support. Stuart Woolf has argued that, in ancien regime Europe, families were often small in size due to the late age of marriage, high infant mortality and the early despatch of children as servants and apprentices. In France, nuclear, extended and 'stem' family structures existed in different regions, as well as in different cycles in the history of a particular family. In the Midi, it was not uncommon to find two couples, parents and a married son or daughter, living under the same roof. In Brittany, one might find two or three brothers, or brothers-in-law, signing joint leases. Big farms, in particular, needed many hands to make them efficient. Studies on Limousin and the Auvergne show that different regions, with different geographic and economic characteristics, contained different family sizes and structures. In wine-growing areas, for example, nuclear families were common while extended families could be found in many mountainous regions.[12]

Jean-Louis Flandrin advances the argument that, despite the undoubted influence of the family home, the village square may have been a more influential space for teaching young people about sexuality, love and romance. Ideas would surely have been disseminated more rapidly in the streets and fields than in the home, particularly at a time when reading and readable material was becoming available, and communication between towns and villages was becoming easier. Anne Fillon's discovery of a manuscript depicting the life of a young weaver, Louis Simon, living in a small village in the Maine-et-Loire in mid-century confirms the validity of this suggestion. The love affair between Louis and Anne Chapeau, his eventual bride, was a drama played in the grounds of the local church and the street, as well as in the home. The action involved the participation of *la jeunesse*, the village youth culture that influenced the course of true love as much as the family. There was also the influence of the new literary culture, as well as the new consumerism. Louis was a customer of *la bibliothèque bleu*, the travelling libraries transported by itinerant booksellers (*colporteurs*). He was also an eager participant in the 'new consumerism', buying his wife dresses, rings and baubles to impress her. Louis and Anne's courtship was the stuff of romantic novels: 'Misunderstandings, wounded pride, reproaches, tears and tiffs, letters supposedly ending their relationship . . . accusations and betrayals . . . a fine history of passionate love.'[13]

But does all this add up to a 'sexual revolution' during the second half of the eighteenth century? If the answer is yes, how do we explain it? There were certainly marked changes in sexual behaviour: significant increases in the number of unmarried men and women, pre-nuptial pregnancies and illegitimacy rates, especially in the urban sector and among the poorer sections of the community. It has been estimated that, during the 1720s, bachelors and spinsters constituted 8.5 per cent of the total population, with 5 per cent living in the countryside. By the end of the century, it is probable that celibacy rates had doubled, with the highest increase occurring in the towns. In 1761, the consul of Arlès said the reason so many young people

151

were not marrying was rising poverty: ' all too often, it is the fear of destitution that prevents *le peuple* from marrying'. A contributory explanation,
however, would be that the religious and cultural controls, symbolised
by the *prêtre*, the *père* and peer groups, that were still operating relatively
successfully in the countryside were much less effective in the towns. In
rural areas, illegitimacy rates only increased from 1 to 1.9 per cent over the
course of the century: a general figure for urban areas would be nearer 8 per
cent. The highest increase was recorded in industrial centres like Lille – from
4.5 per cent in the 1740s to 12.5 by the 1780s. According to Roger Chartier,
by 1789 illegitimacy rates in big cities oscillated between 6 and 12 per cent.[14]

Pre-nuptial pregnancies also increased during the second half of the century. Daniel Roche rashly offers us general figures that indicate a rise in the
number of couples indulging in sex before marriage – 20 per cent in 1700
rising to 30 per cent by 1789. Statistics for particular regions and towns again
suggest that a complex set of socio-economic and cultural factors were at
work. In the regions of Berry, the Touraine, Beauvais and the Normandy
bocage the figures for pre-nuptial pregnancies are around 5 per cent, but they
rise from 10 to 14 per cent over the century for the poor village of Sennely-
en-Sologne. In the small town of Meulan, there was a rise from 8 per cent in
the 1730s to 12 per cent by 1790. Once again, it was the big, industrial cities,
such as Lyon and Rouen, with 20 per cent pre-nuptial pregnancies by 1789,
that registered the biggest change; one suburb of Rouen, Sotteville-les-Rouen,
recorded an exceptional 30 per cent rise. It is generally agreed that servants
and working girls in the towns were most at risk from unwanted pregnancies. Domestic servants were more likely to indulge in pre-marital sex than
any other comparable group, since they were deprived of immediate family
support and married later than artisans. Marriage was the ultimate goal, and
the reason for 'surrendering' to their lovers. Sarah Maza tells us that the
female servants she has studied 'only yielded to the man who harassed them
because they sincerely believed that this (the sexual act) was a first step
toward securing a marriage partner'.[15] The clergy sermonised, with some
justification, about the collapse of the moral order, but a general hypothesis,
linking sexual licence with late marriages and the difficulty of becoming
a property-owner, has also been advanced for the 1400s, another 'era of com-
paratively free sexuality'. In any historical period, it is a mistake to divorce
'sin' from socio-economic circumstance.[16]

Later marriage ages, a decline in the authority of the Church and the
family, rising levels of poverty and the difficulty of getting a home together
all help to explain why more young people from the lower classes, especially
in the towns, were indulging in more sex outside marriage. But what about
the aristocracy and the bourgeoisie? And what about the love 'that dared not
speak its name' under the ancien regime – homosexuality? The answer to
the first question would seem to be that sex for the upper classes before

marriage was denied to most women but available – without serious condemnation – to men and women after marriage. The aristocracy took the lead from Louis XV whose capacity for sex was in inverse proportion to his capacity for hard work. Once married, most aristocratic, or would-be aristocratic men and women, 'continued the tradition of courtly extramarital relationships, in which a lover or mistress was the natural object of passion'. Marriage for the aristocracy was obviously more a matter of calculation than romantic attachment. For the unmarried aristocratic or upper bourgeois daughter, an illegitimate birth would spell disaster on a major scale, which is why so many daughters were closeted in convents until they were of marriageable age, which was much younger than the age for girls from the popular classes. The convent was the institutionalised chastity-belt for aristocratic girls. The aristocracy married early, but led the way in restricting family size – an average of 2.7 children from 1700 to 1749 dropping to two per family by 1790.[17] Many rich, bourgeois marriages pursued a similar course, although religious and social conventions appear to have weighed more heavily upon the consciences of the robe nobility and the 'middling bourgeoisie'. After all, illegitimate offspring were far more acceptable to kings and peers than they were to the eighteenth-century bourgeoisie, especially if the latter had been caught in the embrace of Jansenism as well as that of Venus. One should record, however, that, unlike Louis XIV, Louis XV did not legitimise any of his bastard children, and refused them access to Versailles.

Finally, there were those sexual acts and love affairs between same-sex partners under the ancien regime 'that dared not speak their name', indeed, those which were only allowed to speak *sotto voce* until fairly recently. For the American film director, Woody Allen, the act of masturbation was 'making love to someone you really like'; for eighteenth-century divines, such trite comments bordered on perversion, evidence of spiritual, and physical, anorexia. It must be remembered that the fundamental Christian purpose of marriage for the Church was procreation, hence the strident denunciation of both masturbation and homosexuality. According to the book of Genesis, God had struck Onan dead for 'spilling his seed' on the floor rather than using it to impregnate his sister-in-law after his wife's death. Hence, sexual activity as a means of personal enjoyment, whether inside or outside marriage, was a sin. For the divine right theorist, Bossuet, masturbation was 'an abominable crime'. However, episcopal thunderbolts against this 'crime against God' and procreation did not, apparently, prevent parishioners from sinning on an impressive scale. In 1744, the bishop of Bordeaux reported that young men in his diocese did not regard masturbation as a sin, an indication that many people opted for common sense rather than the Council of Trent. A revealing sign of the times?[18] Did a more 'enlightened' attitude towards sexuality reflect a more individualist approach to existentialist problems? Some of the *philosophes* thought it did. The liberated individual was he or she who had cast off the burdens imposed upon them by organised religion, including the heavy baggage of sexual abstinence and repression. For many of their critics, sexual perversion was known as *le crime des philosophes*.

Masturbation did not attract the death penalty; homosexuality did. The Church denounced all kinds of fornication as 'mortal sins', although it distinguished between 'sins of the flesh', like adultery, and 'unnatural sins' such as bestiality and sodomy, including acts between persons of different sex. Homosexuals were transgressing against the 'natural order' as defined in biblical texts. It is difficult to estimate the scale of homosexuality, since the cases that came to court were few and far between. Merry Wiesner notes that, 'the actual trials or accusations of female homosexuality which have come to light [throughout Europe] are extremely rare'. It has always been the case that state authority has always been more tolerant of female than male homosexuality, usually turning two blind eyes to lesbianism, possibly because it is not referred to in the Bible and is not associated with the denial of procreation. Certainly, the guidance given to priests and monks in the eighteenth century was to view lesbian acts less harshly than male same-sex acts. Interestingly, penance was harsher if the women involved were nuns or had been accused of using 'sex toys'. Of the few cases of lesbianism that did come to court, 'most involved transvestite dress, or women who had usurped male prerogatives, another reminder that the ancien regime was, in power terms, a man's world'. The most famous case to come to court was, of course, that of Marie Antoinette, accused of a variety of sexual crimes including lesbianism and incest. Lynn Hunt's neo-Freudian analysis of the Queen's ordeal and subsequent execution is used to support her contentious thesis that the Revolutionary 'band of brothers' did not want 'the sisters' to follow their lead in assuming the mantle of political sovereignty.[19]

There is sufficient evidence to suggest that homosexuality was not uncommon, especially among the upper classes. Saint Simon refers to gays at the Court of Louis XIV, with one of the king's sons taking the lead with the chevalier de Lorraine. Cases of transvestism were also recorded, the most famous involving the chevalier d'Eon, who provoked widespread comment and press speculation during his stay in England as a government official in 1752. D'Eon took to wearing women's clothes in public during the 1760s. He died in 1810 and was found to be a man 'but with female characteristics'. In his wide-ranging study, *Wages of Sin*, Peter Allen locates society's condemnation of homosexuals within the historical context of the association of sin with disease. He argues that, from the ostracism of medieval lepers to the contemporary lack of sympathy on the part of many critics of homosexuality for the victims of Aids, society has often identified certain diseases with the wrath of God, or Nature.[20] This was unquestionably the approach adopted by the ancien regime Church, Catholic and Protestant. It was also the attitude of a few savants who enlisted science in the service of their campaign against sexual deviance and women's claim to gender equality. As we shall see, mid-eighteenth-century science and 'philosophy' occasionally combined to imprison as well as to liberate the individual, the choice often depending upon social rank, education, gender and sexual behaviour.

Medicine and health

Death as the 'wages of sin' was an explanation proffered by many eighteenth-century doctors, if only because they were ignorant of the pathology of venereal diseases, indeed, ignorant of the pathology of most diseases. Nothing in the history of the ancien regime surprises or shocks one more than the continuation of medieval approaches to the practice of medicine. It is true that improvements were recorded in surgical practice, midwifery and, towards the very end of the century, in the treatment of mental illness. Jones and Brockliss also argue that there was a gradual, ideological shift from a medieval 'Galenist' to an 'iatro-mechanist' conception of medical practice. The latter was clearly influenced by applied Newtonian theories on the movement of matter, and may well have heralded a new era of empirical medical enquiry.[21] Despite these indications of a more modern approach to medical care, however, far too many physicians risked purging and bleeding their patients into the next world. The majority of the population – fortunately too poor to pay the fees demanded by most professional physicians – continued to treat themselves, relying on traditional remedies and the assistance of the village blacksmith to set bones, the village 'wise-woman' to deliver babies and travelling quacks to provide the latest 'miracle cures'.

The relationship between 'elite' and 'popular' medicine has provoked lively debate and provided revealing glimpses into the cultures of both worlds. Mathew Ramsay suggests that there were 'grey areas' between elite physicians, surgeons and apothecaries. The mass of the people only saw the divide separating an elite order of classically trained and expensive doctors from the thousands of untrained, or semi-trained, practitioners to the poor. Country-dwellers, as well as many of the poor in the towns, were obliged to rely on traditional, homespun remedies: they could rarely obtain, or indeed pay for, anything else. As Ramsey concludes, the medical profession in 1789, 'had yet to win a substantial popular clientele'. The poorer sections of the rural community first sought treatment from neighbours with a reputation for healing, including the *curé*. If this failed, they might turn to the legions of travelling empirics, charlatans, quacks, 'teeth-pullers' and faith healers. Ramsay divides popular healers into two categories – itinerary and sedentary – explaining that the 'classic charlatanism' of the seventeenth and early eighteenth centuries flourished in an 'era of mercantile capitalism in the commercial centres, market towns and fairs'. By the late eighteenth century, popular healers were advertising in local and regional gazettes. In 1785, monsieur Le Brun used the *Affiche du Mans* to promise an 'appropriate remedy for [treating] ruptures in the two sexes'. Many travelling medicine men and women used techniques common to the 'snake-oil salesmen' of the American West, affecting a certain learning and professional training, and talking down to their potential customers.[22]

The ailments and diseases which popular healers promised to cure reveal a great deal about the more common diseases suffered during the ancien regime, which included cataracts, hernias and broken bones. 'Bone-setters' (*bailleuls* or *rebouteurs*) were to be found in most localities, frequently forming a bridge between elite and popular medicine. In a few places, executioners offered to mend broken bones as well as to break them! The executioner at Le Mans added the following to his trade description – 'bourgeois de la ville et chirurgien restaurateur'. Most 'bone-setters', however, were blacksmiths and farriers, although shepherds occasionally make an appearance. The most common ailments, fevers, stomach upsets, infections, were usually dealt with by local figures: in Chavagne (Brittany), 'a butcher practised medicine while his wife worked as a midwife'. *Maiges* were members of local communities who often specialised in dealing with specific problems like cataracts; *toucheurs* healed sprains, as well as treating burns and wounds. The reputation of some popular practitioners spread further afield, like that of a madame Allemant, living in a village in Champagne, who had appointed 'urine agents' to attract clients for miles around. Many of the treatments provided were probably lethal. A tanner from the Perche region in the 1780s sold an eye wash that contained alum and 'green vitriol' laced with dog dung! The unofficial practices of priests and friars enjoyed the unique, and more salutary, advantage of having God on their side.[23]

However, if treatment at the hands of many a popular practitioner could be dangerous, that offered by many elite doctors was, all too often, deadly. To diagnose a particular disease, physicians consulted patients' stools, vomit and spittle. The most common form of treatment, after various powders and pills, was bloodletting on a truly horrific scale, and if veins were not emptied, stomachs and bowels were. Virtually every patient, from women recovering after childbirth to victims of smallpox, was subjected to this universal panacea. A doctor's bill for the Tardy family in 1691 reveals something of the suffering inflicted on patients. Madame Tardy was bled through incisions in her arms on 12, 13 and 18 July, followed by bleeding from the veins of her feet on 22 July. Intermittently, she was given pills and 'potions' including one that acted as a purgative. On 8 September, the doctor bled madame Tardy's husband! The Beauvais surgeon, Jean-Baptiste Langlet, who also, like so many of his fellow surgeons, occasionally doubled-up as a physician, bled a madame Breteuil twice and performed enemas on three occasions during the first three days of an attack of smallpox. No fewer than 11 more enemas were administered before the poor women was left – curiously still alive – in peace.[24]

Ideas may have been changing in the medical academies, but, on the ground, medieval practices were still all too common.

More effective 'winds of change' could be recorded in the studies of scientists and statisticians as the state began to worry – unnecessarily as it proved – about the consequences of disease and possible population decline. Gradually, attitudes toward the concept of death began to change. For John McManners, this existentialist shift represents 'one of the most revolutionary and neglected aspects of the thought of the Enlightenment, the beginning of the statistical study of human living and dying'.[25] This comment reminds us that the late Enlightenment was, in large measure, an exercise in applied social science, with the 17 volumes of the *Encyclopédie* providing the text-books. Claude Milanese's study of 'apparent death' confirms the major contribution made by Enlightenment thinkers to the changing concept of death. In 1732, the Dutch surgeon, Jacques-Bénigne Winslow, published his *Exposition anatomique de la structure du corps humain*, which sought to undermine the classical and medieval notion of life and death as two separate and opposed entities. Life was based on the principle of the union of body and soul; death was the result of their separation. But Winslow argued – to the consternation of the papacy – that there was a grey area between life and death, an 'apparent death' from which supposedly 'dead' persons could be resuscitated. In 1749, Georges-Louis Leclerc de Buffon, arguably the greatest of the late Enlightenment thinkers and someone who resented being lumped together with the self-styled *philosophes*, began the publication of his *Histoire naturelle de l'homme*. In this extremely influential work, Buffon argued that life was a vital, physical force, 'one that we can almost measure, increasing and decreasing according to very precise laws, a physical force in every way similar to other forces'.[26] Shades of Isaac Newton fall over the Enlightenment once again! Buffon sought to take the sting out of death, which came 'agreeably', gradually draining away one's 'vital force'. By the end of the century, 'Vitalism' had developed into a very influential medical theory, popularised by Paul-Joseph Barthez (1734–1806) and fellow doctors at the Montpellier Faculty of Medicine.

These debates over the meaning of life and death were not academic, existentialist exercises: they promoted social change. More care began to be taken when burying persons too precipitately following accidents on roads and rivers. In 1767, the Amsterdam *Société de secours aux noyés* was formed, and, five years later, a similar society was set up in Paris. Changing notions on the meaning of life and death also exerted an influence on government and the general public. Gradually, a concern for public and personal health became fashionable. An increasing minority of the population began to realise that lifespans, at the margins, were not preordained, another stage in the development of an anthropocentric, as opposed to a theocentric, society. Rebecca Spang's innovative and interesting work on the appearance and evolution of the restaurant in France after the 1760s provides a case in point. The word 'restaurant' originally referred to the 'restorative' drinks and soups that were served in the earliest eating establishments. 'Nouvelle cuisine' is not really that new! It became *à la mode* in France during the 1760s and 1770s. The 'restaurateur' Jean-François Vacossin invited people with delicate chests to try his menu that included 'only those dishes that contribute to the conservation and re-establishment of good health'. Roze de Chantoiseau, one of the founders of the French restaurant, was also a member of the salons, *deuxième division*. He may just have been one of the influences determining the diet of madame Geoffrin, founder of a salon – *première division* – who attributed her good health to 'a careful and parsimonious diet'.[27]

During the latter part of the eighteenth century, air quality also became a matter of public concern, providing another example of the positive consequences of the alliance between science, medicine and government. Sewers were filled in, roads were widened, medieval walls pulled down, all in the pursuit of clean and fresh air. The building boom during the last decades of the ancien regime reflected a new concern for the environment, at least for the rich. Henceforth, clean air, like wholesome food, would be available on a class basis. As usual, Sébastien Mercier proves to be our best guide. In his *Tableau de Paris*, he raises the case of the Parisian *hôtel Dieu*, where everything was 'pestilential, on account of its humid and airless atmosphere'. As a result, open wounds became gangrenous, Mercier explained, and one in five of the hospital's patients died. Mercier and his enlightened campaigners advocated the opening of windows in public hospitals and private houses, to improve public and private hygiene. Too many houses had 'magasins de corruption' – a wonderful euphemism for early toilets – from which 'infected vapours poured forth', with urine, faeces and other decaying matter thrown into the streets at night to poison entire neighbourhoods.[28] For Mercier, civilisation began at home, especially in the toilet. In fact, toilets – referred to as 'secret comforts' – had been introduced in Holland during the seventeenth century, prompting one cultural historian to conclude that 'The secretions of the body were being privatised along with the cogitations of the mind.' Daniel Roche has argued that other aspects of personal hygiene were also being affected, 'personal habits and methods of behaviour, linked to the wider use of lingerie, were being altered and diffused.'[29]

A final indication of the widespread concern for health was the campaign to move cemeteries from the centre of urban areas. In 1763, a royal decree had ordered new cemeteries to be opened outside the walls of Paris. By the 1780s, the fear of disease spreading from existing burial sites in the capital had created a campaign for the removal of human remains to sites outside the city walls. In 1787, Dr Francis Thiery published *La vie de l'homme respectée et défendue dans ses derniers moments*, a work that included a proposal for the building of mortuaries to prevent 'exhalations' from corpses. Once again,

Mercier joined the ranks of the enlightened, complaining about the 'cadaverous odours that one senses in every church'. He then allowed his vivid imagination to dwell on the 20,000 cadavers resting inside the walls of the capital and the funerals that had taken place over the past 1,200 years. The removal from churches of the bones of the dead is a poignant metaphor for the shift of medieval ideas relating to human beings, body and soul.[30]

Literacy and education

One of the most significant cultural changes to be recorded during the eighteenth century was a marked advance in literacy, associated with a massive expansion of primary education. Paradoxically, as we noted in chapter two, it was not the enlightened *philosophes* but the benighted servants of the Church who provided much of the impetus for change. Their objective, however, was certainly not to make Enlightenment literature accessible to the masses but 'to create Christians, teach the rudiments of the faith, and shape their moral character'.[31] The state, continually haunted by the spread of 'heresy' during the first half of the century, then forced to compete in an increasingly commercial and literate world, offered rather grudging support. Religion was far too important a method of social control to be left to Jansenists and Protestants, while the predatory progress of England on the world stage, highlighted by her historic victory during the Seven Years War, would prompt enlightened royalist ministers to recognise the need for radical change.

Only 29 per cent of adult males and just 14 per cent of the female population could sign their marriage registers around 1700. By 1789, these percentages had risen to 47 and 27 per cent respectively. If we analyse these statistics by region and social class, we find that, broadly speaking, 'northern and north-eastern France was able to read and write by the end of the eighteenth century, at a time when the other France was just embarking upon the process of catching up'. In a few departments of the west and south – Finistère, Ariège, Ardèche, Hautes-Pyrénées – literacy rates doubled, but from a very low base. In general terms, these changes sharpened the contrast between an increasingly literate and commercialised north and east, and a more backward and stagnant south and west.[32] The legendary 'two Frances', divided by a line running from Saint Malo in the west to Geneva in the east, was being created in the schoolroom and the market place. As Colin Jones has remarked, 'Intellectual exchange – *le commerce des esprits* – worked best among the literate and the urbane, social elite and in the kind of commercial society which France was fast becoming.'[33]

Winds of change were slow to blow through France's two dozen universities, encumbered as they were by their medieval and ecclesiastical inheritance. Senior academics frequently spent more time censoring heresy than stimulating intellectual exchange. The influence of the Jesuits was undermined by the attack on the Order during the early 1760s, but given the control exercised by the parlements over university affairs, Jesuits had never dominated university life, especially in Paris. It was the *collèges*, discussed in chapter two, which moved in the direction dictated by the winds of intellectual and commercial exchange: the number of students attending universities – around 13,000 in 1789 – did not change significantly over the century. As one might expect, recruitment to universities came predominantly from the sons of professional, office-holding families, especially for those taking up law – they represented 65 per cent of the students entering the university of Douai in the mid-1770s and 77 per cent of those at the university of Nancy between 1782 and 1789.[34] However, most bourgeois families sent their sons to *collèges*, the rich, legal bourgeoisie of Paris ensuring their own intellectual replication by choosing the famous *collèges* of Louis-le-Grand, Harcourt and Juilly. The 22 law faculties in France turned out around 1,000 law graduates each year. The rise of a more professionalised and commercialised society meant that theology became a less attractive option over the century. University degrees became the preserve of noble archbishops and bishops. Almost all French bishops by 1789 had taken not only the *baccalauréat en théologie*, but also the university *licence*. McManners suggests that there was an improvement in the quality of courses in theology, but concludes that the most glittering academic prizes went to candidates with the longest noble genealogy. By 1789, only one in ten of French *curés* had pursued a doctoral course.[35] Class divisions, again *within* the three orders of the realm, were widened by degrees of educational attainment, primarily favouring the rise, and strengthening the social and professional pre-eminence, of the bourgeoisie.

In most parts of the country, including rural areas in touch with urban commerce and culture, the slow but significant spread of literacy during the century stimulated, and was stimulated by, the shift from a medieval manuscript to a modern print culture. The official production of books increased perceptibly during the second half of the seventeenth century, from an average of around 200 a year in the 1700s to 300 in 1750, rising to 729 in 1764 and 896 in 1770. It then fell to 527 in 1780 as the more reactionary court circles endeavoured, Canute-like, to turn the tide. Confronted with a growing public demand for reading material, publishers began to produce cheap editions of what is currently referred to in France as *livres des poches*. Transferring the site of information – which was now being delivered increasingly through the medium of French not Latin – from the mouths of priests to the pages of a book which could be carried around in the public's pocket completed a cultural revolution that had spanned the fifteenth to the eighteenth centuries. Mercier, of course, was fully aware of the significance of this historic change, criticising the government for seeking to censor booksellers and poor *colporteurs*.[36] One of Robert Darnton's signal contributions to the 'history of the book' concerns the importance and extent of publications smuggled into France from abroad. The Swiss *Société typographique de Neuchâtel*, for example, supplied relatively cheap editions of best-sellers, official and unofficial, to any enterprising French bookseller. In 1778, one of their salesmen, Jean-François Favarger, 'travelled by horse, flogging encyclopaedias and everything else in the publisher's stock, for six months along an itinerary that went through nearly all the major towns of southern and central France'.[37]

After 1750, more bookshelves belonging to nobles and bourgeois, as well as the ledges of the more literate artisans and farmers, began to feature novels, travel books and works of natural history, rather than the traditional almanacs and 'lives of the saints'. Those belonging to the financially and culturally well endowed would have included many, if not all, of the 17 volumes of the *Encyclopédie*, as well as Voltaire's more popular tomes. Novels from the pen of the popular Madame Riccoboni, such as the *Lettres de Sophie*, 'which appealed to an educated but not especially highbrow readership', were not only bought, but actually read, especially by women. A wide class and gender cross-section of readers queued up for Rousseau's *Nouvelle Héloïse* and the *Confessions*, even after his death in 1778. A leading bookseller (and client of the Swiss *Société typographique*) in Reims, Alphonse Petit, was being pestered in the early 1780s for copies of the Abbé Raynal's *Histoire philosophique et politique des établissements et du commerce des européens dans les deux Indes* as well as for Mercier's *Tableau de Paris*. Significantly, both works were highly critical of the government. One merchant in Nantes said that his business colleagues, who were not, he admitted, avid readers, found Raynal's work moving as well as informative: 'reading him, you feel that your heart has been set on fire'.[38] It was a compliment often paid to Rousseau.

As is the case today, sex attracted many more readers than philosophy, though Darnton has argued that eighteenth-century 'dirty books', such as *Margot la ravadeuse*, *Les lauriers ecclésiastiques*, and the *Histoire de Dom B*, provided readers with the best of both worlds. The marquis de Sade would stand at the end of a distinguished line of eighteenth-century exponents of the 'liberationist' *philosophe-pornographe*, one that included both Diderot and Voltaire. If there was an increase in the number of pornographic works, there was a corresponding decrease in the number of religious publications, the stock-in-trade of the early eighteenth-century *colporteur*. One-third of all books printed in 1720 could be described as religious works, a percentage that fell to one-quarter by 1750 and to one-tenth by the 1780s. The clerical Cassandras of the Catholic Church were now lining-up in the pulpit to say, 'We told you so. More reading means less faith!' And more books on the market were only a part of the problem. There was also the increase in the number of newspapers, periodicals, pamphlets, broadsheets and local advertising *affiches* being published each year. Such publications reached that mass illiterate and semi-literate audience accustomed to being lectured at from the pulpit, but which was now eager to hear someone read to them about current political intrigues, financial scandals, highway robberies and, of course, Marie Antoinette's 'outrageous sex-life' and equally outrageously expensive diamond necklaces. This is not to say that the eighteenth-century equivalents of today's tabloids had made a real impact upon the general public by 1789. Reading was not the favourite pastime of physically exhausted farmers. The 1790–92 enquiry into peasant reading material by the indefatigable abbé Grégoire found that politics and crime still came a poor second to the traditional material of the *Bibliothèque bleu* – pious works, almanacs and books on magic.[39] (We should, perhaps, question the validity of Grégoire's enquiry since it was a foolish peasant who told abbés the truth about what they read, thought and heard!)

The impact of cultural change upon the countryside must remain something of a mystery: certainly, for the mass of the poorer peasantry, the ability to read or write was not paramount. For the richer urban artisan, the landed, professional, administrative and commercial bourgeoisie, as well as for many of the sons of aristocratic families, on the other hand, education became almost as important by the second half of the eighteenth century as birth or wealth. Those who were most interested in court politics continued to subscribe to France's official newspaper, the *Gazette de France* (first published in the 1630s); those who thought God came first took either the Jansenist *Nouvelles ecclésiastiques*, or the more establishment, Jesuit periodical, the *Mémoires de Trévoux*. After 1750, such publications had to compete with more controversial periodicals such as Fréron's *Année littéraire*, which appeared eight times a year and ran from 1754 to 1790. Jack Censer has suggested that handwritten *nouvelles à la main*, like the *Correspondance secrète* and the *Espion anglais*, frequently provided the most forthright political coverage. During the last decades of the ancien regime, lawyers began to convert private scandals into public *causes célèbres*, shaping opinion by publishing accounts of judicial cases. As for newspapers and pamphlets, their revolutionary impact, according to Jeremy Popkin, was not really to be felt until the Revolution. The number of newspapers did increase from five in 1750 to 19 by 1785, but most of these, like the *Courrier du Bas-Rhin*, were published abroad. The number of periodicals, on the other hand, increased four-fold (to 80) during the same period. It is worth repeating, however, that, especially in the countryside, 'Orality, acting as a form of interpretation, had to be very, very prevalent.'[40]

The 'book of the Enlightenment' was, of course, the *Encyclopédie*: 'it stands as one of the great achievements of the human spirit and the written word'.[41] Begun in 1751, it comprised 17 volumes of text and 11 volumes of plates when it was finished 21 years later. It was to be printed, reprinted, pirated and counterfeited, incarcerated in the Bastille and then reprieved to become one of the world's iconic publications. Its stature as a monument to European scholarship is reflected in the fact that, today, its articles are cited far more frequently than they are read. It transformed its publisher, Charles Panckoucke, into France's first press baron. The Herculean labours in commissioning and organising the 70,000 or so articles included in the *Encyclopédie* almost drove its chief editor, Denis Diderot, mad. Jean d'Alembert, his co-editor at the beginning of the venture, had the good sense to retire before signs of his own possible insanity became evident.

One of the 'turning-points at which the Bourbon monarchy failed to turn' was the seizure and 'imprisonment' of 6,000 copies of the *Encyclopédie* in 1770, part of chancellor Maupeou's 'despotism'. For Maupeou, as well as for a few of the more enlightened ministers of the crown, the prioritisation of reason over revealed truth threatened the very foundations of the Bourbon monarchy, as reconstituted by Louis XIV. One of the main objectives of the *Encyclopédie* was, indeed, to break the link that united throne and altar, adopting, as its main tool, the methodology of science and reason. Man was defined in relation to Nature, his work and thoughts directed towards the improvement of individuals on earth, rather than their chances of everlasting life in heaven. This was an epochal shift, its long-term dynamic energised by the post-Renaissance European scientific and intellectual revolution. The *Encyclopédie* may not have had the sociological and theoretical coherence of Marx's *Das Kapital*, and it certainly did not have as its principal objective the revolutionary aim of politicising the masses. Its appearance, however, constituted a revolutionary moment in the intellectual and secular history of Europe and parts of the wider world.

The eventual release (in 1774) of copies of the *Encyclopédie* from the Bastille revealed that many highly placed and influential figures, belonging to both throne and altar, had tasted the forbidden fruit and found it to be bittersweet. It is hardly surprising that, given its original price of 980 *livres* for the folio edition – or even its bargain basement offer of 289 *livres* for the quarto edition – subscribers to the *Encyclopédie* constituted a 'heteregenous public of nobles, clerics, and that group usually described as the non-Marxist, *bourgeoisie d'ancien régime'*.[42] From the outset, its fate had depended upon the favourable reactions of Louis XV's mistress, madame de Pompadour, and the minister responsible for censorship, Malesherbes, both of whom, for very different reasons, were convinced that if the monarchy were to survive it simply could not ignore the advance of scientific and technological knowledge. Many *philosophes*, as well as a handful of government ministers and advisers, realised this and fought to protect those critics who wanted to reconstruct the monarchical house that Louis XIV had built, not raze it to the ground. It has to be remembered that the majority of French Catholic intellectuals, and not just the Jansenists, had many quarrels to pick with the Church of Rome. It is all too easy to caricature sincere Catholics such as Henri-Léonard Bertin, one of Louis XV's favourite and longest-serving ministers, as religious fundamentalists, or *dévots*, when they were, in fact, outspoken critics of the papacy and those at court who denounced all *philosophes* and physiocrats as lost souls. We shall examine this important issue in more detail in the following chapter.

It is important to note at this point, however, that the ramifications of the cultural upheaval that shook mid- to late eighteenth century French society extended far beyond adverse reactions to the works of eminent *philosophes*. Many of the latter were little more than erudite *rapporteurs* of what was being discussed in the emerging 'public sphere', the salons, provincial academies, freemason lodges, coffee shops and reading rooms. This is what really worried the profoundly paternalist government of Louis XV, this increasing tendency on the part of many social and intellectual groups, *recruited from an expanding social base* to institutionalise their opposition to certain government policies, in other words, to say in public what they had long thought in private.

Ever since Alexis de Tocqueville argued in *The Ancien Regime and the Revolution* that the phenomenon of intellectuals creating an alternative power base (outside the traditional sites covered by the monarchy) marked a significant stage in the collapse of the ancien regime, controversy has surrounded the concept of a new 'public opinion' that operated within a new 'public sphere'. For some historians, institutionalised public voices had been heard during the Renaissance, echoing those famous orators of the Greek city states; for others, they were present in the private clubs of the late seventeenth century, such as the *Académie de Luxembourg*. Roger Chartier has argued that it was the physiocrats, not the *philosophes*, who refined the idea of 'public opinion', replacing woolly references to Paris as 'le mâitre de l'opinion publique' with the notion of opinion as something that had been tested and clarified through a process of critical public discussion.[43] But it was Jürgen Habermas who really put the Marxist cat among the liberal, cultural pigeons by associating the mid-eighteenth century public sphere with the expanding capitalist and commercial bourgeoisie. For Habermas, true public opinion could only be expressed in the new public sphere, 'an intermediary structure between the political system . . . and the private sectors'. Only when this had taken place were people able to 'reach a reasoned consensus worthy of the name of public opinion'. It took a generation for Habermas's thesis (first published in German in 1962) to awaken the critical spirit of Anglo-Saxon historians, but, once digested, it provoked wide-ranging and fruitful discussion.[44]

The most fashionable building that had been constructed in the new public sphere was the salon, in which bourgeois *savoir-faire* combined with noble *savoir-vivre* to produce a unique blend of wit, polite conversation and intellectual exchange. Hélvetius described this distinctive genre of French philosophy as 'the art of dilating on everything without wasting one's time becoming an expert on any one thing'. It was customary for influential and intelligent women to preside over the proceedings of the salon. Madame Geoffrin's reunions met in her luxurious mansion in the fashionable rue Saint Honoré on Wednesdays. It was madame Geoffrin who helped d'Alembert, co-editor of the *Encyclopédie*, become a member of the prestigious *Académie Française*, suggesting, rightly, that the salon belonged more to the aristocratic past than to the democratic future. Daniel Gordon places an intriguing, through not always convincing, spin on this notion, arguing that the idea of progress itself may be traced back to the conversation-pieces of the salons. For many cultural historians, attracted to what has been termed 'the linguistic turn', language, discourse and a 'culture of civility', possessed the power to shape ideologies.[45]

Gordon's work – which rejects simplistic linkages between the Enlightenment salons of the 1760s and the Jacobin popular societies of the 1790s – does address the important question raised by Daniel Roche: how did the conversation-pieces of the salon – uttered in very comfortable surroundings – influence the wider public? The answer is necessarily complicated, predicated, as it is, upon the atomised nature of these 'fluid and fleeting' gatherings of intellectuals and their camp followers. Those who attended madame Geoffrin's salon were not always the regulars seen at the reunions organised by madame Lespinasse, or the dinners held by madame du Deffand, the latter's aunt and sometime protector. Nonetheless, it is argued, the salons were important in the general dissemination of new ideas and the spread of the critical spirit of enquiry. They may have been unduly influenced by the aristocratic past, but they were certainly not isolated from the emerging capitalist and commercial society that was changing the world around them. Indeed, commercial exchanges are said to have facilitated democratic opinions. It is also important to note the evolution of the salon as the reign of Louis XV gave way to that of his successor. The comte de Ségur was one of many who acknowledged the shift from aristocratic *sensibilité* to bourgeois practicality: 'our *moeurs*', he wrote, 'become less frivolous, but also less polite . . . Politics gained from this, but society lost.' This was a genteel way of saying that increasing numbers of ordinary people were beginning to walk more freely through the marbled halls of the aristocratic *cité*.[46]

Between the publication of Diderot and d'Alembert's *Encyclopédie* in the 1750s and 1760s and the appearance of Charles Panckoucke's more manageable *Encyclopédie méthodique* on the eve of the Revolution, knowledge became far more institutionalised, compartmentalised and commodified, yet another route leading to a more democratic society. Learned societies and academies were founded in almost every large provincial town, extending the boundaries of the public sphere. Of the 73 principal contributors to Panckoucke's *Encyclopédie méthodique*, 15 belonged to the *Académie des sciences*, 7 to the more prestigious *Académie française*, 8 to the *Société royale d'agriculture*, and 18 to the *Société royale de médecine*.[47] Montpellier's *Académie des sciences* published its proceedings and met once a week to discuss 'religion, fossils, phlogiston, and the latest discoveries on everything from geography to anatomy'. By 1789, 75 per cent of provincial towns with populations of over 20,000 inhabitants included an academy within their walls.[48] Tens of thousands of self-styled *gens de lettres* were now members of the hundreds of academies, museums and literary and agricultural societies that opened their doors each year. There were six libraries and reading rooms in Nantes alone, patronised, in the main by merchants and shipowners. *La France profonde* was gradually changing into *La France un peu savante*, especially in the towns.

In Margaret Jacob's opinion, modern civil society was invented during the Enlightenment in these new enclaves of sociability, 'of which freemasony was the most avowedly constitutional and aggressively civic'. And not only did freemasonry play a constructive role in turning savants into citizens, it also helped to democratise the public sphere. In the first place, freemason lodges were, according to Jacob, mainly secular bodies. Government ministers distrusted 'secret societies', whether patronised by freemasons or journeymen, because it was in these institutions that the oaths and rituals ordinarily associated with religion were transmuted into secular and democratic form. Freemasons established constitutional forms of self-government, complete with laws, elections and representatives; they were cells of modern democracy. It was true that aristocrats, even princes of the blood such as the duc d'Orléans, presided over national freemasonry organisations, but it should be noted that, during the Revolution, the royalist duc d'Orléans would be reborn as the republican 'Philippe Egalité'! As early as the 1740s, the Grand Master had announced that freemasons, including 'men as diverse and humble as gardeners, Negro trumpeters, and small merchants' would combine to form 'in the course of time a totally spiritual nation, where without denigrating from the various duties required by different states [or conditions], one [nevertheless] creates a new people'. This caveat concerning social rank and place was typical of pre-Revolutionary radical discourse. In the new, still monarchist, 'republic of all the virtues', everyone would still be required to know their place in society.[49] 'Open discourse', like truth, was revolutionary, the most democratic form of social intercourse, one that could not, eventually, be confined to the palaces of princes or the salons of *philosophes*. And there would be around a thousand lodges in France, with between 50,000 and 100,000 members, by 1789.

Philosophes and the people

Since the relationship between power and *le peuple* provides the main focus of this work, it is appropriate that we should end this chapter with an explanation of the attitude of the *philosophes* towards *le peuple* in general and women in particular. To reach any meaningful conclusion we must appreciate, in the first place, the difficulty of drawing rigid lines between 'elite' and 'popular' cultures; secondly, we need to remind ourselves of Jonathan Israel's contention that the Enlightenment was a diverse movement, characterised, for Israel, by its Newtonian, neo-Cartesian, Leibnitio-Wolffian and radical divisions rather than by its unity; and, thirdly, that time and circumstance altered the agenda of the *philosophes* and their supporters, the concerns of Voltaire in the 1750s being substantially different from those of Condorcet in 1789.[50]

On the first issue, Pieter Spierenburg is one of those who argue, convincingly, that sharp contrasts between elite and popular cultures are inadmissible, given the permeability and diversity of ancien regime social groups and the distinction between Parisian and provincial cultures, as well as that between urban and rural cultures. It is, nonetheless, possible to identify certain broad, characteristic features of what Spierenberg refers to as the 'greater tradition' of the ruling elites as opposed to the 'lesser tradition' of popular culture – for example, the importance of the family, the village *communauté* and the church.[51] Popular responses and attitudes had developed over centuries; they were not 'a piece of soft wax' upon which the *philosophes* could make their mark'.[52] In his work on artisans and journeymen, Michael Sonenscher has drawn our attention to the importance they attached to legal precedents and civil jurisprudence, concluding that, in a sense, they formed 'the other face of the Enlightenment: a body of commonplace rhetoric, established doctrine and familiar platitudes . . . a silent counterpoint to the programmes, projects and public manifestos produced by its Enlightenment critics'.[53] For the masses, the daily struggle for survival, their limited cultural and intellectual reference points, the many tongues in which they spoke, all militated against cultural unity. Although the culture of the Catholic Church was deeply embedded in the countryside, the post-Tridentine Church's broader mission during the seventeenth and eighteenth centuries – to acculturate the masses and maintain their subordinate place in society – was never a complete success. As for the influence of the Voltaires and the Diderots, Gabriel Audisio believes that 'the countryside hardly participated in the *siècle des Lumières*'.[54]

Audisio's comment may be exaggerated, but it is true that the *conservative* Enlightenment had very little to say to peasants: most mid-century *philosophes* wrote them off, literally and metaphorically, until such time as the Goddess of Reason could spread her wings over the countryside. This attitude was not dissimilar to that held by propertied educated white elites in Africa and southern America towards illiterate and semi-literate peasants until recent decades: 'the vote, yes, but not in our lifetime'. It was Voltaire, the seigneur of Ferney, who wrote that '*le peuple* should be instructed and not educated. They are not capable of being educated. It seems to me that there is a place in society for ignorant beggars.'[55] Many of the invaluable plates in Diderot's *Encyclopédie* relating to the world of work reveal an enthusiasm for reducing the input of skilled labour; many of the articles referring to working people provide evidence of that 'class distinction which lay at the heart of the *Encyclopédie*'.[56] Hierarchies of labour were calibrated with reference to education and intelligence. The entry on *artisans* includes the following: 'one says of a good cobbler that he is a good artisan, but one says of a good watchmaker that he is a great *artiste*'. Interestingly, the entry for *le peuple* explains how its meaning had changed over time. In past centuries, it explains, the term was used to describe 'the most useful, the most valuable, the most respectable part of the nation' but, things had allegedly changed by the 1750s: '*le peuple* now refers only to workers (*ouvriers*) and farm workers (*laboureurs*) who live in cottages and work from dawn to dusk'. It is, however, typical of the *Encyclopédie* that we should hear the occasional dissonant note in this dominant theme of elite contempt for working people. 'Why can't we ensure that they have some time for leisure?', the author of the entry on *le peuple* asks, 'time to travel a little for these workers who are crippled by work and taxes and who have no spare time to think?' Finally, the term *citoyen* appears in the *Encylopédie* and is defined as 'a bourgeois', an intelligent property-owner capable of filling a post on a municipality, thus excluding 'the great unwashed'. We shall argue that it was the half-hearted attempt to include the latter in the political process during the Jacobin Terror that finally destroyed the fragile alliance of the bourgeoisie and *le peuple* that had characterised the opening years of the Revolution. Democracy would prove too heady a potion for the emerging French bourgeoisie to swallow in 1789.

The above comments on elite attitudes towards *le peuple* provide supporting evidence for the argument that the Enlightenment did not always speak with one voice. One significant exception to this rule concerns attitudes towards women: on this there was more unanimity. In the *Encyclopédie* the word *femme* is defined as 'the partner of a husband', adding that 'all European laws and customs agree that authority is vested in the husband. A wife must necessarily be subordinate to her husband and obey his orders.' We are even informed that Moses never referred to a woman's soul! In his didactic novel *Emile*, Rousseau argued that men had only been saddled with short sentences behind their gender bars, whilst women had been sentenced to life imprisonment: 'the male is male only at certain moments; the female is female for life'.[57] Montesquieu, an ambivalent advocate of women's rights, does object to the 'enslavement, subordination and ideological humiliation' of women in the *Lettres persanes*, but, in the same work, he condemns the frivolous lives of aristocratic women and the petticoat politics in which they indulge. In book three, chapter nine of his famous *Esprit des lois,* he argues that 'Paternal authority is and should be perpetuated in the marital power of the husband, just as it was in Roman Law'. Diderot thought that women were physiologically unstable, slaves to their biological sexuality and related passions. Madeline Gutwirth makes the appropriate association between Diderot's emancipatory notions on sexuality in his *Supplément à Bougainville* and eighteenth-century bourgeois morality in general, concluding that 'both regard female sexuality and procreation as the domains to be recontained, to be tamed'.[58] For the majority of the *philosophes*, hell had no fury like a woman aroused!

These dismissive and often demeaning attitudes towards women on the part of the *philosophes* were buttressed by the prevailing corpus of eighteenth-century scientific 'knowledge'. According to Thomas Laqueur, a 'rising cultural status for science and medicine allowed the "truths of biology" to replace divinely ordained hierarchies and immemorial custom as the bases for the creation or redistribution of power relations between men and women'.[59] Perhaps 'reinforce' rather than 'replace' would be more accurate, since the subordination, the 'otherness' of women, continued to be deeply embedded in the teachings of the Catholic Church. Nonetheless, it was the reconceptualisation of women's minds, bodies and social roles that Mary Wollstonecraft would condemn in her *Rights of Women*. With Stenon and de Graaf's discovery in 1673 that women possessed ovaries, active, procreative power seemed to have slipped away from men. It was not long, however, before Leuwenboeck and Hartseeker employed their microscopes to discover that Aristotle had been right all along – it was the male sperm that contained 'pre-formed' human beings.[60] A women's body was once again relegated to the position of a foetal container.

The contemporary notion that women possessed rights over their own bodies was one that would have been laughed out of church. If a child was 'unwanted', and, for obvious reasons, this was not uncommon, especially among the poor, it was invariably the woman who had to confront the harrowing choice of aborting or abandoning her child. Jacques Gélis is not sure whether the increase in abortions from the sixteenth century was actually the result of more cases being reported to the authorities or not, but, whatever the truth, the darkest 'secrètes funestes' of the ancien regime were not related to private contraceptive methods, but to the variety of methods adopted to get rid of children by parents who could not afford to raise them. Gélis notes that statistics on infanticide are notoriously difficult to obtain and evaluate, but that those relating to abandonment are 'frightening'. More than 400,000 infants were dumped in the Maison de la Couche in Paris between 1670 and 1789, with a peak year in 1772 of over 7,000. It was not only the 'spectre of the child' that hung over the Enlightenment, but the spectre of women dying during and after childbirth. The duc de Saint-Simon suggests in his memoirs that the wife of one of Louis XIV's ministers, Jérôme de Pontchartrain, died at 29 following the birth of her sixth child because the couple had had too many children too quickly.[61] It was a tragedy that was to be repeated a thousand times during the eighteenth century, and for long afterwards. How many thousands of women, from the duchesse d'Orléans to poor peasants, died following childbirth, often having been 'bled' by a physician? 'La maladie des femmes', indeed!

Intellectual elites were obviously not ignorant of the sheer scale of the personal tragedies suffered by women. The case against the majority of *philosophes*, including Voltaire and Diderot, is that they employed their favourite weapons, Reason and Nature, not just to maintain, but to legitimise on 'scientific' grounds, the subordinate position of women in society; to give secular benediction, in fact, to received theological and biological wisdom on the matter. Dorinda Outram, emphasising the widely acknowledged contradiction between the universal and the particular values held by the *philosophes*, reminds us of the debates 'that focused on the physical constitution of the female sex and on the importance of women's role as mothers.' In these debates, she writes, 'science and medicine contributed an increasingly important voice'.[62]

The conservative wing of the Enlightenment did little to advance the claims of the poor to a real stake in power: it did even less to advance society's conception of women from that ordained by Saint Augustine well over a millenium earlier. Augustine constructed a tripartite world: 'One, the greatest, is the universal world of which we are the particles . . . the other two, the smaller superior world of man, and the smaller inferior world of women.' [63] Merry Wiesner is right. According to the elites who ran France: 'Women's subjection was inherent in their very being and was present from creation . . . Most reformers accepted Eve's principal responsibility for the Fall.'[64] When it came to the poor in general, and women in particular, the *philosophes*, for all their anticlericalism, did very little to raise them above the status they are accorded in the New Testament.

Suggested reading

Allen, P.L. *The Wages of Sin: Sex and Disease, Past and Present* (Chicago, 2000).

Cowans, J. 'Habermas and French History: the Public Sphere and the Problem of Political Legitimacy', *French History* Vol 13 (1992).

Farr, J. *Sexuality and Authority in Burgundy, 1550–1730* (Oxford, 1995).

Hunt, L. 'The Many Bodies of Marie Antoinette', in L. Hunt (ed.) *Eroticism and the Body Politic* (London, 1991).

Jacob, M. *Living the Enlightenment: Freemasonry and Politics in Eighteenth-Century Europe* (Oxford, 1991).

McManners, J. *Death and the Enlightenment: Christians and Unbelievers in Eighteenth-Century France* (Oxford, 1981).

O'Day, R. *The Family and Family Relationships, 1500–1900* (New York, 1994).

Outram, D. *The Enlightenment* (Cambridge, 1995).

Popkin, J. *Revolutionary News: The Press in France, 1789–99* (London, 1990).

Porter, R. *The Enlightenment* (London, 1990).

Ramsay, M. *Professional and Popular Medicine in France, 1770–1830: The Social World of Medical Practice* (Cambridge, 1988).

Chapter 7

'Enlightenments' and the state

During one of the more depressing periods of the Seven Years War (1756–63) with England, Louis XV asked his controller general, Henri Bertin, what he might do to rally support in the country. Bertin answered: 'Sire, we must inoculate the French with *l'esprit chinois'*. The comment appears to be flippant, but Bertin was serious. His 30-year long correspondence with a group of French Jesuit missionaries in Peking constitutes an important contribution to the European Enlightenment. It also provides us with a remarkable insight into the mindset of one of Louis XV's key ministers at a time when crucial decisions affecting the nature of Bourbon absolutism were being taken. We should not underestimate the importance of the 'Chinese connection', for Bertin was by no means alone in his passion for all things Chinese, especially Confucian philosophy. Leading *philosophes* and physiocrats, from Leibnitz to Quesnay, cited Chinese government, philosophy and economics as models to be imitated by Europeans. There was nothing remarkable about this, given that, between 1735 and 1799, China was ruled by the 'Celestial Emperor', Kien-long, arguably the greatest Emperor in Chinese history. To many European politicians and *philosophes*, Kien-Long, who ruled a country with a population ten times as great as that of France, appeared to be the very model of a 'modern' Enlightened Despot. He was regarded as a ruler whose success might provide a solution to the great, political puzzle of the eighteenth century – how to initiate radical reform without destabilising the political and social foundations of absolute monarchy. Defeat in the Seven Years War with Britain provided fertile ground for a reassessment of the fundamental principles upon which the French monarchy rested.[1]

During the 1760s, the duc de Choiseul would struggle to introduce a liberal reform movement designed to rescue the monarchy from the humiliating defeat of the Seven Years War. England, moving in the direction of free trade and aristocratic, constitutional government, would be the model for Choiseul, not China. His ultimate aim, however, was also to strengthen the defences of a monarchy under siege, even if this meant unpalatable compromises with princes of the blood, parlements and provincial estates, all demanding to have their voices heard in the new public arena. Boosting the economy through free trade measures would eventually increase the fiscal strength of the Crown, taxes being the lifeblood of a regime that rested ultimately, upon its capacity to wage war. Reforms of the army and navy represented the flip side of Choiseul's programme of post-war reconstruction, with a war of revenge against England as a not too distant prize. But what of the reaction of the millions of urban and rural workers who would be obliged to suffer the consequences of free-trade policies? A more effective and national programme of repression, comparable to the 'Great Confinement' of the 1720s, would have to be introduced by modernising and expanding the forerunner of today's *Gendarmerie Nationale*, the *maréchaussée*. However, Choiseul would fail to win the unqualified support either of the king or of the aristocratic cliques that continued to dominate court life. His policies would also precipitate one of the most widespread manifestations of social unrest during the eighteenth century, a more important cause behind the resort to 'Maupeou's despotism' in 1770 than many historians have suggested.

Choiseul and the lessons of defeat

On the world stage, an incoherent foreign policy during the 1730s and 1740s had exposed the fundamental dilemma that would continue to confront France until the decolonisation of European empires in the 1950s – was she, primarily, a continental or a colonial power? The wars of the Polish and Austrian Successions had revealed a return to the priorities that had characterised the foreign policy of Louis XIV – dynastic interests and the increasing influence at court of the traditional nobility of the sword.[2] The Polish War (1733–5) had begun with a conflict between the French and Russian governments over the succession to the Polish throne, which the French lost. It ended in something of a stalemate. Louis XV failed to secure the Polish throne for his son-in-law, Stanislas, who was granted the province of Lorraine as a consolation prize until it passed to France in the 1760s. The most significant shift in European relations was the rapprochement between Austria and France that led to the Third Treaty of Vienna in 1738, a 'diplomatic revolution' in the making, since Austria had always been regarded as France's principal enemy.

The War of the Austrian Succession (1740–8) revealed further shifts in the European balance of power. In the first place, there was the emergence of Prussia as a Great Power under Frederick the Great. It was Frederick's seizure of the Austrian province of Silesia in December 1740, just a few weeks after the 23-year-old Maria-Theresa had ascended the Austrian throne, that changed the European scene for ever. Faithful – for the last time during the ancien regime – to the traditional policy of Louis XIV, France had allied herself to Prussia, hoping to prevent Maria-Theresa's husband, the son of the duke of Tuscany, being crowned as Holy Roman Emperor. The relative decline of the House of Habsburg was accentuated by the accession of the French candidate, Charles Albert of Bavaria, the first non-Habsburg to wear the imperial crown in three centuries (although Austria, under Maria-Theresa, would eventually regain control over who wore this rather tarnished crown). Early campaigns had boosted the stock at Versailles of the comte de Belle-Île, but the fortunes of war had swung against the French as England won the battle of Dettingen (27 June 1743) and an Austrian offensive reconquered lost territory. The duc de Richelieu had tried to turn the tide by supporting the invasion of Britain by the Jacobite Pretender, Charles Edward Stuart, in 1745, but futile, romantic gestures were going out of fashion. Fortunately, the much-celebrated French victory at the battle of Fontenoy on 11 May 1745, together with the successful manoeuvres of the cautious Marshal Saxe in the Netherlands, meant that France emerged from the war with her head held high, even though her pockets were empty.

Long before the Treaty of Aix-la-Chapelle had ended the war on 18 October 1748, the more perceptive of Louis XV's ministers had begun to realise that France was deploying too many of her resources on the continent. In a revealing *mémoire politique* from the minister of the navy, Maurepas, in September 1745, the king was told that national greatness increasingly depended upon income from world trade. To triumph in Europe, France would have to challenge England overseas. As we saw in chapter four, France had been constructing a colonial empire since the seventeenth century, although the marked expansion of her overseas trade only dated from the 1720s. During the following decades, many French possessions abroad had been fortified, including Louisbourg on Cape Breton (the island that guarded the approach to the cod fishing-grounds off Newfoundland); the forts that stretched along the eastern bank of the Mississippi river in the American colonies; and Pondicherry, France's principal trading-post in India.[3] But French weakness abroad was not just military or commercial, it was demographic: she had only 60,000, as opposed to England's 1.5 million, colonists in North America, and England's aggressive policies had ensured that the theatre of conflict would now be global. The Treaty of Aix-la-Chapelle would prove to be but a staging post on the way to the real 'first world war', better known as the Seven Years War.

Reasons of state dictated that more money would now be spent on the navy in order to protect the colonies. By the 1750s, 60 per cent of the budget intended for the armed forces in England went to the navy. In direct contrast, the minister who had pressed hardest for increased funds for the French navy, Maurepas, had been dismissed in 1749 by a court cabal led by the duc de Richelieu and a new court favourite, madame de Pompadour. Pompadour would play a significant, though not decisive, role in securing the 'Diplomatic Revolution' that would finally tie France to her traditional enemy, Austria, until the Revolution of 1789.[4] The first Treaty of Versailles between the two powers was announced on 1 May 1756, just three months after England and Prussia had signed the Convention of Westminster. It would prove to be a disaster for France. Instead of spending money on rebuilding the navy, France would now have to provide 100,000 men and 30 million *livres* in subsidies to help Austria regain Silesia! But Louis had been hankering after an Austrian alliance for some time, the only way, according to the king, to obtain a lasting peace and maintain the Catholic religion. We should remember that for Louis XV peace and the defence of the Catholic religion were matters of considerable personal importance, especially as the fear of death began to take precedence over the frenzy of sex.

During the 1750s, however, peace proved to be elusive, given Pitt the Elder's determination that Britannia should rule the waves and Frederick the Great's determination that Austria should be cut down to his size. The Seven Years War would provide definitive proof that France did not have the necessary reserves of men and money to fight on the seas, in the colonies and on the continent. Despite notable victories, such as that against German troops at Minden on 1 August 1759, she would emerge extremely bloody, if not completely bowed. Three battles, in three different theatres of war, would change the course of world history between 1756 and 1763: the battle of Plassey in India in June 1757, which guaranteed that an English flag – albeit hoisted on an East Indies Company pole – would replace the *fleur de lys* in the Indian subcontinent; the battle of Rossbach on 5 November 1757, when the French army was defeated by a Prussian force half its size; and General Wolfe's triumph over the marquis de Montcalm at Quebec on 13 September 1759, which opened the way for English domination of what is now Canada. Over the next few decades, the English East Indies flag would replace its French equivalent along the quaysides of Canton, and influence over China would be all but lost, at least for a century. Cartographers were already beginning to colour their maps of the world in red.

The Seven Years War would not only change global balances of power, it would also place a question mark over the survival of the Bourbon state. However, the Treaty of Paris that officially ended the war on 10 February 1763 proved to be far less disastrous than France had feared, thanks, in part, to the negotiating skills of that feisty, intelligent minister of foreign affairs, Etienne-François, duc de Choiseul. France lost Canada and the island of Cape Breton, her settlements east of the Mississippi, Grenada, Saint-Vincent, Dominica and Tobago in the Caribbean, Senegal in Africa and almost all of her conquests in India, as well as those in the German states of Hanover, Hesse and Brunswick. Minorca was returned to the English, and the huge French territory of Louisiana ceded to Spain. Serious as these losses were, France still retained her rights to fish for cod off Newfoundland, together with the islands of Saint-Pierre and Miquelon. The far more lucrative sugar and coffee islands of Guadeloupe and Martinique were returned to France, along with Cayenne and Guyana. Finally, France was also allowed to retain footholds in several Indian trading posts, as well as control of the slaving port on the island of La Gorée off Senegal. France remained a maritime, colonial and slaving power of some stature.[5]

In 1761, the duc de Choiseul had added the portfolios of the navy and the army to his control of foreign affairs. Far from being daunted by this unprecedented accretion of power, he appeared to revel in them, just as he revelled in accumulating massive wealth, mistresses and enemies at court. His partnership with madame de Pompadour, the equally intelligent pageant-mistress of the Versailles follies, who had deserted the king's bed to make room for sexier models, confirmed that court politics continued to be discussed in the boudoir as well as the boardroom. Choiseul's personal plan for the reconstruction of the monarchy was founded, in large measure, upon an imitation of those English virtues that had proved their value in the Seven Years War – popular patriotism, a French version of 'parliamentary govern-ment' and free trade where appropriate. He realised that the Seven Years War had produced a new form of patriotism, 'formulated with the assistance of a modern vocabulary', one that was being used in the expanding public sphere. Conscious that France had to reform or die, Choiseul embarked upon a policy of 'transparence', working in harmony with the new phenomenon of an increasingly literate and informed public opinion. In his recent bio-graphy of Choiseul, Chaussinand-Nogaret actually refers to him as one of the founding fathers of the French Left! Although anachronistic, this provocat-ive claim does, at least, focus attention on the fundamental political battle of the 1760s – reform *à l'anglaise* or reaction *à la monarchie Louis quatorzième*.[6]

To achieve his goals, Choiseul sought the assistance of selected *philosophes* and physiocrats. If the Seven Years War marks a turning point in the political and military history of the ancien regime, it also signals a new phase in the history of the Enlightenment. Early *philosophes*, such as Montesquieu and Voltaire, had been anti-war and pro-English. Voltaire had even been a pen-sioner of Frederick the Great, responsible for the massive humiliation of the French army at Rossbach in 1757. However, after the initial shocks of defeat, war would create a new spirit of patriotic nationalism, eroding much of the support enjoyed by the *philosophes*. In addition, fate – or the thickness of the king's clothing – had decreed that, in January 1757, an attempt to assassin-ate Louis XV would fail. Some Jansenists accused their 'international' Jesuit opponents of encouraging the assassin – a poor, domestic servant named Damiens – to commit an act of regicide; others suggested that the 'impious and immoral' opinions of the *philosophes* were to blame. It is more likely that poverty and misery explain Damiens's action, as he insisted. A massive crowd had gathered to watch the wretched man being tortured and chopped up in public, as if his terrible suffering and blood might expiate the sins of a regime that had lost its street credibility. The grisly, royal show did help to secure a new, temporary, lease of popularity for the king. However, it would also embitter relations between Choiseul's faction and the *dévôts* as the Jesuit

175

Order, which had made far too many enemies amongst the members of the parlements and the *philosophes*, was accused of being Damiens's mentor. By 1764, the Jesuits would be expelled from public life, much to the chagrin of the *dévôt* faction.

The Damiens affair jolted the government into adopting a more aggressive stance. It began by enlisting many more talented propagandists and playwrights to discredit its enemies. In October 1757, the favourite royal propagandist, Jacob Moreau, had published his clever, vicious satire on what he called 'les cacouacs' (Greek for malicious troublemakers) – a 'savage nation' of *philosophes* and their acolytes who allegedly lived in a mythical world of their own making. D'Alembert wrote to Voltaire to say that Moreau's work would prove to be just the beginning of an 'atrocious campaign' against them. He was right. In his contributions to the monarchist *Moniteur français*, Moreau now insisted that to be a true citizen one also had to be a patriot. On 2 May 1760, Charles Palissot's play, *Les philosophes*, also ridiculed the intellectual pretensions of the latter. In one of the scenes, a servant (who had just read one of Rousseau's works praising 'the natural savage') enters on all fours, eating a lettuce! The play, produced at the *Comédie-Francaise*, proved to be a howling success.[7]

The fact that criticism of Voltaire is muted in Palissot's play, underlines the many divisions within the *philosophe* camp, some of which were replicated among ministers at Versailles: both Palissot and Voltaire lined up with Choiseul. D'Alembert had already dismissed Voltaire as a political chameleon, 'Monsieur Multiforme', while Rousseau and Voltaire had learned to hate each other's innards over the years. Didier Masseau is absolutely right to place Rousseau, by the 1760s, in 'the anti-*philosophe*' camp.[8] Choiseul was clever enough to exploit these divisions. He and madame de Pompadour were sympathetic to many of the ideas popularised by the moderate, *conservative* wing of the Enlightenment. Voltaire had long favoured the cause of a strong monarchy. He had begged Choiseul to give him some diplomatic mission, and was occasionally writing propaganda on behalf of the government. For his part, Choiseul was a cynic, an agnostic at best, or, as Voltaire put it, 'He is one of us', explaining that 'The cause of the king is the cause of the *philosophes*.' It is little wonder that Choiseul made bitter enemies among the *dévôt* faction, which included the queen, for whom the Roman Catholic Church provided, in theory at least, the necessary, moral foundation for the nation.

Choiseul preferred patriotism to prayer. He surfed the waves of resentment and humiliation that followed the defeat of the Seven Years War to create a new sense of national identity, beginning with the armed forces. The legislation he introduced between 10 December 1762 and 1 May 1768 was a bold attempt to 'nationalise' a disparate collection of aristocratic, semi-private army and navy units. Soldiers were no longer to be recruited by individual, aristocratic officers, but by the state, each commune selecting its quota by lot – the widely hated and feared *milice*. Regiments and companies would be named after provinces, not after their aristocratic captains. Choiseul also chipped away at venality in the armed forces, prioritising merit and experience over the right to purchase a commission, a radical and contentious reform that the comte de Saint-German would take further in 1776. A brilliant engineer, Gribeauval, revolutionised the practice of warfare with artillery reforms that would survive the Revolutionary and Napoleonic period. Military schools and academies were opened to improve officer training.

Many of these reforms would crash against the rocks of tradition and privilege, especially those that applied to the navy. One of his successors as Secretary of State for the Navy, Bourgeois de Boynes, would introduce more radical measures, such as the creation in 1772 of an *Ecole royale de marine* in Le Havre. Nonetheless, it was Choiseul who began the process of improving the recruitment and training of the royal navy's officer corps, which, since the days of Louis XIV, had been something of a 'family affair', with sons following in their father's footsteps, wives getting good pensions and offspring being educated at the state's expense. Although the 1760s proved to be one of the great decades in the history of French overseas exploration – epitomised by the publication in 1771 of Bougainville's *Voyage autour du monde* – little of this adventurous spirit and experience before the mast seems to have seized the rulers of the king's navy. Choiseul did try to shake the rigging by appointing a young army officer, the comte d'Estaing, to command the marines. More significant was the choice of a mathematician, Etienne Bezout, to reform officer education. The influence of 'le Bezout', as his education programme would be called, would last for a century.[9]

Finally, two events highlight the emergence, and government exploitation, of the new patriotism that rose from the ashes of the Seven Years War – Choiseul's appeal for money to build ships of the line, and the spectacular success of a patriotic, backs-to-the wall play entitled *The Siege of Calais*. In 1761, Choiseul had appealed, successfully, to the rich Estates of Languedoc for a contribution towards the construction of new warships. Soon, other provincial estates, town councils, tax farmers and tens of thousands of ordinary individuals announced that they also wished to subscribe. By 1766, no fewer than 16 ships of the line had been launched. To promote his campaign, Choiseul had been bold enough to sail, metaphorically, into the public sphere. The government sponsored *l'Année littéraire*, edited by the popular journalist, Elie-Catherine Fréron, expressed the patriotic sentiment that 'There is not a single reader who does not wish to see the words "HONNEUR FRANÇAIS" inscribed, in gold letters, on our flags and standards.' National leaders, from Louis XIV to Charles de Gaulle, have realised that *la gloire* is one of the categorical imperatives of the French, national psyche.

The Siege of Calais, by Pierre-Laurent Buirette de Belloy, was the script that dramatised the birth of the New France. One of the most popular, patriotic tragedies of the entire century, its plot reveals the shift that had occurred in popular conceptions of the relationship between the monarchy and the emerging nation. Set in the fourteenth century, during the reigns of Edward III of England and Philip de Valois of France, the play is profoundly anglophobe, depicting Edward as a bloodthirsty monster, hell-bent on the destruction of France. The parallel with the defeat of the Seven Years War is, of course, inescapable, driven home by the final message that patriotism alone could save a nation. The significant point, however, is the emergence of *le peuple*, led by the bourgeois mayor of Calais, as the true saviours of France. The only noble, the comte d'Harcourt, turns out to be a traitor. Henri Bertin and Jacob Moreau, government minister and government 'historiographer' respectively, would draw upon de Belloy's play for their ideological reconstruction of the monarchy. Forget Montesquieu and his aristocratic, *parlementaire* 'intermediaries' between the king and his people. The salvation of the monarchy now lay in the hands of the middle classes, not, it should be noted, the untutored masses. Choiseul, for obvious reasons, thought highly of the play, while Louis XV instructed the *Comédie-Française* to organise a free performance for the poor of Paris. On 12 March 1765, Savoyard chimney sweeps, charcoal burners and fishwives applauded de Belloy's play with unrestrained enthusiasm. But was the monarchy, in its desperate bid for survival, conjuring up forces that it might ultimately fail to control? Does de Belloy's play move us a couple of steps closer to the concept of the Revolutionary 'nation-in-arms', as opposed to Choiseul's 'monarchy-on-its-last-legs'?[10]

Economic growth: from state regulation towards free trade

As we saw in chapter four, the reign of Louis XV coincided with a period of unparalleled economic growth. In both the agricultural and the industrial sectors, France pursued her specific form of development – islands of capitalist modernity expanding within a sea of pre-capitalist forms of production and market relationships. Despite the defeat of the Seven Years War, France continued to exhibit remarkable resilience and competed well with England, if not in terms of *per capita* income or output, then certainly in global trade as well as in certain industrial and commercial sectors of the economy. Choiseul was astute enough to perceive the link between economic and political freedom that was encouraging political and constitutional change in Europe and across the Atlantic. His liberal policies were introduced during a period of world economic expansion.

The dominance of a seigneurial and communal system of production, one that included millions of subsistence farmers and sharecroppers, as well as hundreds of thousands of serfs, helps to explain why France remained a net importer of grain. Nonetheless, although vast tracts of the countryside would remain immune to change during the second half of the century, significant developments did occur, especially in richer farming regions. A marked increase in population would produce a rise in farm rents, with the more entrepreneurial *fermier* or *laboureur* benefiting at the expense of the small-owner. By the 1790s, land prices, when compared with those recorded in the 1720s, had doubled, in a few cases, tripled. Rich farmers producing for expanding urban markets would now find it easier to buy out small farmers catering for a village economy. The latter would eventually be forced into sharecropping and/or protoindustrial manufacturing; those further down the social scale would join the ranks of the rural proletariat. There was also the expansion of regional, national and international markets for wines and spirits that increased opportunities for micro-producers in Languedoc and Provence, Burgundy and the Bordelais, as well as along the Rhone and Loire valleys.[11] Two examples taken from contrasting agricultural regions will illustrate the changing face of farming. At Lapeyrouse near Toulouse, large farms (over 100 hectares) had accounted for less than 15 per cent of the land in the 1680s, a percentage that would double by the 1780s. On a smaller scale, a detailed study of the seigneury of Marigny-sur-Ouche, south of Dijon, highlights the elimination of the small, independent peasant. In 1735, the communities of Barbirey, Saint-Jean-de-Boeuf, Jaugey and Saint-Victor had included only 14 subsistence farmers (under five hectares); by 1785, this figure would rise to 66.[12]

The industrial sector also benefited from greater concentration of production, and there was some technological innovation, although the latter was more evident in the production of textiles and luxury goods than in the heavy industrial sector. Coal production rose from 50,000–75,000 tonnes in 1700 to 600,000 by 1790, but even one of France's most enterprising coal masters, Pierre-François Tubeuf, had not introduced steam engines to his pits by this date. There was also a significant increase in the production of iron, particularly in the Franche-Comté and Lorraine regions. However, the increase in this case was modest, when compared with that of England. The 65,000 tonnes produced in the early 1770s did not even satisfy home demand, underlining the fact that traditional methods of production were reaching their limits.[13]

The absence of revolutionary change in the heavy industrial sector, however, needs to be balanced by the relative success achieved in the production of textile products and luxury goods. State-sponsored enterprises, such as the Saint-Gobain glassworks, the Gobelins tapestries and the Sèvres porcelain works were profitable, employed large workforces and set benchmarks for luxury trades throughout Europe. There is also the striking success of the French cotton industry. Indian printed cottons had been imported since the end of the sixteenth century, illustrating both the early technical superiority of so-called 'subject races' and the international division of trade that dated back, in some sectors, to medieval times. Cotton goods were being manufactured in France throughout the eighteenth century, but Denis Woronoff dates 'the take off' to around 1760, describing it as 'the ultimate expression of the *élan* that runs through the eighteenth century'. Only two cotton factories could be found between Rouen and Bolbec in the 1750s; there would be 50 by 1789. Throughout the country, 300 printed cloth manufacturers, employing 25,000 workers and producing some 550,000 pieces a year, were operating by this date. Lyon had established its international reputation as a producer of luxury silk articles by the beginning of the eighteenth century, but it was only after the 1750s that its poorer sister to the south, Nîmes, began to supply the international market with cheaper products. A decade later 3,600 looms would be clattering away in this historic textile city. In 1762, a Parisian merchant, Santerre, transferred his gauze factory to the north-eastern region of France around Saint-Quentin. By 1789, 1,400 of his looms would be engaged in the production of mixed silk and cotton gauzes. The mechanisation and technical skills that transformed many of these industries were imported from abroad – Kay's flying shuttle transformed cotton production; Frey and Jeanjacquet in Rouen and Oberkampf in Jouy introduced new techniques to the printed cloth industry; Wilkinson improved iron production in the Nantes region. However, the development of an urban, factory-based, industrial sector *à l'anglaise* continued to be impeded by France's rural protoindustrial textile industry, far greater in size and output than its English counterpart. In the long, competitive struggle for supremacy, or even parity, with England, France was obliged to play to her peculiar strengths.[14]

The decree of 7 September 1762 authorised 'the inhabitants of the countryside, as well as those in places which have no guilds, to spin every kind of material, to manufacture every kind of material, and to finish articles in accordance with government regulations'. This was the kind of freedom that won the plaudits of the physiocrats. The monopoly that early modern urban guilds had exercised – theoretically at least – over production had ended, although government regulation had not. The edict was more the recognition of a *fait accompli* than a revolutionary new departure: rural 'domestic industry' for international markets had been operating from medieval times. Nonetheless, we should not underestimate the significance of the 1762 decree. It provoked howls of protest from diehard guild workers in urban, and a few rural, centres of production, fearful that their skills, and employment opportunities, would now be challenged by the growing reserve army of semi-skilled and unskilled workers. Quite a few urban manufacturers, anxious to retain control of products and prices through the established, corporative guild system, also expressed their anxiety. But cheap, mass-produced articles were in great demand, at home and abroad: top quality was no longer the paramount consideration. 'Producing for urban *négociants* who were trying to sell their goods in distant markets, people realised that their futures depended as much upon the effects of international competition or the rhythms of large-scale, commercial transactions as they did upon the fluctuations of cereal prices'. The international capitalist times were, indeed, changing.[15]

More international trade meant more jobs, and the separation of the poor peasantry from the land would provide the necessary reservoir of cheap labour for manufacturers. Protoindustrial production would be big business by 1789, and, in some sectors, it would get even bigger during the early nineteenth century. In the pays de Caux outside Rouen, the new, relatively cheap cottons and mixed linen-cotton articles would provide employment for tens of thousands of workers who produced 166,000 pieces of fabric in 1732, but 543,000 by 1781. By 1795, linen manufacturers in the five northern provinces of Hainaut, Flanders, Artois, Cambrésis and Picardy would be providing a livelihood for no fewer than one and a half million people, the families of 'flax-growers, spinners, weavers, merchants, bleachers, and finishers'. The textile industry also employed hundreds of thousands of workers in the southern province of Languedoc.[16]

The growth of international trade altered circuits of exchange as the century progressed, attracting them westwards to the Americas and eastwards to Africa, India and the Far East, although, for most firms, Mediterranean and northern European markets would furnish the bulk of their business dealings, especially for those specialising in the re-export trade. In 1716, France's European trade had accounted for 91 per cent of exports and 66 per cent of imports; by 1787, these percentages had not fallen dramatically – 82.8 and 57.5 per cent respectively. Of the 9,500 kilogrammes of coffee that arrived in French ports in 1790, 7,940 kilogrammes would be re-exported. The re-export of all colonial goods rose from 18 to 33 per cent of total exports between 1716 and 1787. According to Pluchon, the Ottoman Empire had become 'a satellite economy' of France by the 1770s.[17]

Surprisingly, the expansion of France's colonial trade did not suffer markedly from the defeat of the Seven Years War. In 1720, France's share of world trade had been just 8 per cent, compared with England's 15 per cent: by 1780, France's share had risen to 12 per cent while England's had dropped to 12 per cent. Colonial trade made a major contribution to this reversal of fortune. Although it had increased by 119 per cent between 1730 and 1740, and by 71 per cent from 1740 to 1745, the period from 1765 to 1776 also witnessed the fastest rate of growth of any sector of the French economy – almost 80 per cent. By value, France's colonial trade was now nearly three times the size of any other sector of overseas trade. The most lucrative trade was conducted with the French West Indies, with Saint Domingue effortlessly taking first prize. By the 1780s, this island alone would be producing more sugar than the whole of the British West Indies. The value of all

181

imported colonial goods increased tenfold between 1716–20 and 1775. The ports of Bordeaux, Nantes and Rouen (which received the lion's share of trade with the Atlantic) were transformed during the eighteenth century. However, England was exporting far more industrial goods. By 1789, industrial exports would account for just 40 per cent of total French colonial trade as opposed to around two-thirds of English colonial exports.[18]

Increased trade and mass production meant that the luxuries once enjoyed by the few could now be imitated by the many. Although one suspects that contemporary concerns have exaggerated the consumerist mentality of the eighteenth-century shopper, the debate over a possible 'consumer revolution' in France has raised important issues. Cissie Fairchilds has suggested that the century from approximately 1750 to 1850 should be seen as a distinct period in French economic history, a period when the French economy was responding to a new consumer demand. Much of this demand centred on the 'populuxe' market, 'fans, snuff boxes and articles which added a touch of class to the life of a journeyman or domestic servant'. Paris, and a few provincial centres, specialised in these items. Mercers in the capital were selling everything by the 1780s 'from furniture and fine art through clothing and dry goods to kitchen utensils and pins'. One of the most innovative centres of production was the fashion industry presided over by the *marchandes des modes*, with their retinue of seamstresses and embroiders. There were colonies of fan-makers in the rue Quincampoix operating within their own subculture. For Michael Sonenscher, 'fashion was . . . a vital defence for a state which entrusted its fate to the market for internationally traded goods'. It could 'generate regular cycles of new products, continually shifting the boundaries between necessities, conveniences and luxuries . . . create the combination of high living standards and shared values . . . associated with Holland and England.'[19]

A pertinent question for our study of 'power and the people', however, is, what was the impact of economic growth and consumerism upon the relationship between the powerful and the powerless? This was one issue that was sharpening antagonisms within the *philosophe* camp by the 1770s. For Voltaire, like many liberals today, wealth conferred benefits on everyone, and if the rich benefited more than the poor, then that was the natural order of things, but then Voltaire was a seigneur who enjoyed the good life, a friend of bankers, financiers and *négociants*. Rousseau, of course, praised the virtues of relative poverty. His influence upon the most perceptive social historians of the late eighteenth century, Sébastien Mercier and Restif de la Bretonne, is striking. The former complains that, by the 1780s, the monarchy was robbing the poor to pay its aristocratic hangers-on: 'The heirs of the old nobility then walk around Paris with their diamonds, their lace, their gold plates and sumptuous carriages.' If the rich had everything they wanted to embellish their lives, very little trickled down to 'la nation en gros', the millions of the urban and rural poor. Restif drove the point home: 'Any advantage the rich acquire [from luxury goods] . . . favours the increase of wealth and perpetuates social inequality.'[20] The argument continues in the twenty-first century.

In case it is thought that the Rousseauesque sympathies of Mercier and Restif have affected our judgement, we should leave the last word to the widely respected, contemporary historian of consumerism, Daniel Roche. In his absorbing analysis of 'the culture of appearances' (which includes diet, clothes, housing and furniture), he stresses that it would be naïve to suppose that the 'consumer revolution' of the eighteenth century blessed rich and poor alike. If there was a revolution in production and demand, there was certainly no radical change in social inequality: 'The luxury which displayed the power of the super-rich remained therefore a major problem in the old society.'[21] It is tempting to suggest that it would remain *the* social problem for the France of Louis XVI.

In 1767, the Scottish economic theorist, Sir James Steuart, wrote that 'Trade and industry are in vogue; and their establishment is occasioning a wonderful fermentation with the remaining fierceness of the feudal constitution'.[22] Unlike many recent historians, Steuart was happy to use the term 'feudal' to describe the 'constitution' of France. The main purpose of his comment, however, was to indicate how capitalism was undermining what remained of feudal structures and mentalities in England and on the continent. In France, the free trade policies pursued by Choiseul would certainly cause 'a wonderful fermentation' in matters pertaining to trade and industry. They would also accelerate the process of undermining the 'feudal constitution'. Le Roy Ladurie asserts that John Law's radical economic policies in the 1720s had marked 'a decisive break' with those that had been favoured by Louis XIV's renowned minister, Colbert. Whatever the validity of this assertion, there were a few similarities between policies introduced by the duc d'Orléans and John Law during the Regency and those favoured by Choiseul in the 1760s. But would it be yet another example of '*plus ça change* . . .'?[23] Or, to be more precise, could economic modernisation succeed without radical changes in the sphere of aristocratic government and a seigneurial system of land ownership?

Colbert's system had been influenced by mercantilist theories. Mercantilism was an early, monetarist system that linked the exchange of goods to the circulation of precious metals. The global amount of both money and goods in circulation at any given time was thought to be constant, and the aim of a sophisticated economic system was to ensure that imports did not cost more than a country received from exports. Following this general principle would ensure a 'favourable balance of trade' and a healthy reserve of hard cash. However, by mid-century, many critics were pointing out that mercantilism had not brought success in the struggle with England. Pitt had won the Seven Years War, it was alleged, by riding on the back of free trade.

Physiocratic theory had triumphed over mercantilism in France by mid-century. Influential physiocrats, such as Quesnay (madame de Pompadour's doctor) and his disciples, such as Pierre Samuel Du Pont de Nemours, appeared to be offering a new way forward. In 1758, Quesnay had published his influential *Tableau économique*, followed, in 1767, by *Physiocratie*. Echoing the political thought of most Enlightenment gurus, these two works laid particular emphasis upon the need for a strong monarchy. Physiocracy would supply the economic component of Enlightened Despotism. The question in this case was, would doctor Quesnay's cure be more dangerous than the disease? In some respects, physiocratic ideas reassured ministers raised in an absolutist, Catholic and rural culture. They were advised, for example, to concentrate more on the countryside than the colonies. The young Du Pont de Nemours argued that money should be invested in land – the essential source of a country's wealth for physiocrats – not placed under the mattress by *rentiers*, 'the lowest and one of the most dangerous classes that can exist in a state'.[24] Free trade, within France at least, would free the productive capacity of that rural 'Prometheus Unbound', the countryside, *if* seigneurial constraints were removed, but this was a very big 'if' indeed. Quesnay argued that a single tax, falling equitably – if not equally – on all social classes, would provide 300 million *livres* a year for the royal treasury. Traditional restraints would have to be removed in town and country: medieval guilds abolished; medieval farming methods, such as village rights to free pasture land (*vaine pâture*), discouraged. Freedom for reforming capitalist land-owners was the message. But all this implied a policy of taxing the privileged orders. Could the monarchy seriously adopt such a policy when aristocratic elites continued to dominate the top positions in both Church and state? It was a tall, political and socio-economic order.

Voltaire and his friends had been singing the praises of commercial capitalism for many years. Although the 'sage of Ferney' had occasionally denounced colonial expansion, the frequent citations of his description of Canada as 'those few acres of snow' is not typical. He had, in fact, invested some of his own money in the Caribbean trade. Both Voltaire and Quesnay had applauded Bertin's choice of China as a model for France. Here was a country that supported rural landowners; one whose emperor, Kien-long, was known as the 'chef des cultivateurs'. After all, France was not England, imprisoned within a process of rapid industrialisation. French economic, cultural and social strengths were rooted in the soil. Immediately after the Seven Years War, the ex-controller-general, Bertin, and a future controller-general, Jacques Turgot, had dispatched two converted Chinese Catholic missionaries, Ko and Yang, to Peking to discover everything they could about the 'Celestial Empire'. The twenty-year correspondence between Ko, Yang and Bertin provides us with an appreciation of the influences that helped to shape royal policy in the 1760s and 1770s.[25]

Choiseul shared physiocratic opinion on the benefits to be derived from the liberalisation of trade and industry, although he rejected the more revolutionary implications of Quesnay's attack upon seigneurialism. It seems that Louis XV (encouraged, no doubt, by madame de Pompadour) had read Quesnay's *Tableau économique*, and, like several of his ministers, was prepared to go with the flow. The controller-general, Henri Bertin, was a cautious convert, responsible in the early 1760s for the establishment of a dozen or so Societies of Agriculture in various parts of the country. Daniel Trudaine, an *Intendant de finance*, and one of the most effective of all Louis XV's officials, worked tirelessly to promote industrial growth and improve the nation's transport system. Between 1750 and 1774, some 25,000 kilometres of roads and canals would be constructed. A few provincial officials like Bertin's colleague, Jacques Turgot, Intendant of Limousin in the 1760s, had tried, rather successfully, to put physiocratic theory into practice. He had relaxed controls on the grain trade, encouraged industry and commerce and lifted a few feudal burdens, such as forced peasant labour on the roads (*corvée*), off the backs of the peasantry.[26]

Choiseul was not, then, without support and, until her untimely death in 1764, he could usually count on the invaluable assistance of madame de Pompadour. However, it was the dynamism and drive of France's own 'iron duke' that converted intellectual pressure into royal policy. In 1762, as we have seen, the French countryside was opened up to manufacturers. On 25 May 1763, the government took the momentous step of freeing the grain throughout the country, and this was followed in August 1764 by an even more radical move – allowing the export of grain from some 27 ports. In the same year, Choiseul relaxed some of the restrictions governing overseas trade and, in 1769, the trading monopoly held by the *Compagnie des Indes* was abolished. Together with his modernisation of the armed forces and the rural mounted constabulary, the *maréchaussée*, Choiseul had masterminded one the most significant reform movements in the history of the Bourbon monarchy.

However, circumstances had favoured reform in the early and middle years of the 1760s. The post-war disgust with the defeat of the Seven Years War, together with a series of good harvests, had provided a 'window of opportunity' for a strong-willed politician who had answers to seemingly intractable problems. But that window would close as circumstances changed and opposition towards Choiseul at court grew more confident and vociferous. And when the crisis came, Louis XV would prove that he was hardly 'a man for all seasons', just the good ones! One of the apparently insoluble problems concerned the historic shift towards free trade. While this may have been a blessing for many – prosperous farmers, grain merchants and exporters, and manufacturers of certain mass-produced textile products – it proved to be a disaster for the great majority of the urban and rural poor. Free trade was not a universal blessing, even for many employers. Two examples illustrating this point must suffice here – manufacturers and guild workers in Lille, and the grain trade in Paris and Rouen.

As textile manufacture expanded in the countryside, relationships between many established urban centres and their satellite *bourgs* and villages became more antagonistic. Gail Bossenga's study of Lille and its hinterland provides us with a case in point. During the second half of the eighteenth century, bitter rivalry developed between the city, with its long tradition of textile and ceramic production, and the neighbouring *bourgs* of Tourcoing and Roubaix. As a border town, Lille enjoyed certain customs privileges relating to foreign trade which elicited jealousy from surrounding manufacturing centres. Tourcoing, for example, sought its own privileges, including a monopoly over the production of flannel cloth. The decree of 1762 ordered Lille to end its opposition to the expansion of rival centres of production such as Tourcoing. The order provoked bitter opposition in Lille, and implementation of the decree had to be suspended for three years. Many manufacturers also resisted attacks on the guilds, which they used 'to restrict the number of looms operated by master wool weavers, to keep manufacturing inside the city, and to shut out brokers and non-native wholesalers in order to maintain their communal dominance'. In Lille, as in Paris and many other urban centres, merchants often 'transformed the guilds into bourgeois tools'.[27] Guild workers also competed with non-guild workers for jobs, thus undermining any incipient working-class solidarity.

Judith Miller's work on state intervention in the grain trade in northern France reveals that, due to fierce popular opposition, the introduction of market policies took a great deal of time and no small measure of ideological compromise. Indeed, 'a moderate form of free trade' would not be definitively implemented until the 1860s! Miller argues that the practice of provisioning markets on the ground was more about 'sleight of hand' than about Adam Smith's 'invisible hand' of the market. For example, in 1757, the authorities in Rouen, worried about consumer concerns over high prices, persuaded a local miller to sell grain below the market price by offering him a subsidy – in private. In 1768, the president of the parlement of Rouen paid merchants (who were naturally reluctant to bring their grain to market if it meant selling at a loss) to sell their wares at a 'popular' price. Gradually, a two-tier system emerged – market prices for the rich and subsidised sales for the poor.[28]

Steven Kaplan's impressive studies of merchants and grain markets also distinguish the regulated 'market place' from the free trade 'market principle'. The central market of les Halles in Paris organised the transport of flour, fish, vegetables and flowers along a thousand arterial roads and alleyways inside and outside the capital. A 'staggering array of local officials' were used by Intendants, as well as by officials of the provincial parlements, to ensure that adequate supplies of grain reached the market place and that they were sold at prices customers could afford. Two thousand mills worked to supply Paris with bread; the famous grain-producing region of Pontoise alone had 136 watermills and 29 windmills. More 'economic milling' would be introduced after 1770, reducing the amount of grain necessary to feed an individual for one year by one-third. In the opinion of the eighteenth-century populariser of the humble potato, Parmentier, 'no single achievement in the century of the Enlightenment was more important'.[29] However, particularly in periods of dearth, the unsophisticated application of free trade in grain and sales of bread at prices dictated by the open market would lead only to riot and rebellion. Popular economics favoured regulation, anti-hoarding laws, 'the just price' – they were the constituent elements of a 'moral' rather than a market economy.

For the consumer, bread was more a matter for police than philosophy. Without cheap bread, as important to the survival of poor Frenchmen and women as the potato was to their Irish counterparts, the economy could not function. There appears to be a gene in the cultural DNA of twentieth-century French citizens that evokes past horrors of mass starvation, which explains why the humble baguette has assumed almost iconic significance. The owner of any *boulangerie* in Paris or Rouen today will tell you, in no uncertain terms, that the price of bread remains a matter of government concern.

Maupeou's 'enlightened absolutism'

It is no coincidence that the second phase of the eighteenth-century 'Great Confinement' of the poor occurred during the late 1760s and the early 1770s. The consequences of free market policies and adverse climatic conditions combined during this period to produce widespread social unrest, mainly in the countryside. The monarchy responded by tightening the screws of its repressive machine. However, between 1770 and 1774, the 'Triumvirate', comprising the chancellor, Maupeou, the controller-general, the abbé Terray, and the minister for foreign affairs, the duc d'Aiguillon, also introduced what we may describe as more enlightened programmes to tackle the 'social problem'. They represented a belated, and temporary, victory for Henri Bertin and Jacob Moreau, who had been pressing, since the 1750s, for an ideological reappraisal of the foundations of absolute monarchy, a reappraisal that would be legitimized by historical precedent and sealed by the emasculation of the parlements. The *dévôt* faction, short on enlightenment, but glad to be rid of the agnostic Choiseul who had struck up too cosy a deal with the parlements, threw in their vote, securing the active support of Louis XV by presenting him with a beautiful, new mistress, madame du Barry. The real prize for the king, however, was nothing less than the survival of absolute monarchy, as opposed to the aristocratic form of constitutional monarchy that the parlements had been inching towards ever since the Regency of the duc d'Orléans in 1715.

Jacob Moreau, the royal historiographer, was one of those rare breeds, a Jansenist-trained critic of the parlements. In 1760, he had written a memorandum that represented, in the words of Keith Baker, 'A powerful blueprint for ideological action in defence of the absolute monarchy'.[30] The previous year, Etienne de Silhouette had asked Moreau to start thinking about the creation of a government archive that could be used by ministers and government supporters to defend the Crown against its increasingly vocal critics, spearheaded by the parlements. By 1763, Moreau's labours had already produced a depot consisting of 1,500 volumes and cartons of judicial, administrative and legal documents, finally housed in the *Bibliothèque du roi*. For the rest of his life, Moreau, supported at every step by Bertin, would create a massive, official archive in order to 'assert the foundations of true political authority in France'. It would represent a labour of love, one to which Moreau dedicated his entire life. 'Enlightened absolutism' rested upon a determined and prolonged effort to fashion a new ideology for Bourbon rule, something that is too often overlooked.

Henri Bertin's enforced resignation as controller-general in 1763 had by no means ended his influence at court. Indeed, his importance to Louis XV was signalled by the creation of a unique secretaryship of state, a patchwork quilt of ministerial responsibilities that covered several departments. Throughout the period described by the government's critics as 'Maupeou's despotism', Bertin would continue to be a close confidant of the king and a senior member of the king's inner council, as well as a member of the *Conseil des finances*. Lucien Laugier points out that even the abbé Terray did not dare to challenge Bertin directly.[31] What is missing from most appraisals of Bertin's career is a detailed assessment and evaluation of his 'Chinese connection', or what Bertin referred to as his *Correspondance littéraire*. The expression was employed to describe the hundreds of letters exchanged between Bertin and the Jesuits of the French mission in Peking between 1765 and 1792. The term would also be used by Moreau to identify the work of the monks of the Benedictine order of Saint-Maur – his 'literary correspondents' – who laboured, during the same period, in several religious and private houses to unearth, translate and copy thousands of the historical documents that would constitute Moreau's royal archive. They both tried to react positively to currents of political change and secularisation sweeping Europe, not least by reinventing moribund monastic institutions as serious centres of scholarship. It would be a fundamental error to dismiss all royal ministers, and Jesuits, as unenlightened reactionaries, incapable of adapting policies to the changing times. The appropriate questions to ask are, how far was the enlightened minority at court prepared to go, or how far would they be allowed to go? They certainly appreciated that a modernisation of absolutism would entail a secularisation of its political philosophy and the establishment of closer links with the public. It was a pity, though hardly a surprise, that Louis XV always found the attractions of his royal harem – the notorious *parc aux cerfs* – more enticing than the occasional tour of the provinces to drum up public support for his ministers.

The radical aspect of Bertin and Moreau's modernisation involved a closer relationship with the emerging bourgeoisie and a more distant relationship with the aristocratic parlements. This new ideological stance would reflect themes treated in de Belloy's smash hit, *The Siege of Calais*. The evidence for this is to be found not only in the voluminous *Collection Moreau* but also in the *Collection Périgord*, both housed in the manuscript section of the *Bibiliothèque nationale*. For example, volume 68 of the latter collection contains a remarkable article, over 300 pages long, written in the early 1770s and co-signed by Bertin and Moreau. Entitled *Mémoire sur la constitution politique de la ville et cité de Périgord,* it traces the 'bourgeois' defence of Périgord (Bertin's home town) against foreign invaders and feudal lords since the Middle Ages. Its heroes are the propertied bourgeoisie; its villains 'anarchic' feudal seigneurs. It dismisses the 'representative' destabilising claims of intermediary bodies like the parlements in favour of the sovereign uniting his people in accordance with the historic laws of the kingdom. 'Where does the unity of France lie?' the document asks. 'It is not in possessions, but in the action of the power that protects them; because this power is a unitary one and its actions must always be guided by justice. Justice that tells us that Government is not a destructive but a tutelary force. Liberty and Property, these are the rights of subjects; Protection and Direction, these are the rights of the Prince'. This is the political philosophy that would inform Louis XV's uncompromising attacks on the parlements in the late 1760s.

The tone of the above article is post-Montesquieu and pre-Sièyes and, in its dismissal of the historic claims of the parlements, even 'despotic'. Towards the end of his life, in 1792, Bertin would bemoan the fact that Louis XIV and his successor had not pursued the logic of this historical analysis. If only they had embraced the cause of a third estate *that included the robe nobility* with more enthusiasm, France might not have collapsed into the 'anarchy' of the Revolution. Bertin was travelling on the right historic road, even if he wanted to end his journey before reaching the sign that led to 'constitutional monarchy'. The tragedy of the Bourbon monarchy during the second half of the eighteenth century was that it cast too many glances backward at the aristocratic, seigneurial and ecclesiastical socio-political system of Louis XIV and too few forward to the constitutional alliance of 'King and (bourgeois) Third Estate'. Without the mediation of the bourgeoisie, the monarchy would be unable to preside over the emerging capitalist system. One reason why embracing a bourgeois–robe noble alliance proved so difficult was that the princes of the blood, led by the house of Orléans, but followed eagerly by the Conti and the Soubise clans, frequently preferred to back the parlements rather than the Crown in times of political crisis.[32] The problem was that the parlements were never quite sure which line to take on matters of constitutional government. What really matters, however, as Marisa Linton has indicated, is that it was 'clear from the time of the Maupeou coup that the jurisdictional quarrel between the *Parlements* and ministers had generated the idea of the legitimacy of civic virtue as an authority for political participation in the minds of people who followed the debate'.[33]

Circumstances dictated that these domestic political and ideological matters would head the agenda drawn up by the so-called 'Triumvirate' in 1770. For one thing, a shortage of cash meant that France did not have the choice of sacrificing internal security for foreign adventure. In any case, Louis XIV – a pupil of the pacific Cardinal Fleury at heart – was increasingly opposed to military action. The immediate cause of Choiseul's dismissal in December 1770 would be the duke's flirtation with the idea of challenging England's predatory designs on the Falkland Islands. A consequence of this docile approach to foreign affairs, however, was a loss of power and prestige on the continent as Russia, Prussia and Austria began the process of partitioning Poland in 1772 and Russia defeated France's traditional ally Turkey in the Balkans. In July 1774, Turkey was forced to sign one of the most important treaties of the eighteenth century, that of Kutchuk-Kainardji. Relegating the problems associated with these long-term shifts in the balance of European power to a future date, Maupeou and his colleagues struggled to save the country from bankruptcy and popular violence. As controller-general at a time of national crisis, the abbé Terray did what circumstances, not ideology, obliged him to do – severely curtail the freedom of the grain trade and declare a partial bankruptcy. However, to force through these two key policies, he would have to cut off, rather than clip, the wings of the parlements. On this point, the pragmatism of the Triumvirate coincided with the principles of the 'enlightened absolutists', Bertin, Moreau and their supporters. For utilitarian and ideological reasons, the constitutional claims of the parlements would have to be challenged and defeated.

Two interrelated problems poisoned the relationship between the French Crown and the parlements after the 1750s – finance and political sovereignty. The struggles over religious issues (often a mask for political and jurisdictional differences) lost their venom following the collapse of the Jesuit Order. Both parties fought to control the purse strings, which, in turn, controlled the levers of political power. Recently, a distinguished team of scholars, headed by Richard Bonney, has produced a most valuable collection of essays on the fiscal history of Europe. One of its principal conclusions was that 'The motor of fiscal change in France, as for all the main European monarchies, was expenditure on war.' Great powers, in ancient and modern history, are, in the final analysis, killing machines and without control of taxation, these machines cannot run smoothly. Tim Le Goff believes that 'a common set of assumptions and a common approach to fiscal and financial problems' characterised all administrations in France from the 1720s to the Revolution, and they all failed for the same reason – 'their inability to deal with post-war, short-term debts'. Non-loan revenues had contributed only 67 per cent of the costs incurred in the War of the Austrian Succession and just 49 per cent of the costs associated with the Seven Years War. War debt was higher in Britain, but, as John Bosher has argued, the British government, closer to its financial and commercial elites, could raise loans at lower rates of interest. Bourbon absolutism mortgaged its power and authority during the eighteenth century at too high a rate.[34]

A second, major conclusion to be drawn from the work of Richard Bonney and his colleagues is that, for all the inroads cut into the bastions of noble and ecclesiastical privilege, gross fiscal inequality between rich and poor remained a constant feature of ancien regime government and society. To compound this fiscal felony, taxes collected from the peasantry, as well as from those bourgeois who did not enjoy tax exemptions, were recycled at the court of Versailles to further enrich the privileged few that paid little or no taxes. The *taille*, the basic direct tax, fell overwhelmingly on the peasantry, and although extraordinary taxes – the *capitation* (first levied in the 1690s) and the *vingtième* (that replaced the *dixième* in 1749) – were levied on nobles, they did not significantly adjust the inequitable balance between the privileged and non-privileged. For example, Michael Kwass's study of government taxation in the Caen region concludes that privileged groups were indeed obliged to pay 'a mildly burdensome *capitation* in the eighteenth century'. However, this tax (which fell on all subjects) also 'augmented what was already a heavy tax burden for commoners', adding 37 per cent over the century to the existing burden of the *taille*, that rose, nationally, from 30 million *livres* in 1699 to 64 million by the 1780s. The clergy, owning some of the richest land in France, had been excluded from the *dixième* extraordinary tax altogether. They had also escaped a realistic contribution to the *capitation* by buying out their liability with a lump sum of 24 million *livres* in 1710. It was impossible for the provincial estates (which levied their own taxation as opposed to the *pays d'états* where taxes were levied directly by government officials) to pull off a scam of this magnitude. But the estates also made regular deals with the government to pay a lump sum, thus ensuring that, yet again, the Crown sacrificed its 'future revenues for the short-term fix of a cash advance'. No wonder Kwass asks whether or not we should describe the ancien regime as a 'welfare state for the privileged'. These, not the politics of aristocratic factionalism and favouritism, were the issues that would ultimately determine the fate of the Bourbon monarchy in the eighteenth century.[35]

Were the parlements truly defenders of privilege? For all their professional, juridical and constitutional *gravitas*, and commitment, the answer is an unequivocal yes. Their membership was drawn almost exclusively from the ranks of the robe and sword nobility; much of their personal wealth was founded upon seigneurial dues and landed rents; their ideological mentor was Montesquieu, the champion of noble intermediary political bodies created to defend the nation against despotic government. One of their greatest fears was the introduction of a land survey (*cadastre*) that would lead to the revaluation of estates for tax purposes. In 1763, during his period as controller-general, Henri Bertin had tried to introduce a new survey, eliciting the predictable negative response from the parlements throughout the country. Swann tells us that there were 'Howls of protest', indicating that 'he had struck a privileged nerve'.[36] Bertin was forced to give up his idea of replacing extraordinary taxes with a land tax and fall back upon temporary expedients. Serious attempts to tax the privileged orders entailed serious consequences, including the charge of 'despotism' that soiled the reputation of Maupeou and his colleagues. Money made from the ownership of land was usually invested in the equivalent of today's government gilt-edged securities – bonds placed with the Paris *hôtel de ville*. It is significant that the abbé Terray's partial bankruptcy in 1770 did not target this form of investment. All this is not to argue that the parlements did not provide a vital check on government 'despotism'. Their reluctance to agree to increased taxation, after all, was something that even the peasantry could applaud.

Arguments between the monarchy and the parlements over who was to blame for successive financial crises – wasteful royal expenditure and antiquated methods of tax collection or tax avoidance by the country's privileged classes – became increasingly common during the middle decades of the eighteenth century. This was hardly surprising given France's involvement in three wars. During the 1760s, royal demands for increased taxation to pay off war debts frequently developed into constitutional struggles over the status and rights of the parlements, evoking comparisons with the conflict between Charles I and the English parliament a century earlier. Conscious that the historic victory of absolutism in France had prevented the evolution of a single parliament based on the English model, the Paris parlement and the twelve provincial parlements began to make worrying comments about speaking with one voice, the so-called *union des classes*. There was never much chance that union would have been achieved, given the assumption – hotly contested by the provincial parlements – that, in the final analysis, it was the Paris parlement who spoke for the king, who, in turn, spoke for France. Nonetheless, the immediate *political* background to Maupeou's 'coup' was a revolt by the most aristocratic and fiercely independent of all the provincial parlements, that of Brittany. The Paris parlement provided opportunistic support.

In 1765, Brittany provided the stage for a dress rehearsal for Maupeou's assault on the parlements five years later. A quarrel over fiscal and constitutional policy between Louis XV's military commander in Rennes, the duc d'Aiguillon, and a leading figure in the Breton parlement, La Chalotais, led to the arrest and subsequent internal exile of the latter. The magistrates of the parlement were dismissed and replaced by the king's nominees, a procedure that Maupeou would follow with regard to the Paris parlement in 1771. This dispute between an expansionist central state and one of the most independent provincial parlements rapidly developed into a prolonged and extremely damaging personal joust between d'Aiguillon and La Chalotais. The affair was poisoned by allegations that the latter had obtained letters from a former mistress of Louis XV. Satirists and pamphleteers were presented with the two weapons they most coveted to assault the court – a constitutional crisis and Louis XV's sex life. When the Paris parlement decided to throw its weight on the side of the Bretons, the court, which had previously set up a committee to discuss the problem of the parlements, decided to fight back. The so-called 'flagellation' of the Paris parlement during a special session convened by Louis XV on 3 March 1766 was directed at all the French parlements, particularly those at Rennes, Rouen and Pau, whose *remonstrances* against the king's actions had been the most provocative.[37]

Louis began by stating, in a truly regal manner, that 'he would not permit the formation of an association [of the parlements] in his kingdom that could degenerate into a *confédération de résistance*'. He stressed that sovereignty belonged to the king alone and that the recent claims of the Paris parlement to 'represent' the nation were contrary to the fundamental laws of the kingdom. It is important to note, as William Doyle has argued, that the king did not deny the historic and constitutional rights of the parlements to comment on legislation and to advise the Crown, but these rights had to be expressed with the moderation and humility owed to a sovereign. This extraordinary royal session of 3 March constituted the high water mark of French absolutism *à la Louis XV*. It proclaimed the constitutional bases of 'enlightened absolutism', attempting to distinguish them from 'royal despotism'. Unfortunately for the court, the parlements and their supporters were not minded to accept Louis XV's *dictat*. The feud between d'Aiguillon and La Chalotais continued for several years, envenomed with show trials and appeals by La Chalotais to be tried by his peers in the Paris parlement. As was usually the case, Louis XV failed to maintain his resolute stance. In 1769, for example, the members of the *old* parlement in Rennes were recalled to the delight of the local inhabitants. By 1770, d'Aiguillon was a member of the government, along with Maupeou, while La Chalotais's supporters, incensed at the imprisonment of their hero in the Bastille (he was subsequently condemned to internal exile in Saintes), were planning their revenge.[38]

Michel Antoine suggests that the country was descending into anarchy: 'It was becoming impossible to govern . . . In order to mask the decay of the old judicial system, the robe nobility [in the parlements] was trying to seize power, threatening the constitution of the kingdom by bringing down the monarchy.'[39] Overstated, but not without some substance. The 'enlightened absolutists' certainly believed that the parlements had become the primary obstacle to the implementation of their programme. When, in the summer of 1770, Louis XV was accused of naked 'despotism' for halting the trial of the duc d'Aiguillon by the Paris parlement, the court began to prepare for a final showdown. On 20 January 1771, the members of the parlement were exiled to the provinces, marking the beginning of what was truly a major judicial and constitutional revolution. The judicial and political powers of the parlements throughout France were severely curtailed, although some rights of *remonstrance* were allowed. New courts of justice were created with new magistrates replacing those who had led the resistance against Versailles. Venality was abolished and salaries replaced the old, corrupt system of offering gifts (bribes?) to magistrates. Despite the prediction of the king's enemies, the new courts of justice proved to be not only effective, but popular. The earth did not tremble, and, by 1774, the Crown appeared to have triumphed in this historic conflict. Terray's economic reforms had almost succeeded in balancing the books; the censorship imposed upon the press and the more radical *philosophes* appeared to have blunted the edge of public criticism. Maupeou was even planning a programme of educational reform.

Unfortunately, according to historians sympathetic to the royalist cause, fate then intervened to undermine the longer-term success of 'Maupeou's revolution'. Pierre Gaxotte believed that the last chance to save absolute monarchy in France was lost with the downfall of Maupeou and the abbé Terray, not with the subsequent failure of the physiocrat fellow-traveller, Jacques Turgot. Even if, for the sake of an interesting argument, we agree that absolutism could have been saved in 1770, it could only have been done so by attacking the roots of the mass discontent that was afflicting the countryside. It was the *agrarian problem* that lay at the heart of the dilemmas confronting governments during the ancien regime, and it was the agrarian problem that would continue to pose the most acute difficulties for Revolutionary administrations. One of the reasons for the popularity of the parlements was their opposition to radical free-trade policies, as Jacques Turgot would discover to his cost in 1775.

Repression and social rebellion

Although many spotlights have been focused on the ideological, political, fiscal and economic struggles of the 1760s and 1770s, much of the history of social unrest and rebellion remains obscure. In 1774, the *curé* of the parish of Athis in Normandy expressed his alarm at the growing divide between rich and poor in the region of Bayeux: 'Day-labourers, manual workers, craftsmen, and all those whose profession furnishes not much more than subsistence and clothing are those who become beggars . . . their only resort is to take up the staff and the pack, which they do even more readily when their father has done the same.'[40] At the heart of the good *curé's* concerns for the poorer members of his flock was the remarkable demographic and economic boom of the 1760s that had facilitated the introduction of free-trade policies. At the top end of the social scale, the boom had produced a rise in farm rents and increased profit margins for the agricultural goods produced by rich *fermiers* and *laboureurs*. At the opposite end, high rates of population growth in many rural areas had increased the demand for land, leading to the fragmentation of small properties and the gradual displacement of subsistence farmers. Proletarianisation, frequently through the route of protoindustrial labour, awaited those who were forced to accept wage increases that failed to keep pace with rising prices.

The series of bad harvests at the end of the 1760s had compounded the structural problems affecting the countryside, provoking the traditional backlash of grain riots and attacks on property. Worrying reports, accompanied by proposed solutions, had reached the government via the Intendants and the new Societies of Agriculture. One physiocratic reformer, Guillaume Le Trosne, submitted a treatise to the Society of Agriculture in Lyon in the early 1770s that painted an extremely alarming picture of robbery, murder and the reappearance of armed gangs. Le Trosne's report has a relevance to contemporary debates on unemployment and social welfare, in particular his proposal for what we know as 'welfare to work' programmes. Placing the poor in hospitals in times of recession, Le Trosne wrote, is to mistake the root cause of the problem, that 'vagabonds are essentially enemies of work . . . It is assuredly not work that is lacking but the good will to work.'[41] The charitable impulse was being replaced by more utilitarian and 'market friendly' solutions, a switch that necessarily entailed greater state control. According to an eighteenth-century provincial administrator, governments would now have to 'provide for the subsistence of the people, without which there will be neither law nor the forces of order to contain it'.[42] It constituted a law of eighteenth-century government, and it was one that would be tested to the limit from 1768 to 1775. This was a period that produced one of the most widespread social crises in French history, comparable with those of 1709–10 and 1788–9.

The Russian historian, Anatoli Ado, informs us that 'From the 1770s, subsistence problems assumed massive proportions . . . In 1773, they coincided with the general political crisis provoked by Maupeou's reforms.' Riots occurred in many parts of Languedoc, followed, from the autumn of 1774 to the spring of 1775, by revolts in the south-west and the centre of France, from Toulouse to Limoges. From 1777, there would be a recurrence of social unrest in Languedoc, as well as revolts in Quercy. According to Ado, these struggles set the poor against the richer members of the third estate – grain merchants, landowners, millers and substantial *fermiers*, many of whom benefited from collecting seigneurial and ecclesiastical dues. During the last years of the 1760s, armed bands appeared in the Haute Auvergne and Gévaudan, as well as in the provinces of Dauphiné and Languedoc. One band in the Haute Auvergne was led by a former lieutenant of Louis Mandrin, one of France's legendary criminals. Mandrin and his armed followers had terrorised tax collectors and customs officers throughout seven provinces, stretching from Burgundy to Dauphiné, during the 1750s. He was the last of the legendary 'Robin Hood' figures of the ancien regime, a popular icon, immortalised in story and song. The scope of his activities, and the almost universal sympathy he evoked amongst the common people, calls into question the belief that there were no uprisings between 1715 and 1789 that were in any way comparable to the great tax revolts of the previous century.[43]

Poor peasants could, and did, muster serious resistance to what were, for the rich, liberal reforms. Hilton Root has provided chapter and verse to describe the collective resistance of the peasantry in Burgundy, founded upon their shrewd exploitation of the law.[44] Ado's work addresses one of the crucial questions relating to peasant culture. What impact did cultural change exert upon the countryside during the last decades of the century? Although far more research is required before definitive conclusions can be reached, he suggests, for example, that the significant rise in literacy rates recorded during the century facilitated access to an increasing number of books and pamphlets that were critical of both liberal reforms and feudal exploitation. Rural 'Grub Street' authors, like Augustin Rouier, published works aimed at the peasantry that 'attacked the feudal regime, denounced the exploitation of peasants by seigneurs and bourgeois', whilst praising the patriarchal Utopia of a 'popular monarchy'.[45] In order to assess the true significance and character of these pre-Revolutionary disturbances, far more work needs to be done in archives that house the records of the poor, beginning with those of the seigneurial courts of justice and the *maréchaussée*.

Choiseul's repressive measures, which had been launched as early as 1760, were an understandable response to this widespread breakdown in law and order. They represent a continuation, involving an expansion of state involvement, of the programme of poor relief and vagrancy that had begun during the 'Great Confinement' of the 1720s. The policies adopted by Choiseul, however, were different in two respects. First, they were laced with a fairly weak dose of Enlightenment sympathy for the victims of social change and upheaval. The sick, the aged and the 'deserving poor' would receive a Christian minimum of state assistance, the able-bodied 'undeserving poor' would be imprisoned and, if they chose to take the vagabond's escape route to robbery and violence, despatched to the galleys or hung. Second, they were aimed, in no small measure, at protecting the successful rural property-owner, from the failed sharecropper and day-labourer, for whom begging, vagrancy and theft appeared to be the only alternatives to starvation. One of the most profound, and politically significant, changes to affect French society during the eighteenth century, as the culture of seigneurial paternalism was gradually eroded by the much harsher culture of the emerging capitalist and commercial world, was an increase in class rivalry *within* the ranks of the French peasantry.

This new approach to the problem of law and order required a radical reorganisation of France's rural constabulary, the *maréchaussée*. Originally created as a military police force, controlled by the Intendant, legislation passed in 1670 had extended its jurisdiction to cover crimes committed by civilians, especially those associated with highway robbery, and popular disturbances. Offenders could now be tried in the *maréchaussée*'s own courts, the *prévôtés*. In August 1764, the constabulary was given the right to set up and control *dépôts* for arrested criminals. The galleys were reintroduced as a penalty, although the time served in these floating hells was reduced to three years. The 1764 bill contained a provision stating that offenders who had been beggars for over six months would lose the right to have 'their respectable character and conduct . . . attested to by persons of dignity and trust'. These attestations of good character were essential passports to employment in ancien regime France. In 1768, reflecting the growing rural unrest referred to above, Choiseul announced that 200 new brigades would be added to the existing force, bringing the total to 760. By 1776, the *maréchaussée* would be composed of 33 *prévôts*, 112 lieutenants and 3,986 men (an increase of 1,160 since 1764), divided into 955 brigades.

Choiseul's police reforms, building on the work of his predecessors, allayed some of the fears of the rich whilst aggravating the plight of the poor. The quality, in terms of literacy and personal commitment, of recruits to the *maréchaussée* might have been of a low standard, and far too many of its members might have been addicted to alcohol, but most experts agree that Choiseul had acted to restore the authority of the government in the countryside at a time when anarchy appeared to be only a bad harvest away. At the end of 1773, government figures indicated that 72,025 persons had been arrested and that of this number 58,000 had been imprisoned and 968 condemned to the galleys. Although there was talk of the need for enlightened measures to be taken against the poor, it is obvious that those arrested under the Great Confinement of the 1760s and early 1770s were treated as harshly as those arrested in the 1720s. For every offender imprisoned in harsh Hanoverian England, three or four were interned in France.[46] Schwarz concludes that if the reorganisation of the *maréchaussée* was a success in many regards, 'its very purpose testified also to one of the most evident failings of French government and society at the time, the failure to revamp its

197

hopelessly outmoded system of poor relief'.[47] Both Turgot in the mid-1770s and the legislators of the Revolution almost a generation later would fail, hopelessly, to tackle this huge problem of poverty and the crime it engendered.

Suggested reading

Baker, K. 'Controlling French History: The Ideological Arsenal of Jacob-Nicolas Moreau', *Inventing the French Revolution* (Cambridge, 1990).

Bonney, R. (ed.), *Economic Systems and State Finance* (Oxford, 1995).

Bossenga, G. *The Politics of Privilege: Old Regime and Revolution in Lille* (Cambridge, 1991).

Fairchilds, C. 'The production and marketing of populuxe goods in eighteenth-century Paris', in J. Brewer and R. Porter (eds.) *Production and the World of Goods* (London, 1991), pp. 230–42.

Kaplan, S. *Provisioning Paris: Merchants and Millers in the Grain and Flour Trade During the Eighteenth Century* (Cornell University Press, 1984).

Kley, D. Van *The Damiens Affair and the Unravelling of the Ancien Régime, 1750–1770* (Princeton, 1984).

Lewis, G. 'Henri-Léonard Bertin and the Fate of the French Monarchy: The Chinese Connection', in W. Doyle and M. Crook, A. (eds.) *Essays in Honour of Norman Hampson* (2004).

Linton, M. 'The Rhetoric of Virtue and the *Parlements*, 1770–1775', *French History* Vol 9 (1995).

Miller, J. *Mastering the Market: The State and the Grain Trade in Northern France, 1710–1860* (Cambridge, 1999).

Roche, D. *A History of Everyday Things: The Birth of Consumption in France, 1600–1800* (Cambridge, 2000).

Sonenscher, M. 'Fashion's Empire: Trade and Power in Early Eighteenth-century France', in R. Fox and A. Turner (eds.) *Luxury Trades and Consumerism in Ancien Régime Paris* (Aldershot, 1998).

Swann, J. 'Politics: Louis XV', in W. Doyle (ed.) *Old Regime France* (Oxford, 2001).

PART THREE

Reform and reaction

The fact that France would be celebrating the birth of the First French Republic in just two decades would have shocked courtiers attending the coronation ceremony of Louis XVI in 1775. A few of the military nobility of the sword might not have been surprised, however, given the rising profile of those damned, 'liberal', reforming ministers. One of the king's first decisions had been to place such a minister, Ann Robert Jacques Turgot, in charge of the nation's finances, which, thanks largely to a few good harvests and the abbé Terray's good housekeeping, were in reasonably good shape. By the late spring of 1776, however, friends of the old guard at court had secured Turgot's political demise. It proved to be a pyrrhic victory. By the summer of 1789, the Bastille was being stormed and the most serious peasant revolt of the eighteenth century, the Great Fear, was trampling over France's 'feudal constitution'. The poor had followed the nobility and the bourgeoisie into the public sphere, pitchforks, rather than printed manifestos, tucked under their arms.

Chapter 8

'New ideological wine into old constitutional bottles': reform and reaction, 1774–91

Social reform: from Turgot to Necker, 1774–81

Revolution was never an inevitable scenario, but Turgot's failure did suggest that marrying liberal capitalism to Bourbon monarchism would be an extremely risky process. The policies pursued by Henri Bertin and the abbé Terray had also suggested that, for those we shall henceforth refer to as the 'enlightened-monarchists', tackling the problem of mass poverty would have to be high on the political agenda. To achieve their goal, the power of the parlements would have to be curtailed so that the necessary fiscal and land reforms could be introduced. The abbé Terray had explained to the comte de Périgord in November 1772 that he was determined to introduce reforms in the commercial and agricultural sector. However, this did not mean 'that I will tolerate grain prices rising excessively so that big landowners can enrich themselves at the cost of the poor, who have to survive on the poor wages they receive'. Even more revelatory of the disturbing relationship between free trade policies and 'the social question' was Terray's comment that whenever he was called to intervene in the market, 'I shall do so because I am always conscious of the interests of the masses (*la multitude*), for whom bread is their main, often their only, source of nourishment, and whose seditious actions, when bread is scarce, can destroy empires.'[1]

Jacques Turgot's manifesto was based upon the introduction of free trade, labour and market liberalisation, tempered with policies aimed at ameliorating the suffering of the poor, an overall programme that bears a remarkable similarity to those pursued today by European governments. However, contemporary attitudes towards the poor are markedly different from those adopted in the 1770s. Liberal social and economic policies in Turgot's day had to begin by elevating the status of manual labour, unleashing, in the process, the political potential of the poor. Henceforth, *le peuple* would be divided into those who sought to raise their ignoble condition through hard work – *le bon peuple* – and those who did not – *le mauvais peuple*. The abbé Mably argued that the king should do what God had seemingly failed to do – guarantee a living for all his subjects. Mably was one of those rare radicals

201

of the Enlightenment who, along with Rousseau, D'Holbach and the *curé* Meslier, urged ordinary people to fight for their rights if governments refused to address this issue.[2]

Turgot's programme did include radical fiscal, constitutional *and* social reform. Unfortunately, his appointment coincided with the recall of the magistrates who had sat in the pre-Maupeou parlements, since Louis was anxious to court popularity for a monarchy that had lost its street credibility, a matter of increasing importance in this period of the late Enlightenment. Initially, Turgot had argued against restoring the powers of the parlements, but his resolve had been weakened by the man Louis XVI had chosen as his personal mentor, the comte de Maurepas. The return of both Maurepas, who had been forced out of office by madame de Pompadour as long ago as 1749, and the parlements, which insisted, rightly, that their constitutional pedigree could be traced back to the fourteenth century, provides us with a prime example of new, ideological wine being poured into old, cobwebby, court and constitutional bottles. Not surprising, then, that Turgot's reign as controller-general was to be short and stormy. Appointed on 24 August 1774 and forced to resign on 12 May 1776, he became a victim of the contradictions that had characterised government policy since the death of Louis XIV. Should the France of Louis XV and XVI be a slightly modernised version of France under Louis XIV, or should serious constitutional change be introduced? Should France fight England on the world stage, or should she be content with continental hegemony? Finally, a contradiction that was becoming sharper during the second half of the century: given the introduction of free trade policies, should the state simply rely on force to suppress popular opposition, or should it replace the decaying institutions of Church and private charity with a national programme of social reform?

Turgot and Necker would both confront these fundamental issues, although their approach would be different, more a question of means, perhaps, rather than ends. It is difficult to place Turgot in any convenient political pigeon-hole. Often described as a physiocrat, he was by no means an uncritical supporter of Quesnay and Du Pont de Nemours. He did share the predilection of the physiocrats for strong government, but placed far greater emphasis on the need to stimulate commerce and industry, as well as agriculture. The fundamental issue for Turgot was that which confronted all reforming government ministers – how to resolve the problems raised by the contra-diction between the implementation of a *laissez-faire* economic programme and improving the condition of the masses. Turgot was convinced – like Adam Smith, whose *Wealth of Nations* was published during Turgot's period in office – that the 'invisible hand' of the market would confer prosperity and freedom upon producers and consumers alike – over the long term. However, in the short term, something constructive and meaningful would have to be offered to poor consumers, something that did not include, Turgot insisted, going soft on popular violence.[3]

The reaction to three of Turgot's policies reflects the complexity of the issues involved and the strength of the opposition he faced: the reintroduction, on 20 September 1774, of freedom of the grain trade; his opposition to the medieval character of Louis XVI's coronation in June 1775; and the 'Six Edicts', registered by the Paris parlement on 12 March 1776.

The reintroduction of free trade was a brave move: it immediately nailed Turgot's colours to the *laissez-faire* mast. How could one go on defending policies that produced surpluses of grain in one part of France and famine in another, he asked? Why should grain merchants not sell directly to individuals or store grain in warehouses for emergency use? All this appeared to be self-evident to rich grain producers and merchants, less so to the millions of poor consumers who accused grain merchants and government ministers of making fortunes out of grain speculation. As for hoarding grain that could be sold when prices rose, this was contrary to all justice, the actions of perfidious and amoral *monopoleurs* and *affameurs*, those 'leeches' who drained the blood of the poor. It was during this period that the traditional and popular myth of a 'famine pact' concocted by corrupt ministers won new followers.

Unfortunately, the harvest of 1774–5 failed in many parts of France. Turgot also had to deal with an extremely serious cattle epidemic, one that decimated entire herds, although it was the food riots, affecting the regions of Burgundy and the Île-de-France in particular, that posed the most serious problems for the government. From the spring of 1775, consumers in the rich, grain-producing areas around Paris, were being asked to pay 14–16 *sous* for their four-pound loaf, double the customary price. From the end of March, to the first months of May, serious rioting occurred from Champagne and Burgundy to small market towns along the river Oise around Paris. At the end of April, what became known as the 'Flour War' reached the very gates of Versailles, where Louis XVI was forced to address agitated crowds. Government officials and merchants were attacked; wagons and barges were blocked as they moved food supplies from one region to another; grain was seized and sold at a price people could afford (*taxation populaire*). Women frequently took the initiative, emphasising their particular role in food riots as well as the difficulty of feeding their families. A typical example was the riot at the market of Beaumont-sur-Oise on 22 April where a group of women wrestled a sack grain from a man who had paid, in their opinion, too high a price for it. The mounted constabulary (*maréchaussée*) managed to retrieve it, provoking a furious reaction from the women who shouted, 'We shall see what happens next week!'[4] Turgot kept his nerve, and – what was more important – so did the king, on this occasion. *Pour décourager les autres*, two men, a wigmaker and a textile worker, were hung on 11 May from a high gibbet on the place de Grève, outside the town hall in Paris. The Flour War was virtually over, but sporadic outbursts of unrest in the countryside continued.

A month later, Louis XV1 was crowned in Reims with all the pomp and circumstance of a medieval monarch. He was anointed with the holy oil that had allegedly sanctified Clovis. In an act that moved the king a few steps towards divinity, he 'cured' 2,400 sufferers from scrofula. The clergy, anxious about the spread of irreligion and unsettling talk about granting civic rights to Protestants, insisted that the coronation oath should include the king's post-Reformation duty to 'extirpate heresy'. The intolerance of the majority of the French clergy remained a major obstacle to religious toleration, as it did to democratic reform. The customary practice of allowing ordinary people to attend the ceremony, recognition of the bond that linked the monarch to his people, was omitted in 1775. Turgot, a materialist by persuasion, had favoured a simple, 'modern' service, convinced that, in an increasingly secular age, the close association of throne and altar would have to be exchanged – sooner rather than later – for one based on an alliance of throne and nation.[5]

But Turgot's reforms were provoking serious opposition at court and in the country. The parlement of Paris only agreed to his Six Edicts on 12 March 1776 under duress; elderly court favourites like Maurepas (eighty-one when he died in 1781) and the foreign minister, the comte de Vergennes, regarded them as a direct attack upon the social foundations of absolute monarchy. Four of the edicts dealt with the further deregulation of markets in the capital, but it was the two remaining edicts that created the anti-Turgot coalition responsible for his resignation in May. The first abolished the privileges and statutes governing almost all the guilds. Turgot believed that the guilds were a major obstacle to the expansion of commerce and industry, discriminating, as many did, against female and foreign (especially English) workers. In other words, labour markets had also to be deregulated. But this, in the eyes of Turgot's critics, was an attack upon the corporate structures of the French state – 'today the guilds, tomorrow the parlements!' was the fear. Turgot, in response, informed the king that his edict, 'after that which established the freedom of the grain trade, represents one of the most important acts in the amelioration, indeed in the regeneration, of the kingdom'.[6] The edict that commuted the peasants' feudal obligation to build and repair the country's roads (the *corvée*) into a money payment, paid by the privileged and unprivileged orders alike, was again criticised as a direct attack on the fiscal privileges of the nobility, the thin end of a very thick anti-feudal wedge. Turgot, and other enlightened absolutists, were indeed trying to undermine the particularist, corporate and venal character of French government and society.

Too many enemies with too many privileged axes to grind eventually secured Turgot's fall. They were encouraged by the fact that his liberal free-market policies did not enjoy the support of the mass of the working population. But, however we weigh the evidence, it is a mistake to associate the fall of the Bourbon regime with any particular minister, Choiseul, Turgot, Necker or Calonne. The problems were long term and structural, with *les privilégiés*, from princes of the blood, magistrates of the parlements and court financiers placed at one extreme, and the mass of the exploited poor at the other. Peers and princes of the blood revealed their opposition to the policies of the enlightened-monarchists throughout this period, boycotting Maupeou's reconstituted parlement and plotting to get rid of Turgot. On 29 January 1776, the prince de Conti, exhibiting the traditional, frondeur behaviour of his family, rushed to the Paris parlement to lead the opposition against the Six Edicts. As for the parlements, even the reconstituted parlement of Bordeaux had protested against Terray's tax reforms in 1772, deepening splits with the Triumvirate. In 1776, the Paris parlement led the protests against the abolition of the guilds and the commutation of the *corvée*. One magistrate, who was to make something of a name for himself, Jacques Duval d'Eprésmesnil, expressed the opinion that those who were going around preaching the virtues of free trade in everything were no better than the Jesuits.[7] Lucien Laugier's unflattering portrait of Turgot argues that his only consistent support came from a handful of *philosophes* and physiocrats, and that, in any case, the abbé Terray and Turgot's successor, Jacques Necker, were both better at running the country's finances, as well as being more sympathetic to the needs of the poor.[8]

Jacques Necker, a Protestant Swiss banker, appears to be an odd choice as 'director of finance' (his faith meant that he could not be given the actual title of controller-general). But investors had confidence in him, since Necker enjoyed the reputation of being something of a financial wizard. However, in recent years, he has also emerged as a man who possessed genuine social concern. In the financial sphere, he continued the work of Terray and Turgot, endeavouring to balance the books, not by raising taxes, but by lowering interest payments on loans, improving the fiscal system and reducing the wasteful expenditure of the royal household. These were not 'revolutionary' expedients; they did not seriously challenge the privileged position of the nobility, apart from increasing, slightly, the burden of the *vingtième* tax. Nonetheless, with the help of some creative accounting, they did help Necker to balance the books; indeed, his famous balance sheet, the *Compte rendu*, published in 1781, actually envisaged a surplus of income over expenditure of 10 million *livres*. This was more than enough to attract loans at cheaper rates than had been possible hitherto. In terms of social policy, both monsieur and madame Necker were active social reformers. The latter was a tireless campaigner on behalf of hospitals and charitable institutions for the poor. In 1775, her husband had published a pamphlet entitled *Sur la législation et le commerce des grains* which suggested a compromise on free trade that would have protected the interests of the poor. Necker argued that free trade should be allowed when grain prices fell below 30 *livres* a *setier*, with price controls being reintroduced once they had risen above this figure. This was a minister who, whatever the flaws in his economic theory, had the courage to confront the 64,000 *livre* question – how could one introduce a liberal economic programme without aggravating the miserable plight of millions of the king's subjects.

Encouraging Necker's attempts at social reform was the realisation that the poor were finding a voice that was being heard in the public sphere. Jean Nicolas's national enquiry into popular movements has established that, although there was no national revolt on the scale of the Great Fear of 1789, anti-seigneurial riots, involving attacks on enclosures and pigeon-lofts, and assaults on seigneurial agents, increased markedly between the 1760s and the Revolution. In the Bordeaux region, the years 1773–4 had witnessed 'the most intense period of armed unrest before the Revolution . . . unrest [that] was caused by the problem of subsistence'.[9] To explain why Necker's social policy failed to match the scale of the problem, we need to place it within the long-term evolution of government repression and rising levels of crime. Repression in France during the 1760s and 1770s was harsher than in Hanoverian England.[10] In certain regions, especially those with high migrant populations, the arrest of impoverished individuals and families seeking work had actually increased after Turgot's dismissal. In many places, repression depended upon the numerical strength and leadership of the rural constabulary, as well as the financial rewards that were introduced for capturing delinquents. For Turgot, as for the archbishop of Toulouse, Loménie de Brienne, *dépôts de mendicité* were 'hideous . . . asylums more horrible than criminal prisons'.[11]

Several studies on the social history of crime covering the second half of the century emphasise the link between poverty, starvation and theft. Nicole Castan's research reveals that, in the south, theft was 'multiform and omnipresent'. On average, over two-thirds of the criminal cases in Bordeaux, Aix, Rouen, Toulouse, Nîmes and Grenoble were related to theft. On the eve of the Revolution, some 60 per cent of the death sentences passed by provincial courts concerned non-violent crimes, again mostly thefts. Richard Andrews has established that thefts accounted for approximately three-quarters of the crimes prosecuted by the criminal courts of the *Châtelet* and the Paris *parlement* from 1735 to 1789.[12] To obtain a more complete pictutre, more research needs to be undertaken on the provincial courts – particularly the provost courts attached to the mounted constabulary – which possessed the right to pass sentences without appeal. Such courts invariably took a far less humanitarian approach than the appeal courts attached to the parlements. The socio-cultural research of Jean Quéniart and his students at Rennes University has indicated the way forward.[13]

Neither Turgot nor Necker were allowed to implement fully their plans designed to ameliorate the condition of the poor. In August 1775, Saint-Priest, the Intendant of Languedoc had informed Turgot that 'vagabonds and beggars are a terrible plague for the countryside'. He wanted to transform the ghastly *dépôts de mendicité* into workshops for the poor, thus anticipating the Revolutionary association of poverty with unemployment and liberal economic reforms. Turgot's reply was that he was planning to close down all but five of the *dépôts* in France, sending younger delinquents to the army, but he fell from power before these radical, if desirable, measures could be implemented in full. Necker's plans – which again were never fully implemented – reveal a better understanding of the causes of mass poverty. In a letter written to the Intendant of Montpellier on 10 December 1777, he drew a necessary distinction between regions with large-scale farms (*pays de grande culture*), such as the Île-de-France and Burgundy, and regions in the centre, the south and the west characterised by small farms and sharecropping (*pays de petite culture*). In the former, landowners were rich enough to carry the burden of assisting the poor, Necker claimed. In the latter, regions of overpopulation and land-hunger, the great majority of landowners were not rich and were often forced to make tenants and farm labourers work for subsistence wages. One serious frost or hailstorm could transform the latter into wandering beggars.

However, the Intendant's reply revealed how difficult it was for a centralising state to impose its will on particularist provincial estates. He explained that he had very little money to set up charitable workshops, just 351,700 *livres* to cover nearly 3,000 communities. Funds from the *capitation* tax could not be tapped because the Estates of Languedoc had paid a lump sum to escape the charge. He could not squeeze any money out of the Church because the province had 23 bishops who would all resist the suggestion 'that the civil administration should poke its nose into charitable matters'.[14] Nonetheless, the inmates of the *dépôts* appear to have changed by the 1780s, largely because hospitals were too short of cash to admit the poor and needy. Take the *dépôt* set up in Grenoble, for example. Opened in 1768, its customary clientele were vagabonds, thieves and prostitutes, but, by the 1780s, it was also admitting illegitimate and orphaned children as well as a few 'honest paupers'. The cost to the government for housing the 9,000 individuals – one-third of them female – who were received, or incarcerated, between 1768 and 1789 was over 60,000 *livres* a year. The Grenoble *dépôt* may not have been a haven of peace and rest, but, given its secondary role as an annexe to the city's *hôpital-général*, it did make some contribution to the monarchy's laudable, but lamentably conceived and implemented, programme of social welfare.[15] It is conceivable that a strong monarch could have strengthened the hands of reforming ministers. Louis XVI was not that kind of monarch. Immature political ingénues, both Louis and Marie Antoinette, were peculiarly ill-suited to the task of refereeing this historic contest between a centralising, modern state and privileged, corporate, ecclesiastic and provincial bodies. John Hardman argues that Louis (only 21 years old in 1776) was not simply a pawn in the hands of his ministers, and this is undoubtedly true.[16] However, confronted with the crisis surrounding the dismissal of Turgot in 1776, Louis XVI had revealed that when it came to washing his hands, he could have given Pontius Pilate a lesson or two! As for Marie Antoinette, alienated by Turgot's attempts to reduce the massive 33-million-*livres* annual budget of the royal household, she began her disastrous career as 'the Queen of factions' by supporting the return of the duc de Choiseul. She would do much the same when Necker's dismissal was being discussed in May 1781.

Significantly, however, both Turgot and Necker were forced out of office on account of another historic contest, one as old as the fourteenth-century Paris parlement – the rivalry between England and France. On 19 April 1775, the confrontation between the English army and American rebels at Lexington had marked the beginning of the American War of Independence. The comte de Maurepas, encouraged by the faction around the exiled Choiseul and supported by Marie Antoinette and her coterie, seized the opportunity for revenge against England for the defeat of the Seven Years War. The Spanish, France's Bourbon allies, wanted to get Gibraltar back from the English (as they still do!) Vergennes, France's ageing foreign minister, first allowed money and volunteers to be sent, secretly, to America, and then drifted gradually into declarations of open warfare. It was an historic mistake. Here was an absolute monarchy, fighting for its own survival, about to borrow almost 1,000 million *livres* to support the creation of an American Republic 3,000 miles away. Necker had been dubious about the enterprise from the beginning and, in 1781, he pressed to be given control of the armed forces, in the forlorn hope that he might prevent further acts of diplomatic lunacy. His request was refused and Necker resigned. A few more misguided steps had been taken on the road to '1789'.[17]

'Liaisons dangereuses': political and cultural crossroads during the 1780s

Roger Chartier has suggested that we should isolate politics from both the philosophical thought of the period and the actions of government in order to 'reinvest the intellectual sociability of the century with a political content'. It is a valuable suggestion, given that there were no modern political parties in France to give this intellectual sociability ideological substance. The arrival of a more political age is personified in the career of the *philosophe*, Jean Antoine-Nicolas Caritat de Condorcet, who was only in his forties in 1789, a time when 'The winds of historical change began to rise . . . The time of the philosopher had passed. The time of the politician had arrived.' The late eighteenth century recorded remarkable political and constitutional change in many European countries, as well as across the Atlantic. Keith Baker has drawn our attention to the urgency with which the French Constituent Assembly of 1789 would seek 'to define and distinguish, with an eye to the American models, their own views of the meaning of a declaration of rights . . .'[18] This was, after all, the 'Age of the Atlantic Revolution'.

The universalist message of Enlightenment, for all its social conservatism, had undermined the authority of an aristocratic caste since the 1750s. From the early 1770s, Maupeou, Turgot and Necker had begun to challenge the political powers of the aristocratic parlements by threatening to create a far more representative system of local and provincial government. In August 1775, Turgot had commissioned 'a remarkable document', the *Mémoire des municipalités*, that advocated, for the first time, the creation of elected consultative local and provincial assemblies, specifically designed as alternatives to the parlements and provincial estates. Munro Price has described Turgot's efforts as 'the first systematic blueprint for France's transformation into an enlightened absolute monarchy'. In his memorandum of 1778, Necker visualised the creation of provincial assemblies throughout France, with equal numbers of clerics and nobles, a doubling of the representation of the third estate and a system of voting by head. It is true that only two assemblies would see the light of day, those of Berry in 1778 and Haute-Guienne a year later, but an extremely important precedent had been created, one that would exert an impact upon the history of the Estates General of 1789.[19] Enlightened-monarchists, such as Jacob Moreau – who had been appointed as tutor to Louis XVI – had been toying with the idea of calling an Estates General of the realm since the 1760s. But many of Moreau's unreconstructed royalist critics were profoundly worried that championing this new, more representative – if not truly democratic – political culture might unleash the spectre they all feared – a *social* revolution leading to the destruction of the aristocratic and feudal basis of the Bourbon monarchy. This was, indeed, the Achilles heel of the enlightened-monarchist. Moreau himself was certainly more 'monarchist' than 'enlightened' when it came to representative democracy.

The political content that emerged from 'the intellectual sociability' of the period – separable from, but also informing, the work of enlightened-monarchist ministers – included the ideas and opinions that were being aired in salons and academies, masonic lodges, coffee houses, newspapers and pamphlets. The public sphere was expanding, providing space 'in which to experiment and elaborate a democratic sociability that would find its most complete and explicit form in Jacobinism'. Aristocratic salons and academies had lost some of their veneer, conceding pride of place to more democratic forms of 'intellectual sociability', cafés, lodges and clubs modelled on English prototypes. Debates in the salon presided over by madame Necker in the 1780s were directed more towards more practical and social issues than had been the case in the salons of madame Deffand. A national press was emerging. Colin Jones speculates that a total newspaper circulation of 15,000 before 1750 may have risen to 60,000 by the mid-1780s. Given the increase in the number of reading rooms, coffee houses and clubs, the total number of readers might have been 'anything between a quarter and half a million individuals'. Masonic lodges, those 'laboratories of citizenship', had increased in number from 44 in the 1740s to 1,000 by 1789, boosting membership to anything between 50,000 and 100,000.[20]

If, as David Garrioch and Sarah Maza have argued, we should not yet correlate this new, more democratic 'intellectual sociability' with a bourgeoisie conscious of its separate class identity, French society was nonetheless becoming far more anti-aristocratic, surely a necessary stage in the process of creating a distinct bourgeois class. However, Maza has suggested that 'While the new idea of a "society" distinct from the polity did emerge in eighteenth-century France, it retained features strongly reminiscent of the absolutist synthesis.' But this was, indeed, the political and socio-cultural consummation devoutly wished for by the enlightened-monarchists – a classless society united in its love for the monarch and rejecting the atheism and immorality associated with an aristocratic caste.[21] Two famous literary works captured this anti-aristocratic mood – Caron de Beaumarchais's *Marriage of Figaro* and Choderlos de Laclos's *Les liaisons dangereuses*. The former was written in 1778, but, as a result of royal censorship, not performed at the Comédie-Française until April 1784. The plot – a wily servant, Figaro, unmasks the cynical and lustful actions of his master, a grand seigneur, count Almaviva – celebrated a long theatrical tradition of masters being outwitted by their servants. The message of the play – an attack on the values of hereditary nobility and state repression – was also hardly original. What made *Figaro* a box-office success was the wit and humour of its author, allied to the fact that, in the eyes of a late eighteenth-century Parisian audience, the butt of most of the jokes was a tasteless and cynical nobility that had lost its *raison d'être*.

Caron de Beaumarchais was himself a noble, and a rich one. He had bought the prestigious venal office of a *secrétaire du roi* for over 100,000 *livres*. What riled him was the fact that, through the lorgnette of a *real* noble of the blood, he was but a talented scribbler, a speculator, a man who made money by gun-running for the American rebels. Wealth could buy noble titles, but only birth ensured unfettered access to aristocratic society. More titles of nobility (4,000 of them) were bought, or conferred by royal patent, under Louis XVI than under his predecessor. But, although they might bring fame and fortune in the magisterial, financial, legal or industrial world for many, they could not secure a top job in the Church, the army, the navy or the government. Under Louis XVI, the velvet cushions that surrounded throne and altar, as well as many of those filled by the high magistrates of the parlements, were increasingly reserved for hereditary sword nobles. All of France's 139 bishops in 1789 were nobles, some of them living lives of princely grandeur. Many of Louis XVI's ministers, like the Ségurs and the Castries, were chosen from the ranks of the sword nobility; three-fifths of the magistrates in the parlement of Aix were sword nobles in the 1780s as opposed to two-fifths in 1715. And yet, as Albert Soboul wrote over 40 years ago: 'The feudal aristocracy seemed to be in a state of decadence . . . It was becoming poorer and poorer, with the Court nobility ruining itself at Versailles and the provincial nobles leading aimless lives on their lands.'[22] Mozart's operatic version of Beaumarchais's play, impregnated with masonic symbols and meanings (but often racist and anti-feminist, and thus a true reflection of the conservative wing of the Enlightenment!), would reflect the opinions of the German *philosophes*, Fichte and Lessing, that freemasonry existed to develop a culture of common humanity, not a code of caste distinction, throughout the world.[23]

Choderlos de Laclos's novel, *Les liaisons dangereuses*, was more acidic in tone than Beaumarchais's play, far more corrosive in its examination of aristocratic values and vices. If *Figaro* was about sexual conquest, *Liaisons* was about sexual exploitation and perversion, especially the perversion of the aristocratic soul. Moreover, and more controversially, it suggested that when it came to perverted human values, women could stoop as low to conquer as men. Of the two spiders constructing their social and sexual webs of corruption, the marquise de Merteuil and the vicomte de Valmont, the former is the more deadly. The idea that women could rival men in sexual perversion deeply offended one of France's most widely read novelists, Madame Riccoboni, friend of the English actor, David Garrick, and author of best-selling romantic novels like *Lettres de Fanny Butler* (1757). A character such as de Merteuil could never have crept between the covers of a Riccoboni novel! Riccoboni's correspondence with Laclos reveals what was at stake – the literary assassination of the virtuous, domestic female constructed by Rousseau and Riccoboni since the 1750s. She accused Laclos in 1782 of creating an aberrant monster in de Merteuil; of 'providing strangers with a revolting vision of the morals of his nation'. 'Change your system, monsieur,' Riccoboni begged Laclos, 'or you will live burdened with the curse of half the world.'[24] The request was made more in sadness than in hope, for, as Madame Riccoboni herself confessed, she was a women of mature years, no longer in tune with the *esprit de siècle*.

The longing for social cohesion and a *patrie* founded upon loving family values was accompanied by a Rousseauesque rejection of a conspicuous wealth (*luxe*) that could purchase only depravity. The literature of the period is replete with references to the corrupting influence of money and its association with sexual immorality. Sébastien Mercier laments the fact that 50 million *livres* a year was spent on Parisian prostitutes, but just three million on charitable gifts. He praises the work of his contemporary, Restif de la Bretonne, who, in *Le paysan perverti*, records the temptations awaiting the innocent visitor to the capital: 'Ah! You happy republicans,' Mercier exclaims. 'Protect the moral purity that you find in your peaceful homes, that reward of happiness and domestic virtue.'[25] Madame Riccoboni had, allegedly, missed the point. It was precisely the *esprit* of the *fin de siècle* that was rotten.

Madeleine Gutwirth argues that *Les liaisons dangereuses* was 'rooted in contemporary preoccupations and formulations about women and sexuality', the main onslaught being directed against the immorality of the traditional nobility. For Gutwirth, the 1780s was a decade that set the distinction between the 'public male' and the 'domestic female' in concrete. Lynne Friedli tells us that passing legislation concerning erotic practices between women was thought unnecessary; 'they continued to move between the fluctuating boundaries of medical and pornographic discourse, where they flourish still'. Marie Antoinette moved between the 'fluctuating boundaries' of *luxe* and sexual licence, condemned, justifiably, for arranging a 700,000 *livres* annual pension for her favourites, the Polignacs, in 1780; condemned, unjustifiably, for wanting to purchase a million-*livre* necklace in the Diamond Necklace Affair five years later. This was a time when 'the Austrian bitch' became the favourite target for political pornographers, their publications rising exponentially between 1774 and 1789. In 1783, 534 copies of the scandalous *Essais historiques sur la vie de Marie-Antoinette* were destroyed in the Bastille by the government. Many of them concentrated on the queen's alleged sexual activities, including lesbianism. In her Freudian interpretation of these grotesque attacks on Marie Antoinette, Lynn Hunt suggests that the republican ideal of virtue during the Revolution would become 'homosocial', based on 'a notion of fraternity between men in which women were relegated to the realm of domesticity' – the queen as a regal victim of the Enlightenment's anti-feminism. There certainly was an unhealthy obsession with, and fear of, homosexuality and transsexuality during the 1780s. Marie Antoinette was accused of 'dissimulation', a peculiarly feminine and aristocratic trait aimed at 'effeminising' the male of the species. We should be cautious, however, about placing too much emphasis on the political impact of pornography. In a recent article, Vivian Gruder has accused feminist historians – as well as Robert Darnton – of underestimating the gullibility of the public: ' "Political pornography" was a handmaiden to politics, following in its path, an instrument in a preceding and larger political combat.'[26]

Feminist concerns were certainly being voiced during the cultural upheavals of the 1780s; indeed, Jane Abray has dared to suggest that 'even the image of the happy homemaker had begun to quiver' before 1789.[27] And, unlike many male sympathisers, feminist propagandists extended the hand of friendship to the masses. The *Journal des dames* extolled the virtues of the new *drame bourgeois*, expressing the hope that it might 'lead the illiterate people out of ignorance and slavery'. One of its editors, Madame de Beaumer, specifically espoused the cause of women of the popular classes. She also subscribed to the masonic vision of universality, that most effective solvent of class distinctions reflective of a changing capitalist and consumerist age.[28] Both Mercier, who wrote plays that included working-class characters, and Condorcet joined the ranks of a new phalanx of late *philosophes* whose writings extended beyond the male middle-class boundaries established by earlier colleagues. In 1788, Condorcet would publish a warning shot over the bows of male chauvinists with his *Très humble remonstrances des femmes françaises.*

If the values and historical claims of the noble second estate were clearly being challenged by the eve of the Revolution, it is hardly surprising that, given the aristocratic control of the Church, those of the clerical first estate were also under threat. John McManners suggests that 'the process by which the old monolithic Christian order was being eroded needs a name; probably the best to use is "laicisation", reserving "de-Christianisation" for the drastic purposive attack of the Revolution'. The process of erosion had been lengthy and complicated, involving the challenge to the unity of western Christendom during the Reformation; the rise of scientific and intellectual enquiry covering the period from the Renaissance to the Revolution; and the long-term advance of capitalism and urbanisation. By the end of the eighteenth century, the foundations of a new lay social and cultural order had well and truly been laid. The evidence was an almost universal detestation of the Church tithe; fewer people attending Easter mass and fewer sons of the bourgeoisie entering the priesthood; fewer provisions for the foundation of masses for the souls of the dead in wills; fewer names of saints being chosen for their children by parents; and fewer lessons in schools and colleges on religious affairs.[29]

The course of the Revolution of 1789 was to be profoundly affected by the waning authority of the Catholic Church. Remove religion and you deprive the ancien regime of its inner core and the Revolution of one of its main internal dynamics. This was a worry that had often disturbed the slumbers of enlightened-monarchists such as Jacob Moreau and Henri Bertin. The relationship between government, religion and social order had always been of fundamental concern to both men as they wrestled with the problem of renovating the Bourbon monarchy. For them, the scandal and sensationalism surrounding the 'animal magnetist', Franz Anton Mesmer, who arrived in Paris in 1778 with the message that heavenly bodies acted on all living creatures by the emission of a fluid that could penetrate all matter, was proof of what people might believe when it was announced that 'God is dead'. Bertin, as a result of his prolonged and erudite exchanges with the French Jesuit priest living in Peking, Joseph Amiot, had even toyed with the idea of employing Confucian philosophy – washed in the transforming waters of

Jesuit theology – to fill the moral space left by a departed deity. One should not be totally shocked by this: Voltaire had once described Confucius as 'the Chinese Socrates'. Confucianism promoted personal perfection, love of one's fellow man and woman and that all-important 'submission to legitimate authority'.[30] It may have been an exotic substitute for Catholicism, but speculation about its values reflects the seriousness of the struggle that was being waged in favour of a purified morality – and a revivified society!

The fiscal and financial crisis of the ancien regime

The nature of the economic crisis that preceded the Revolution has always attracted fierce debate. Was it 'contingent', the result of fiscal and political ineptitude, allied to the accident of two bad harvests? Or was it 'structural', related to changing patterns of world trade and the impact of the widely hated feudal system that underpinned the Bourbon regime? The focus of the debate has usually revolved around the statistical research of Ernest Labrousse, who argued that France experienced a long-term depression from around 1778 to 1787, followed by a short-term crisis that reached its peak in 1789. The collapse of the monarchy, in Labrousse's view, was inextricably linked to this long-term structural crisis, especially in the agricultural sector.[31] David Parker has insisted that, in 1788, 'the structural weaknesses of the French economy reasserted themselves in a major subsistence crisis which sent grain prices soaring with traumatic consequences for the textile industry and those dependent on it. A large part of the French population were still locked into social structures which continued to prevent them, as they had done for two centuries, from contributing to economic development either as producers or consumers.' However, Colin Jones is more cautious, convinced that 'many aspects of the economic difficulties seem to have had more to do with unwise government policies than with problems gestating over the *longue durée*'.[32] Our view will be that Parker's assessment is substantially correct, but that Jones's comments provide the necessary modification.

Most scholars would agree that the exact timing of the Revolution was determined by adverse climatic conditions. Louis Cullen refers to 'the weather in late 1788 and early 1789 which, in a succession of snow falls, ice-blocked rivers and catastrophic thaw, created havoc for months'. He also links the harvest failures of these years with a psychological reaction that 'created in people's minds an overwhelming and hypnotic sense of foreboding which acquired a momentum of its own as an apparent physical parallel to the all too palpable political crisis'.[33] The crisis, of course, was provoked by the cost of French participation in the War of American Independence. The Treaty of Versailles between England and France had ended the war in September 1783, with France receiving little in compensation but revenge for the crippling defeat of the Seven Years War. In this case, revenge was to taste rather bitter. The war had cost around a billion *livres*, raising the old problem of debt repayment. From 1751 to 1788, the cost of servicing debts, incurred primarily in war, had risen from 28 per cent of total expenditure to 49.3 per cent. According to François Crouzet, the new controller-general, Calonne, should have declared a partial bankruptcy in 1783 and then continued the work of reforming the fiscal system. Instead, he fell back upon the fatal expedient of borrowing at high rates of interest. Between 1783 and November 1787, the government borrowed no less than 570.4 million *livres*. On the eve of the Revolution, it was facing a deficit of more than 160 million *livres*, with repayment of the Crown's debts absorbing over two-fifths of government spending.[34]

France's European foreign policy further weakened her position. By 1787, France's reputation had fallen abroad and she was on the verge of financial bankruptcy at home. The date of 17 August 1787 marked the beginning of an upheaval on the European continent comparable to the domestic crisis of 20 August 1786 in France when Calonne had informed Louis XVI that the country was drifting into insolvency. It was on this date that Turkey declared war on Russia, a war that provided a window of opportunity for Prussia's invasion (supported by the English) of the United Provinces in the autumn of 1787. Tim Blanning believes that 'If the rest of Europe had not been ablaze, from the North Sea to the Black Sea, with wars and rumours of wars, the Revolution would have developed very differently.'[35] The United Provinces was being torn apart by a struggle between the princely House of Orange and republican 'patriots', encouraged by the triumph of their American counterparts. The French, on the verge of bankruptcy and revolution, were impotent to intervene. The United Provinces, in 1787, was the geographic intersection where a misguided foreign policy collided with a ruinous fiscal system. On the high seas, England was now ruling the waves. Choiseul, taking his cue from William Pitt, had been right in the 1760s to perceive that 'in the present state of Europe, it is colonies, trade and, in consequence, sea power which must determine the balance of power upon the continent'.[36] Choiseul had always believed that France's control of Europe was related to her strength at sea and that, sooner rather than later, France and England would be forced into war. Spending on the navy would increase from just 25 million *livres* in 1774 to between 150 and 200 million by the 1780s. However, it was all too late to purchase imperial glory. French trading interests were collapsing in the Caribbean and China, as well as in India. By the 1780s, only a few French ships were to be seen moored along the quays of Canton, their former berths seized by the English in search of Chinese tea, silks and porcelain. The same collapse of a French presence was apparent in India where France now had just five trading posts representing little more than a sad 'acknowledgement of Enlightenment France's failure to embrace power and glory overseas'.[37]

Cardinal Fleury, Bertin, Turgot and Necker had preferred a continental peace to a global war. Unfortunately, confronted by England's aggressive policy world wide, the war party at Court believed that the option was never really available.

As a direct result of changes in the emerging capitalist world, especially the rise of English power, many markets worldwide had been closed to the French after the Seven Years War. By the late 1770s, her balance of trade was recording a deficit. Many sectors of the massive textile industry would suffer considerable losses from changing patterns of world trade. As early as 1778, the silk industry in Languedoc was being adversely affected by a Spanish edict prohibiting the sale of French goods in its colonies. In Nîmes, the Spanish government's decree of 23 December 1786, prohibiting the import of foreign silk stockings, was described by the city's merchants 'as a mortal wound'. James Thomson has charted the 'painful and protracted decline' of the woollen industry in Clermont-de-Lodève after the 1750s, adding that 'a similar pattern has been observed in many other industrial centres of France'. The effects of the Eden Treaty of 1786 unquestionably exacerbated a problem that had its roots in the 1770s and 1780s. The intentions of liberal policy makers such as Du Pont de Nemours were sound, but the timing was appalling. Declining textile towns, such as Elbeuf, that manufactured linen, woollen and cotton articles, now had to compete with the modernised machinery of Manchester, as well as the even lower-wage economies of Scotland and Ireland.[38] Of course, not all industries experienced long-term decline, as Louis Cullen's work on the wine trade and the buoyancy of some sectors – by no means all – of the colonial trade illustrate, but these tended to be notable exceptions to a fairly general rule. Did the agricultural sector, which produced almost three-quarters of the country's gross national product, also experience a structural crisis in the 1770s and 1780s? The answer for Labrousse, given his thesis of a *general* crisis of the ancien regime economy, had to be yes: agriculture was 'the motor of the pre-industrial economy'. French agriculture did experience 'a cycle of extreme instability', beginning in 1782, and punctuated only by the bumper harvest of 1787. Peter Jones concludes that the agrarian downturn really began in 1785, not 1788–9, with floods and droughts, cattle disease and crop failures aggravating 'those *structural* [my italics] weaknesses in the rural economy which Labrousse had identified'.[39]

In general terms, then, Labrousse was right: there *was* a long-term structural crisis of the ancien regime economy. And there is one component of that crisis that this work has sought to highlight – mass poverty, a constant, expanding blight on the landscape. Sébastien Mercier focused upon the suffering of those who were herded into the new *dépôts de mendicité* during the second Great Confinement of the poor between 1768 and the Revolution. In one of his many angry indictments, he writes that 'The atrocious and barbaric fashion in which they were treated from 1769 to 1772 will leave an indelible stain on a century that has been described as "human and enlightened". It seemed as if we were trying to exterminate them . . . they died in almost every *dépôt*, those prisons where indigence was punished as a crime.'[40] Poverty, constructed on human structures of misery and, all too often, horror, was, and would remain, a cancer in the French body politic. While many bishops lived like princes, paupers were subjected to harrowing punishments for stealing a few *sous* from the offertory box in their churches. Take the not untypical case of the 35-year-old farm labourer, Jacques le Bihan, arrested in the Breton *bailliage* of Auray in 1764. Accused of stealing money from churches, the soles of his feet were burned on nine occasions before he 'confessed' his crimes. He was then taken, dressed in a white robe and tied hand and foot, to be 'hung and strangled' on the place des Lices in Rennes.[41] There is good evidence – the abolition of torture, for example – that the judicial system had became somewhat less inhumane by 1789, but for the tens of thousands of wretches detained in the *dépôts* or dispatched to the galleys, life often meant a hell on earth. Kathryn Norberg in her study of poverty in Grenoble acknowledges the contribution of the Enlightenment to the march of human progress, but concludes that, in Grenoble, 'the late eighteenth century saw no sweeping innovations in poor relief and certainly no increase in the number of individuals receiving assistance'.[42]

Urban poverty was frequently imported from the countryside. David Andress, referring to the 1780s, sums up the plight of the impoverished peasantry: 'This group may have amounted to over half of the rural population, and had seen the price of basic food-stuffs outstrip wages substantially over the previous decades. Tenant farmers . . . were caught in a "scissors" of poor crop prices and rising rents. Even those fortunate enough to own their own farms . . . could not escape the burdens that the wider social system put on the agricultural population.'[43] John Markoff has identified a rising curve of peasant revolt during the last decades of the ancien regime. Basing his conclusions upon the pioneering work of Jean Nicolas and Guy Lemarchand, he informs us that 'From low levels during much of the century, apart from a spike around the famine of 1709, one sees clearly that the curve of conflict starts to rise in the 1760s. There is a sharp peak, the highest in the century so far, at the Flour War of 1775, and although the trajectory falls back afterward, it remains above its pre-1760s level and then begins a new, accelerating dizzy ascent in the late 1780s.'[44] A Bourbon regime that had failed to adjust in time to the dawn of a new era was unquestionably being undermined by the mass actions of the poor. From 1789 to 1791, a conservative bourgeois and noble elite would be propelled by the exigencies of state formation and the legacy of the humanitarian, radical Enlightenment into an unforeseen, and ultimately unsustainable, alliance with the radical Left to confront, if not to solve, this major social problem.

The bourgeois–popular revolution of 1789–91: 'mixed messages'

Edmund Burke in his best-seller, *Reflections on the French Revolution*, spotted as early as 1790 the most fateful 'mixed message' of the Revolution – the incompatibility of universal, or what Burke called 'metaphysical', truths with the very particular, individual property rights of the predominantly bourgeois ruling elite. The days of absolute monarchy were numbered when controller-general Calonne placed his project of reform on Louis XVI's desk in November 1786, a project described by William Doyle as 'the most radical and comprehensive plan of reform in the monarchy's history'.[45] It reflected the reforming efforts of the enlightened-monarchists from Bertin to Necker, including, as it did, a more equitable taxation system, the reform of provincial government and the reintroduction of free trade principles. It would provide the blueprint for the bourgeois–popular revolution of 1789 to 1791. However, Louis XVI's failure to provide solid support for Calonne, a failure that drove him into a deep and prolonged depression, would place his royal feet on the steps of the guillotine by January 1793. By 1789, Marie Antoinette was sitting in the king's inner council.[46]

Calonne had attempted to implement his reforms in February 1787 by using the political fig leaf of an 'Assembly of Notables' – 144 predominantly noble delegates, divided into seven committees, each chaired by a prince of the blood. Distrustful both of Calonne and his administration, the Assembly called into question two of the controller-general's main proposals – the tax to be levied on all landowners, irrespective of rank, and the creation of the new assemblies. On 8 April, the king, reluctantly, dismissed Calonne in favour of the queen's nominee, Loménie de Brienne. However, Brienne also failed to get unqualified support from the Assembly of Notables and, on 25 May, the archbishop terminated their meetings. Having been forced into the now fatal expedient of borrowing at high interest rates, Brienne turned for support to the parlements. It was not forthcoming. For the next eighteen months, the court was obliged to fight an exhausting battle against the thirteen parlements and the majority of the provincial estates, culminating in Louis XVI's historic agreement to convoke a meeting of the Estates General of the realm. Scheduled for 4 May 1789, it would be the first meeting of the Estates for 175 years.

For Louis XVI, there were very few alternatives. The court and its enemies had been revisiting old battlefields since the fall of Necker who, significantly, had to be recalled to deal with the threat of government bankruptcy in August 1788. On 3 May 1788, the Paris parlement had issued its famous 'Fundamental Laws of the Kingdom', which stated that France had always been a constitutional monarchy. The court replied with the May Edicts, an imitation by the Chancellor, Lamoignon, of Maupeou's short-lived plan to curtail the judicial and political powers of the parlements. Over the summer, the Assembly of the Clergy joined the chorus of aristocratic opposition to reform by launching 'a farrago of recriminations'. It offered less than a quarter of the financial grant requested by the king, and, for good measure, denounced the court's recent Edict of Toleration for Protestants. Finally, the Princes of the Blood delivered the unkindest cut of all by publishing a memorandum in December 1788 reminding the king that he was, first and foremost, an aristocrat, duty bound to defend the sanctity of the feudal system. In the light of all this, it is difficult to disagree with Albert Soboul's conclusion that 'The aristocracy did indeed start the struggle against absolute monarchy and they involved the Third Estate in the campaign, but they did so with the clear intention of establishing on the ruins of absolutism their own political power and of ensuring that their social privileges were not endangered.'[47]

This aristocratic opposition was cutting its own throat: the France of 1789 was not the France of 1614. The rapid and revolutionary sequence of events of 1788 and early 1789 further developed the political consciousness of the nation, whilst the threat of bankruptcy, recession and mass famine radicalised, and temporarily united, both the bourgeoisie and *le peuple*. A new raucous, radical voice could be heard, loud and clear, in the gardens of the Palais Royal, where the duc d'Orléans – soon to be known as 'Philippe Egalité' – choreographed opposition to Versailles. For his pains, he would follow his king to the guillotine in 1793! According to Jeremy Popkin, at least 767 pamphlets were issued between 8 May and 25 September 1788, rising to 2,639 during the first four months of 1789.[48] The most famous pamphlet of the time, the abbé Sieyès's *What is the Third Estate*, achieved that most remarkable act of political alchemy, transforming the third estate into 'the nation', with the poor and women as honorary attendants. For Sieyès, the nobility had 'ceased to be the monstrous feudal reality that could oppress people with impunity . . . it is now no more than a shadow, and this shadow will seek in vain to terrify an entire nation'. The political voice of the new nation-in-waiting was also heard in provincial cities like Grenoble, where, in July 1788, an assembly was set up in Vizille with the third estate receiving roughly the same number of seats as the clerical first and noble second estate. This issue of the 'doubling' of the third estate, along with the question of voting by head or by estate, would top the political agenda by the end of 1788.

Ironically, it was the government that took what proved to be the most revolutionary decisions of the period. Subjected to intense pressure, it agreed, on 27 December 1788, to double the representation of the third estate. This was a smart move, given that the Paris parlement had rejected this demand on 21 September (it subsequently reversed this judgement, but the damage had been done). Neither court nor parlement, however, had the courage to tackle the crucial question of how the Estates General would vote, by head or by order. Just as pregnant with revolutionary consequences – although the court was only following the procedures of 1614 – was the decision to allow every parish and corporation in the land to draw up notebooks of grievances (*cahiers de doléances*). Peter McPhee describes this decision as 'the decisive moment in the mass politicisation of social friction'.[49] The *cahiers* would provide the scripts for the 1,177 delegates to the Estates General in May 1789. The result of the remarkably democratic elections of early 1789 was an Estates General composed, originally, of 604 third estate deputies, exclusively bourgeois and predominantly lawyers, office-holders and landowners; 278 noble deputies, drawn mainly from the provinces; and 295 clerical deputies. Two points are worth noting: only 6 per cent of the members of the second estate were not sword nobles, but three-quarters of the clerical first estate were parish priests, sympathetic to the plight of their parishioners.[50]

From 1789 to 1791, the deputies to the Estates General would achieve something just short of miraculous – the root-and branch modernisation of France. Its first, unforeseen, task would be to overcome the resistance of the court and its traditional aristocratic supporters. On 17 June, the Estates General decided to call itself the 'National Assembly'. At a stroke, power passed from the first two estates to the third, dominated by the legal, professional and land-owning bourgeoisie. Over the next few days, this historic victory over the monarchy, weakened by a divided court and the death of the dauphin, would be confirmed by the defection to the third estate of a majority of parish priests, as well as by that of a minority of nobles. On 27 June, the king accepted, temporarily, defeat, although he continued to defend the values and privileges of the aristocracy. Indeed, rumours that the court had ordered troops into the capital to overthrow the 'National Assembly' provoked the popular uprising that was to assume iconic significance, the Storming of the Bastille on 14 July.[51] The *quatorze juillet* is still celebrated today, as well it might be. It witnessed the emergence of the politicised Parisian crowd – predominantly artisans and shopkeepers; it supplied the *coup de grâce* to absolute monarchy in France; it provoked, or supported, a series of municipal mini-revolutions throughout the country; and it marked the birth of the counter-revolution as many of the princes and their retainers fled abroad.

Parallel with this show of strength, a massive rural revolt was sweeping through most of France – the Great Fear of the spring and summer of 1789. The threat forced the deputies ensconced at Versailles to declare, on 4 August, 'the abolition of feudalism'. The fears expressed by the abbé Terray almost 20 years earlier had been realised – the people had overthrown an empire! On 24 August, a 'Declaration of the Rights of Man and the Citizen', influenced by American precedents, enshrined the principles upon which the new order would be established. One of the most influential pieces of parchment in modern history, it introduced political and religious freedoms, as well as equality before the law. Nonetheless, it contained several 'mixed messages', as Keith Baker has argued. For example, article one declared that men were born free and equal in rights, but did this egalitarian statement apply to women and did it promise voting rights to all citizens? Article seven defined the law as an expression of the 'General Will', but would this Rousseau-esque concept provide legitimation for the allegedly 'totalitarian' Jacobin Terror of 1793–4?[52]

The agenda of the National Assembly – or the 'Constituent Assembly' as it decided to call itself after 9 July – was long and immensely challenging. In the first place, it had to redraw the administrative map of France and modernise the judicial system. Second, it would have to establish a new framework of legislation relating to property rights following the 'abolition of feudalism' in town and country. Third, given its decision to nationalise Church property, it would have to introduce a new civil constitution of the clergy. Fourth, it would have to tackle the problem of unemployment and mass poverty. Finally, there was the small matter of legalising the transformation of France from an absolute to a constitutional monarchy. A lawyer from Arras, Maximilien Robespierre, summed up the task succinctly: it was simply a matter of 'complete regeneration' involving the creation 'of a new people'![53]

The collapse of the monarchy entailed the collapse of its legal and administrative infrastructure – parlements, provincial estates, Intendants, local government, public corporations. All disappeared, virtually overnight. From being one of the most centralised administrative states in Europe, France would become, for three years, at least, one of the most decentralised. The law of 14 December 1789 created a new system of local municipalities with elected mayors and councillors. The laws of 22 December 1789 and 15 January 1790 abolished provinces and replaced them with 83 departments, each with its subdivisions of districts, cantons and communes. This structure has lasted, with a few significant alterations, to the present day. The judicial system was also given a radical and permanent overhaul. In the civil sphere, elected justices of the peace would be introduced in each canton on 16 August 1790, with three elected – not venal – judges sitting in district courts above them. During the course of 1790, criminal law was modernised with the creation of police courts at communal and cantonal level, criminal courts at the level of the department and, on 27 November, a Supreme Court of Appeal in Paris. The election of judges and the introduction of a jury system created the foundation of a modern judicial system. Along with the sweeping administrative reforms, these changes involved a major transfer of power from the king to the tax-paying people. The personnel of municipalities and courts of justice may not have changed in certain towns and villages, but all officials were now to be *elected*. The decentralisation of power involved, however, would favour the growth of political opposition to the Revolution if things went wrong, which they did.

The 'enlightened-monarchists of 1789' – unlike many recent revisionist historians – had experienced no problem identifying the link between feudal forms of rents and land ownership and the political power of the aristocracy as one of the main causes of disaffection with the monarchy. The monarchy had abolished serfdom on its own lands and was seeking, cautiously, a compromise with the nobility over the 'vestiges of feudalism' on their property. However, stiff opposition, from noble and bourgeois owners of seigneurial fiefs, had prevented root and branch reform. From 1789 to 1793, the peasantry, assisted by the outbreak of war in April 1792 and the consequent political radicalisation of the Revolution, would achieve what the most enlightened of the enlightened monarchists had hoped to achieve – the abolition of feudalism.

George Lefebvre's classic study of the Great Fear has established its causes, course and consequences – the autonomous nature of peasant revolt; the unco-ordinated, multi-pronged assault affecting many provinces (primarily in the north-east, the centre and the south) on *chateaux* and their feudal charters; the 'panics' unleashed by the largely unfounded fear of 'brigands' and foreign troops; and the alleged 'aristocratic plots' against the Revolution.[54] Recent research has served only to fill in the gaps and to modify a few of Lefebvre's major conclusions. Two of the latter are of particular interest to us – the argument that the Fear was not primarily motivated by anti-seigneurial sentiment, and the link between the Fear and pre-Revolutionary poverty and crime.

On the first point, there does not appear to have been a close relationship between the exaction of heavy feudal dues and outbreaks of the Great Fear. In John Markoff's opinion, dues did not increase significantly during the second half of the century. Peter Jones also argues that 'the issue [of anti-seigneurialism] scarcely acted as a fixative to the degree that Lefebvre would have us accept'. On the second point, Timothy Tackett has recently suggested that Lefebvre underplayed 'the extraordinary scope of the subsistence crisis and revolts in the spring of 1789', arguing that 'the overwhelming preoccupation of the rioters . . . was the shortage of food'. It was only *after* the Great Fear of 1789 that seigneurialism would become the 'target of choice' for the peasantry. Anti-seigneurial attacks would represent one-third of all peasant insurrections between the autumn of 1789 and 1793, with 62 per cent of anti-seigneurial riots occurring in the more impoverished south. However, subsistence riots came a fairly close second. This modification of Lefebvre's argument strengthens our claim that mass poverty and the fear of starvation played a significant role in fuelling peasant protest throughout the period from the 1770s to the Jacobin Terror of 1793. Hatred of feudal dues, which would lodge in the peasant psyche for half a century, was based on the need to satisfy the pangs of hunger, not the political programmes of anti-aristocratic campaigners.[55]

The problem for the Constituent Assembly's Feudal Committee after the 4 August (when feudalism was alleged to have been abolished *'in its entirety'*) was how to distinguish between dues that truly belonged to the feudal past and dues that were related to modern land contracts. Revolutions are invariably about bringing the past up to date rather than configuring the future! The solution, announced by the Committee between March and May 1790, was that dues involving all forms of personal servitude and feudal rights – the *cens* (the due paid in recognition of a seigneur's authority), work on the lord's estate, exclusive noble hunting rights, etc. – would be abolished outright. However, payments directly related to the rental, purchase or sale of land – the *champart*, *lods et ventes* and *banalités* – would have to be redeemed at 20 or 25 times their annual value. Now, for tenants and small-owning peasants in particular, feudal dues were feudal dues and no amount of legal chicanery or wordplay would justify their continued existence. Resentment over this crucial matter would turn to rebellion in many departments when it was later decreed that tenants would have to pay the Church tithe (*dîme*), which had also been 'abolished', in principle if it had been included in contracts with ecclesiastical or lay landlords signed before 1789. In May, riots swept through the recently created department of the Lot and several other departments, as publication of the government's decrees reached peasant communities. For Markoff, the 'dialectic' between a government keen to protect the legal rights of property-owners (especially bourgeois property-owners who had bought 'feudal' seigneuries before the Revolution) and peasant communities convinced that the tithe and many seigneurial dues belonged to the oppressive 'feudal past', would exert a powerful influence upon the Revolution until the 'time of the lords' was actually ended in 1793.

From late 1789, the optimism that had accompanied the expected abolition of all feudal dues, without redemption payments, was maximised by the prospect of purchasing a few acres of land from the massive sale of Church, and later *émigré*, property. In the short term, the 'nationalisation' on 2 November 1789 of around two billion *livres'* worth of ecclesiastical land would naturally induce 'a quickening in the land market'; it would 'nurture the property-owning ambition of the rural poor'.[56] The sale of 'National Lands', as the confiscated Church and *émigré* property would be described, unquestionably represents a major social revolution. The problem for the poorer peasants in particular was that they failed to get their expected share. It is true that hundreds of thousands of peasants, mainly those that already owned some land, joined the biggest land-rush in French history. Lefebvre estimated that, in the new department of the Nord, as much as 25 per cent of cultivable land was sold as National Lands, with the peasantry and the bourgeoisie sharing the spoils between them. However, this was something of an exception to the rule. Until the summer of 1792, land was sold at auction and, unless peasant communities banded together (which some did), they had precious little chance of turning the historic tide of bourgeois land purchase. In the Corbières region of southern France, for example, 'merchants from Carcassonne, Limoux, and Narbonne, bought up a disproportionate share of church property, with rural labourers acquiring less than 1 per cent of the value of the land sold'. Recent work conducted by Peter Jones provides further evidence that the bourgeoisie were the principal winners in this greatest land sale of the century.[57]

The Catholic Church lost not only its land but also its independence during the Revolution. It was necessary, therefore, to create a new structure for the governance of the Church. The result was the Civil Constitution of the Clergy, ratified by the Constituent Assembly on 12 July 1790. Influenced by the anti-clerical principles of the Enlightenment, it sought to rebaptise the French people in the waters of science and rationalism. For this reason alone, it would fail to win majority support, either in Rome or amongst the majority of the faithful. In the long term, it would produce 'a seismic fault in the political geology of the French revolution, provoking repeated tremors throughout every section of French society down to Napoleon's Concordat with the Papacy in 1802'. Nigel Aston has recently insisted upon the virulence of the Revolutionary attack upon the Catholic Church.[58] A final settlement for the Protestant and Jewish minorities (*c*.600,000 and 40,000 respectively) would also have to wait for Napoleon's 'tidying-up' of the Revolution, although both minorities had been granted full religious and voting rights by September 1791.

Many of the articles of the Constitution attracted considerable support – increased salaries for parish priests, the attack on non-residence, even the new Gallican (anti-papal) tone of the document. However, the seizure of Church property and the abolition of all archbishoprics, as well as 50 bishoprics alienated the upper clergy, whilst the decision that bishops and *curés* would be elected, by believers and unbelievers alike, failed to attract the support of the majority of the clergy. If only the Assembly had called a general council of the Catholic Church and allowed the Constitution to bed down with time, but time is inevitably in short supply during revolutions; there was also the fear that other corporate bodies would demand a say in what was happening. To speed up the clock of acceptance, the Assembly made the fatal mistake of ramming the settlement down the throats of the clergy. On 27 November 1790, clerics had to swear an Oath of Allegiance to the new Constitution. Only seven members of the upper clergy would take the oath, compared with just over half of the lower clergy. It is difficult to draw any general conclusions from the map of acceptance and rejection of the oath, although rejection was more widespread in the west, north-east and the southern Massif Central. Decisions, for or against, depended upon 'broader cultural assumptions and opinions of fellow citizens and fellow clergymen across whole pays or provinces'.[59]

The fears and resentments arising from the redemption of feudal dues and the Civil Constitution of the Clergy would not have provided fertile soil for anti-revolutionary, or subsequent counter-revolutionary, movements had it not been for the persistence of economic recession and unemployment. The effects of the deep recession of 1788–9 were exacerbated by the fiscal and financial policies of the Constituent Assembly. In the course of 1790–1, the Assembly agreed to the introduction of a new tax structure. It consisted of a land tax (*contribution foncière*), a poll or personal tax (*contribution mobilière et personelle*) and a tax on business (the *patente*). Indirect taxes, such as those on salt and drink, were abolished between 1789 and 1796, representing a considerable loss to the Treasury. The immediate problem, however, was that the responsibility for assessing and levying the new taxes fell upon the new municipalities, meaning that, in some cases, revenue would not be forthcoming until 1792. In 1791, the land tax only brought in 34 million *livres* in place of the budgeted 300 million. Richard Bonney states that 'tax collection did not become really effective, nor were revenues stabilised, at least in nominal terms, until 1797'.[60]

The deputies (conscious of their own financial investments?) refused to bridge the yawning financial gap by declaring a state bankruptcy, choosing instead to fund the cost of reorganising the kingdom by the introduction of paper money backed by the value of the land they had just 'acquired' from the Church. Thus, the financial floodgates were opened to the 'Great Inflation' that would adversely affect the course of the Revolution until the late 1790s. To facilitate the sale of Church lands, the government used the paper money they had invented called *assignats*. The original intention was that state creditors would be paid off in *assignats* that they would then exchange for National Lands (the *assignats* would then be returned to a specially created office to be destroyed). It was an ingenious, but ultimately disastrous, experiment, primarily because, instead of restricting the use of the *assignats* to pay off state debts, successive administrations would print notes worth billions of *livres* to finance war and the reconstruction of the state. Inflation followed as night follows day. It did not become an acute problem until late in 1792, but, from the outset, the nation was wary of paper money (grandfathers told alarming tales of 'John Law's experiment' in the 1710s to their children!). Hard cash began to be hoarded and commerce suffered accordingly.

Finally, the reintroduction of Turgot's liberal economic policies, masterminded by his disciple, Du Pont de Nemours, worsened the plight of the poor.[61] In August–September 1789, the Assembly reintroduced free trade in grain (Necker had refused this option in 1788). Lifting controls on the cost of basic food supplies during a period of mass unemployment and inflation was bound to aggravate the suffering of the poor. It was, nonetheless, totally consistent with the 'abolition of feudalism' in the countryside and the introduction of new property law founded upon individual, private contracts. Also consistent, but hotly contested by masters and men alike, was the passing of the Allarde Law on 2 March 1791 which abolished all corporations and guild masterships, thus implementing, posthumously, one of Turgot's cherished policies. Persistent strikes and demonstrations by urban and rural workers explain the introduction on 14 June of the 'bourgeois' anti-strike legislation that introduced a free market in labour – the *Loi Chapelier*. The law would remain on the statute book for almost a century. Jacques Turgot would obviously have been rejoicing, rather than revolving, in his grave.

But what about the flip side of Turgot's programme of 'enlightened reform' – social welfare? It was not forgotten by the influential *'monarchien'* faction in the Constituent Assembly which, in several important regards, attempted to implement the programme of the enlightened-monarchists of the ancien regime. The day before the famous 'night of 4 August', the *monarchien* deputy, Malouet, pressed the Assembly to discharge its responsibilities towards the unemployed masses. Malouet's speech was couched in terms that Terray, Turgot and Necker would all have applauded: poverty was an inevitable plague, but it was the duty of a civilised state to assist those in need. The Constituent Assembly, imbued with the spirit of the conservative Enlightenment, and alarmed at the scale of popular opposition to the Revolution, decided to act. On 21 January 1790, it set up a *Comité de mendicité* (the emphasis on the elimination of begging rather than poverty is significant). It had nineteen members, and was chaired by a liberal noble, the duc de La Rochefoucauld-Liancourt, friend of the radical *philosophe*, Condorcet. The committee would meet on 70 occasions and compile an impressive archive of statistics and reports that would produce the ammunition for the Revolution's assault on poverty until 1795. The Committee's three main achievements were to reveal, in some detail, the extent of poverty in France, to identify why the ancien regime system of charity had collapsed and to suggest what constructive measures should be adopted to remedy the situation. By 1791, replies to questionnaires from 51 departments had established the shocking statistic that France sheltered no fewer than 1,928,064 beggars within its borders. The causes were obvious – mass unemployment, the collapse of traditional forms of Christian charity and the financial collapse of hospitals deprived now of income from feudal dues, tithes and rents, and, of course, the inevitable consequences of disease and old age. Many proposed solutions to the problem were discussed, including the creation of saving banks and insurance societies offering policies to cover the sick and elderly, as well as charitable workshops.

Reports on the latter emphasise the scale of the social crisis in 1790–1, although the possibility of permanent state assistance sharply divided radicals from conservatives in the Constituent Assembly. Many deputies were disturbed to learn that the government was allocating 50,000 *livres* to pay the unemployed in the department of the Isère to dig ditches and build flood defences and that another 150,000 *livres* had been earmarked for work on the canal de Beaucaire. In June 1791, Liancourt reported that the situation was out of control: the capital alone was spending 900,000 *livres* a month to pay its 31,000 male and female workers. However, pity for the poor tended to evaporate by 1791 as charitable workshops became sites for political demonstrations. Exaggerated hopes discussed the previous year, that the discredited *dépôts de mendicité* could be transformed into 'old peoples' homes', collapsed. Given the financial and political difficulties of the time, as well as the existence of an increasingly conservative faction in the Constituent Assembly, it is hardly surprising that Liancourt and his well-meaning colleagues managed to construct neither a radical system of social services, nor a coherent attitude towards the poor. But the problem would not go away. It would reappear on the agenda of the National Convention.[62]

By the spring of 1791, the political consensus that had been forged between moderate bourgeois and liberal noble deputies sitting in the Assembly was beginning to crack under the strain of the political and social contradictions inherent in their reform programme. Nobles, led by the marquis de Lafayette and the comte de Mirabeau, desperately worked to bridge the gaps created by a court under pressure, from inside and outside France, to crush the Revolution, and an increasingly vocal Popular Movement. Mirabeau's early death on 2 April 1791 followed reasonably well-founded accusations that he had sold himself to the court. Lafayette lived on to lose another day. Both politicians were deeply concerned about mounting popular violence. As in the summer of 1789, the main threat came from the countryside. Anatoli Ado sums up the position succinctly: 'The "radical bourgeois" and the anti-ancien regime peasant producer . . . were both opposed to the moderate bourgeoisie and the liberal nobility, still attached, in so many ways, to feudal and semi-feudal forms of social relationships, and increasingly concerned about the fate of private property . . . Food riots led by poor, starving peasants, demonstrations in favour of price-fixing and a controlled economy, strikes organised by rural workers, all provoked widespread fears'.[63] And dissatisfaction was not confined to land-hungry peasants and unemployed workers. By the summer of 1791, hereditary nobility had been abolished, swelling the ranks of the *émigrés*, and the state had recognised the religious and civic rights of Protestants, thus driving more Catholics into the anti-Revolutionary camp. Elections for local and departmental offices had provoked new rivalries and divisions in many towns and villages. The new municipal district and quite conservative departmental councils were receiving an increasing volume of complaints about taxes, redemption dues, tithes, disputes over common lands, unemployment and high food prices.

It was in response to this growing chorus of discontent that an urban and rural Popular Movement began to assume political and organisational shape. Shaken by the violent manifestations of popular power during the Great Fear and the Storming of the Bastille, the majority of deputies in the Constituent Assembly had tried to convince the mass of the population that the Revolution was over and that everyone should abandon the barricades. A draconian law had been introduced as early as 21 October 1789, following violent protests in the capital. Significantly, the protest had taken the form of a food riot, culminating in the lynching of a baker. The fear of popular violence helps to explain why the deputies decided to divide voters into 'active' and 'passive' citizens, the latter, ironically, being those most prone to indulge in public protest! On 22 December, the Assembly, working on the new Constitution, disenfranchised 40 per cent of the adult male population – women, of course, were completely excluded from the political arena. 'Active' citizens would qualify for the vote by paying the equivalent in direct taxes of three days' work. These fortunate citizens would then choose 'electors', who merited their exalted position by paying the equivalent of 10 days' work in annual taxes. Deputies to the future Legislative Assembly could only be selected from the ranks of those who paid over 50 *livres* in taxes. Malcolm Crook is undoubtedly right to remind us that this system of voting still made France the most democratic country in Europe. Nonetheless, as Maximilien Robespierre and the sanguinary editor of the *Ami du peuple*, Jean-Paul Marat, pointed out, 'an aristocracy of wealth' had, effectively, replaced 'an aristocracy of birth'.[64]

The powerhouses of the Popular Movement that would overthrow the Bourbon monarchy on 10 August 1792 were the popular clubs and administrative and electoral bodies created by the Revolution since 1789. However, the most influential organisation to flourish during the early years of the Revolution was the predominately bourgeois Jacobin Club. From its headquarters in the rue Saint-Honoré, lawyers like Brissot and Robespierre would broadcast their political principles to hundreds of clubs throughout France, as well as to many throughout the world. The Cordelier Club, more popular in composition, would build more bridges with the poor, as well as with female activists. There were also the 48 Sections into which Paris had been divided in 1790 for electoral and administrative affairs. During the summer of 1792, they would be invaded by those supposedly quiescent 'passive' citizens, allying themselves to slightly more affluent radical artisans and craftsmen to form the sansculottes (a description that separated them from those who wore the breeches [*culottes*] of the bourgeoisie). A barometer of the rising political atmosphere throughout France was the increase in the number of provincial clubs affiliated to the Jacobin Club in Paris – 20 in January 1790, 300 by January 1791 and mushrooming to 900 by July of the same year. A handful of women activists formed their own clubs: the *Fraternal Society of the Two Sexes* allowed men and women to participate in political discussion on an (almost) equal basis. Feisty, feminist journalists like Louise Kéralio, co-editor of the *Mercure national* with her husband, François Robert, supported them. The work of an impressive array of feminist historians (see also chapter nine) has transformed *'les tricoteuses'* from cobwebby, Dickensian caricatures to early pioneers in the historic struggle for women's rights, personified in England by Mary Wollstonecraft.[65]

History is littered with 'if onlys' but, if only the Constitution of 1791 had created a constitutional monarchy on the English model, could war and the Jacobin Terror of 1793–4 have been avoided? It seems improbable. In any case, the court, bolstered by increasing internal discontent and external prompting from absolutist European regimes, refused to accept the idea of a constitutional monarchy. By June 1790, the first significant manifestation of organised counter-revolution had occurred in Nîmes, a bloody encounter that left several hundred Catholic royalists dead in the streets. The so-called 'bagarre de Nîmes' evoked the horrors of the sixteenth-century Wars of Religion, and its consequences were to shape the course of the Revolution in much of south-eastern France throughout the 1790s. Significantly, the massacre occurred during an electoral campaign, revealing the explosive mix of religion and politics that can still shake the foundations of 'modern' states. Throughout 1790 and 1791, class war in Lyon, France's second city, divided the rich from the poor sections of this wealthy manufacturing and mercantile city, with the former adopting an increasingly royalist, if not counter-revolutionary stance.[66] Abroad, the princes and a sizeable minority of the nobility, joined by a few bourgeois, had been creating a very loose confederation of counter-revolutionary camps in England, Germany, Italy and Switzerland. From Turin and Koblenz, agents of the comte d'Artois and the comte de Provence pestered foreign courts for shelter, money and, with the connivance of Louis XVI and Marie Antoinette, promises of armed intervention in French affairs.

A second reason for the rejection of a constitutional monarchy based on the English model was the refusal of the majority of deputies in the Constituent Assembly to countenance the notion of an aristocratic upper house. It is true that the Constitution, finally approved in 1791, had endowed the king with considerable powers. He could, for example, chose his own ministers outside of the Assembly and delay legislation for several years through the device of a 'suspensive veto'. Nonetheless, all this could not mask the fact that effective power had passed to the people, or, rather, to 'the propertied people'. The decree of 10 October 1790 stated that Louis was 'King of the French', theoretically 'by the grace of God', but, in practice, he ruled 'by the constitutional law of the state'. Members of the constituent assembly, the administration and the judiciary were now elected, not appointed by the Crown. Furthermore, it was the Assembly that initiated legislation, leaving the Crown to provide only its royal rubber stamp. As for the aristocracy, they were identified with a feudal regime that had been 'abolished in its entirety'. It was hardly conceivable, therefore, that its power should be reconstituted in the architectural shape of a 'House of Lords'.

Three events now concentrated the political mind of the nation. On 21 June 1791, Louis XVI and Marie Antoinette finally made their break for freedom, planning, eventually, to join the Austrian army in the Netherlands. Typical of the ineptitude they had so frequently manifested since 1774, they only got as far as the town of Varennes in north-eastern France. The conservative groups in the Assembly invented the fiction that the royal family had been abducted. It fooled only those who were terrified of the Revolution slipping into the bloody hands of 'passive' citizens. On 17 July, a republican demonstration on the Champs-de-Mars, organised by the Cordelier Club, was savagely broken up by the bourgeois National Guard. Some 50 demonstrators were killed – more 'blood of the martyrs'! On 27 August, the Prussian and Austrian rulers issued their Declaration of Pillnitz, threatening, somewhat weakly, to wreak vengeance on the French if a hair of Louis XVI's head was removed. The French crisis had been internationalised. These three events sharply divided the bourgeois–noble political elite. On 15 July, the division had already assumed institutional form with the decision of the majority of conservative members to withdraw from the Jacobin Club to form the Feuillant faction.

On 30 September 1791, the Constituent Assembly ended its Herculean labours. The Legislative Assembly that replaced it was supposed to implement the legislation already passed. In fact, its brief twelve-month history only provided a passage to foreign war and the establishment of the First French Republic.

Suggested reading

Andress, D. *French Society in Revolution* (Manchester, 1999).

Aston, N. *Religion and Revolution in France, 1780–1804* (Washington, D.C., 2000).

Bell, D. *The Cult of the Nation in France: Inventing Nationalism, 1680–1800* (London, 2001), chapters five and six.

Crook, M. *Elections in the French Revolution* (Cambridge, 1996).

Cullen, L. 'History, Economic Crisis, and Revolution: Understanding Eighteenth-century France', *Economic History Review*, Vol 46 (1993).

Doyle, W. *The Oxford History of the French Revolution* (Oxford, 1989).

Forrest, A. *The Revolution and the Poor* (Oxford, 1981).

Hardman, J. *Louis XVI* (London, 2000).

Jones, C. *The Great Nation: France from Louis XV to Napoleon* (London, 2002), chapters nine to eleven.

Jones, P. *Liberty and Locality in Revolutionary France: Six Villages Compared* (Cambridge, 2003).

Lewis, G. *The French Revolution: Rethinking the Debate* (London, 1993).

Lucas, C. 'Nobles, Bourgeois, and the Origins of the French Revolution', *Past and Present*, Vol 60 (1973).

Price, M. *The Fall of the French Monarchy: Louis XVI, Marie Antoinette and the Baron de Breteuil* (London, 2002).

Tackett, T. *Religion, Revolution and Regional Culture in Eighteenth-Century France: the Ecclesiastical Oath of 1791* (Princeton, 1986).

Woloch, I. *The New Regime: Transformations of the French Civic Order* (New York, 1994).

Chapter 9

War and dictatorship

Eighteenth-century European states were ultimately shaped by economic and military power. In France, financial and fiscal deficiencies had precipitated the Revolution, whilst the military marathon with her English and European enemies between 1792 and 1815 would finally determine, *grosso modo*, the contours of the country we know today. During the wars of Louis XIV and those of the Revolution and Napoleonic Empire, mass armies of up to 750,000 men transformed the character of French society: millions of French men, women and children died as a direct result of war and its outriders, disease and famine. Roughly 1,500,000 people would be killed between 1792 and 1815. An eminent French economic historian has even claimed that the 'Second Hundred Years War' (covering the period from the reign of Louis XIV to that of Napoleon) transformed France into 'a weak, poor, backward, wretched and unhappy country'.[1] It is imperative, therefore, that, before studying the course of the Revolution in greater detail, we should make some general observations about the impact of war on Revolutionary politics and society. It is no coincidence, after all, that France's national anthem, written by Rouget de Lisle in 1792, is a hymn of praise to war.

The Revolutionary conflict began on 20 April 1792 with a declaration of war on Austria. There was an interlude in hostilities with the Peace of Amiens, from March 1802 to May 1803, which proved to be simply a breathing space before another 12 years of warfare. Identifying the causes of the war on Austria reveal the geographic reach of the problems that were to transform a national revolution into 'the greatest conflict in the history of the world until that time'.[2] They include an atavistic hostility to the Franco-Austrian alliance of 1756, sharpened by Marie Antoinette's treachery; the *émigré* military camps set up on France's north-eastern borders; and the European alliance system. Jacques Brissot, the loudest advocate for war in the Legislative Assembly, successfully stirred the blood of his fellow deputies by warning them that 'We cannot be calm until Europe, all of Europe, is in flames.'[3] It soon would be, with the heat being felt around the rest of the trading world.

The daunting task of securing victory against the major European powers involved a revolution within the Revolution. The regiments of just 170,000 men inherited from the ancien regime had to be transformed into a modern national army – the 'nation-in-arms'. The foundations for this transformation would be laid during the 1790s, although it was Napoleon who was to complete the task.[4] The historic victory over the Prussians at Valmy on 20 September 1792 was won, in the main, by the regular troops of the line. However, the thousands of volunteers that had rushed to the colours to save the Revolution had unquestionably bolstered the army's morale. General Custine's troops went on to liberate the north-eastern fortress towns of Verdun and Longwy before occupying the Rhineland in October, whilst general Dumouriez's men marched into the Austrian Netherlands (the future Belgium) to defeat the Austrians at Jemappes on 6 November. In the east, the French had taken the Swiss town of Basle a week earlier. The Revolution had been saved, but the volunteers, who left the army in droves at the end of their contracts in December, could not have realised that Valmy and Jemappes had been just the first skirmishes of a very long war. On 21 February 1793, having declared war on England and Holland on the first of the month, and faced with the resurgence of Prussian and Austrian power, the military committee of the National Convention (20 September to 26 October 1795) decided to amalgamate regular and volunteer troops. Although full integration would take years, demi-brigades were gradually created from the union of one battalion of regulars with two battalions of volunteers, an important first step towards a unified Revolutionary army.

Given that it would have to take on, at one time or another, all of the European Great Powers, this 'new model army' would have to be increased in size as well as reorganised. The departure of the first batch of volunteers had reduced the army from *c*.400,000 men at the beginning of December 1792 to *c*.220,000 by February of the following year. To fill the gap, the government decided to call for a levy of 300,000 men on 24 February 1793, followed in August by the announcement of a *levée en masse*. These momentous decisions would transform the nature of modern warfare as well as the French state; they would also transform the social and political objectives of the Revolution. The *levée* accelerated the process of gearing up the entire nation for war through a programme of requisitioning that included men, munitions, food and horses; it would transform economic strategy through the suspension of free-market policies and the substitution of emergency regulations and price-fixing. The cost would prove too high for those communities that had already been alienated by the religious and land policies of the Revolution. The massive rebellion in the west of France, known to history as the Vendée, would erupt as a direct result of the *levée*.

The path of the Revolution would also be diverted from its original course by the existence, from day one, of armed counter-revolution, inside and outside France. On the day following the fall of the Bastille, in fact, the comte d'Artois had emigrated, signalling the birth of the counter-revolution abroad. The first organised counter-revolutionary movement on French soil raised its standard in the southern town of Nîmes in the summer of 1790. Lyon became a site for counter-revolution from around the same period. Many districts in lower Languedoc and Provence would be affected by outbreaks of the counter-revolutionary virus throughout the 1790s. The scale and significance of these rebellions in the south-east should never be underestimated, but it was the explosive counter-revolutionary movements known as the Vendée and the *'chouannerie'* in western France that would pose the greater threat to the Republic. The revolt in the Vendée (a short-hand expression for Catholic royalist uprisings in the department of the Vendée itself, as well as those in the neighbouring departments of Deux-Sèvres, Maine-et-Loire, Mayenne, and Sarthe) assumed alarming proportions for the government in March 1793, following the announcement of the *levée*. The *chouannerie* (a word derived from the cry of an owl, appropriate for rebels operating by night) was a guerrilla war affecting a few of the Breton departments to the north-west. Although counter-revolutionary activities, degenerating into sporadic violence and crime in some instances, would persist both in the west and the south-east until the reign of Napoleon, the grave military threat they posed had ended by 1796.[5]

The counter-revolution abroad obviously encouraged Catholic royalist resistance within French borders: *émigré* divisions would also fight alongside the Prussians and the Austrians. Munro Price's recent study of the baron de Breteuil – Louis XVI's agent abroad – makes it clear that, although the various *émigré* camps spent much of their time plotting the downfall of the Revolution, support from European courts was only forthcoming when it suited them.[6] *Émigré* invasions of France were rare, and usually ended in disaster, as was the case with the Quibéron expedition to the coast of southern Brittany at the end of June 1795. Of the 3,000 invaders, 1,000 were captured by general Hoche's men, 640 of whom were shot.[7] The history of the émigrés abroad, however, was not all doom and gloom. The English did take over the important naval base of Toulon from 28 August 1793 with some *émigré* assistance, although it was only held until December.[8] A few *émigré* journalists, such as Mallet du Pan, were advocating compromise with the Revolution by the mid-1790s, arguing in favour of a return to something like the constitutional monarchy of 1791. Their advice went unheeded, dooming the monarchist cause to a generation in the wilderness. The history of the *émigrés* in England and on the continent is one of political failure and, in most cases, personal disillusionment and sadness. More than two-thirds of those who took refuge in England during the Revolution had made their peace with Napoleon by 1802.[9]

The combination of foreign war and internal counter-revolution largely dictated the ideological course of the Revolution after 1792, pushing it to the left during the successive military crises from the spring of 1792 to the spring of 1794, then swinging the political pendulum back to the political centre-ground once those crises had been overcome. The treachery of the court and the threat of foreign invasion prompted the fall of the monarchy on 10 August 1792 and the subsequent September Massacres in which around 1,200 prisoners were brutally put to death. This bloody event would help to shape elite responses towards 'the mob' for the rest of the Revolution. The adverse course of the war after September pushed the Revolution further to the left. The military defeats of the spring of 1793, together with the outbreak of the Vendéan rebellion, fatally undermined the authority of the moderate Girondin faction that had reassumed power after the inauguration of the Republic on 20 September 1792. The treachery of the Girondin general, Dumouriez, who fled to the Austrian camp soon after the defeat of Neerwinden on 18 March 1793, encouraged the Jacobin–sansculotte alliance which would form the basis of the Terror from June 1793 to July 1794. In contrast, the reoccupation of Belgium after the battle of Fleurus on 26 June 1794 (8 Messidor Year 11 according to the new 'Revolutionary Calendar' introduced by the Convention on 24 November 1793) increased pressure to end the Terror, precipitating the end of the Jacobin–sansculotte alliance a few weeks later. Finally, during the regime of the Directory (3 November 1795–10 November 1799), the army would intervene on several occasions to repress internal rebellions and correct violent electoral swings to left and right. France was, in effect, being run by the army well before Napoleon Bonaparte began the transformation of France from a parliamentary democracy to a military dictatorship in November 1799.[10]

The pre-eminent role played by the army obviously distorted the natural evolution of civilian government in France, as elsewhere in Europe. War between 1793 and 1815, for example, accelerated the long process of creating the modern fiscal state: it 'wove the European network of national states, and preparation for war created the internal structures within it. The wars of the French Revolution and Empire capped this trend . . . With the nation-in-arms a state's extractive power rose accordingly.'[11] Unfortunately, the English government's 'extractive power' would prove far superior to that of the French. The result, for France, would be a return to socially regressive forms of taxation. Although, due to their association with the inequitable levy of taxes during the ancien regime, many indirect taxes were abolished during the early stages of the Revolution, they would be reintroduced to fund the wars of the Directory and Napoleonic Empire.[12] The higher profile of recruiting-sergeants and tax officials explains, in large measure, why the bulk of the French population would become apathetic towards, or actively opposed to, the Revolution by the late 1790s. Alan Forrest considers it 'surprising how many of the men in the revolutionary and especially in the Napoleonic armies seem to have considered the option of deserting at one time or another'.[13]

During the first years of war, however, when the Revolution was in serious danger of collapsing in the face of external and internal attack, the defining character of the military machine constructed by the recruitment of volunteers and the *levée en masse* had been dedication to *la patrie*, not desertion. We shall argue that the motivation behind this newly minted patriotism was not simply a natural wish to defend one's country, but the expectation of social reform, especially from 1792 to 1794 when Girondin and Jacobin administrations held the reins of power. Social revolution during the early 1790s would strengthen national political institutions and mobilise the population and resources to meet the demands of an expanding state and military machine. In other words, the early leaders of the Revolution succeeded where the enlightened-monarchists had failed – they modernised the political and administrative structures of France by defeating 'reactionary' forces at home and abroad. This was the major achievement of the Revolution. The cost, to the bourgeois governing elite, whose class formation was being advanced during the 1790s, was social reform. They were forced to address the issue of mass poverty, and they did – until 1795. Unlike the American War of Independence, the French Revolution contained a revolutionary *social* message. The war unlocked that message. The republican historian, George Michon, wrote that, in 1792, 'War was willed *solely* [my italics] to act as a diversion for social problems which were becoming more serious with every day that passed.' An exaggeration, perhaps, but Michon undoubtedly had a point.[14]

The Revolution not only posed a threat to traditional elites in France, it challenged the aristocratic social order throughout Europe and its dependencies. The threat had become quite evident to Edmund Burke – a dedicated opponent of the Revolution – by 1796. In his *Letter on a Regicide Peace*, he argued that England was at war 'with a system, which, by its essence, is inimical to all other governments . . . It is with an *armed doctrine* that we are at war. To us it is a Colossus which bestrides our [English] channel.'[15] Burke's reaction should be evaluated within the context of the 'Second Hundred Years War' between France and England. His words were music to the ears of those in England who were constantly seeking ideological legitimation for their successful struggle to control the late eighteenth-century global capitalist market.[16]

The rise and fall of the Jacobin–sansculotte alliance, 1792–4

The French Revolution was the first of those modern revolutions that witnessed the rapid transformation of a society's state and class structures, accompanied by, and in part accomplished through, popular revolts from below.[17] In this section, we shall focus upon the relationship between Jacobinism, its ideology increasingly shaped by the emerging bourgeois state, and sansculottism, the first organised political movement in French history to represent *le peuple* (as defined in chapter five).

Jacobinism has been defined, on the one hand, as a prototype of twentieth-century Bolshevism, and, on the other, as 'a model for modern democrats'. Patrice Higonnet attempts to bridge the apparently unbridgeable gap by suggesting that we should separate Jacobinism's inner core, created during the absolutist ancien regime, from its outer shell, constructed after the outbreak of war in 1792. For François Furet, the inner core of the Jacobins was Jean-Jacques Rousseau's 'totalitarian democracy'; the heirs of the Jacobins were the Bolsheviks of 1917. Higonnet rejects this simplistic analysis, arguing convincingly that it was the circumstances of war, counter-revolution and confusion over class identity that eventually discredited the Jacobins' 'ecumenical worldview' and democratic credentials as 'enlightened libertarians'.[18] Jacobins were indeed democrats, but with a penchant for Rousseauesque theories on 'popular sovereignty'; they were educated urban property-owners; free marketeers, but with a preference for small-scale capitalism and land ownership; patriots, but, initially, sensitive to the rights of other nations. Before war and counter-revolution changed the rules of political engagement, Maximilien Robespierre had voted for the abolition of the death penalty and against any declaration of war against France's enemies.

The Jacobin-dominated 'Revolutionary Government' of 1793–4 derived its political strength from its alliance with the Popular Movement, as well as from its nationwide network of clubs and popular societies. When this network disintegrated after the spring of 1794, Jacobin domination would be imperilled. It was in the Jacobin 'mother-club' in the rue Saint-Honoré that the sansculotte red cap of liberty – the *bonnet rouge* – was transformed by the summer of 1792, 'from a factional badge to a national, republican emblem, an evolution which corresponds to the elevation of the Jacobins to a central role in government'.[19] The six thousand or so Jacobin clubs, or popular societies affiliated to the Jacobins, created between 1789 and 1794 would attract around a million members. These are staggering figures for eighteenth-century political engagement; they illustrate Jacobin domination of the Revolution by 1793. However, it was the alliance between Jacobin and sansculotte organisations that ensured the victory of the former over their Girondin enemies in the National Convention. From 29 May to 2 June, sansculotte-dominated Sections stormed the Convention, forcing the assembly to decree the arrest of 29 Girondin deputies, thus paving the way for the installation of the Jacobin Terror. It should be noted, however, that the institutions of the Terror – the powerful Committee of Public Safety (6 April 1793), the police Committee of General Security (25 November 1791), the Revolutionary Tribunal and the representants-on-mission to the departments (10 March 1793) – had all been created before the Jacobins assumed power. Terror was the politically illegitimate child of the marriage between war and Revolution, not war and Jacobinism.

The Girondin faction had enjoyed two relatively brief and always contested periods of influence in government, from March to June 1792 and from September 1792 to the spring of 1793. In terms of education, social class or, indeed, patriotism, there was little to distinguish a Girondin from a Jacobin. It was geography, electoral history and, primarily, attitudes towards *le peuple* that separated Girondins from Jacobins by late 1792. In the elections to the National Convention in September 1792, Jacobin candidates had swept the board in Paris, whilst – as their name suggests – Girondin candidates had been successful in the region around the Gironde river in the south-west of France. To over-simplify, Jacobins thus became Parisian 'centralisers'; Girondins, provincial 'federalists'. In order to acquire power, as well as to indulge their genuine, Rousseauesque sympathies for the poor, the Jacobins had taken control of Paris with the support of the sansculotte Popular Movement. The Girondins, on the other hand, had evinced little sympathy for the revolutionary social and political claims of the sansculottes, often dismissing both Jacobins and their sansculotte supporters as 'anarchists', 'levellers' and 'drinkers of blood' (*buveurs de sang*), constantly evoking the horrors of the 1792 September Massacres. The September Massacres, in the course of which well over a thousand inmates of several Paris prisons had been hacked to death by 'organised' committees of sansculottes, left a permanent stain on the reputation of the Popular Movement. Girondin–Jacobin rivalry on this issue was but the latest chapter in the narrative of elite responses to the violent invasion of the political public sphere by the lower orders of society. The massacres, which occurred when Paris was threatened with foreign invasion, have also led gifted historians like Simon Schama to the specious conclusion that popular 'violence was the motor of the Revolution'.[20]

Their inability to resolve three major crises explain the downfall of the Girondins: Louis XVI's execution (he had been a prisoner since the 10 August), the conduct of the war and the continuation of the ancien regime conflict between bourgeois free-trade economics and popular demands for a regulated economy. On the first issue, the Convention agreed to a man that Louis XVI was guilty of treason; the only matter for discussion concerned his sentence. The Girondins vacillated before supporting the motion for a popular referendum on the death penalty. The Convention rejected this motion by 424 votes to 283, and then went on to vote, by 387 votes to 334, in favour of the death penalty. On 21 January 1793, the king met his death, bravely, on what is now the Place de Concorde. On the second issue, the outbreak of the Vendéan counter-revolution in March coincided with the entry of England and Spain into the war and the defeat of General Dumouriez at Neerwinden on the eighteenth of the month. Dumouriez, a supporter of the Girondins, threatened to march his troops on Paris in order to crush the Popular Movement before choosing the far less risky option of deserting to the Austrians. Finally, with the Revolution's paper money, the *assignats*, falling to half their face value, unemployment and food riots added a worrying social dimension, fuelling the insurrectionary actions of the Parisian Sections. By July, the Jacobin Triumvirate of Robespierre, Couthon and Saint-Just had joined the Committee of Public Safety. In September, two advocates of 'legal' (legitimised by the Convention), as opposed to popular, terror, Billaud-Varenne and Collot d'Herbois, had also been admitted. This marked the peak of the Jacobin–sansculotte alliance, dedicated to the resolution of one of the greatest national emergencies in French history.[21]

The chance of a successful outcome appeared to be remote. Austrian and Prussian troops had invaded France from the north and north-east, while Spanish and Piedmontese armies had crossed into France from the south. In the west, Vendéan counter-revolutionary forces were advancing towards Nantes. To add to this tale of military woe, defeated Girondin supporters in the south and west had organised a 'Federalist Revolt' against Paris, attracting considerable support in large commercial cities such as Marseille, Bordeaux and Caen. Although something of a damp squib from a military perspective, the Federalist movement represented a direct challenge to the popular democracy advocated by the Jacobin–sansculotte alliance. On 13 and 17 July, Jean-Paul Marat and Joseph Chalier, heroes of the Popular Movement in Paris and Lyon respectively, were killed by opponents of the Jacobin Revolution. Throughout that summer of 1793, Paris was a city in crisis: 'In such a situation the news spread by 1,000 newspaper street-sellers was embellished by word of mouth, creating a city crackling with a potent mixture of rumour, optimism, and suspicion.'[22]

These were the circumstances that empowered the Popular Movement. *Aristocrates* and *modérés* – terms referring by this time to anyone who was not actively working for the Jacobin version of the Revolution – were hounded and expelled from popular societies. By the autumn, the sansculottes would seal their victory by attaching popular societies (*sociétés sectionnaires*) to most of the 48 Parisian Sections. They would become the mainsprings of the sansculotte revolutionary movement until the early spring of 1794. Demands for 'direct democracy' legitimated invasions of the Convention, if 'mandated' national deputies did not implement the 'general will' of the people. Sansculotte organisations supported the 'sacred right of insurrection': once the people had risen, it became the embodiment of all justice. The September Massacres would be excused on these grounds. *Le peuple* were now not just stage extras, but leading actors in the Revolutionary drama. For the mass of uncommitted deputies in the Convention (the Plain), however, the lower orders were still 'strolling players' whose contracts would have to be short term.

The economic and social ideas of the sansculottes also challenged received wisdom on the relationship between the individual, community and politics.

A few were shared, and articulated, by Robespierre, a critical, rather than a devoted, follower of Rousseau. For *l'Incorruptible* (as cynics described him), the *primary* object of any civilised society was the provision of work and food for its citizens. This *droit à l'existence* became a cherished mantra for sansculotte spokesmen, some of whom questioned the social and economic benefits of an expanding consumerist market, just as opponents of Turgot had criticised his liberal 'free-market' programme in the 1770s. By the early spring of 1793, the National Convention was receiving petitions for a ceiling on price-rises, from urban and rural consumers. In the south-east, continual rural insurrections were organised by poor and landless peasants reacting 'to shortages and spiralling prices by intervening in the market-place'.[23] This was 'déjà vu all over again', this cycle of free markets followed by demands for a regulated economy that characterises French economic history after the 1750s. On 4 May, the Girondins were forced to introduce the first ceiling on prices. It lacked sansculotte teeth, and was followed by the Jacobin 'General Maximum of Prices and Wages' only introduced, it should be noted, after a sansculotte invasion of the National Convention on 29 September 1793. The adoption of the revealing term 'sansculottes' (those who dressed as working men rather than as bourgeois) highlighted their sense of possessing a separate identity as skilled and semi-skilled artisans, small shopkeepers, clerks and journeymen. However, it is their declared sympathy for the poorer members of society, not a precise calibration of their place within the bourgeoisie (a minority of sansculottes were fairly wealthy employers), that gave them their street credibility. Sansculotte ideas frequently reflected – somewhat inchoately – more than a century of *radical* Enlightenment thought. They were influenced by thinkers from Spinoza to Rousseau, adapting their ideas to the political culture of the early 1790s.[24]

On gender issues, most sansculottes shared the general opinion, of most men *and women*, that politics was a man's business. There were, it is true, around 50 Jacobin women's clubs, and a minority of sansculottes – supporters of the Enragés for example – encouraged female – but not necessarily feminist – political participation. Nonetheless, critical, feminist voices could be heard, contributing to the social revolution that '1789' had unleashed. In September 1791, Olympe de Gouges, a butcher's daughter, had published a pioneering document, *Déclaration des droits de la femme et de la citoyenne*. It contained everything that male activists did not care to hear – men were 'bloated with science', anxious 'to command as a despot a sex that is in the full possession of its intellectual faculties'. Etta Palm d'Aelders was an active feminist who had been welcomed in Condorcet's salon as well as in the most progressive revolutionary club in Paris, the *Cercle social*, founded in January 1790 by the abbé Fauchet. This still, small voice of revolutionary, feminist activism could also be heard, quite clearly, during the debates of the society of revolutionary-republican women, founded by Claire Lacombe (significantly, perhaps, a sometime actress like Olympe de Gouges) and Pauline Léon. The liaison between this society and the Enragés frightened Jacobins and unreconstructed sansculottes alike. Women played a far more influential role outside the doors of popular societies, in streets and market places, participating in riots outside bakers' shops. It was the influence of ordinary mothers and housewives, seamstresses and domestic servants, that helped to shape the *social* agenda of the Jacobin–sansculotte alliance, especially in issues concerning wages, food prices and rents, as well as divorce, which was actually introduced on 20 September 1792. [25]

Once in power, the Jacobins had little choice but to convert this kind of pressure into a social programme that would secure the allegiance of the urban and rural masses for the war effort. If the Jacobins were patriots, the sansculottes – again often prompted by women – were super-patriots, *le peuple en armes*. The famous *levée en masse* of 23 August 1793, for example, was a watered down version of sansculotte demands for the entire population, male and female, to take up arms against traitors. Much of the work of the Sections, which effectively ran the local government of Paris under the aegis of the Commune, a body elected from the 48 Sections, was devoted to recruiting volunteers for the war against foreign armies and the counter-revolution. They collected arms, uniforms and saltpetre for making gun-powder; they distributed money to wives and orphans of soldiers killed in battle; they pressurised the National Convention to support the Terror, vital instrument of the war effort. It is true that, *when all else had failed*, the strength of the Parisian Popular Movement depended upon force and the threat of violence. That perceptive analyst of revolutionary violence, Richard Cobb, understood that the 48 Sections were 'powerful, even dangerous, because they controlled the artillery companies and could give the orders to trundle out the cannon . . . as a final argument when all else failed'.[26] Jacobin politicians often went into battle with a sansculotte pike poking into their backs.

The 'Revolutionary Government', officially constituted on 10 October 1793, had learned the hard lesson that it should not imitate the actions of the Girondins who had confused 'the situation of a people in revolution with that of a people with a settled government'.[27] Many popular demands would have to be met: they would have to adopt the strategy of embracing – with at least one arm – the common people. They were encouraged to do so by the Enragé and Hébertist factions, supporters of a social revolution backed by Terror. In June, Jacques Roux, spokesman for the Enragés, demanded that hoarders and speculators should be punished with the death penalty. A cursory glance through the bold, bloody and bawdy pages of Hébert's news-paper, the *Père Duchesne* and Marat's *Ami du peuple* during this period spread the printed word that liberal capitalism was the root cause of popular misery. On 4 June, Marat accused the defeated Girondins of being the lackeys of 'capitalists, the large property holders, the wholesale merchants, the

241

bankers, the engrossers, the speculators, the public blood-suckers'.[28] The public propaganda of the 'Revolutionary Government' would have to contain a critical paragraph or two on the evils of unfettered capitalism.

If there was one document that fitted this bill admirably, it was the Constitution of 1793, agreed by the Convention on 24 June. It denounced the 'unpatriotic rich'; it declared that governments had the duty to provide not only public assistance, but work; it legitimised the right of popular insurrection; and it introduced the principle of annual elections and ratification of government policy by popular assemblies. This was a truly revolutionary document, not only for its own time, *but for any time*. It was, of course, never implemented! On 26 July 1793, despite the misgivings of the Plain, the Convention decreed that the hoarding of basic food supplies should become a capital offence, and, on 9 August, even agreed to set up 'national warehouses' to store emergency supplies of grain. The sansculotte Sections applauded, but, aware that words came easily to politicians, demanded that 'the will of the people' should actually be implemented. On 5 September, the Sections again invaded the Convention, demanding a regulated economy and a tightening of the terrorist screw. They were successful – for the last time. A General Maximum of Wages and Prices was introduced, fixing the former at 50 per cent above their 1790 levels, and the latter at one-third higher. On the political front, popular paramilitary *'armées révolutionnaires'* were created, eventually numbering around 40,000 men, with divisions formed in most departments. On 17 September, a draconian Law of Suspects was introduced, dramatically increasing the number of arrested men and women brought before the Revolutionary Tribunal. The Popular Movement had reached the apogee of its power.

That power had extorted very significant social and economic concessions from the 'Revolutionary Government', spearheaded now by the Robespierrist-dominated Committee of Public Safety. Let us begin with those secured by the peasantry, which had provided the main dynamic behind revolutionary social change since the Great Fear of 1789. A new Rural Code had been intro-duced in September–October 1791, but it had done little to appease peasant hunger for land. In most cases, it had merely confirmed the status quo, allowing pre-Revolutionary practices to continue, including the enclosure of land where landowners were powerful enough to insist upon it. What was required was the total abolition of the feudal land system, thus, it was hoped, making more land available for small farmers and the poor. During the spring and summer of 1792, a major rebellion had broken out in the south-east, which, when combined with the revolutionary action of the Parisian Sections, had precipitated the collapse of the Bourbon monarchy on 10 August. It had been this combination of rural and urban rebellion – the Great Fear and the Storming of the Bastille – that had transformed the political and economic crisis of 1789 into a social revolution. In turn, the combination of rural and urban insurrection in 1792 led directly to the introduction of the very important decrees of 20–5 August, ending the payment of all feudal dues to seigneurs, unless title deeds could be produced to prove their 'non-feudal' origins. In most instances, this was an impossible task. Following the passage of this legislation, anti-seigneurial activity in the countryside would abate.

Renewed peasant unrest in the late winter of 1792–3 was characterised by a shift towards the acquisition and redistribution of land. Peasant land-hunger posed a major threat to large-scale property-owners in pro-revolutionary and counter-revolutionary regions. On the 18 March, the Girondins had introduced the death penalty for those preaching any form of agrarian communism (the *loi agraire*). Once in power, the Jacobins, although sharing property-owners' disdain for land seizures, were forced to introduce real concessions. In the period 3–10 June, they passed a series of measures, including provisions for the poor to rent small plots of former Church and *émigré* land, as well as legislation permitting the division of common lands. The latter could be divided amongst the heads of households if one-third of the villagers agreed. On 17 July, it was announced that *all* feudal dues were to be abolished and all feudal charters destroyed. It was the end of an era.[29]

What had not ended, of course, was the affliction that was visited upon the poorest sections of rural and urban society – the problem of mass poverty; indeed, in many instances, the Revolution had only exacerbated it. The work of the *Comité de mendicité* from 1790 had undoubtedly encouraged a more humanitarian approach to unemployment and poverty, and the Revolutionary Government did make a genuine attempt to convert words into action by the introduction of several radical schemes of poor relief. There was, for example, the ambitious decree of 28 June 1793 that promised state assistance for pauper children, foundlings, the aged and the indigent. Illegitimate children were given full civic rights, including rights of inheritance. Sections and popular societies throughout France were eager to implement these decrees, and did, indeed, organise effective relief programmes. However, they also demanded far more radical measures to extinguish poverty. It was this pressure that secured some state assistance for the poor and the elderly, as well as the occasional scheme for the distribution of *émigré* property seized by the government – see, for example, the decrees of 26 February–3 March 1794 (8–13 Ventôse Year 11). Crowning these measures was the Great Register of National Assistance announced on 11 May 1794 (22 Floréal Year 11). According to Alan Forrest, this scheme represented 'the most ambitious dream of the Revolution'. Significantly, the Register was targeted on the *rural* poor. Government money was promised for 'deserving' peasants and artisans who were either chronically sick or aged, as well as to widows and mothers of large families. Departmental administrators were given the unenviable task of choosing the lucky few that would receive assistance.[30]

But, as the sansculottes were only too aware, it was easy to announce reforms, but far more difficult to implement them, especially in times of war. Buying the support of hostile communities had to take pride of place, with victims of war and counter-revolution, as well as the families of soldiers killed or injured at the front, receiving the lion's share of state-financed relief. The Jacobins would find it impossible to implement a social revolution and defeat their internal and external enemies. By 1795, many of the dreams of genuine reformers were turning into nightmares. Infants put out to wet nurses continued to die in unacceptable numbers. In Limoges, three out of five children did not live to see their third birthday. Hospitals collapsed as their income from feudal dues and tithes disappeared and their staff, drawn, in the main, from the ranks of the priesthood and female nursing orders, were imprisoned and even guillotined. The hospital of Saint-André in Bordeaux had lost one-third of its income during the first few years of the Revolution. Furthermore, the traditional distinction between the 'deserving' and the 'undeserving poor' meant that the foul cells of the *dépôts de mendicité* continued to be reserved for the latter. A few vagabonds were even deported to Madagascar. The alleviation of mass poverty demanded long-term solutions, and revolutionary regimes are, by definition, short term.[31]

In the light of the above, it is tempting to dismiss Jacobin social policy as opportunistic, if not downright cynical. This would be to commit a fundamental error about revolutions in general, and the Jacobins in particular. The compulsive, admittedly long-term, drive to 'regenerate' the human race, to create '*l'homme nouveau*' was common to Girondins and Jacobins alike. For Mona Ozouf, education was central to Jacobinism's discourse of regeneration, but, as she explains, 'all the revolutionaries invested the educational issue with enormous symbolic significance'.[32] On 21 December 1792, a deputy stood up in the Convention to plead for a 'second revolution in heads and hearts', a system that would subject the French to 'physical exercises, parades, festivals, "morality lessons", the reading and memorisation of key political texts, and the singing of patriotic songs'. Immediately, an image of modern communist and fascist propaganda machines springs to mind. However, the deputy who made this speech was a moderate, not a Jacobin 'terrorist'. He was Rabaut de Saint-Etienne, the enlightened son of the famous founding father of the eighteenth-century Protestant Church, Paul Rabaut, and he would die in a few months on the scaffold.[33] On 13 July 1793, Robespierre (on behalf of the 'martyred Lepeletier de Saint Fargeau', assassinated as a regicide the previous January) presented an education plan to the Convention. It was followed, on 29 Frimaire 11 (19 December), by Gabriel Bouquier's education bill introducing the principle of obligatory primary education. What is striking about both sets of proposals was the degree of state control and political indoctrination that they contained, but, again, this was not an unusual approach during a revolution.

State-sponsored 'Regeneration' characterised the work of the great painter Jacques-Louis David, a member of the Committee of General Security for a time, and responsible for masterminding the great fêtes of the Jacobin Republic. During the Fête of Unity and Indivisibility held on 10 August 1793, the crowd had to pass five points chosen to imitate the stations of the cross, 'worshipping' at the shrines of Nature and Liberty and refreshing themselves at 'fountains of regeneration'. In the process, it was expected that the 'great unwashed' would be cleansed in the purifying waters of bourgeois enlightenment. Lynn Hunt provides an iconographical example of this process of bringing the general public into line. During the Fête of Unity, a revolutionary, rather macho image of Hercules was used to represent the people; a year later, it was replaced by a far more classical and restrained image for the Fête of the Supreme Being. In the meantime, 'the people . . . had been brought under control'.[34] In fact, exercising control over popular organisations proved to be difficult. The Committee of Public Safety, having resorted to brutal terrorist methods to conquer the counter-revolution in the Vendée, would not feel confident enough, first to cut the Popular Movement down to size, then to confront the anti-Robespierrist factions in the Convention, until the spring of 1794.

It was during the 'anarchic' autumn and winter of 1793, that the Popular Movement really tried to push its power beyond the limits imposed on the Revolutionary Government by political, economic and military circumstances. As time passed, the Committee of Public Safety realised that its principal, historic task would be to save the Revolution and the country, not govern in the interests of the Popular Movement. On 10 October, the National Convention virtually handed over control of the country, temporarily, to the Committee. It was now a question of winning back 'the hearts and minds' of millions of citizens, especially in the countryside, whose allegiance was being sorely tested by the intrusive and often violent actions of a minority of representatives-on-mission, popular societies and departmental *armées révolutionnaires*, the praetorian guard of the Terror. The National Convention had been pressurised into creating the Parisian *armée révolutionnaire*, composed of some 6,000 militant sansculottes, by the sansculotte *journée* of 2 June 1793. By the autumn, over 50 departments had copied the capital's example.

Several representatives-on-mission, dispatched as agents of the government to the provinces, had become the political lords and masters of all they surveyed, purging and 'energising' local popular societies, organising the repression and executions of 'suspects', loosely defined. From his headquarters in Nantes, Jean-Baptiste Carrier supervised the drowning of hundreds of priests in the river Loire; in Lyon, the representatives-on-mission, Joseph Fouché and Jean-Marie Collot d'Herbois, were jointly responsible for the execution of almost 2,000 'enemies of the Republic'. The *armées révolutionnaires* (often created by enthusiastic representatives-on-mission) were essential accomplices in this brutal repression, cogs in the machinery of the Terror, the Terror on the move, the Terror in the village, as Richard Cobb put it. They represented every militant sansculotte's dream – the guillotine on wheels, casting its long, tall shadow over grain hoarders, counter-revolutionary priests and the ubiquitous 'foreign spy'.[35] The *armées* and the representatives-on-mission were the principle architects of 'dechristianisation', the movement that swept through France in that bloody autumn and winter of 1793. The representative, Joseph Fouché (destined to become Napoleon's Minister of Police), had set the official process rolling with the closure of churches in the department of the Nièvre. His action was then copied by the Paris Commune that chose to replace God in the cathedral of Notre-Dame with a 'Goddess of Reason', in the shapely form of an actress. In a meeting of the popular society of the Gravilliers Section, a seven-year-old boy, whose father had been killed at the front, was brought to the lectern to announce the closure of all the Section's churches, describing them as 'lairs frequented by ravenous animals that devour the people's daily bread'.[36] In the department of the Loire, the representative-on-mission, Claude Javoques, was actively converting churches into 'Temples of Reason'. One of the reasons behind Javoques's action, as indeed behind many acts of dechristianisation, was the pressing need to secure precious metals, obtained from church bells and ornaments, for the war effort.[37] Mars, not Robespierre, was the real deity of the Terror.

For the Committee of Public Safety, however, this reign of terror in the countryside was proving counter-productive: the process of winning back the country for the Revolution, now synonymous with the nation, had to begin in earnest. On 21 November 1793 (1 Frimaire Year 11), Robespierre stunned many activists by denouncing dechristianisation as 'aristocratic'. A fortnight later, he delivered the *coup de grâce* – the decree of 4 December (14 Frimaire). If the Constitution of 1793 had represented the 'Constitution of the Popular Movement', the decree of 4 December represented the 'Constitution of the Revolutionary Government'. According to Albert Soboul, 'it shattered the impetus built up by the popular leadership'.[38] Although the National Convention would remain the 'sole centre of government', the Committee of Public Safety now became its instrument for centralising and bureaucratising the Revolution. Popular societies were forbidden to correspond with each other; representatives-on-mission were recalled; all departmental *armées révolutionnaires* were to be disbanded. Henceforward, a new local official, the *agent national*, charged with the responsibility of communicating with the Committee every ten days, would rule in every district of France. It all marked the beginning of divorce proceedings for the Jacobin–sansculotte marriage that had underpinned the early work of the Revolutionary Government.

In securing its brief monopoly of power, the Revolutionary Government had enjoyed the support of a silent, but very powerful, partner – the bureaucratic, centralising French state. The growth of state power gradually paralysed the critical spirit and political militancy of the Parisian masses. John Bosher's account of this 'new Leviathan' focuses upon the considerable expansion of salaried civil servants and the 'grand scale' of the Revolution's dealings with war suppliers and bankers, both underlining 'the importance of the state as the dispenser of economic and political power'.[39] The most important, if shadowy, dispenser of economic and financial power was the minister of finance, Pierre-Joseph Cambon. In January 1790, the Constituent Assembly had created a *comité de liquidation* to settle the massive debts bequeathed by the ancien regime. It was divided into nine sections and staffed by no fewer than 280 clerks. Although the plan was to settle with the state's creditors by 1793, in fact the work was to drag on until 1810. The refusal to resolve the situation by declaring a state bankruptcy tied the hands, and feet, of every Revolutionary government, but the Committee of Public Safety, in particular, suffered, given that Cambon exploited the situation on behalf of himself and 'speculators and profiteers of all shapes and sizes'. Despite the favourable military situation, the *assignat* had fallen to half of its face value by the time Robespierre fell on 9 Thermidor Year 11 (27 July 1794). In his famous speech to the Convention the previous day, Robespierre had launched a bitter attack on Cambon, accusing him of favouring wealthy creditors at the expense of the poor who had been driven 'to ruin and despair' through the uncontrolled emission of *assignats*.[40] It was an acute observation on the impossibility of introducing major social reforms while trying to finance a European war.

The 'unpatriotic' bankers and financiers, vilified so frequently by the Enragés and the Hébertistes, were not figments of the over-heated imaginations of the sansculottes. As Morris Slavin has argued, 'there was an insoluble contradiction between an economic system based on *laissez-faire* and an attempt to regulate it by price controls and by the direct intervention of the state in market relations'.[41] This very same fundamental problem had bedevilled the policies of enlightened-monarchist ministers during the ancien regime, from Choiseul to Necker. Barère's proposal for a relaxation of the Maximum of Prices on 21 February 1794 (3 Ventôse Year 11) and the introduction of a new maximum level for wages (that cut the income of many wage-earners by one-third) just four days before the Robespierrists fell, reveal a significant shift of power from workers and consumers to employers and producers. Robespierre's eve-of-death appeal to the Jacobin Club to expel the 'sansculotte' members of the Committee of Public Safety, Billaud-Varenne and Collot d'Herbois, drives the point home.

The process of dismantling the machinery of popular Terror and replacing it with state Terror had begun with the 'Constitution of the Revolutionary

Government' on 4 December 1793 and continued with the execution of the Hébertistes and the Dantonistes in February–March 1794. The former had sought, clumsily, to defend, and occasionally to extend, the Terror; the latter, led by a chastened and recently married Danton, had championed the cause of ending the war and, therefore, the Terror. Just as the Stalinist state machine would deal, mercilessly, with the 'left' and 'right' opposition in the late 1920s, so the far less murderous Robespierrist machine in 1794 sought to secure central control in France. The Hébertistes were guillotined on 24 March 1794 (4 Germinal Year 11), the Dantonistes, just under a fortnight later. 'The sheep having lost their shepherds', as one police spy described the situation to the Committee of Public Safety, the sansculottes began to close down, 'voluntarily', the militant popular societies that they had attached to the Sections. In April, the Committee of Public Safety created its own police bureau, much to the chagrin of its sister Committee of General Security. On 10 May (21 Floréal), the Committee of Public Safety replaced the sansculotte mayor of Paris, Jean-Nicolas Pache, with its own nominee, Jean-Baptiste Fleuriot-Lescot. The Fête of the Supreme Being on 8 June was the spiritual complement to the materialist benefits promised under the Committee's national register of pensions that had been announced on 11 May. It was an escape hatch for the government that allowed people of all religious persuasions to worship the same deity. It might – just might – win back the Catholic vote in the countryside. However, Robespierre's decision to lead the procession proved to be a great error, providing evidence for his growing band of enemies in the corridors of power that he was setting himself up as a 'new Pontiff'. A month later, the infamous 'Law of 22 Prairial' (10 June) drastically curtailed civil liberties, by depriving prisoners brought before the Revolutionary Tribunal of the right to defend themselves.

The Committee of Public Safety appeared to be master of all it surveyed, but Robespierre's control over the state machine was never comparable to that which Stalin would enjoy in Russia. Norman Hampson is right to insist that historians have too often exaggerated Robespierre's authority: 'He never exercised any departmental responsibility, and his influence on policymaking was confined to a few initiatives . . .'[42] What did boost the authority of the Committee of Public Safety during the spring and summer of 1794 was military success over both the counter-revolution in the west and the Austrians in the Low Countries. The triumph of Republican troops at the battle of Fleurus on 26 June (8 Messidor) marked the end of the Austrian threat and the beginning of French imperialism in Europe. At the same time, however, it removed much of the rationale for the continuation of the 'Great Terror'. This was the essential dilemma confronting the Robespierristes. As Barère tried to bring the worried, warring factions within the two great Committees together, some of the recalled – and threatened

– representatives-on-mission, such as Fouché, began to plot Robespierre's downfall. During this critical period, Robespierre, having survived one assassination attempt, chose to absent himself from the meetings of the Committee of Public Safety. His famous speech to the Convention on 26 July (8 Thermidor) denouncing 'state enemies' unleashed the coup that led to his execution the following day. Weakened and confused by the campaign launched against them by the Committee of Public Safety, the sansculottes failed to muster enough support to save the Robespierristes. The Jacobin–sansculotte alliance was buried on the day that Robespierre, along with over 70 of his supporters, went to the guillotine. It proved to be the last great 'show trial' of the Revolution.

Albert Soboul and Patrice Higonnet – constructing their arguments on very different ideological premises – are right to argue that the Jacobins did not rest on 'a solid class basis'.[43] The Revolutionary Government was a war, not a class, dictatorship. Given the critical military situation of 1793–4, the dialectic of Terror and war was bound to exert more influence upon the evolution of Jacobin ideology than the class dialectic, founded upon changing modes of production, between 'the bourgeoisie' and 'the working class'. Until the advent of Gaullism in the 1960s, Jacobinism would continue to be identified with the ideology of a centralised, nationalist France, not with a particular class. This does not mean, however, that class antagonisms did not contribute to the collapse of the Jacobin–sansculotte alliance. There were class differences *within* the ranks of the sansculotterie, between wealthy master artisans and unskilled workers, for example. The dictatorship of the Revolutionary Government entailed the collapse of the institutions of the Popular Movement and with them, the collapse of the 'ambitious dreams' of alleviating, if not eradicating, poverty. Hannah Arendt argued that, sadly from her political perspective, 'The transformation of the Rights of Man into the rights of the sans-culottes was the turning point not only of the French Revolution but of all revolutions that were to come.'[44] The principle of equal rights had only been advanced by the bourgeoisie in 1789 so as to defeat aristocratic privilege; they had only contemplated a theoretical equality in the eyes of the law to govern their relationship with the Popular Movement. Although the objectives of the Popular Movement were necessarily diverted by the war crisis of 1792–4, the sansculottes remained focused upon the creation of a more democratic and equal society encompassing a serious attack on poverty. Contrary to the opinion of Arendt, we would argue that the defeat of the sansculottes, whose cause would be definitively lost during the reign of the wealthy bourgeoisie after 1795, involved a defeat for the 'Rights of the Common Man'. Herein lies the root cause of the failure of both the French Revolution and modern, 'free market' capitalism, to achieve real, as opposed to theoretical, democracy.

Le peuple, counter-revolution and the bourgeois state

Martyn Lyons was right to think that 'Studying the Revolution without considering the Counter-Revolution is like watching somebody shadow-boxing,' if only because, by the end of the 1790s, millions of French men and women were echoing the words of William Wordsworth (who had welcomed the early phase of the Revolution):

> Now do I feel how I have been deceived,
> Reading of Nations and their works, in faith,
> Faith given to vanity and emptiness.[45]

From the very beginning of the Revolution, tens of thousands of 'counter-revolutionaries' – nobles and priests, as well as ordinary citizens, rich and poor – had opposed, on ideological grounds, the replacement of the ancien regime by a secular, centralising bourgeois state, but they had represented a relatively small minority of the population. Of far greater concern to the Revolutionary elites was the massive increase between 1789 and 1793 in the number of those who turned against the Revolution. These numbers had increased exponentially as new administrative and legal structures were introduced, the Civil Constitution of the Clergy drastically reduced the power of the Catholic Church, the bourgeoisie took the lion's share of Church and *émigré* property, tithes and feudal dues continued to be levied (albeit under new names), new taxes began to kick in, then war, followed by the final collapse of the Bourbon monarchy, straining waning sympathies to breaking point. The existence of a counter-revolution abroad exploited growing discontent by encouraging the formation of Catholic–royalist conspiracies and coups, such as the marquis de la Rouerie's *Association bretonne*, founded in 1791, and François Froment's movement in lower Languedoc, organised a year earlier. However, the counter-revolution in exile placed its real hopes of crushing the Revolution in the hands of European princes, not in popular uprisings, save for a few, ill-conceived plots sanctioned by the comte d'Artois. The *émigrés* were well aware that the great majority of 'commoner counter-revolutionaries' had little affection for aristocratic titles, tithes or feudal dues. Contempt for the untutored masses was shared by both noble and bourgeois elites.

It was the European war that transformed widespread discontent into open civil war, based, primarily, in the west and the south-east. Occasional bouts of counter-revolutionary fever also infected big commercial and manufacturing cities like Lyon, Marseille, Bordeaux and Caen, but urban uprisings were much easier to crush militarily. Of the two predominantly rural centres of counter-revolution, the Vendée posed, by far, the greatest military threat to a Republic that was, it should be remembered, only a few months old. The signal for the insurrection in the Vendée was the announcement on 24 February 1793 of the levy of 300,000 men for the army. It was only a fortnight later that protest in many parts of western France 'metamorphosed into thunderous waves of civil disobedience: attacks on National Guardsmen, republican mayors and constitutional clergy [those who had taken the oath to the Constitution in 1791] and, above all, outright refusal to join the armed forces'.[46] In common with young men in many other parts of France, the peasants and artisans of the west were prepared, if pushed, to live with the Revolution, but not to die for it. When recruiting agents arrived in the village of Saint-Alban, 400 kilometres to the south-east of the Vendée, they were greeted with abuse from crowds of young men shouting, 'Vive le roi! Au diable la nation! Vivent les émigrants!', a revealing glimpse of the components that went into the making of a counter-revolution by 1793. The Charrier counter-revolutionary insurrection that broke out in the region a couple of months later was a direct product of this anti-conscription revolt.[47]

But why, then, did so many citizens who shared a common concern about the way the Revolution was developing decide *not* to join counter-revolutionary movements? Charles Tilly's answer is that the advance of state power engendered a series of anti-bourgeois counter-revolutions only 'where pre-existing rivalries placed a well-connected bloc in opposition to the expanding bourgeois state'.[48] This hypothesis merits serious consideration. In both the counter-revolutionary areas of the west and the south-east, religious, separatist and socio-economic forces had combined, over long periods of time, to create 'well-connected blocs' that challenged the incursion of the bourgeois state and the advance of large-scale, mercantile capitalism. Although localised insurrections *within* the counter-revolutionary movements of the west and the south-east exhibited features that were unique, these particular 'blocs' were common to all of them.

Throughout this study, we have stressed the overwhelming importance of religion. It is hardly surprising, therefore, that, almost everywhere, the language of counter-revolution would be biblical, especially in the countryside where the Catholic Church formed the keystone of western European civilisation. Every serious study of counter-revolution has to address the question of religion; disagreements focus solely on the degree of importance one should attach to it. In the south-east, there is common agreement that it was central to the outbreak, the course and the character of counter-revolutionary insurrections. The history of many regions of lower Languedoc had been moulded by two centuries of bloody, Catholic–Protestant conflict, just as the history of Northern Ireland has been shaped by sectarian rivalry to the present day. The town of Nîmes in the department of the Gard – one-third of whose population was Protestant – had been seen as the 'Mecca of Protestants' in France since the birth of Calvinism in the early sixteenth century. Until the 1760s, Protestants had been executed, forced to emigrate and, until as late as 1787, denied full civic rights. The Revolution of 1789 promised, if not revenge, then certainly redress. A minority of rich Protestant merchants had

increasingly dominated the financial and manufacturing life of the department during the latter part of the ancien regime. The introduction in 1789
of an electoral system based on wealth rather than birth provided the
opportunity to exchange wealth for political power. Supporters of the old
Catholic and royalist order resisted. On 13–14 June 1790, around 300 Catholic
workers were brutally massacred by Protestant National Guardsmen, aided
and abetted by Protestant peasants and artisans from the surrounding
hills. It was symbolic that the killing should have started outside the bishop's
palace, commandeered for the elections that would ultimately transfer political
power from the majority Catholic to the minority Protestant community.
This so-called *bagarre de Nîmes* laid the foundations for sporadic, Catholic
royalist plots and insurrections that would continue throughout the 1790s.
Blood would flow again after the fall of Napoleon in 1815 when the Catholic community would reverse the decision of 1790, killing over a hundred
Protestants in the process.[49]

In the west of France, some Vendéan rebels died wearing images of the
'sacred heart of Jesus'. In many parts of the region, Catholicism was the matrix
of the social and cultural networks that united thousands of small, scattered,
rural communities. Most of the Catholic communities that turned counter-
revolutionary had welcomed the Revolution in 1789 as eagerly as those that
remained loyal to the Revolution. For the former, it was the assault on Church
property and the introduction of the Civil Constitution of the Clergy in 1790
that marked a crucial turning point. The number of priests who rejected the
enforced clerical oath to the Constitution was higher in the Vendée than
in any other region of France. Throughout the Revolution, 'and especially
during the crisis of the Civil Constitution of the Clergy in 1792/3, the rural
municipalities and the peasants bombarded the authorities with petitions
demanding the return of their former clerics'. This was true for both the
Vendée and Upper Brittany where, from 1793 to 1796, the *chouannerie* would
keep the fires of the counter-revolution alight.[50]

Apart from the peasant families who died in battle, priests were the first
victims of the savage military repression of the Vendée during the winter of
1793–4. On 16 November, 80 priests were pushed into small boats, deliber-
ately holed beneath the waterline, and drowned in the fast-flowing River
Loire. Several hundred more would meet their watery grave in subsequent
noyades de Nantes. The representative-on-mission ultimately responsible for
these crimes, which left a permanent stain on the reputation of the First
French Republic, was Jean-Baptiste Carrier. In his recent illuminating study
of the Vendéan revolt, Alain Gérard argues that Carrier was a true representative of a Republic that, by 1793, had moved on from facing the hard facts
of modernising France to embrace the 'fantasies' of 'regenerating' human
beings. Jacobin Terror, in the hands of 'born again' terrorists like Carrier, it is
argued, offered death as the only form of 'purification', although they killed

out of the purist of motives, 'par principe d'humanité'. It is more likely that pressures of war and the reality – not the 'fantasy' – of counter-revolutionary violence (a few Vendéan rebels were also *aficionados* of human butchery) explain the horrors of the Vendée. But, whichever interpretation one chooses, the true horror is the fact that more than 140,000 Vendéan men, women and children died in this brutal civil war.[51]

As for the relationship between separatism and counter-revolution, it is relevant to note that the two most independent provinces under the ancien régime (described as such by Alexis de Tocqueville in his *The Ancien Regime and the Revolution*) were Brittany in the west and Languedoc in the south-east. The scourge of enlightened monarchist ministers before 1789, geographically the most distant from Paris, proud of their unique customs, traditions and, indeed, languages, both provinces had been bastions of aristocratic and ecclesiastical power and fiscal independence. The abbé Grégoire's linguistic enquiry in 1790 revealed that, whereas the French language was widely understood in the centre, north and east, in much of Brittany and Languedoc it was regarded as a foreign language. Apart from the Breton and Occitan languages, there were 30, mutually incomprehensible, patois dialects spoken in pre-Revolutionary France. Even today, there are Breton and Occitan separatist movements that bear continued witness to the power of historic cultural traditions. Apart from seeking to change the way that country people thought, the Jacobins would also try to change the way they spoke, planning to force national acceptance of the French language.[52] A good motto for Revolutionary Jacobinism would be 'Too much, too soon'! Illiteracy compounded the linguistic problem for Revolutionary administrators. After all, it was not much use translating Gascon patois into French if the majority of inhabitants could not read either! Universal primary education was the answer provided here, but it would take a very long time to implement national schemes of education. Meanwhile, religion, with priests instructing through the medium of patois, continued to fill the cultural gap. In the Île-et-Vilaine region of upper Brittany, the prefect pointed out in 1801 that 'an urban, literate culture did not penetrate very deeply, if at all, into the isolated homes of [the] Breton countryside'. Vendéan families were not born to be more *'fanatique'* than peasant/artisan families in regions that accepted the Revolution. The problem was that in many of the remote rural regions of Brittany, elites – priests, nobles and notables – were their brokers with the outside world. In upper Brittany, for example, where the vast majority of priests refused to take the clerical oath to the new religious settlement, 'priests aligned themselves with the rural community and thus became symbols of the solidarity of the community against outsiders.'[53]

The third distinctive feature, common to both the western and the south-eastern counter-revolutions, was the link between protest, poverty and protoindustrialisation. The popular counter-revolution was not 'capitalist'; indeed, in its rejection of bourgeois economic principles it had affinities with the Parisian sansculottes. By the mid-nineteenth century, a popular, anti-capitalist, Catholic royalist party had emerged in lower Languedoc, known as *la Montagne blanche* (as opposed to the Jacobin '*Montagne rouge*'). Brian Fitzpatrick has traced the origins and ideology of this party back to the Catholic royalist movements of the 1790s.[54] Fitzpatrick agrees with the conclusions provided in most studies of counter-revolutionary movements in the west that had been published in the 1960s – that poverty was a vital cause of protest. Marcel Faucheux's work stressed the difference between the relative prosperity of the republican-dominated plains south of Fontenay-le-Comte and the poverty of the royalist-controlled countryside in the department of the Vendée. Varying reactions to the disruption caused by urban cultural and economic domination of the countryside are central to the explanations provided by Paul Bois and Charles Tilly in their studies of counter-revolution in the departments of the Sarthe and the Maine-et-Loire.[55] Donald Sutherland's study of the *chouannerie* in upper Brittany argues that 'the typical *chouan* was most likely to have been a young man in his early twenties, a peasant, farmhand, or village artisan by trade, who came from one of the poorer families which had been living in the region for some time'.[56]

Tessie Liu's recent book on the Cholet district of the Maine-et-Loire department resolves some of the ambiguities surrounding the relationship between protoindustrial communities and their support for, or opposition to, counter-revolutionary protest. In general terms, Liu agrees that the relationship between protoindustrialisation and poverty has long been underestimated: sweated labour as an alternative to technological input, the exploitation of entire families performing mind-numbing tasks of human repetitive behaviour, was, indeed, 'a sign of poverty and long-term immisceration'. Problems arise when we try to explain why some proto-industrial communities remained loyal to the Revolution whilst others were converted to the counter-revolutionary cause. For Liu, it was 'the logic and the process of rural transformation that is at issue'.[57] We must look at the struggle for control of the putting-out process between urban merchants and village artisans and small merchants; we must consider the *extent* of mercantile penetration of the countryside. For example, Paul Bois argues that the protoindustrialised eastern districts of the department of the Sarthe remained loyal to the Revolution because the bourgeoisie had long succeeded in imposing their domination over the region. However, one cannot gen-eralise from single examples. The protoindustrialised Mauges district of the Maine-et-Loire department, for example, which produced for the world market, became a major centre of counter-revolution.

To solve this apparent puzzle we need to look at other variables, especially religion. The protoindustrialised communities of the Gardonnenque region of lower Languedoc remained loyal – for the most part – to the Revolution because it was a *Protestant* enclave, depending for work on *Protestant* merchants in Nîmes. In 1790, the *éminence grise* of the counter-revolution in Nîmes, François Froment, accused these merchants of providing work only for Protestants in the hills, 'who live more cheaply than those [Catholic workers] in the towns and can therefore offer to produce finished goods more cheaply'.[58] In this example, fierce competition confronting merchants and manufacturers fighting to protect profit margins during a period of economic stagnation, combined with religious prejudice and revolutionary circumstance, produced a protracted struggle that would blight the lives of the inhabitants of lower Languedoc for decades.

The exclusion of the people from power

'What are you trying to say? That the Republic existed during the reign of Terror? . . . That the representatives-on-mission who visited fire, the sword, devastation and death upon France were republicans?' With these words from *Le Nouveau Paris*, written in 1798, Louis Sébastien Mercier expresses the sentiments of the conservative Enlightenment and Revolution *vis-à-vis* the common people, disassociating them from the First French Republic which now became the political property of the wealthy, cultured property-owners of France. 'We fear popular politics and democracy', Mercier concluded, 'because they are too close to mob rule,' a comment that might have been made by Voltaire.[59] The deputy, Jean-Denis Lanjuinais, agreed: 'The time for toadying to the people is past . . . which of us wants to witness for a second time the spectacle of political assemblies given over to crass ignorance, to contemptible greed or vile drunkeness?'[60]

The period between the overthrow of the Robespierrists and the inauguration of the Directory in November 1795 – commonly referred to as the 'Thermidorean Regime' – prepared the ground for the exclusion of the masses from national political life. Much of the legislation relating to the Jacobin Terror, including the General Maximum, was repealed; the Jacobin Club itself was closed down, the Parisian Sections were disbanded. The Popular Movement, physically and psychologically exhausted by two years of total war, was finally crushed following two abortive uprisings in Germinal and Prairial Year III (1 April and 20 May 1795). The streets of Paris and the provinces, once the parade grounds of the sansculottes, were now invaded by the gilded offspring of the wealthy bourgeoisie – the *muscadins* and the *merveilleuses* – some displaying openly royalist sentiments. In parts of the south of France a royalist 'White Terror' exacted a bloody revenge against

Jacobin supporters of the 'Red Terror' throughout the summer of 1795. This bloody reaction finally convinced the post-Robespierrist deputies in the National Convention that a new Constitution must return the masses, royalist and republican, to their rightful place – spectators of the political scene. This was by no means the first time that attempts had been made to 'terminer la Révolution', in other words, to silence the voice of *le peuple*. The death penalty had been introduced as a response to public riots as early as the autumn of 1789. What was missing at that time was the *collective* will of the bourgeoisie and reliable armed support. In 1795, both of these desiderata were present. The main task of the Constitution of 1795 would be to make the First French Republic safe for plutocracy, with the help of the army. To avoid any threat of 'military dictatorship', the executive would be composed of five civilian 'Directors', periodically re-elected; the legislature would be bicameral, comprising a Council of 500 and a Council of Elders (aged forty years and over!); voting would be indirect, a system of primary and secondary assemblies, producing an electoral college of just 30,000 electors. This elite 'college of the wealthy' effectively determined who ran the country. A similar process of exclusion was underway at the local level. The focus of local administration was moved from the municipality to the much larger geographic unit, the canton. Thousands of municipalities would be silenced: 'about 87 per cent of villages [would be] deprived of their mayors, municipal officers and aldermen'.[61]

A 'cultural Thermidor' accompanied these constitutional and administrative changes.[62] There had been an unparalleled expansion in the number of printing presses and book dealers since 1789. Cultural gurus of the Directory, such as the abbé Grégoire, would now provide substantial government subsidies for writers and printers who published 'improving' works of literature and politics. Primary education, a battleground then – as now – between Catholic private and state public schools, was ignored in favour of the secondary and tertiary sectors. The Daunou legislation of 25 October 1795 (3 Brumaire Year IV) laid down the framework for the future: support for the *grandes écoles*, which remain the most prestigious establishments in the higher education field, and the creation of the *écoles centrales*, the forerunners of today's *lycées*. The Directory also encouraged the use of fêtes, processions and the planting of liberty trees to sell the message of a moderate and patriotic revolution to the masses, as well as to promote the secularisation of the state through lay education, state marriages and the rejection of Catholicism as a state religion. Anti-clericalism – the safeguard against the return of lands seized from the Catholic Church – became one of the defining characteristics of Directorial rule.

Elitist, rather than populist, measures were encouraged by the economics of war and free markets. With a million men under arms, war was exceptionally costly, even when it was partly financed by fleecing the populations of countries that had just been 'liberated'. To balance the books, the finance minister, Dominique-Vincent Ramel, embarked upon a thorough overhaul of France's fiscal system towards the end of 1797, shifting much of the burden of taxation from the rich to the poor in the process. Tax schedules were changed, a new tax on doors and windows was introduced, old indirect taxes on food, alcohol and tobacco (*plus ça change* . . . !) were reintroduced. In Donald Sutherland's opinion, under the pressures of war and financial collapse, the Revolution would end up by refashioning 'a social inequality every bit as daunting as that of the old regime'.[63] The rich, however, did not have it all their own way. On 30 September 1797 (9 Vendémiaire Year V), the government, in desperate financial circumstances, repudiated two-thirds of its national debt. The Directory's days were numbered when many of its natural supporters found that their purses were two-thirds lighter after this partial bankruptcy.

Critics of the Directory also increased in number as a result of the widespread corruption that accompanied the shift from public to private management of the economy. Howard Brown, describing the Directory's policy as 'the drive to privatise', suggests that the government's method of financing war was an eighteenth-century equivalent of the 'twentieth-century military/industrial complex'.[64] Fortunes were there to be made and mansions to be built out of currency speculation, land deals and government contracts. Bankers, currency dealers, war contractors and *négociants* would dominate the list of the 150 highest taxpayers in Paris by 1808; Lecouteulx de Canteleu, a banker who had been arrested during the Terror, returned to public life and became the first president of the Bank of France under Napoleon.[65] Even for Mercier, conscience of the *bien pensant* bourgeoisie, bankers and currency dealers were outside the pale of free-market economics. He described the unofficial stock exchange in the Palais-Royal as 'the temple where speculation empties the public purse, condemning entire families to starvation'. However, Mercier believed that the effects of the controlled economy associated with the Jacobin–sansculotte alliance of Year II had been equally pernicious. When the Thermidorean regime abolished most of the controls on trade, including the 'sansculotte' General Maximum of Prices and Wages, on 24 December 1794 (4 Nivôse Year III), Mercier was ecstatic. He celebrated 'the end of workers' demands for higher wages', the end of 'the homicidal law of the Maximum' and the end of the Paris Commune's plan 'to create anarchy through the introduction of 'universal famine'!'[66]

In fact, the abolition of price controls combined in 1794–5 with one of the worst eighteenth-century winters on record to produce mass misery on a scale only comparable with that of 1709. Richard Cobb charted the social map of misery for us from an analysis of police records relating to violent deaths during the period 1795 to 1801. It shows that, in 1795, Parisian mortality rates reached the record figure of 30,000. His detailed study of

404 cases covering the period 1795 to 1801 reveals that poor workers living in lodging houses accounted for the great majority of suicides. Commenting on the personal belongings retrieved by the police, Cobb provides a Goya-esque evocation of 'the harlequin colours of the very poor, as they walked in rainbow clothing, as if to defy death', including the women who chose to die on Sundays, 'wearing their pathetic best, as if they were going [or had just been?] to mass'. Cobb's description of death in Paris reveals a post-revolutionary, almost Darwinian, landscape of deprivation and despair during the late 1790s.[67] The worst years for the poor throughout France were between 1795 and 1797 when war and economic stagnation weighed most heavily on the unreconstructed finances of the state. Many hospitals, short of cash and staff, were in a desperate state. Nursing staff, especially the *Soeurs grises*, were returning by 1795, but many sources of private charity had dried up. Once again, war aggravated the situation, diverting resources earmarked for civilians towards the casualties of war. Even in Limoges, far from any war zone, the total patient list of 885 in June 1795 included 142 soldiers. War, a stagnating economy and the end of state assistance spelled 'disaster' for those last refuges of the poor, the *dépôts de mendicité*. In 1796, the *dépôt* in Lyon had a deficit of 800,000 *livres*, and, two years later, it lacked the funds to bury its dead. Official reports from this period also indicate that the system of wet nursing had collapsed for financial reasons in many localities. In 1799, the director of one of the foundling hospitals in the Eure department reported that members of his staff were picking up dead babies left on the outside steps.[68]

Little wonder, then, that these profound and long-term political and social problems provoked violent insurrectionary movements throughout the period of the Directory. They would explain, in large measure, the collapse of the regime in 1799. Even at the level of high politics, the history of the Directory, from the outset, is one of instability, plots and *coups d'états*. On 5 October 1795 (13 Vendémiaire Year IV), a royalist insurrection in Paris, protesting against the decision that two-thirds of the members of the outgoing National Convention would be allowed to retain their seats in the new legislature, had to be crushed – with the help of a certain Napoleon Bonaparte. The decision had been prompted by the fear on the part of the Directors that free and fair elections would return a royalist majority. From the beginning, then, elections were being rigged. Severely circumscribed in 1795, the choice of the electors would be 'severely repudiated in the Year V [1797] and . . . blatantly distorted in the Year VIII [1798]'.[69] In 1797, the election of 177 'royalist' deputies was annulled; the following year, it was the turn of successful Jacobin candidates to be set aside. In November 1799, Napoleon's *coup d'état* would put an end to what had become an electoral farce.

The undisputed fact was that, by 1795, there was no national consensus upon which a stable parliamentary democracy could be constructed. The chances of a compromise between royalists and republicans were nullified by the attitude of the monarchy in exile, led by the comte de Provence, the future Louis XVIII. His Declaration of Verona on 24 June 1795 (6 Messidor Year III) was an uncompromising statement that promised to restore ancien regime privileges and execute regicides (had he been tutored about the Restoration period of English history in 1660?). It is true that the exiled Bourbons were, to some extent, pawns of the European Powers, but, as in 1791, the Bourbons had refused to countenance the possibility of becoming constitutional monarchs, a mistake of historic proportions. On the left, the chances of a compromise between the bourgeois leaders of the Republic and the Popular Movement had virtually disappeared with the collapse of the Jacobin–sansculotte alliance. Many ex-sansculottes had been forced underground. Of these survivors, Gracchus Babeuf, editor of the little-read *Tribun du peuple*, would bequeath the richest legacy to the history of socialist theory, in spite of the fact that his 'Conspiracy of the Equals' collapsed ignominiously with his arrest in May 1796 and subsequent execution a year later. Claims, by some left-wing historians, that Babeuf was the 'first, modern communist' are not without theoretical foundation, although, strongly influenced by the somewhat Utopian theorising of Rousseau and Mably, Babouvism had more in common with eighteenth-century sansculotte ideas on the state ownership and distribution – not production – of goods.[70] The historical significance of Babouvism in 1796 was its rejection of popular democratic institutions in favour of the temporary dictatorship of a centralised elite, a concept that obviously invites comparisons with Leninist political theory. This rejection reflects the popular disenchantment with the corrupt political system of the Directory, the loss of social *égalité*. The loss of *liberté* and *fraternité* would follow under Napoleon.

For the mass of the French population, excluded from these somewhat recherché debates, politics had become an irrelevant pastime by the late 1790s. Colin Jones believes that 'The rural world passed through hell and high water' during this period.[71] The comment is especially relevant to the condition of the landless or land-poor strata of the peasantry. Those with some cash to spare had done well out of the sale of National Lands; those with surplus produce did well out of rising prices after 1795. Obviously, neither of these benefits was available to those without cash or land. In addition, the loss of many European and world markets spelled misery for hundreds of thousands of rural, and urban, protoindustrial workers. Olwen Hufton suggests that women, not men, bore the heavier burden. For Hufton, it was hardly surprising that a large percentage of the poor, female population, for whom life was a 'grisly lottery', should have embraced the *Catholic* royalist cause during the 1790s. What had the Revolution done for them? The decree of 21 February 1795 had introduced freedom of worship, but only in private buildings served by priests faithful to the regime. But women refused, in most localities, to recognise priests loyal to Grégoire's Constitutional Church. Is it surprising, then, that many of them sheltered the counter-revolutionary bands of *chouans* in the west and the *enfans de Jésus* in the south-east? The state 'had intruded too far and women entered the public arena to push it back and won'.[72] Ordinary people, indeed, ordinary women, *did* shape politics at the end of the eighteenth century, just as they had done under the monarchy before 1789. In 1801, Napoleon would be forced to return France to the Vatican fold, if only as the black sheep of the universal family.

The hopes of royalists, too, were kept alive during the late 1790s, in many cases by the resistance of the poor and the disinherited, whether as *chouans* in the west or by the Catholic royalists in the south-east. It is true that many of these Catholic royalist bands did participate in gratuitous killing and criminal activity, particularly after the Directory had destroyed the hopes of a legitimate royalist takeover of power by the *coup d'état* of September 1797. Mercier argued that a 'mob' was a mob, whatever its ideological cover: 'the killers paid by the aristocracy [in 1797] to serve its cause were the same as those who had sold themselves to the Robespierrists'.[73] But this is little more than another example of the massive condescension of the powerful against the powerless. Our study of insurrections in the departments of the Gard and Ardèche in south-eastern France between the 1780s and the 1800s reveals a continuity of conflict – 'anti-Bourbon' in the 1780s, 'anti-revolutionary' after 1789 – founded upon the very real socio-economic hardships experienced by small farming and protoindustrial communities. Whether we are dealing with the *Masques armés* revolt, led by the so-called *'procureurs des pauvres'*, in 1783, or with the royalist insurrections of 1790–93, or the guerrilla warfare of the *égorgeurs du Midi* during the late 1790s, we find the presence of poor artisans and farmers, textile workers, male and female, and, after 1793, the odd priest, son of the local squire and, of course, army deserters. The names of the same small towns and villages in this poor region of protoindustrialised workers and mini-farms recur in the official reports of riots and rebellion throughout the 1780s and 1790s.[74]

The most important piece of legislation to be passed in the dying days of the Directorial regime was the Jourdan Law of 5 September 1798 (19 Fructidor Year VII). It marked the introduction of conscription for the armed forces, rather than periodic levies. A few weeks later, the state called for the conscription of 200,000 more men for the army. The Revolutionary state, which had been announced with the promise of bringing peace and equality to all Europe, was now committing itself to looting its neighbours and forcing a military dictatorship on its own people. Isser Woloch concludes that 'Military conscription . . . became the one issue that truly threatened civic peace, that produced mass resistance of a sustained, endemic character.'[75] The choice for many poor young men by 1799 was either to be killed by the army or to join it.

Suggested reading

Forrest, A. *Napoleon's Men: The Soldiers of the Revolution and Empire* (London, 2002).

Gough, H. *The Terror in the French Revolution* (London, 1998).

Hampson, N. 'Robespierre and the Terror', in C. Haydon and W. Doyle (eds.) *Robespierre* (Cambridge, 1999).

Higonnet, P. *Goodness Beyond Virtue: Jacobins during the French Revolution* (Cambridge, Mass., 1998).

Hufton, O. 'In Search of Counter-Revolution Women', in G. Kates (ed.) *The French Revolution: Recent Debates and New Controversies* (London, 1997).

Lyons, M. *France under the Directory* (Cambridge, 1975).

Scott, S. *The Response of the Royal Army to the French Revolution: The Role and Development of the Line Army, 1787–93* (Oxford, 1978).

Skocpol, T. *States and Social Revolution: A Comparative Analysis of France, Russia, and China* (Cambridge, 1979).

Slavin, M. *The Making of an Insurrection: Parisian Sections and the Gironde* (Cambridge, Mass., 1986).

Sutherland, D. *The Chouans: The Social Origins of Popular Counter-Revolution in Upper Brittany, 1770–1796* (Oxford, 1982).

Conclusion

The publication of Napoleon's Civil Code on 21 March 1804 confirmed, from a legal standpoint, the demise of the ancien regime. Under Napoleon's chairmanship, it collated 'a myriad of local statutes into a coherent code, based on a compromise between Roman and common law, and stands as one of the regime's greatest achievements'.[1] It also confirmed that the internecine political and social struggles of the Revolution were over, not definitively, but certainly in the forms they had assumed during the 1790s. Counterbalancing Napoleon's creation of a militarised, increasingly anti-democratic regime, the Civil Code would provide a legal and a *national* foundation for civil society in France that would endure well into the twentieth century. Pierre Goubert has even suggested that 'the juridical unification of the country, first sketched by Louis XIV . . . represents the true legacy of the Revolution'.[2]

In socio-political terms, the code confirmed the decline, if not the fall, of the French nobility: around half of its property had been confiscated; it had lost well over 1,000 of its members; at least 16,000 nobles had emigrated. For the large majority who had survived, there was the ever-present reality that 'The abolition of feudalism had ended their unreflecting dominance over local politics . . .'[3] The electoral lists for 1830 reveal that 40 per cent of the noble families of the 1780s had either disappeared or were no longer wealthy enough to pay the 200 *francs* annual direct taxes to qualify for voting rights. Balzac has one of his aristocratic characters launch a tirade against her fellow nobles, suggesting that they were 'mad for wishing to remain in the fifteenth century when we are in the nineteenth. There is no longer a nobility. Napoleon's *Code Civil* killed it off – just as cannon killed off feudalism! You will be a lot more noble when you have some money!'[4] The quotation is an accurate reflection of what had happened in France since 1789 – the peasantry had destroyed what remained of feudalism; Napoleon had legalised its historic victory over the nobility.

The creation of a new 'service nobility' during Napoleon's First Empire would do little to mask the political and social reality that, in terms of its hegemonic power and influence, 'the age of the aristocracy' had ended and the 'age of the bourgeoisie' had begun. This 'rise of the bourgeoisie' had obviously occurred over several centuries: the Revolution had cleared the ground for its ultimate victory with the defeat of both the aristocracy and *le peuple*. The collapse of the Bourbon monarchy and its aristocratic supporters by 1792, however, had created the demand for some other form of political legitimacy, a substitute for the absolutist state. For François Furet, Napoleon Bonaparte became 'the ultimate incarnation of that crisis of political representation that was the essence of the Revolution'.[5] To claim that 'political representation' formed the 'essence' of the Revolution is, of course, the revisionist way of underestimating the significance of social change during the Revolution. What is undeniable is that if the Revolution did profoundly affect social relationships, it also failed to create a stable political system. The Jacobin period and the Napoleonic Empire provided an interim solution by substituting the dictatorship of a militarised state for representative democracy. Between the end of the Jacobin parliamentary dictatorship in 1794 and the beginning of Napoleon's military dictatorship in 1799, the very foundations of the state had begun to collapse.

An interim, authoritarian solution was necessary because, as in most examples of total war, the rules governing France's fledgling, representative democracy had to be suspended. France's dominant bourgeois elites had not yet donned their full middle-class attire – parliamentary government, religious toleration, equality before the law, free markets and free speech. By the end of the 1790s, these elites were still fearful of losing the massive gains they had acquired from the sale of Church lands and the seizure of *émigré* property, and this fear had been aggravated by sporadic rebellions on the part of the dispossessed and disenfranchised masses. The nerves of the bourgeoisie were steadied, and the power of the French bourgeois state immeasurably increased, with the announcement of the religious settlement with the papacy, which reversed several centuries of subservience to Rome. The Concordat of 1802, together with the Organic Articles that Napoleon appended to the original agreement, transformed the French Gallican Church into a department of state. It was an epochal event. Napoleon would now choose the new bishops and priests; the pope could only 'invest' them with his official blessing. The salaries of the clergy would be paid by the state. Catholicism had ceased to be the official religion of France; henceforth it would be described, accurately, as 'the religion of the majority of Frenchmen'. The Protestant and Jewish Churches would be granted separate recognition and organisation. A minority of Catholics was distinctly unimpressed with these changes, and a few even rejected the settlement out of hand, forming themselves into a small, schismatic sect – *la petite église*. But at least the majority had now been welcomed back into the universal Roman Catholic fold, and – of more immediate interest to Napoleon and the bourgeoisie – the counter-revolution had lost one of its main sources of recruitment. Napoleon had bridged one of the deepest chasms opened up by the Revolution. That bridge would not be dismantled again until the separation of Church and state in 1905.

As we noted above, the Concordat was followed, two years later, with the legal settlement that provided the bourgeoisie with the further reassurance it was seeking – the Civil Code. More than any other provision in this historic document, it was the legalisation of the massive transfer of Church and *émigré* property to the bourgeoisie, as well as to the wealthier peasantry, that attracted support for Napoleon. Modern social revolutions, especially the French, the Russian and the Chinese, have been propelled by demands for land reform. On this fundamental issue, Napoleon was the executor of the Revolution's 'last will and testament' which promised, eventually, to transfer political power – and the land upon which it was founded – to the bourgeoisie. Former noble landowners would also be welcome to a share in this historic deal, so long as they accepted the loss of their feudal rights.

The crises and conflicts generated by the Revolution and Empire 'spectacularly accelerated the process' of creating a cohesive bourgeois class, although they 'probably altered the form it took'.[6] As Michael Mann has argued: 'Not even revolutionary politics flow simply from the conflict between classes already "out there" in civil society. The class actors aroused during the French Revolution barely existed before the Revolution. They were created by its power process – partly because militant ideologists worked hard to mobilise class sentiments, but mostly because they were unintentionally fostered by political power relations'.[7] Class identity is not a fixed 'structure' but an unfolding process. It was only after the Revolution of 1830 and the abdication of Charles X, the last of the Bourbon kings, that a French middle class, forged in the crucible of protracted struggles with the aristocracy and the lower orders, could be clearly identified.[8]

However, the French bourgeoisie that emerged from the Revolution and Napoleonic Empire was not only created by bloody social conflict but also by its dependence upon the French state, a dependence which has distinguished its history from that of the British middle class to the present day. Throughout the ancien regime, wealthy bourgeois had looked to the monarchy for social advancement and, especially during the second half of the eighteenth century, for greater economic freedom. We saw in chapter seven how, following the seismic shock of defeat during the Seven Years War, enlightened monarchists within – and without – the monarchy had responded by becoming more receptive to bourgeois, liberal capitalist ideas. Encouraged by physiocratic reforming ministers like Jacques Turgot, the monarchy had moved, hesitantly, in the direction of economic and political reform – free trade, free speech, religious toleration, elected provincial assemblies, all these were now placed on the court's 'agenda for change'. Unfortunately, the weakness of Louis XVI, the strength of aristocratic resistance at Versailles, as well as in the parlements and the Church, and the understandable resistance of the poor had all worked against the introduction of a 'Glorious Revolution' along English lines. In 1789, and again in 1795 with Louis XVIII's Declaration of Verona, the Bourbon regime would chose to remain loyal to its 'faithful aristocracy' rather than desert it for the far less faithful bourgeoisie.

The monarchy's task had been complicated by the fact that France was a 'warrior state': by the late eighteenth century, its reach extended to the farthest corners of Europe and the wider world. In Fernand Braudel's opinion, events from the ninth to the fifteenth century had proved that 'Without Europe, there could be no France'; and he extended his claim to cover contemporary France: 'Europe is our family, the condition for our existence.'[9] The French state had been conceived and raised on the European battlefield; it had been 'born again' under the warrior king, Louis XIV, 'a prince who was born for the happiness of France and of all Europe', according to the duc de Saint-Simon.[10] Unfortunately, Britain – embarked upon its historic world quest to become 'Great Britain' – did not share Saint-Simon's enthusiasm for the Sun King. The almost inevitable result was that France became embroiled in the Seven Years War, the American War of Independence and, from 1792, a generation of bloody conflict with Great Britain and her continental allies. During the 1790s, revolution and war fused to create a 'nation-state', led by the Revolutionary bourgeoisie. John Bosher, in a chapter entitled 'The New Leviathan', has explained how, between 1795 and 1815, a 'national civil service (a Ministry of the Interior was created in April 1791), especially the national treasury . . . [managed] to enforce a greater measure of state control than the Bourbons had achieved'.[11] The nature of the French state, and of the bourgeoisie, was transformed by war, culminating in the military dictatorships of the Jacobins and Napoleon Bonaparte. The latter 'had studied war, he had experienced it, he was born of it, and it never ceased to shape his life' and, we might add, the shape of France's civil society.[12] But Napoleon's reach had exceeded his grasp. France emerged from this final episode of the 'Second Hundred Years War' exhausted, lacking, as she did, the political and financial institutions, and the social stability, to defeat her traditional enemy.

The arranged marriage of the French bourgeoisie to the Revolutionary military state was also clearly visible at local level. The recent research conducted by Peter Jones and David Garrioch makes this abundantly clear. Garrioch argues that 'it was the state, crowned by the Revolution, that acted as midwife for the new local elite: providing employment and encouragement for industry; showering honors on men of science and of property; closing off the way to political participation [of *le peuple*] and admitting the few to favor and influence'. Jones suggests that the crucial ingredient in the Revolutionary settlement for the peasantry was equality before the law, and concludes that the Revolution had given villages real political power and, although this power was certainly not 'democratic', it had 'substantially remedied the rural inferiority complex'.[13] Control of the countryside, however, was now more firmly placed in the hands of the rural bourgeoisie than it had been during the ancien regime. The cost, in terms of cash and military casualties, would alienate many of the poorer sections of the rural community from the Revolutionary settlement.

The final link in the chain that bound the Revolutionary bourgeoisie to the Napoleonic regime was economic. A distinctive feature of the Revolutionary state bureaucracy, as opposed to its ancien regime predominantly noble counterpart, was that it tended to marry widely into business circles, 'forming a bourgeoisie that was socially, ideologically, and politically more united than the pre-revolutionary middle class'.[14] Napoleon not only encouraged these liaisons, he also provided financiers, manufacturers and wealthy farmers with rich pickings from the financing, arming, outfitting and feeding of his armies. Compensation for the loss of France's overseas empire would be found in the acquisition of a continental empire and the expansion of an internal market. For the bourgeoisie, the Concordat, the Code and the Continental Blockade – the last favouring the expansion of French trade with conquered European countries – replaced the Revolutionary trinity of 'Liberty, Equality and Fraternity'.

A decade of foreign and civil wars after 1792 obviously damaged French economic performance. Agricultural levels of production were lower in 1800 than they had been in the late 1780s; industrial production had fallen to about 60 per cent of pre-Revolutionary performance; foreign trade had been severely affected. This was bad enough, but, in 1803, Napoleon would sell off the huge Louisiana territories to America for a handful of dollars, effectively ending the history of France's first colonial empire. It has to be remembered, however, that foreign trade had suffered from the loss of colonies to the English and the closure of Spanish markets from the 1770s. It is also vital, when relating the importance of the Revolutionary period to the long-term performance of the French economy, to bear in mind the geographic, demographic and economic structures of *la France profonde*. For example, while the population of England increased by 133 per cent between 1680 and 1830, that of France rose by just 39 per cent. There can be no doubt that Revolutionary legislation – the end of feudal dues and the tithe, the end of internal customs barriers and river tolls, the creation of the National Bank and the introduction of a metric system, and anti-strike legislation – moved the economy in the direction of modern capitalism. However, ancien regime France could not be transformed overnight: the above legislation would take decades to bed down. Atlantic ports such as Bordeaux, whose population fell from 110,000 in the early 1790s to just over 90,000 in 1815, would take decades to recover. It was not all gloom and doom, of course. The rich had become richer during the Directory; war provided an impetus for the textile and metallurgical industries; many Parisian suppliers of luxury and cotton goods made healthy profits during the Directory and Empire.[15]

It was what happened in the rural, rather than the urban, sector, however, that prompted Le Goff and Sutherland to describe the period of the Revolution and Empire as 'a lost generation for economic growth and development'. One of the causes of this alleged loss was the huge volume of Church and *émigré* land that came on the open market in the 1790s. Paul Butel agrees: 'We cannot over-emphasize the diversion of capital [from trade and industry] towards agriculture as merchants increasingly became landlords. The most important developments in this respect arose from the sale of *biens nationaux* between 1791 and 1800.' Many professional and commercial bourgeois in Bordeaux, for example – like the Lamothe family we discussed at the end of chapter four – invested their money in land. One of the attractions was the profit that might be found, and the social cachet that certainly was to be found, in purchasing a country estate that included a vineyard. This was a move that married their interest in 'living nobly', occasionally in a château, with their penchant for safe forms of investment. Social status around the 1800s was often 'château-bottled'! According to Le Goff and Sutherland, viticulture, an industry that had expanded significantly before the Revolution, was one of the very few in the French countryside to provide 'some signs of dynamism in an otherwise stagnant rural economy at the end of the Empire'.[16]

Given the considerable risks associated with investing during periods of revolution and war, allied to the fact that land was the principal gift bestowed by the Revolution on the bourgeoisie during the 1790s, it is hardly surprising that the French took a different route to modern capitalism than the English. English elites had acquired a considerable volume of their lands as a result of Henry VIII's sale of the monasteries and the handouts associated with English revolutions of the seventeenth century. Between 1760 and 1820 they would be enclosing millions of acres of the countryside, dispossessing small-owners and cottagers of their 'immemorial' rights in the process. The French bourgeoisie had also been acquiring land in the seventeenth and eighteenth centuries, but it was the seizure of Church and *émigré* property during the Revolution that really swung the balance of landed power in their favour. However, given the fact that the Revolution had also benefited the small peasantry, it would take time, and a revolution in attitudes, before any kind of 'agrarian revolution' would occur in France. In other words, the 'triumph of the bourgeoisie' was never uncontested in the countryside. It was the strength of, and the persistent challenge from, the peasantry that helped – perhaps more than any other single factor – to shape the character of French capitalism. The land owned by the peasantry increased during the 1790s from approximately 30 to 40 per cent, while the number of peasant owner-occupiers rose by one-third.

Patrick O'Brien has pointed out that 'By abolishing seigneurial dues and suppressing tithes, the Revolutionaries also transferred agricultural income back to those who farmed the land. At a stroke, the tax and judicial reforms of the 1790s lightened the burdens on the peasantry and enhanced their capacity to prosper on small plots of land.'[17] The Napoleonic Code of 1804 would strengthen partible inheritance and encourage young people to stay on the land. Le Goff and Sutherland suggest that 'by entrenching the rights of millions of smallholders and making it difficult to alter the old communal rights, the Revolution may have slowed down the pace of rural economic transformation and put a brake on the movement of labour into the cities and the factories'. Anatoli Ado, on the other hand, admits that capitalist development in the French countryside was 'retarded' during the Revolution and Empire, but argues that the fault (if such it be) lay with the lack of entrepreneurial dynamism on the part of large estate owners, not with the small-owning peasantry, many of whom were eager to expand their farms but lacked the capital to do so.[18]

No French government, from Choiseul in the 1760s to Napoleon 40 years later was prepared to challenge head-on the resistance of peasant communities. Bertin and Terray had warned Turgot in the mid-1770s to move cautiously when seeking to introduce legislation on enclosures. The Rural Code of 1791, introduced at a time of alarming peasant rebellions, had introduced the first of many compromises between (bourgeois) 'individual' and (peasant) 'collective' systems of farming. In effect, the law stipulated that 'individual' and 'collective' practices could continue, if customary practice sanctioned it. In a predominantly rural society composed of millions of small farmers and farm labourers, all governments found it extremely difficult to legalise the enclosure of farmland in the interests of the wealthy landowners. An exhaustive enquiry carried out between 1812 and 1814 did condemn collective practices, 'yet in the next breath set out procedures for local exemptions that undercut the major premise'.[19] As late as 1945, poor farmers in the French countryside had to be 'bought out', with subsidies and pensions, before any 'progress' was achieved. The bourgeoisie may have triumphed in the towns as a result of the Revolution, but their domination of the countryside was always contested by the peasantry, and, in some parts of France, still is!

Whether in the towns or the countryside, the Napoleonic Code would confirm what the Revolution – *after 1793* – had decided about women: that their legal and social position should be inferior to that of men. The Code not only overturned the divorce laws of 1792, but denied women the right to sign legally binding contracts or to buy or sell property in their own names. The rights and social position of illegitimate children were also downgraded. The law on adultery envisaged imprisonment for women accused of this assault upon their husband's honour, while being far more forgiving to men. This legislation would not be significantly altered until 1975. Madame de Stael, who once accused Napoleon of presiding over 'a garrison where misery and boredom ruled', wrote that 'Since the Revolution men have found it politically and morally useful to reduce women to the most absurd mediocrity.'[20] Dorinda Outram has quarried the innovative writing of cultural historians to reveal how the process of women's exclusion from the public sphere had been secularised by 1804: 'It was the Revolution that 'brought into being the stoical male figure as the archetypal public actor, dissociated from Christian reference points, and serving to exclude the "peripheral" political groups, such as women and sansculottes, from access to dignified heroic personification which was at the heart of the struggle for control of power in Revolutionary politics.'[21] We argued in chapter two that the fundamental cause of women's subordination to men was the teaching of many of the world's most influential religions. In a recent newspaper article, Polly Toynbee agreed: 'Judaism, Islam, and Christianity are defined by hatred of women's bodies'.[22]

It is important to distinguish the earlier from the later period of the Revolution when discussing the bodies or minds of women. There was a brief interlude between 1789 and 1793 when it appeared that the Revolution would create its own space for the elevation of women in society and politics. The space occupied by women in the public sphere was significantly enlarged by their participation in political clubs and societies, while legislation that promised them some form of equality *vis-à-vis* men – such as the divorce law of 1792 – was gradually being introduced. Ultimately, however, the male bourgeois elite that controlled the political fate of the nation, coupled with the increasing militarisation of the Revolution, reversed the process. Joan Scott has argued that 'the structure of modern republican politics can be construed as part of an elaborate defence against women's power and public presence'. Although this was written in 1988, few women in France, or in many other 'modern' societies, would say today that the battle for equality has been won.[23]

The importance of the French state in the reconstruction of society and politics before and after 1789 has been a constant theme throughout our study. Some feminist historians have insisted upon its contribution in the reshaping of a woman's place in nineteenth-century France. Naomi Schor, for example, has argued that 'Because of the widespread feminisation of republican iconography in France, the nineteenth-century heroine, in contradistinction to her eighteenth-century predecessor, is always inhabited by the uncanny shadow of the state whose very laws serve to silence and oppress her.'[24] We would add that it was the militarisation of the state – an almost inevitable consequence of modern revolutions – that played a significant role in this process. War has traditionally been, primarily, a male pursuit, and the rise of war to the top of the state's agenda in 1792 closed many of the spaces in the public sphere that '1789' had begun to open.

According to Le Goff and Sutherland, 'The financing of the war and the Terror, and the impact of civil disturbances . . . put a new burden on the neglected majority of the population, the countrymen and women so despised by the *sans-culottes*.'[25] It is difficult to avoid the conclusion that the mass of the poor, male and female, in town and country, gained precious little from the Revolution. Richard Cobb, the best analyst of the Revolutionary popular mind, wrote in 1970 that the fears and panics that haunted the lives of the poor during the early years of the Revolution, and that fuelled so many revolutionary rebellions, were fully justified. Referring to the terrible famine of the winter of 1795 he writes: 'It was, it is true, the last time in French history that a disaster on quite such a scale occurred, but, as it turned out, the sans-culotte had every reason to look in fear to the immediate future and to tremble for the morrow.'[26] This was no exaggeration. By the late 1790s, even the ancien regime hospitals that had offered some hope to the sick and the dying were in crisis. According to Michael Kwass, Louis XIV had created 'a type of welfare state for the privileged'.[27] Our argument throughout this work has been that one of the striking, and ultimately fatal, failures of ancien regime and Revolutionary administrations was the inability to create anything approaching a sustainable, substitute 'welfare state' for the working classes.

The French state, recreated under the Revolution and Napoleon, became a more efficient police state than that of the ancien regime. Anti-coalition laws, such as the *loi Chapelier* of 1791 began the process of subjugating workers and expanding the power of employers. Under Napoleon, workers would be obliged to carry their passbooks (*livrets*) containing details of their identity and work records; conversation in cafés, cabarets, freemason lodges and journeymen's halls would now be recorded and reported more efficiently than they had been under the ancien regime. In the countryside, hundreds of thousands of protoindustrial workers were entering what Didier Terrier has described as the second phase of the protoindustrialisation process, which lasted from *c*.1800 to 1880. It was a phase that would produce a 'proletariat atypique', one that desperately tried to keep one foot on the land, the other reluctantly being pushed in the direction of the factory gate. He adds that the expansion of protoindustrial forms of production after 1800 would enable France 'to follow a road that was clearly different from that taken by England, thanks to the elaboration of an industrial process which can be said to have passed 'almost unnoticed'.[28]

For rich and poor alike, however, it was war that helped to destroy that vision of a reformed state that had been the dream of a few enlightened monarchists during the ancien regime and the programme of so many Revolutionaries from 1789 to 1792. It is ironic, but revealing, that Maximilien Robespierre, *éminence grise* of the Jacobin Terror, should have denounced bellicose orators like Jacques Brissot as allies of a treacherous court before war broke out in 1792. For Isser Woloch, one of the cruellest ironies of the entire period was the fact that 'state power marshalled by the revolution of 1789 should in the end have achieved its greatest impact with Napoleonic conscription'; and that this machine 'arguably produced the most disastrous result of the French Revolution by virtue of the mass slaughter it facilitated'.[29]

Glossary

aides indirect taxes on commodities, especially wines and spirits.

assignat revolutionary paper currency first introduced in 1790, originally backed by the sale of Church property.

bailliage jurisdiction of royal judicial court (referred to as *sénéchaussée* in the south).

banalités monopolies involving payments by the peasantry for use of the seigneur's ovens, mills and winepresses.

bourgeois urban property-owner enjoying certain rights and privileges, including the right to vote and to avoid military service.

cahiers de doléances notebooks of grievances drawn up by communities throughout France in preparation for the meeting of the Estates General in the spring of 1789.

chambre des comptes one of the nine finance offices of the crown.

champart seigneurial due levied on the harvests of the peasantry, usually paid in kind and often quite onerous (referred to as the *tasque* in parts of the south).

colporteur itinerant bookseller.

compagnon a skilled artisan or 'journeyman', many of whom had worked in several provincial towns to improve their skills (the *'tour de France'*).

corvées forced labour on seigneurial estates or on government roads.

cour des aides one of the four fiscal and customs' offices of the crown.

cour des monnaies one of the two royal mints.

curé not a curate (who was called, confusingly, a *vicaire*), but the parish priest.

dépôts de mendicité workhouses to confine beggars, vagabonds and often prostitutes after the late 1760s.

dîme ecclesiastical tithe.

élection subdivision of the *généralité*.

fermier used for a tenant farmer, as well as for someone who collected taxes, tithes or dues for a landlord.

franc-fief the payment made to the crown by a non-noble who purchased noble property.

gabelle ancien regime salt tax, much hated by the people.

généralité main fiscal and administrative unit of ancien regime France.

hôpital-général ancien regime institution that was more of a poorhouse than a modern hospital.

hôtel-Dieu a hospital that cared for the sick, especially the elderly and the poor.

Intendant ancien regime agent of the crown in each *généralité*; forerunner of the Napoleonic Prefect.

laboureur usually refers to a wealthy farmer.

livre (tournois) basic unit of currency during the ancien regime. A *sou* was worth 12 *deniers;* a *livre* (increasingly referred to as the *franc* after 1789) was worth 20 *sous;* and three *livres* made one *écu*.

lods et ventes a seigneurial due, often heavy, that was levied on the purchase and sale of property.

maréchaussée mounted police force that operated primarily in the countryside.

métayage sharecropping, quite widespread in France, especially in the south.

noblesse de l'épée the 'sword nobility', whose noble status had been acquired – often in the medieval past – through military prowess.

noblesse de robe the 'nobility of the robe', whose noble status was acquired through service in the royal bureaucracy.

parlements highest courts of appeal under the ancien regime, but also possessing political powers that acted as a check on royal 'despotism'. There were 13 parlements, the most influential being the parlement of Paris.

pays d'élection ancien regime regions which did not possess provincial estates. They covered most of France and were administered directly from Versailles.

pays d'états ancien regime regions, situated on the periphery of France, that possessed provincial estates. They had limited powers of self-government, such as the right to levy taxes.

philosophes philosophers and men of letters associated with the French Enlightenment.

physiocrates economic theorists during the period of the Enlightenment.

rentier property-owner living off private investments, interest on loans, bonds and government securities.

sansculotte a political activist in the 48 Parisian sections, especially during the Jacobin Terror, 1793–4. Many were master craftsmen, journeymen and shopkeepers.

sociétés populaires political clubs created during the early years of the Revolution and patronised by the sansculottes.

taille the main government tax levied under the ancien regime.

Notes

Introduction

1 James McMillan, 'Social History, New Cultural History, and the Rediscovery of Politics', *Journal of Modern History*, Vol 66 (1994), p. 761.
2 Pierre Goubert and Daniel Roche, *Les Français et l'ancien régime*, 2 vols (Paris, 1984, 1991), Vol I, *La société et l'état* (1984), p. 49.
3 Peter Campbell, *Power and Politics in Old Regime France, 1720–45* (London, 1996), p. 318.
4 Guy Sorman, *Une belle journée en France* (Paris, 1998), p. 80.
5 Peter McPhee, *A Social History of France 1780–1880* (London, 1992), p. 3.
6 Arthur Young, *Travels in France and Italy* (London, 1976), p. 107.
7 Jonathan Israel, *Radical Enlightenment: Philosophy and the Making of Modernity 1650–1750* (Oxford, 2001), p. 271.

Chapter 1

1 Peter Burke, *The Fabrication of Louis XIV* (London, 1992), p. 77; Francois-Xavier Emmanuelli, *État et pouvoirs dans le France XVIe – XVIIIe siècles* (Paris, 1992), p. 20.
2 Pierre Pluchon, *Histoire de la colonisation française*, 2 vols (Paris, 1991), Vol I, *Le premier empire colonial: des origines à la Restauration*, p. 9.
3 Paul Kennedy, *The Rise and Fall of the Great Powers: Economic Change and Military Conflict from 1500 to 2000* (London, 1989), p. 115.
4 Fernand Braudel, *The Identity of France*, 2 vols, translated by Sian Reynolds (New York, 1988,1990), Vol I, *History and Environment*, p. 127.
5 Bernard Lepetit, *The Pre-Industrial Urban System: France 1740–1840* (Cambridge, 1994), pp. 449–502; Braudel, *The Identity of France*, Vol I, chapter six.
6 Voltaire, *The Age of Louis XIV* (London, 1961), p. 2.
7 Michel Antoine, *Louis XV* (Paris, 1989), p. 119.
8 For a representative sample of this school, see the essays in Keith Baker (ed.), *The French Revolution and the Creation of Modern Political Culture*, 3 vols, Vol I, *The Political Culture of the Old Regime* (Oxford, 1987).
9 Goubert and Roche, *Les Français*, Vol I, p. 190.
10 Antoine, *Louis XV*, p. 210.
11 Emmanuelli, *État et pouvoirs*, chapter ten; Richard Bonney, 'Absolutism: What's in a Name', *French History* Vol I (1987), pp. 93–110.
12 Antoine, *Louis XV*, pp. 180–227.
13 David Parker, *Class and State in Ancien Régime France: The Road to Modernity?* (London, 1996), pp. 175–6.
14 Goubert and Roche, *Les Français*, Vol II, pp. 204–8.

15 Parker, *Class and State*, p. 195; Tim Blanning, *The Culture of Power and the Power of Culture* (Oxford, 2002), p. 36.

16 Peter Campbell, *Power and Politics*, pp. 16–20; Susan Kettering, *Patrons, Brokers and Clients in Seventeenth-Century France* (New York, 1986).

17 Perry Anderson, *Lineages of the Absolutist State* (London, 1974), p. 212. Anderson writes: 'the influence of war on its [eastern absolutist] structure was even more preponderant than in the west'. In the east, 'the function of the centralised State was to defend the class position of the feudal nobility against both its rivals abroad and its peasants at home'.

18 John McManners, *Church and Society in Eighteenth-Century France*, 2 vols (Oxford, 1998), Vol I, *The Clerical Establishment and its Social Ramifications*, p. 210.

19 Richard Bonney, *The Limits of Absolutism in Ancien Regime France* (Aldershot, 1995).

20 Peter Burke, *The Fabrication of Louis XIV*, pp. 102–5.

21 McManners, *Church and Society*, Vol II, *The Religion of the People and the Politics of Religion*, pp. 572–9.

22 For a short historiographical essay, see William Doyle, *Jansenism* (London, 2000), pp. 1–4.

23 McManners, *Church and Society*, Vol I, p. 20; Vol II, pp. 387–9.

24 Jeremy Black, *From Louis XIV to Napoleon: The Fate of a Great Power* (London, 1999), p. 53.

25 John B. Collins, *The State in Early Modern France* (Cambridge, 1995), pp. 125–6.

26 Saint-Simon, *Mémoires* (Paris, 1990), 2 vols, Vol I, pp. 290–320.

27 Colin Jones, *The Great Nation: France from Louis XV to Napoleon* (New York, 2002), pp. 40–41.

28 Emmanuel Le Roy Ladurie, *Saint-Simon, ou le système de la Cour* (Paris, 1997), pp. 385–505.

29 Franklin Ford, *The Regrouping of the French Aristocracy after Louis XIV* (New York, 1965), p. 176.

30 Parker, *Class and State*, p. 157.

31 Julian Swann, 'The State and Political Culture' in William Doyle (ed.) *Old Regime France* (Oxford, 2001), p. 160.

32 Pluchon, *Histoire de la colonisation française*, Vol I, pp. 127–9; see also Jeremy Black, *From Louis XIV to Napoleon*, p. 72, who quotes the French ambassador to the Hague as saying that Dubois's foreign policy was good for the Regent, but bad for France.

33 Guy Chaussinand-Nogaret, *Le Cardinal Dubois, 1656–1723* (Paris, 2000), p. 64.

34 Antoine Murphy, *John Law: Economic Theorist and Policy-maker* (Oxford, 1997), p. 213.

35 John Collins, *The State in Early Modern France* (Cambridge, 1995), pp. 168–72.

36 Murphy, *John Law*, p. 87.

37 Black, *From Louis XIV to Napoleon*, pp. 70–4.

38 Jean-Christian Petitfils, *Le Régent* (Paris, 1986), pp. 505–17.

39 Saint-Simon, *Mémoires*, Vol I, pp. 391–2.

40 Petitfils, *Le Régent*, p. 524.

41 Pluchon, *Histoire de la colonisation*, pp. 122–35. Antoine Murphy's conclusion is that 'Law's System certainly bankrupted the creditors of the state. As a debtor,

however, the state was a net gainer', *John Law*, p. 308. See also Petitfils, *Le Régent*, pp. 521–72.

Chapter 2

1 Goubert and Roche, *Les Français*, Vol I, p. 9.
2 McManners, *Church and Society*, Vol I, p. 40.
3 Pluchon, *Histoire de la colonisation*, pp. 163–4.
4 See R. Po-Chia Hsia, *The World of Catholic Renewal* (Cambridge, 1998), pp. 191–3.
5 For a good summary of the Church's wealth, see McManners, *Church and Society*, Vol I, p. 98.
6 Gabriel Audisio, *Les Français d'hier*, 2 vols, Vol I, *Des Paysans, XVe – XIXe siècle* (Paris, 1993), pp. 195–7; McManners, *Church and Society*, Vol I, pp. 95–6.
7 René Baehrel, *Une Croissance: la Basse-Provence rurale, fin du XVIe siècle à 1789* (Paris, 1961), pp. 346–9.
8 Danièle Galland-Boret, 'La propriété en pays Saumurois à la fin de l'ancien régime', in *Les Sentiers de l'histoire locale*, no. 1 (1991), pp. 19–81.
9 Goubert and Roche, *Les Français*, Vol I, p. 376.
10 Emmanuelli, *États et pouvoirs*, pp. 191–3.
11 Gabriel Audisio, *Les Français d'hier*, 2 vols, Vol II, *Des Croyants, XVe – XIXe siècle* (Paris, 1996), pp. 374–5.
12 Raymond Donck, *Vergèze, porte de la Vaunage* (Vergèze, 1987), p. 95.
13 Philippe Joutard, 'The museum of the Desert', in P. Nora (ed.) *Realms of Memory: Rethinking the French Past*, 2 vols, Vol I, *Conflicts and Divisions*, pp. 353–77. There is a small museum dedicated to the memory of Marie Durand in the village of Bouschet-de-Prasles (Ardèche). It became a Mecca for pacifists after the wars of 1914–18 and 1939–45.
14 McManners, *Church and Society*, Vol II, pp. 631–43.
15 Campbell, *Power and Politics*, p. 219.
16 McManners, *Church and Society*, Vol II, p. 471.
17 Campbell, *Power and Politics*, chapters 9–11; Catherine Maire, *Les convulsionnaires de Saint-Médard: miracles, convulsions, et prophéties à Paris au XVIIIe siècle* (Paris, 1985).
18 Julian Swann, 'Parlement, Politics and the *Parti Janséniste*: The *Grand Conseil* Affair', *French History*, Vol IV (1992), pp. 435–61.
19 John Rogister, *Louis XV and the Parlement of Paris, 1737–1755* (Cambridge, 1995), p. 258; William Ward, *Christianity under the Ancien Régime, 1648–1789* (Cambridge, 1999), pp. 31–2, cited by Blanning, *The Culture of Power*, pp. 382–3; Dale Van Kley, *The Damiens Affair and the Unravelling of the Ancien Régime* (Princeton, 1984), part two.
20 McManners, *Church and Society*, Vol I, p. 516.
21 Ibid., p. 217.
22 Goubert and Roche, *Les Français*, Vol I, p. 78.
23 Audisio, *Des Croyants*, pp. 125–6.
24 McManners, *Church and Society*, Vol I, pp. 321–57.
25 Joutard, 'The Museum of the Desert', p. 370.
26 Daniel Robert, *Les Eglises réformées en France*, (Paris, 1961), pp. 1–45.

27 Audisio, *Des Croyants*, p. 173.

28 Kathryn Norberg, *Rich and Poor in Grenoble, 1600–1814* (Berkeley, 1985), pp. 82–5. For fascinating insights into the history of Parisian charitable institutions, visit the Musée de l'Assistance Publique in Paris, 47 quai de Tournelle.

29 Colin Jones, *Charity and Bienfaisance: The Treatment of the Poor in the Montpellier Region, 1740–1815* (Cambridge, 1982), pp. 45–94.

30 Benoît Garnot, *Le peuple au siècle des Lumières* (Paris, 1990), p. 91. On death rates McManners provides figures of 10 per cent for Montpellier in the 1780s, and just under 12 per cent for Nîmes between 1740 and 1785, *Church and Society*, Vol I, pp. 560–1.

31 Philip Thinard, *Sept siècles de bons soins: chronique de l'hôpital de Roanne* (Roanne, 1990), pp. 8–33.

32 Catherine Maire, in Nora, *Realms of Memory*, Vol I, p. 335.

33 David Bell, 'Culture and Religion' in William Doyle (ed.), *Old Regime France* (Oxford, 2001), pp. 89–90.

34 François Furet and Jacques Ozouf, *Reading and Writing: Literacy in France from Calvin to Jules Ferry* (Cambridge, 1982), p. 61.

35 Audisio, *Des Croyants*, pp. 165–6.

36 Roger Chartier, Marie-Madeleine Compère and Dominique Julia (eds.), *Education en France du XVIe au XVIIIe siècle* (Paris, 1976), chapter four.

37 McManners, *Church and Society*, Vol I, p. 517; Goubert and Roche, *Les Français et l'ancien régime*, Vol II, pp. 211–14.

38 Chartier, *et al.*, *Education en France*, p. 200.

39 McManners, *Church and Society*, Vol I, pp. 525–33.

40 Bonnie Anderson and Judith Zinsser, *A History of their Own*, 2 vols, Vol II, *Women in Europe from Prehistory to the Present* (London, 1990), pp. 98–9.

41 McManners, *Church and Society*, Vol I, pp. 510–14; Jean Imbert, *Les Hôpitaux en France* (Paris, 1994), p. 25.

42 Thinard, *Sept siècles de bons soins*, pp. 19–32.

43 Jones and Brockliss, *The Medical World of Early Modern France* (Oxford, 1997), p. 271.

44 Chartier, *et al.*, *Education en France*, pp. 242–3.

45 Françoise Langlois, 'L'Enseignement primaire payant à Paris, 1770–80', *mémoire de maîtrise*, Paris 10, (Nanterre, 1975).

46 McManners, *Church and Society*, Vol I, p. 535.

47 Merry Wiesner, *Women and Gender in Early Modern Europe* (Cambridge, 1993), p. 203.

Chapter 3

1 Gail Bossenga, 'Society', in William Doyle (ed.), *Old Regime France* (Oxford, 2001), p. 63.

2 R. Bonney, 'Early Modern Theories of State Finance', in R. Bonney (ed.) *Economic Systems and State Finance* (Oxford, 1995), pp. 163–229.

3 Jones, *Reform and Revolution*, p. 84; Audisio, *Des Paysans*, pp. 311–25.

4 Emmanuel Le Roy Ladurie, *Histoire du climat depuis l'an mil* (Paris, 1983), pp. 284–7.

5 Moriceau, *Les Fermiers de l'Ile-de-France, XVe–XVIIIe siècle* (Paris, 1994), p. 426; Jones, *Reform and Revolution*, pp. 14–15.

6 George Grantham, 'Jean Meuvret and the Subsistance Problem in Early Modern France', *Journal of Economic History*, Vol 49 (1989), pp. 184–200.

7 Moriceau, *Les Fermiers*, p. 613.

8 Patrick O'Brien, 'Path Dependency, or Why Britain Became an Industrialised Economy Long Before France', *Economic History Review*, Vol 49 (1996), pp. 215–27.

9 Hilton Root, *Peasants and King in Burgundy: Agrarian Foundations of French Absolutism* (Berkeley, 1987), pp. 153–4.

10 Parker, *Class and State*, pp. 264–5; Joel Félix, 'The Economy', in William Doyle (ed.), *Old Regime France*, p. 10.

11 Alfred Cobban, *The Social Interpretation of the French Revolution* (Cambridge, 1964), pp. xiii–xlix; Susan Kettering, *Patrons, Brokers, and Clients in Seventeenth-Century France* (Oxford, 1986).

12 Thomas Kaiser, 'Property, Sovereignty, the Declaration of the Rights of Man, and the Tradition of French Jurisprudence' in Dale Van Kley (ed.), *The French Idea of Freedom: The Old Regime and the Declaration of Rights of 1789* (Stanford, 1994), pp. 300–39.

13 Goubert and Roche, *Les Français*, Vol I, p. 15.

14 Audisio, *Des Paysans*, pp. 33–42.

15 Peter McPhee informs us that, in 1669, 92 families in the diocese of Carcassonne were punished for falsely claiming to be nobles. *Revolution and Environment in Southern France* (Oxford, 1999), p. 24.

16 Franklin Ford, *Robe and Sword: The Regrouping of the French Aristocracy after Louis XIV* (New York, 1965), p. 31; Guy Chaussinand-Nogaret, *The French Nobility in the Eighteenth Century: From Feudalism to Enlightenment* (London, 1985), pp. 29–30.

17 Gail Bossenga, 'Society', pp. 44–5; Chaussinand-Nogaret, *The French Nobility*, pp. 29–30.

18 Chaussinand-Nogaret, *The French Nobility*, pp. 52–3.

19 Richard Andrews, *Law, Magistracy, and Crime in Old Regime Paris, 1735–1789*, 2 vols, (Cambridge, 1994), Vol I, *The System of Criminal Justice*, pp. 237 and 147.

20 Albert Soboul, *The French Revolution, 1787–1799* (London, 1974), p. 38; see also Colin Lucas, 'Nobles, Bourgeois and the Origins of the French Revolution', *Past and Present*, Vol 60 (1973), pp. 84–126.

21 David Bell, *Lawyers and Citizens: The Making of a Political Elite in Old Regime France* (Oxford, 1994), pp. 198–9.

22 Chaussinand-Nogaret, *The French Nobility*, p. 34.

23 Ford, *Robe and Sword*, p. 251.

24 Ibid., pp. 32–3.

25 Le Roy Ladurie, *Saint-Simon*, p. 217.

26 Roger Mettam, *Power and Faction in Louis XIV's France* (New York, 1988), pp. 316–17.

27 Jonathan Israel, *Radical Enlightenment: Philosophy and the Making of Modernity, 1650–1750* (Oxford, 2001), p. 565.

28 L. Boisnard, *La Noblesse dans la tourmente, 1774–1902* (Paris, 1992), p. 34.

29 Jean Meyer, *Noblesses et pouvoirs dans l'Europe d'ancien régime* (Paris, 1973), p. 63.

30 F. Léonard, *L'Armée et ses problèmes au XVIIIe siècle* (Paris, 1958), chapter ten.

31 Doyle, *The Oxford History of the French Revolution* (Oxford, 1989), p. 27.

32 Andrews, *Law, Magistracy and Crime*, Vol I, pp. 144–5.
33 Ford, *Robe and Sword*, pp. 140–4.
34 Parker, *Class and State*, p. 183.
35 Ibid., p. 263.
36 Marquis d'Argenson, *Considérations sur la gouvernement*, written in the 1730s but only published after his dismissal from office by Louis XV in 1747.
37 Audisio, *Des Paysans*, p. 134.
38 Mcphee, *Revolution and Environment*, p. 29; Gwynne Lewis, *The Advent of Modern Capitalism in France: The case of Pierre-François Tubeuf*, pp. 81–3.
39 Natacha Coquéry, *L'Hotêl aristocratique: le marché de luxe à Paris au XVIIIe siècle* (Paris, 1998), p. 150.
40 Daniele Gallard-Boret, *Les Sentiers de l'histoire*, 'Le Coudray-Macouard, un village en Saumurois', (Le Coudray-Macouard, 1996), p. 70.
41 Audisio, *Des Paysans*, p. 135; J. Gallet, *Seigneurs et paysans bretons du Moyen Age à Révolution* (Rennes, 1992), pp. 77–88.
42 Ford, *Robe and Sword*, pp. 162–5.
43 Andrews, *Law, Magistracy, and Crime*, Vol I, p. 274.
44 Mcphee, *Revolution and Environment*, p. 25.
45 Parker, *Class and State*, p. 53.
46 Moriceau, *Les Fermiers*, pp. 773–83.
47 R. Dugrand, *Villes et compagnes en Bas-Languedoc* (Paris, 1963), pp. 537–9.
48 Mcphee, *Revolution and Environment*, pp. 33–4.
49 Peter Jones, *The Peasantry in the French Revolution* (Cambridge, 1988), p. 49.
50 Goubert and Roche, *Les Français*, Vol I, pp. 100–7.
51 Ibid., p. 87.
52 Audisio, *Des Paysans*, p. 35; Mcphee, *Revolution and Environment*, pp. 26–8.
53 L. Vardi, *Land and the Loom: Peasants and Profit in Northern France, 1680–1800* (London, 1993), p. 40; Jones, *The Peasantry*, p. 49; Mcphee, *Revolution and Environment*, p. 25.
54 A. Soboul, *Problèmes paysans de la Révolution française* (Paris, 1976), pp. 100–14; Chaussinand-Nogaret, *The French Nobility*, p. 57.
55 Moriceau, *Les Fermiers*, p. 473, n. 8; Lewis, *The Advent of Modern Capitalism*, p. 143; Audisio, *Des Paysans*, p. 199.
56 Audisio, *Des Paysans*, pp. 37–8.
57 Jean Gallet, *Seigneurs et paysans*, p. 266.
58 Gallet, *Seigneurs et paysans*, p. 140.
59 Hilton Root, *Peasant and King*, p. 158; Peter Jones, *Liberty and Locality in Revolutionary France, 1760–1820* (Cambridge, 2003), pp. 63–74.
60 Jean Bart, 'Les Bourgeois des champs', in P. Bordes (ed.), *Bourgeoisies de province et Révolution* (Grenoble, 1987), p. 157; P. Jones, 'Georges Lefebvre and the Peasant Revolution' in P. Jones (ed.), *The French Revolution in Social and Political Perspective* (London, 1996), pp. 54–71.
61 Audisio, *Des paysans*, p. 269.
62 Moriceau, *Les Fermiers*, pp. 696–700.
63 A. Chambon, *Paysans du Vivarais* (Bourg-les-Valence, 1985), pp. 76–91.
64 Jonathan Dewald, *Pont-St.-Pierre, 1398–1789: Lordship, Community and Capitalism in Early Modern France* (Berkeley, 1987), p. 30.

65 Moriceau, *Les Fermiers*, pp. 704–5.

66 Jean-Pierre Jessene, *Pouvoir au village: Artois, 1760–1848* (Lille,1987), p. 45; Pierre de Saint-Jacob, *Les Paysans de la Bourgogne du Nord au dernier siècle de l'ancien régime* (Paris, 1960), pp. 428–32; R. Robin, 'La nature de l'état à la fin de l'ancien régime: formation sociale, état et transition' in *Dialectiques*, 1–2 (1973); Hilton Root, *Peasants and King*, p. 175.

Chapter 4

1 For the historiographical background, see François Furet, 'The French Revolution Revisited', in Gary Kates (ed.) *The French Revolution: Recent Debates and New Controversies* (London, 1998), pp. 71–90.

2 Elinor Barber, *The Bourgeoisie in Eighteenth-Century France*, p. 20.

3 Soboul, *The French Revolution*, p. 44.

4 Chaussinand-Nogaret, *Histoire des élites* (Paris, 1975), p. 223.

5 David Garrioch, *The Formation of the Parisian Bourgeoisie, 1690–1830* (London, 1996), p. 1. See also Sarah Maza, 'Luxury, Morality, and Social Change: Why There Was No Middle Class Consciousness in Prerevolutionary France', *Journal of Modern History*, Vol 69 (1997), pp. 199–229.

6 Christine Adams, *A Taste for Comfort and Status: A Bourgeois Family in Eighteenth-Century France* (Pennsylvania, 2000), p. 4.

7 Michel Perronnet, 'Bourgeois, "bourgeoisies": les définitions du Dictionnaire de l'Académie', in *Bourgeoisies de province et Révolution* (Grenoble, 1987), p. 27.

8 Doyle, *The Oxford History*, pp. 22–3.

9 Braudel, *The Identity of France*, Vol II, pp. 444–5. Urban population figures are from Bernard Lepetit, *The Pre-Industrial Urban System: France, 1740–1840* (Cambridge, 1994), pp. 449–52.

10 Lepetit, *The Pre-Industrial Urban System*, p. 9.

11 Braudel, *The Identity of France*, Vol I, p. 163.

12 Ibid., Vol II, p. 445.

13 Ladurie, *Saint-Simon ou le système de la Cour*, p. 338.

14 T.J. Markovitch, *Histoire des industries françaises: Les industries lainières de Colbert à la Révolution* (Geneva, 1976); Patrick O'Brien and Caglar Keyder, *Economic Growth in Britain and France, 1780–1914: Two Paths to the Twentieth Century* (London, 1978); Jean-Claude Toutain, 'Le produit de l'agriculture française de 1700 à 1958: la croissance' in *Cahiers de l'Institut de science économique appliquée*, No. 115 (1961), p. 276; François Crouzet, *Britain Ascendant: Comparative Studies in Franco-British Economic History* (Cambridge, 1990); Peter Jones, *Reform and Revolution in France: The Politics of Transition, 1774–1791* (Cambridge, 1995), p. 84.

15 Robert Duplessis, *Transitions to Capitalism in Early Modern France* (Cambridge, 1997), pp. 273–4; François Hincker, *La Révolution française et l'économie* (Paris, 1989), p. 43.

16 Jean-Pierre Poussou, Philippe Bennichon and Xavier Huetz de Lemps (eds.), *Espaces coloniaux et espaces maritimes, XVIIIe siècle* (Paris, 1998), pp. 115–21.

17 Pluchon, *Histoire de la colonisation française*, Vol I, p. 161.

18 Jeremy Black, *Europe and the World, 1650–1830* (London, 2002), p. 71; Arthur Young, *Travels in France* (London, 1976), p. 56.

19 Jones, *Reform and Revolution in France*, p. 99.

20 Braudel, *The Identity of France*, Vol I, p. 32.

21 Louis Cullen, *The Brandy Trade under the Ancien Regime: Regional Specialisation in the Charente* (Cambridge, 1998), p. 45; Thomson, *Clermont-de-Lodève, 1633–1789: Fluctuations in the Prosperity of a Languedocian Cloth-making Town* (Cambridge, 1982).

22 Duplessis, *Transitions to Capitalism*, p. 206.

23 Liana Vardi, *The Land and the Loom*, p. 11.

24 Gay Gullickson, *Spinners and Weavers of Auffay: Rural Industry and the Sexual Division of Labour in a French Village* (Cambridge, 1986), p. 67; Maxine Berg, *The Age of Manufactures, 1700–1820: Industry, Innovation and Work in Britain* (London, 1996), p. 25.

25 James Thomson, *Clermont-de-Lodève, 1663–1789: Fluctuations in the Prosperity of a Languedocian Cloth-Making Town* (Cambridge, 1982), pp. 18–19.

26 Lepetit, *The Pre-industrial Urban System*, p. 375.

27 Cobban, *The Social Interpretation of the French Revolution*, p. 54.

28 Albert Babeau, *Les Bourgeois d'autrefois* (Paris, 1886).

29 Olwen Hufton, *Bayeux in the Eighteenth Century A Social Study* (Oxford, 1967), p. 75; Braudel, *The Identity of France*, Vol II, pp. 447–8; Claude Nières, *Les bourgeois et le pouvoir* (Rennes, 1988), p. 16; Georges Garrier, 'La formation d'un complexe économico-social de type Rhodanien', in Pierre Léon (ed.), *Structures économiques et problèmes sociaux du monde rurale dans la France du sud-est, fin XVII siècle – 1835* (Paris, 1966).

30 Bell, *Lawyers and Citizens*, pp. 27–9.

31 McManners, *Church and Society*, Vol I, p. 326.

32 Nicole Castan, *Les criminels de Languedoc: les exigences d'ordre et les voies du ressentiment dans une société pré-révolutionnaire, 1750–1790* (Toulouse, 1980), pp. 90–95.

33 Jean Nicolas, 'Villageois et "gens d'affaires"', in *Bourgeoisies de province et Révolution: Colloque de Vizille, 1984* (Grenoble, 1987), p. 168.

34 Bell, *Lawyers and Citizens*, pp. 28–9; Henri Sée, *La vie économique et classes sociales en France du XVIIIe siècle* (Paris, 1928), p. 186.

35 Babeau, *Les Bourgeois d'autrefois*, p. 115.

36 Colin Jones, '*Médecins du roi* at the End of the Ancien Regime and in the French Revolution', in Victor Nutton (ed.), *Medicine at Court in Europe, 1500–1837*, (London, 1997), p. 225.

37 Jones and Brockliss, *The Medical World of Early Modern Europe*, chapter eight; Colin Jones, 'Bouche et dents dans l'Encyclopédie' in R. Morrissey and P. Roger (eds.), *L'Encyclopédie: du réseau au livre et du livre au réseau* (Paris, 2001), p. 75.

38 Jones and Brockliss, *The Medical World of Early Modern Europe*, p. 482; Catherine Maillé-Virole, 'La naissance d'une personnage: le médecin parisien à la fin de l'Ancien Régime', in Jean-Pierre Goubert, *La médicalisation de la société française* (Waterloo, Ontario, 1982), pp. 155–63.

39 Didier Masseau, *Les Ennemis des philosophes: anti-philosophes au temps des Lumières* (Paris, 2000), p. 421.

40 Jean Sgard (ed.), *Dictionnaire des journalistes, 1600–1789* (Oxford, 1999), Vol II, pp. 1002–4. Sgard writes that the main conclusion to be drawn from this study is that 'The *Ancien Régime* Press was composed of a nebula in the process of rapid transformation,' p. 1021.

41 Chaussinand-Nogaret, *The French Nobility*, pp. 114–15.

42 A.D. Saint Malo, *Documents pour l'histoire de Saint Malo*, No. 4, pp. 19–20.

43 Pierre Joutard, *Les Cévennes: de la montagne à l'homme* (Toulouse, 1979), p. 219.

44 Goubert and Roche, *Les Français*, Vol II, pp. 173–5.

45 Daniel Roche, *A History of Everyday Things: The Birth of Consumption in France, 1600–1800* (Cambridge, 2000), pp. 44–5.

46 Natacha Coquery, *L'Hôtel aristocratique*, p. 277.

47 A.D. Nîmes, C 511, *État des contribuables sujets au payement du vingtième de l'industrie*, 1760.

48 Vardi, *The Land and the Loom*, pp. 172–5.

49 Barbier, *Journal*, p. 58.

50 Michael Sonenscher, *Work and Wages: Natural Law, Politics and the Eighteenth-Century Community* (Cambridge, 1989), pp. 27, 99. See also David Garrioch, *Neighbourhood and Community in Paris, 1740–1790*, (Cambridge, 1986), pp. 97–115.

51 Saint Léon, *Histoire des corporations*, pp. 411–12; Sonenscher, *Work and Wages*, pp. 175, 204–5; Michael Sonenscher, *The Hatters of Eighteenth-Century France* (Berkeley, 1987), p. 45; Abel Poitrineau, *'Ils travaillent la France': métiers et mentalités du XVIe au XIXe siècle* (Paris, 1992), pp. 22–3.

52 Saint Léon, *Histoire des corporations*, p. 461.

53 Poitrineau, *'Ils travaillent la France'*, p. 14.

54 Adams, *A Taste for Comfort*, p. 28.

55 Paul Bamford, *Privilege and Profit: A Business Family in Eighteenth-Century France* (Philadelphia, 1988).

56 Ibid., pp. xvi, 128.

57 Wiesner, *Women and Gender*, p. 106.

58 Bamford, *Privilege and Profit*, p. 104.

59 André Lespagnol, 'Femmes négociants sous Louis XIV: les conditions complexes d'une promotion provisoire' in *Études réunies en honneur de François Lebrun* (Rennes, 1989).

60 Garrioch, *Neighbourhood and Community*, p. 113.

61 Arlette Farge, *Fragile Lives: Violence, Power and Solidarity in Eighteenth-Century Paris* (Oxford, 1993), pp. 114–17. For a detailed account of the influence exerted by a master printer's wife, see Robert Darnton, *The Great Cat Massacre and Other Episodes in French Cultural History* (London, 1984), pp. 75–104.

62 A.D. Nîmes, C 511, *État des contribuables sujets au payement du vingtième de l'industrie*, 1760.

63 Adams, *A Taste for Comfort and Status*, p. 259.

64 Garrioch, *The Formation of the Parisian Bourgeoisie*, p. 7.

Chapter 5

1 Garnot, *Le peuple*, p. 80.

2 Israel, *Radical Enlightenment*, p. 5.

3 Woolf, *The Poor in Western Europe*, p. 6; Olwen Hufton, *The Poor of Eighteenth-Century France, 1750–1789* (Oxford, 1974), Vol I, pp. 21–4.

4 Goubert and Roche, *Les français*, Vol II, pp. 93–9.

5 Ibid., Vol I, pp. 89–90.
6 Ibid., Vol I, pp. 92–4.
7 Clère, *Les paysans de la Haute-Marne*, pp. 26–68.
8 Gallet, *Seigneurs et paysans*, pp. 167–220.
9 Audisio, *Des paysans*, pp. 198–9.
10 Chambon, *Paysans du Vivarais*, pp. 96–102.
11 Braudel, *The Identity of France*, Vol II, p. 329.
12 McPhee, *Revolution and Environment*, p. 19.
13 Braudel and Labrousse, *Histoire économique*, Vol II, p. 116.
14 *Les sentiers de l'histoire*, pp. 9–18.
15 Vardi, *The Land and the Loom*, p. 31.
16 Chapalain-Nogaret, *Misère et assistance*, pp. 23–5.
17 Vardi, *The Land and the Loom*, p. 23; Terrier, *Les deux âges de la proto-industrie*, p. 148.
18 Maurice Hamon and Dominique Perrin, *Au coeur du XVIIIe siècle industriel: condition ouvrière et tradition villageoise à Saint-Gobain* (Paris, 1993), pp. 12–13; Stanley Chapman and Serge Chassagne, *European Textile Printers in the Eighteenth Century: A Study of Peel and Oberkampf* (London, 1981), pp. 125–46; Serge Chassagne, *Oberkampf: Un entrepreneur Capitliste au siècle des lumieres* (Paris, 1980).
19 Hamon and Perrin, *Au coeur du XVIIIe siècle*, pp. 330–9; Lewis, *The Advent of Modern Capitalism*, pp. 40–6.
20 Audisio, *Des paysans*, p. 184; Woolf, *The Poor in Western Europe*, p. 7; Lewis, *The Advent of Modern Capitalism*, pp. 46–7; Hamon and Perrin, *Au coeur du XVIIIe siècle*, pp. 364–71.
21 Louise Tilly and Joan Scott, *Women, Work and Family* (London, 1989), p. 25.
22 Michael Mann, *The Sources of Social Power* (Cambridge, 1993), 2 vols, Vol I, *The Rise of Classes and Nation-States, 1760–1914*, p. 28.
23 Catherine Lys and Hugo Soly, *Poverty and Capitalism in Pre-Industrial Europe* (Brighton, 1982), p. 108.
24 Gullickson, *The Spinners of Auffay*, p. 216; Peter Kriedte, Hans Medick and Joachim Schlumbohm, *Industrialisation before Industrialisation: Rural Industry in the Genesis of Capitalism* (Cambridge, 1981), pp. 23–37, 38–73; Tessie Liu, *The Weaver's Knot: The Contradictions of Class Struggle and Family Solidarity in Western France, 1756–1914* (New York, 1994), pp. 41–2.
25 Sonenscher, *The World of Wages*, p. 67; Daniel Roche, *The People of Paris: An Essay in Popular Culture in the Eighteenth Century* (Leamington Spa, 1987), p. 71.
26 Christine Truant, *The Rites of Labour: Brotherhoods of Compagnonnage in Old and New Regime France* (New York, 1994), pp. 110–16.
27 Steven Kaplan, *Le meilleur pain du monde: les boulangers de Paris au XVIIIe siècle* (Paris, 1996), pp. 223–4.
28 Darnton, *The Great Cat Massacre*, p. 82.
29 Kaplan, *Le meilleur pain du monde*, p. 213.
30 Louise Tilly and Joan Scott, *Women, Work and Family* (London, 1989). pp. 15–20; Garrioch, *Neighbourhood and Community*, pp. 113–14.
31 Sonenscher, *The World of Wages*, pp. 170–3.
32 Arlette Farge, *Vivre dans la rue à Paris au XVIIIe siècle* (Paris, 1992), pp. 36–7.

33 Louis Sébastien Mercier and Restif de la Bretonne, *Paris le Jour, Paris la Nuit* (Paris, 1990), pp. 57, 159–63.

34 Deborah Simonton, *A History of European Women's Work, 1700 to the Present* (London, 1998), pp. 68–9.

35 Rétif, *Paris le jour*, pp. 771–2.

36 Jeffry Kaplow, *The Names of Kings: The Parisian Laboring Poor in the Eighteenth Century* (New York, 1972), p. 43; Farge, *Vivre dans la rue*, p. 163; Guy Chaussinand-Nogaret, 'La saga des gens de peu: les Parisiens du XVIIIe siècle', *Histoire*, Vol 46 (1982), p. 87.

37 Mercier, *Paris le jour*, p. 178.

38 Jean-Pierre Poussou, 'L'évolution comparée des immigrants Limousine et Auvergnate à Bordeaux au XVIIIe siècle', in *Entre faim et loup: actes de la rencontre inter-universitaire du jeudi 8 avril 1976 à Clermont-Ferrand* (Clermont-Ferrand, 1976), pp. 59–71; Maurice Garden, 'L'emigration du Massif Central vers Lyon dans la seconde moitié du XVIIIe siècle', in *Entre faim et loup*, pp. 33–57.

39 Chapalain-Nogaret, *Misère et assistance*, pp. 137–41; Poitrineau, *Ils Travaillent la France: métiers et mentalités du XVIe au XIXe siècle* (Paris, 1992), pp. 144–9.

40 Sonenscher, *Work and Wages*, pp. 203–4; Robert Schwartz, *The Policing of the Poor in Eighteenth-Century France* (London, 1988), pp. 109–10; Kaplow, *The Names of Kings*, pp. 52–5; Braudel and Labrousse, *Histoire économique*, Vol I, p. 670.

41 Erica-Marie Benabou, *La prostitution et la police des moeurs au XVIIIe* siècle (Paris, 1987), p. 312.

42 Cissie Fairchilds, *Domestic Enemies: Servants and their Masters in Old Regime France* (Baltimore, 1984), p. 2; Chaussinand-Nogaret, 'La saga des gens de peu', p. 187.

43 Jean-Pierre Gutton, *Domestiques et serviteurs dans la France de l'ancien régime* (Paris, 1981) p. 47; Jean Meyer, *Noblesses et pouvoirs dans l'Europe d'ancien régime* (Paris, 1973). Meyer points out that the life of the poor noble was often indistinguishable from that of his peasant neighbours, p. 63.

44 Roche, *The People of Paris*, p. 68; Gallet, *Seigneurs et paysans*, p. 29.

45 Maza, *Servants and Masters*, p. 332; Fairchilds, *Domestic Enemies*, p. 86.

46 Mercier, *Paris le jour*, p. 276.

47 McManners, *Church and Society*, Vol I, pp. 386–7; Coquery, *L'Hôtel aristocratique*.

48 Gutton, *Domestiques et serviteurs*, p. 237.

49 Roche, *The People of Paris*; p. 69; Maza, *Servants and Masters*, pp. 84–5; Fairchilds, *Domestic Enemies*, pp. 55–8; Kaplow, *The Name of Kings*, p. 53.

50 Maza, *Servants and Masters*, p. 335; Mercier, *Paris le jour*, pp. 95–6.

51 Audisio, *Des paysans*, p. 278.

52 Lys and Soly, *Poverty and Capitalism*, p. 109.

53 Schwarz, *The Policing of the Poor*, p. 121.

54 Andrews, *Law, Magistracy and Crime*, pp. 345–58; Michel Foucaud, *Discipline and Punish: Birth of the Prison* (New York, 1979), translated by Alan Sheridan. Randall McGovern, 'Power and Humanity: Foucault among the Historians', in Colin Jones and Roy Porter (eds.), *Reassessing Foucault: Power, Medicine and the Body* (London, 1994), p. 97.

55 Kettering, *French Social History*, pp. 133–4.

56 For this, and much of what follows, see Benabou, *La prostitution*.

57 Antoine, *Louis XV*, p. 46.
58 Duplessis, *Transitions to Capitalism*, pp. 198–201.
59 Pluchon, *Histoire de la colonisation*, pp. 413–22; *Nègres et Juifs au XVIIIe siècle: Le racisme au siècle des Lumières* (Paris, 1984), pp. 65–8.
60 Nigel Aston, 'The Golden Autumn of Gallicism? Religious History and its Place in Current Writing on Eighteenth-Century France', *French History*, Vol 13 (1999), p. 190.
61 Israel, *Radical Enlightenment*, p. 5.
62 Ibid., pp. 265–70.
63 Ibid., p. 494.
64 Maire, p. 308; Doyle, *Jansenism*, p. 39.
65 Sgard (ed.), *Dictionnaire des journalistes*, Vol I, pp. 358–63.
66 Doyle, *Jansenism*, p. 49.
67 Garrioch, *The Formation of the Parisian Bourgeoisie*, p. 36.
68 Donck, *Vergèze*, pp. 141–3.
69 Campbell, *Power and Politics*, p. 200.
70 Petitfils, *Le Régent*, pp. 548–52.

Chapter 6

1 Roy Porter, *The Enlightenment* (London, 1990), p. 21.
2 Jones and Porter (eds.), *Reassessing Foucault: Power, Medicine and the Body* (London, 1994) p. 1; Peter Kaufman, 'Soviet Perspectives on the French Enlightenment and Revolution', *Studies in Eighteenth-Century Culture*, Vol 20 (1990), pp. 115–29; Dorinda Outram, *The Enlightenment* (Cambridge, 1995), p. 95.
3 Roche, *La France des Lumières*, p. 437; Audisio, *Des paysans*, p. 230.
4 Chapalain-Nogaret, *Misère et assistance*, p. 115; René Favier, 'Economic Change', in Benedict (ed.), *Cities and Social Change*, pp. 232–3; Kaplow, *The Names of Kings*, pp. 80–81.
5 Kaplow, *The Names of Kings*, pp. 90–92; Braudel, *The Identity of France*, Vol II, pp. 191–202.
6 Audisio, *Des paysans*, p. 220; Jones and Brockliss, *The Medical World*, pp. 366–7. See also John Brewer and Susan Staves (eds.), *Early Modern Conceptions of Property* (London, 1995).
7 Garnot, *Le Peuple*, pp. 47–8; Audisio, *Des paysans*, p. 232.
8 Madelaine Gutwirth, *The Twilight of the Goddesses: Women and Representation in the Revolutionary Era* (New Brunswick, 1992), p. 50; Jones and Brockliss, *The Medical World*, p. 717.
9 Beatrice Gottlieb, *The Family in the Western World: From the Black Death to the Industrial Age* (Oxford, 1993), p. 52. See also Edward Shorter, 'Capitalism, Culture and Sexuality: Some Competing Models', *Social Science Quarterly*, Vol 53 (1972).
10 James Farr, *Sexuality and Authority in Burgundy, 1550–1730* (Oxford, 1995), pp. 90–97.
11 Rosemary O'Day, *The Family and Family Relationships, 1500–1900* (New York, 1994), p. 23.

12 Woolf, *The Poor in Western Europe*, pp. 14–15; Abel Poitrineau, 'Sur la configuration des familles en Auvergne aux XVIIe et XVIIIe siècles', in *Entre faim et loup*, pp. 81–104; Nicole Lemaître, 'Ussel ou la difficulté de vivre: familles urbaines et rurales aux XVIIe et XVIIIe siècles', in *Entre faim et loup*, pp. 11–17.

13 Jean-Louis Flandrin, *Familles: parenté, maison, sexualité dans l'ancienne société* (Paris, 1984), pp. 40–1; Anne Fillon, *Les trois bagues aux doigts* (Rennes, 1989), p. 135, and *Louis Simon, villageois de l'ancienne France* (Rennes, 1996).

14 Garnot, *Le peuple*, p. 48; Jones and Brockliss, *The Medical World*, pp. 366–7; Audisio, *Des paysans*, pp. 219–20; Jean-Louis Flandrin, *Les amours paysannes: Amour et sexualité dans les campagnes de l'ancienne France (XVIe – XIXe siècles)* (Paris, 1975), pp. 303–18; Chartier, *Les origines culturelles*, p. 125.

15 Goubert and Roche, *Les Français*, Vol II, pp. 136–7; Flandrin, *Les amours paysannes*, pp. 228–31; McManners, *Church and Society*, Vol II, p. 298; Fairchilds, *Domestic Enemies*, p. 82; Maza, *Servants and Masters*, p. 70.

16 Peter Lewis Allen, *The Wages of Sin: Sex and Disease, Past and Present* (Chicago, 2000), p. 45.

17 Pieter Spierenburg, *The Broken Spell: A Cultural and Anthropological History of Preindustrial Europe* (New Brunswick, 1991), p. 237; McManners, *Church and Society*, Vol II, p. 303.

18 McManners, *Church and Society*, Vol II, chapter 33.

19 Benabou, *La prostitution*, p. 433; Weisner, *Women and Gender*, pp. 53–6; Lynn Hunt, 'The Many Bodies of Marie Antoinette', in Lynn Hunt (ed.), *Eroticism and the Body Politic* (London, 1991), pp. 108–30.

20 Lynne Friedli, ' "Passing Women": a Study of Gender Boundaries in the Eighteenth Century', in G. Rousseau and R. Porter (eds.), *Sexual Underworlds of the Enlightenment* (Manchester, 1987), pp. 244–6; Lewis, *The Wages of Sin*, chapters two and six.

21 Galen (129–200 BC) was the Graeco-Roman physician who related 'the symptoms of health and disease to the proper and improper functioning of the forms of the parts of the human body'. Jones and Brockliss, *The Medical World*, p. 85.

22 Mathew Ramsay, *Professional and Popular Medicine in France, 1770–1830: The Social World of Medical Practice* (Cambridge, 1988), pp. 70, 296, and 26.

23 Ibid., pp. 221–36, 179.

24 Thinard, *Sept siècles de bons soins: chronique de l'hôpital de Roanne* (Rouen, 1990), p. 13; Jones and Brockliss, *The Medical World*, p. 569.

25 John McManners, *Death and the Enlightenment: Christians and Unbelievers in Eighteenth-Century France* (Oxford, 1981), p. 94.

26 Milanese, *Mort apparente*, pp. 128–33.

27 Rebecca Spang, *The Invention of the Restaurant: Paris and Modern Gastronomic Culture* (London, 2000), pp. 35, 16.

28 Mercier, *Tableau de Paris*, pp. 139, 49.

29 Spierenburg, *The Broken Spell*, pp. 5–6; D. Roche, *La culture des apparences: une histoire du vêtement, XVIIe–XVIIIe siècle* (Paris, 1989), pp. 149–50.

30 Milanese, *Mort apparente*, pp. 183–91; Mercier, *Tableau de Paris*, p. 49.

31 Audisio, *Des croyants*, p. 167.

32 Furet and Ozouf, *Reading and Writing*, pp. 45, 26.

33 Jones, *The Great Nation*, p. 178.
34 Marie-Madeleine Compère, 'Les universités: d'une cléricature à une autre', in Chartier *et al.*, *L'Education en France*, pp. 276–8; Goubert and Roche, *Les François*, Vol II, pp. 215–17.
35 McManners, *Church and Society*, Vol I, p. 229.
36 Mercier, *Tableau de Paris*, pp. 62–3.
37 Robert Darnton, *The Kiss of Lamourette* (New York, 1990), pp. 143–4.
38 Robert Darnton, *Forbidden Bestsellers of Pre-Revolutionary France* (London, 1996), pp. 28–9, 221.
39 Chartrier, *Les origines culturelles*, p. 200.
40 Jack Censer, 'The Public Divided: How Contemporaries Understood Politics in Eighteenth-Century France', in Christine Adams *et al.* (eds.), *Visions and Revisions of Eighteenth-Century France* (Pennsylvania State University Press, 1997), p. 204; Jeremy Popkin, *Revolutionary News: The Press in France, 1789–99* (London, 1990), chapter one; Sarah Maza, *Private Lives and Public Affairs: The Causes Célèbres of Pre-Revolutionary France* (Berkeley, 1993).
41 Darnton, *L'Aventure de l'encyclopédie, 1775–1800* (Paris, 1982), p. 38.
42 Darnton, *The Business of the Enlightenment*, pp. 283–6.
43 Chartier, *Les Origines culturelles*, pp. 27–8.
44 See John Cowans, 'Habermas and French History: The Public Sphere and the Problem of Political Legitimacy', *French History*, Vol 13 (1992), pp. 134–60.
45 Gordon, *Citizens Without Sovereignty*, pp. 92, 127; see also Dorinda Outram's critique in 'Mere Words', *Journal of Modern History*, Vol 63 (1991), pp. 327–41.
46 Roche, *La France des Lumières*, pp. 399–403.
47 Darnton, *The Business of the Enlightenment*, p. 430.
48 Darnton, *The Great Cat Massacre*, p. 138; Roche, *La France des Lumières*, pp. 394–8.
49 Margaret Jacob, *Living the Enlightenment: Freemasonry and Politics in Eighteenth-Century Europe* (Oxford, 1991), p. 7.
50 Israel, *The Radical Enlightenment*, p. 715.
51 Spierenburg, *The Broken Spell*, pp. 50–4.
52 Chartier, *Les Origines culturelles*, p. 30.
53 Sonenscher, *Work and Wages*, p. 48.
54 Garnot, *Le Peuple*, p. 140; Audisio, *Les Paysans*, pp. 300–10.
55 Garnot, *Le peuple*, p. 138.
56 Jones, *The Great Nation*, p. 185.
57 Outram, *The Enlightenment*, p. 85.
58 Sheila Mason, 'The Riddle of Roxane', in Eva Jacobs *et al.* (eds.), *Women and Society in Eighteenth-Century France* (London, 1979), p. 33; Gutwirth, *Twilight of the Goddesses*, pp. 68–71.
59 Cited in Outram, *The Enlightenment*, pp. 84–5.
60 Roche, *La France des Lumières*, pp. 471–2.
61 Jacques Gélis, *L'Arbre et le fruit: la naissance dans l'occident moderne, XVIe–XIXe siècle* (Paris, 1984), pp. 422–3; Picciola, *Le Comte de Maurepas*, pp. 67–8.
62 Outram, *The Enlightenment*, p. 81.
63 *The Confessions of Saint Augustine*, (London, 1949), p. 192.
64 Wiesner, *Women and Gender*, p. 21.

Chapter 7

1 Gwynne Lewis, 'Henri-Léonard Bertin and the Fate of the Bourbon Monarchy, in Malcolm Crook, William Doyle and Alan Forrest (eds.) *Enlightenment and Revolution: Essays in Honour of Norman Hampson* (Aldershot, 2004), pp. 69–90; Keith Baker, 'Controlling French History: The Ideological Arsenal of Jacob-Nicolas Moreau', in Keith Baker (ed.), *Inventing the French Revolution* (Cambridge, 1990), pp. 59–85; Edmond. Djiembowski, *Gabriel-François Coyer et Jacob-Nicolas Moreau: écrits sur le patriotisme, l'esprit public, et la propagande au milieu du XVIIIe siècle* (La Rochelle, 1997).

2 Campbell, *Power and politics*, p. 170; Picciola, *Le Comte de Maurepas*, pp. 357–72.

3 Black, *Louis XIV to Napoleon*, pp. 78–104; Pluchon, *Histoire de la colonisation française*, pp. 161–90; Poussou, *Espaces coloniaux*, pp. 3–43; Picciola, *Le Comte de Maurepas*, pp. 337–49.

4 André Picciola, *Le Comte de Maurepas: Versailles et l'Europe à la fri de l'Ancien Régime* (Paris, 1999); James Pritchard, *Louis XV's Navy 1748–1762* (Montreal, 1987), p. 372.

5 Fred Anderson, *Crucible of War: The Seven Years War and the Fate of the Empire in British North America, 1754–1766* (London, 2000), pp. 503–6; Guy Chaussinand-Nogaret, *Choiseul, 1719–85: naissance de la Gauche* (Paris, 1998), pp. 146–8.

6 Edmond Dziembowski, *Un nouveau patriotisme français, 1750–1770: La France face à la puissance anglaise à l'époque de la guerre de Sept Ans* (Oxford, 1998), p. 491; Chaussinand-Nogaret, *Choiseul, 1719–85*, pp. 276–7.

7 Dale Van Kley, *The Damiens Affair and the Unravelling of the Ancien Régime, 1750–1770* (Princeton, 1984); Dziembowski, *Un nouveau patriotisme*, pp. 434–44; Didier Masseau, *Les Ennemis des philosophes*, p. 141–56.

8 Masseau, *Les Ennemis des philosophes,* pp. 237–70.

9 Emile Léonard, *L'Armée et ses problèmes au XVIIIe siècle* (Paris, 1958), chapter xi; Michel Vergé-Franceschi, *Marine et éducation sous l'ancien régime* (Paris, 1991), pp. 255–68.

10 Dziembowski, *Un nouveau patriotisme*, pp. 458–86.

11 Duplessis, *Transitions to Capitalism*, p. 146; Cullen, *The Brandy Trade*, p. 47; Thomas Brennan, *Burgundy to Champagne: The Wine Trade in Early Modern France* (London, 1997), chapter one.

12 Parker, *Class and State*, p. 54; Béatrice de Varine, *Villages de la vallée de l'Ouche aux XVIIe et XVIIIe siècles: la seigneurie de Marigny-sur-Ouche* (Roanne, 1979), pp. 245–6.

13 Lewis, *The Advent of Modern Capitalism*, chapter one.

14 Stanley Chapman and Serge Chassagne, *European Textile Printers in the Eighteenth Century* (London, 1981), chapter eight; Denis Woronoff, *Histoire de l'industrie en France du XVIe siècle à nos jours* (Paris, 1994), pp. 92–6, 180–1; Duplessis, *Transitions to Capitalism*, p. 204; Terrier, *Les Deux Âges de la protoindustrialisation*, pp. 21–76.

15 Terrier, *Les Deux Âges de la protoindustrialisation*, p. 13.

16 Braudel, *The Identity of France*, Vol II, pp. 449, 511–15.

17 Poussou, *Espaces coloniaux*, pp. 129–30; Pluchon, *Histoire de la colonisation*, p. 710; Black, *From Louis XIV to Napoleon*, p. 143; Duplessis, *Transitions to Capitalism*, p. 243.

18 Paul Butel, *Européens et espaces maritimes, 1690–1790* (Bordeaux, 1997), pp. 74–5.
19 Cissie Fairchilds, 'The production and marketing of populuxe goods in eighteenth-century Paris', in John Brewer and Roy Porter (eds.), *Production and the World of Goods* (London, 1991), pp. 230–42; Michael Sonenscher, 'Fashion's Empire: Trade and Power in Early Eighteenth-Century France', in Robert Fox and Anthony Turner (eds.), *Luxury Trades and Consumerism in Ancien Régime Paris* (Aldershot, 1998), p. 243; Jones, *The Great Nation*, pp. 349–63.
20 Pluchon, *Histoire de la colonisation*, p. 153; Mercier, *Paris le jour*, p. 36; Restif, *Paris le jour*, p. 910.
21 Daniel Roche, *A History of Everyday Things: The Birth of Consumption in France, 1600–1800* (Cambridge, 2000), p. 254.
22 Richard Bonney (ed.), *Economic Systems and State Finance* (Oxford, 1995), p. 203.
23 Leroy Ladurie, *Saint-Simon*, p. 460; Woronoff, *Histoire de l'industrie*, pp. 47–61.
24 Pierre Joly, *Du Pont de Nemours: Apostle of Liberty and the Promised Land* (Wilmington, Delaware, 1977), pp. 28–9.
25 Lewis, 'Henri-Léonard Bertin', pp. 74–6; M. Antoine, *Louis XV*, pp. 861–3 (1993); Pluchon, *Histoire de la colonisation*, pp. 560–1.
26 Chaussinand-Nogaret, *Choiseul*, 1719–85, p. 176; Louis Cullen, 'History, Economic Crises, and Revolution: Understanding Eighteenth-Century France', *Economic History Review*, Vol 46 (1993), p. 643.
27 Gail Bossenga, *The Politics of Privilege: Old Regime and Revolution in Lille* (Cambridge, 1991), p. 166; Braudel, *The Identity of France*, Vol II, pp. 452–5.
28 Judith Miller, *Mastering the Market: The State and the Grain Trade in Northern France, 1710–1860* (Cambridge, 1999).
29 Steven Kaplan, *Provisioning Paris: Merchants and Millers in the Grain and Flour Trade during the Eighteenth Century* (Cornell U.P., 1984), pp. 34–6, 407–8. See also Kaplan, *The Bakers of Paris and the Bread Question, 1700–1775* (London, 1996).
30 Keith Baker, 'Controlling French History', p. 59.
31 Lucien Laugier, *Un ministère réformateur sous Louis XV: le Triumvirate (1770–1774)* (Paris, 1975), p. 318.
32 Bibliothèque nationale, *Mémoire sur la constitution politique de la ville et cité de Périgord* (Paris, 1775). *Collection Moreau*, Vol 68, p. 310.
33 Marisa Linton, 'The Rhetoric of Virtue and the *Parlements*, 1770–1775', *French History*, Vol 9 (1995), p. 201.
34 Gwynne Lewis, 'Fiscal States: Taxes, War, Privilege and the Emergence of the European Nation-State c.1200–1800', *French History*, Vol 15 (2001), pp. 1–15; Richard Bonney (ed.), *The Rise of the Fiscal State in Europe, c.1200–1815* (Oxford, 1999), p. 161; Tim Le Goff, 'How to Finance an Eighteenth-Century War', in Mark Ormrod *et al.* (eds.), *Crises, Revolutions and Self-Sustained Growth: Essays in European Fiscal History* (Stamford, 1999), pp. 389–90; John Bosher, *From Business to Bureaucracy* (Cambridge, 1970).
35 Michael Kwass, 'A Welfare State for the Privileged?', in Mark Ormrod *et al.* (eds.) *Crises, Revolutions and Self-Sustained Growth*, p. 357; Julian Swann, 'War and Finance in Burgundy in the Reign of Louis XIV, 1661–1715', in *Crises, Revolutions and Self-Sustained Growth*, p. 322.
36 Swann, 'Politics: Louis XV', in *Old Regime France*, pp. 216–17.
37 Jones, *The Great Nation*, pp. 271–9.

38 Antoine, *Louis XV*, chapter 16; William Doyle, 'The Parlements', in Keith Baker (ed.), *The Political Culture of the Old Regime* (Oxford, 1987), pp. 157–67.

39 Antoine, *Louis XV*, p. 906.

40 Schwartz, *Policing the Poor*, pp. 132–3.

41 Ibid., pp. 154–8.

42 Kaplan, *Provisioning Paris*, p. 23.

43 Anatoli Ado, *Paysans en Révolution: terre, pouvoir et jacquerie, 1789–94* (Paris, 1996), pp. 64–93.

44 Root, *Peasants and King*, chapter five.

45 Ado, *Paysans en Révolution*, p. 91.

46 Victor Gatrell, *The Hanging Tree: Execution and the English People, 1770–1868* (Oxford, 1994), p. 7.

47 Robert Schwartz, *Policing the Poor*, pp. 171, 200–9; Ian Cameron, *Crime and Repression in the Auvergne and the Guyenne, 1720–90* (Cambridge, 1981); Benoît Garnot, *Crime et justice aux XVIIe et XVIIIe siècles* (Paris, 2000); Clive Emsley, 'La maréchaussée à la fin de l'ancien régime: note sur la composition du corps', *Revue d'Histoire Moderne et Contemporaine*, pp. 622–44.

Chapter 8

1 Laugier, *Un ministère réformateur*, p. 26; abbé Terray, *Projet d'édit sur la mendicité et l'education du peuple*, B.N., *Fonds français*, 6570.

2 Roche, *La France des Lumières*, pp. 258, 295–6.

3 Jean Pierre Poirier, *Turgot: laissez-faire et progrès social* (Paris, 1999), chapter eight.

4 Ibid., p. 233; Cynthia Bouton, *The Flour War: Gender, Class and Community in Late Ancien Regime French Society* (Pennsylvania, 1993).

5 Munro Price, 'Politics: Louis XVI', in Doyle (ed.), *Old Regime France*, pp. 230–1; McManners, *Church and Society*, Vol I, p. 651.

6 Poirier, *Turgot*, p. 291; Jones, *The Great Nation*, pp. 295–301.

7 Bailey Stone, *The Genesis of the French Revolution: A Global-Historical Interpretation* (Cambridge, 1994), pp. 99–110.

8 Support for Laugier's thesis comes from Eugene White, 'Was There a Solution to the Ancien Régime's Financial Dilemma', *Journal of Economic History*, Vol 49 (1989), pp. 548–59. See also Robert Harris, 'Necker's *Compte rendu* of 1781: A Reconsideration', *Journal of Modern History*, Vol 42 (1970), pp. 161–83, and Bosher, *French Finances*, pp. 142–53.

9 Julian Ruff, *Crime, Justice and Public Order in Old Regime France: The Sénéchaussées of Libourne and Bazas, 1696–1789* (London, 1984), p. 149; Jean Nicolas (ed.), *Mouvement populaire et conscience sociale* (Paris, 1985).

10 Schwartz, *Policing the Poor*, p. 169.

11 Castan, *Les Criminels de Languedoc*, p. 12; Schwartz, *Policing the Poor*, p. 172.

12 Castan, *Les Criminels de Languedoc*, p. 218; Andrews, *Law, Magistracy, and Crime*, pp. 536–47.

13 See Jean Quéniart, *Le Grand Chapelletout: violence, normes, et comportements dans la Bretagne rurale au 18e siècle* (Rennes, 1993).

14 Raymond Molis, 'De la mendicité en Languedoc, 1775–1783', *Annales du Midi*, Vol 52 (1974), pp. 482–500.

15 Norberg, *Rich and Poor in Grenoble*, p. 217.

16 John Hardman, *Louis XVI* (London, 2000), pp. 68–9.

17 Price, *The Fall of the French Monarchy*, p. 22.

18 Roger Chartier, 'The Cultural Origins of the French Revolution', in Schecter (ed.) *The French Revolution*, pp. 79–105; Elizabeth and Robert Badinter, *Condorcet: un intellectual en politique* (Paris, 1988), p. 248; Keith Baker, 'The Idea of a Declaration of Rights', in Gary Kates (ed.), *The French Revolution*, p. 94.

19 Price, 'Politics: Louis XVI', pp. 230–1; Peter Jones, *Reform and Revolution in France: The Politics of Transition, 1774–91* (Cambridge, 1995), pp. 35–9.

20 Chartier, 'The Cultural Origins of the French Revolution', p. 85; Jones, *The Great Nation*, p. 367.

21 Sarah Maza, 'Luxury, Morality, and Social Change: Why There Was No Middle-Class Consciousness in Pre-Revolutionary France', in Schecter (ed.) *The French Revolution*, pp. 175–209. See also David Bell, *The Cult of the Nation in France: Inventing Nationalism, 1680–1800* (London, 2001), p. 68.

22 Soboul, *The French Revolution*, p. 37; Colin Lucas, 'Nobles, Bourgeois, and the Origins of the French Revolution', *Past and Present*, Vol 60 (1973), pp. 84–126.

23 Brigitte Massin, *Mozart: les chemins de l'Europe* (Strasbourg, 1997), pp. 284–5.

24 Gutwirth, *The Twilight of the Goddesses*, p. 164.

25 Mercier, *Paris le jour, Paris la nuit*, p. 128.

26 Gutwirth, *The Twilight of the Goddesses*, pp. 157–8; Lynne Friedli, ' "Passing Women" A Study of Gender Boundaries in the Eighteenth Century', in Rousseau and Porter (eds.), *Sexual Underworlds of the Enlightenment* (Manchester, 1987), pp. 234–60; Lynn Hunt, 'The Many Bodies of Marie Antoinette', in Peter Jones (ed.) *The French Revolution in Social and Political Perspective* (London, 1996), pp. 268–84; Vivian Gruder, 'The Question of Marie-Antoinette: The Queen and Public Opinion Before the Revolution', *French History*, Vol 16 (2002), p. 298.

27 Jane Abray, 'Feminism in the French Revolution', in Peter Jones (ed.) *The French Revolution*, p. 237.

28 Landes, *Women and the Public Sphere*, pp. 58–9.

29 McManners, *Church and Society*, Vol II, p. 117; Michel Vovelle, *The Revolution and the Church: From Reason to the Supreme Being* (London, 1991); Ralph Gibson, *A Social History of French Catholicism, 1780–1914* (London, 1989).

30 Lewis, 'Henri-Léonard Bertin', pp. 88.

31 C.E. Labrousse, *La Crise de l'économie française à la fin de l'ancien régime et au début de la Révolution* (Paris, 1943).

32 Parker, *Class and State*, p. 213; Jones, *The Great Nation*, pp. 350–1. See also James Riley, 'French Finances, 1727–68', *Journal of Modern History*, Vol 59 (1987), p. 235; Louis Cullen, 'History, Economic Crisis, and Revolution: Understanding Eighteenth-Century France', *Economic History Review*, Vol 46 (1993), pp. 635–57;

33 Cullen, *The Brandy Trade*, pp. 47, 57.

34 François Crouzet, *La Grande Inflation: la monnaie en France de Louis XVI à Napoléon* (Paris, 1993), pp. 78–82: Kwass, *Crises, Revolutions and Self-Sustained Growth*, p. 376; Eugene White, 'Was There a Solution to the Ancien Régime's Financial Dilemma?' *Journal of Economic History*, Vol 49 (1989), pp. 545–68.

35 Blanning, *The French Revolutionary Wars*, p. 36.

36 Paul Kennedy, *The Rise and Fall of the Great Powers: Economic Change and Military Conflict from 1500 to 2000* (London, 1989), p. 147.

37 Pluchon, *Histoire de la colonisation*, p. 739.

38 Lewis, *The Second Vendée*, pp. 14–15; James Thomson, *Clermont-de-Lodève, 1633–1789* (Cambridge, 1982), pp. 2–3; Jeffrey Kaplow, *Elbeuf during the Revolutionary Period: History and Social Structure* (Baltimore, 1964), pp. 106–7.

39 Jones, *Reform and Revolution*, pp. 103–4.

40 Mercier, *Paris le jour*, pp. 136–7.

41 Etienne Bataille, *De par le Roy et la justice: chronique judiciare des paroisses d'une sénéchaussée bretonne de la fin au XVIIIe siècle à la Révolution* (Rennes, 1993), pp. 35–99.

42 Norberg, *Rich and Poor in Grenoble*, p, 299.

43 David Andress, *French Society in Revolution, 1789–1799* (Manchester, 1999), p. 19.

44 Markoff, *The Abolition of Feudalism*, p. 26.

45 Doyle, *The Oxford History*, p. 68.

46 Munro, *The Fall of the French Monarchy: Louis XVI, Marie Antoinette and the Baron de Breteuil* (London, 2002), p. 25.

47 Soboul, *The French Revolution*, p. 108; Jones, *The Great Nation*, p. 389.

48 Popkin, *Revolutionary News*, pp. 25–6. See also Hugh Gough, *The Newspaper Press in the French Revolution* (London, 1988).

49 McPhee, *France, 1780–1880*, p. 32.

50 Timothy Tackett, *Becoming a Revolutionary: The Deputies of the French National Assembly and the Emergence of a Revolutionary Culture* (Princeton, NJ, 1996), chapter one.

51 Price, *The Fall of the French Monarchy*, pp. 75–96.

52 Keith Baker, 'The Idea of a Declaration of Rights', p. 196.

53 Bell, *The Cult of the Nation*, p. 156.

54 Georges Lefebvre, *The Great Fear of 1789: Rural Panic in Revolutionary France* (London, 1953).

55 Jones, *Liberty and Locality*, p. 118; Timothy Tackett, 'Collective Panics in the Early French Revolution, 1789–91 A Comparative Perspective', *French History* (2003), pp. 149–71. See also David Hunt, 'Peasant Politics in the French Revolution', *Social History*, Vol 9 (1984), pp. 277–97.

56 Jones, *Liberty and Locality*, p. 247.

57 McPhee, *Revolution and Environment*, pp. 68–9; Jones, *Liberty and Locality*, pp. 245–50.

58 Lewis, *Rethinking the Debate*, p. 61; Nigel Aston, *Religion and Revolution in France, 1780–1804* (Washington, D.C., 2000), p. 167.

59 Timothy Tackett, *Religion, Revolution and Regional Culture in Eighteenth-Century France: the Ecclesiastical Oath of 1791* (Princeton, 1986), pp. 288–300.

60 Bonney, *Rise of the Fiscal State*, p. 150.

61 Joly, *Du Pont de Nemours*, pp. 120–1, 135.

62 Alan Forrest, *La Révolution française et les pauvres* (Paris, 1986), pp. 9–63, English translation *The Revolution and the Poor* (Oxford, 1981).

63 Ado, *Paysans en Révolution*, pp. 254–5.

64 Malcolm Crook, *Elections in the French Revolution* (Cambridge, 1996), p. 39.

65 Andress, *French Society*, chapter five; Lewis, *Rethinking the Debate*, chapter two; Dominique Godineau, *Citoyennes tricoteuses: les femmes du peuple à Paris pendant la Révolution française* (Aix-en-Provence, 1988); Joan Scott, 'French Feminists and the Rights of Man: Olympe de Gouges's Declarations', in Schechter (ed.), *The French Revolution*, p. 235; Sara Melzer and Leslie Rabine, *Rebel Daughters: Women and the French Revolution* (Oxford, 1992).

66 William Edmonds, *Jacobinism and the Revolt of Lyons, 1789–1793* (Oxford, 1990), pp. 89–97.

Chapter 9

1 François Crouzet, 'The Second Hundred Years War: Some Reflections', *French History*, Vol 10 (1996), p. 450.

2 Blanning, *The Origins of the French Revolutionary Wars*, p. 69.

3 Doyle, *The Oxford History*, p. 201.

4 Samuel Scott, *The Response of the Royal Army to the French Revolution: The Role and Development of the Line Army, 1787–93* (Oxford, 1978), p. 208; Alan Forrest, *Napoleon's Men: The Soldiers of the Revolution and Empire* (London, 2002), pp. 7–9.

5 Alain Gérard, *'Par principe d'humanité': La Terreur et la Vendée* (Paris, 1999); Donald Sutherland, *The Chouans: The Social Origins of Popular Counter-Revolution in Upper Brittany, 1770–1796* (Oxford, 1982).

6 Price, *The Fall of the French Monarchy*, chapters 11 and 12; Norman Hampson, *The Perfidy of Albion: French Perceptions of England during the French Revolution* (London, 1998).

7 Maurice Hutt, *Chouannerie and Counter-Revolution: Puisaye, the Princes, and the British Government in the 1790s* (Cambridge, 1983), 2 vols, Vol II, pp. 276–322.

8 Malcolm Crook, *Toulon in War and Revolution: From the* ancien régime *to the Restoration, 1750–1820* (Manchester, 1991), chapter 6.

9 Kirsty Carpenter, *Refugees of the French Revolution: Émigrés in London, 1789–1802* (London, 1999), p. 178.

10 Jonathan Devlin, 'The Directory and the Politics of Military Command: The Army of the Interior in South-Eastern France', *French History*, Vol IV (1990).

11 Tilly, *Coercion, Capital and European States*, pp. 74–85.

12 Peter Mathias and Patrick O'Brien, 'Taxation in Britain and France, 1715–1810', *Journal of European Economic History*, Vol 5 (1976), pp. 601–50.

13 Forrest, *Napoleon's Men*, p. 179.

14 Blanning, *The Origins of the French Revolutionary Wars*, p. 71.

15 See the introduction by Conor Cruise O'Brien to Burke's *Reflections on the French Revolution* (London, 1968), p. 61.

16 See the conflicting interpretations of Theda Skocpol and Immanul Wallerstein on this crucial issue, discussed by Skocpol in *Social Revolutions in the Modern World* (Cambridge, 1996), pp. 46–68.

17 Ibid., p. 1.

18 François Furet, 'Révolution française et tradition jacobine', in Colin Lucas (ed.), *The French Revolution and the Creation of Modern Political Culture*, Vol II, *The Political Culture of the French Revolution*, p. 339; Patrice Higonnet, *Goodness Beyond Virtue: Jacobins during the French Revolution* (Cambridge, Mass., 1998), pp. 1–3.

19 Richard Wrigley, 'Transformations of a Revolutionary Emblem: The Liberty Cap of the French Revolution', *French History*, Vol 11, (1997), p. 147.

20 Simon Schama, *Citizens: A Chronicle of the French Revolution* (London, 1989), p. 859.

21 Hugh Gough, *The Terror in the French Revolution* (London, 1998), chapter four; Peter McPhee, *The French Revolution, 1789–99* (Oxford, 2002), chapter six.

22 McPhee, *The French Revolution*, p. 125.

23 Jones, *The Peasantry in the French Revolution*, p. 121.

24 Andress, *French Society*, pp. 132–3.

25 Higonnet, *Goodness beyond Virtue*, pp. 91–6; Joan Scott, 'French Feminists and the Rights of "Man": Olympe de Gouges's Declarations', in Schechter (ed.) *The French Revolution*, pp. 213–35; Sara Melzer and Leslie Rabine (eds.), *Women and the French Revolution* (Oxford, 1992).

26 Richard Cobb, *The Police and the People: French Popular Protest, 1789–1820* (Oxford, 1970), p. 87.

27 George Rudé (ed.), *Robespierre* (Eaglewood Cliffs, New Jersey, 1967), p. 27.

28 Morris Slavin, *The Making of an Insurrection: Parisian Sections and the Gironde* (Cambridge, Mass., 1986), p. 11.

29 Jones, *Liberty and Locality*, pp. 250–65; Markoff, *The Abolition of Feudalism*, chapter eight.

30 Forrest, *La Révolution française et les pauvres*, p. 127.

31 Ibid., chapters five and seven.

32 Mona Ozouf, 'Regeneration', in François Furet and Mona Ozouf (eds.), *A Critical Dictionary of the French Revolution* (Cambridge, Mass., 1989), p. 785.

33 Bell, *The Cult of the Nation*, pp. 1–2.

34 Lynn Hunt, *Politics, Culture and Class in the French Revolution* (London, 1986), p. 111.

35 Richard Cobb, *Les Armées révolutionnaires: instrument de la Terreur dans les départements, avril 1793-floréal an 11*, 2 vols (Paris, 1961–3), Vol II, chapters one and six.

36 Walter Markov and Albert Soboul, *Die Sansculotten von Paris* (Berlin, 1957), p. 208.

37 Colin Lucas, in *The Structure of the Terror: The Example of Javoques in the Loire* (Oxford, 1973), pp. 184–6.

38 Soboul, *The French Revolution*, p. 355.

39 John Bosher, *The French Revolution* (London, 1989), chapter 11.

40 Henri Guillemin, *Robespierre: politique et mystique* (Paris, 1987), pp. 333–9; Pierre-François Pinaud, 'The Settlement of the Public Debt from the Ancien Régime, 1790–1810', *French History*, Vol V (1991), p. 425.

41 Morris Slavin, *The Hébertistes to the Guillotine: Anatomy of a "Conspiracy" in Revolutionary France* (London, 1994), p. 36.

42 Norman Hampson, 'Robespierre and the Terror', in Colin Haydon and William Doyle (eds.), *Robespierre* (Cambridge, 1999), p. 173.

43 Soboul, *The French Revolution*, pp. 595–605.

44 Arendt, *On Revolution*, p. 61.

45 Martyn Lyons, *France under the Directory* (Cambridge, 1975), p. 37; Wordsworth, *The Prelude*, (1805 text), lines 170–3.

46 Jones, *The Great Nation*, p. 468.

47 Jones, *Liberty and Locality*, p. 142.

48 Tilly, *Coercion, Capital, and European States*, p. 114.

49 Lewis, *The Second Vendée*, chapter six.

50 Donald Sutherland, *The Chouans: The Social Origins of Popular Counter-Revolution in Upper Brittany, 1770–96* (Oxford, 1982), p. 213.

51 Alain Gérard, *'Par principe d'humanité': la Terreur et la Vendée* (Paris, 1999), pp. 266–9, chapter thirteen.

52 Braudel, *The Identity of France*, Vol I, pp. 92–5.

53 Sutherland, *The Chouans*, pp. 27, 311.

54 See Brian Fitzpatrick, *Catholic Royalism in the Department of the Gard, 1814–1852* (Cambridge, 1983).

55 See, for example, Paul Bois, *Les Paysans de l'Ouest* (Le Mans, 1960), Charles Tilly, *The Vendée: A Sociological Analysis of the Counter-Revolution of 1793* (London, 1964); Marcel Faucheux, *L'Insurrection vendéenne de 1793: aspects économiques et sociaux* (Paris, 1964).

56 Sutherland, *Les Chouans*, p. 54.

57 Liu, *The Weaver's Knot*, p. 16.

58 Lewis, *The Second Vendée*, p. 9.

59 Mercier, *Le Nouveau Paris*, pp. 377, 437.

60 Crook, *Elections in the French Revolution*, p. 116.

61 Jones, *Liberty and Locality*, p. 127.

62 Carla Hesse, *Publishing and Cultural Politics in Revolutionary Paris, 1789–1810* (Berkeley, 1991), p. 141.

63 Sutherland, *Taxation, Representation* in Crises and Revolutions, pp. 423–6.

64 Howard Brown, 'A Discredited Regime: The Directory and Army Contracting', *French History*, Vol IV (1990), p. 76.

65 Michel Brugière, *Gestionnaires et profiteurs de la Révolution* (Paris, 1986), pp. 116–32, 227–93; Louis Bergeron, *Banquiers, négociants et manufacturiers parisiens du Directoire à l'Empire* (Paris, 1978).

66 Mercier, *Le Nouveau Paris*, pp. 424, 426.

67 Richard Cobb, *Death in Paris* (Oxford, 1978), pp. 73, 79.

68 Forrest, *La Révolution française et les pauvres*, pp. 111, 137–43, 188–9.

69 Crook, *Elections in the French Revolution*, p. 186.

70 R. Rose, *Gracchus Babeuf: The First Revolutionary Communist* (London, 1978); Claude Mazauric, *Jacobinisme et Révolution* (Paris, 1984), pp. 281–98.

71 Jones, *The Great Nation*, p. 561.

72 Olwen Hufton, 'In Search of Counter-Revolution Women', in Kates (ed.), *The French Revolution*, p. 329.

73 Mercier, *Le Nouveau Paris*, p. 377.

74 Gwynne Lewis, 'Les égorgeurs du département du Gard', in *Religion, Révolution, Contre-Revolution dans le Midi, 1789–1799* (Nîmes, 1990).

75 Woloch, *The New Regime*, p. 432.

Conclusion

1 Michael Broers, *Europe under Napoleon, 1799–1815* (London, 1996), p. 52.

2 Goubert and Roche, *Les Français et l'ancien régime*, Vol I, p. 26.

3 Jones, *The Great Nation*, p. 555; John Dunne, 'The French Nobility and the Revolution: Towards a Virtual Solution to Two Age-Old Problems', *French History*, Vol 17 (2003).

4 Cited by Roger Magraw, *France 1800–1914: A Social History* (London, 2002), p. 26.

5 François Furet, 'Napoleon Bonaparte', in Kates (ed.) *The French Revolution*, p. 349.

6 Garrioch, *The Formation of the Parisian Bourgeoisie*, p. 282.

7 Mann, *The Sources of Social Power*, Vol II, p. 30.

8 Magraw, *France 1800–1914* (London, 2002), p. 34.

9 Braudel, *The Identity of France*, Vol II, p. 165.

10 Saint-Simon, *Mémoires*, Vol I, p. 336.

11 John Bosher, *The French Revolution: A New Interpretation*, (London, 1989), chapter 11.

12 Furet, 'Napoleon Bonaparte', in Kates (ed.), *The French Revolution*, p. 353.

13 Garrioch, *The Formation of the Parisian Bourgeoisie*, p. 244; Jones, *Liberty and Locality*, pp. 270–1.

14 Garrioch, *The Formation of the Parisian Bourgeoisie*, p. 286.

15 Paul Butel, 'Revolution and the Urban Economy: Maritime Cities and Continental Cities', in Alan Forrest and Peter Jones (eds.), *Reshaping France: Town, Country and Region during the French Revolution* (Manchester, 1991), pp. 37–51.

16 Butel, 'Revolution and the Urban Economy', p. 45; Tim Le Goff and Donald Sutherland, 'The Revolution and the Rural Economy', in *Reshaping France*, p. 63.

17 Patrick O'Brien, 'Path Dependency, or Why Britain became an Industrialized and Urbanized Economy long before France', *Economic History Review*, Vol 49 (1996), p. 228.

18 Le Goff and Sutherland, 'The Revolution and the Rural Economy', in *Reshaping France*, p. 52; Anatoli Ado, *Paysans en Révolution*, pp. 450–3.

19 Woloch, *The New Regime*, pp. 155–6.

20 Gutwirth, *The Twilight of the Goddesses*, p. xviii.

21 Dorinda Outram, *The Body in the French Revolution: Sex, Class and Political Culture* (London, 1989), p. 105.

22 The *Guardian*, 28 September 2001, p. 21.

23 Scott, *Women and the Public Sphere*, pp. 203–4.

24 Naomi Schor, 'Triste Amérique: Atala and the Postrevolutionary Construction of Woman', in Melzer and Rabine (eds.), *Rebel Daughters* (Oxford, 1992), p. 139.

25 Le Goff and Sutherland, 'The Revolution and the Rural Economy', p. 46.

26 Cobb, *Police and the People*, p. 321.

27 Kwass, *Crises, Revolutions, and Self-Sustained Growth*, p. 344.

28 Terrier, *Les Deux Âges de la protoindustrialisation*, pp. 148–9.

29 Woloch, *The New Regime*, p. 432.

Index